A HISTORY OF CHRISTIANITY
IN JAPAN

A History of Christianity in Japan

ROMAN CATHOLIC

AND

GREEK ORTHODOX MISSIONS

BY

OTIS CARY, D.D.

For Thirty Years Missionary of the A. B. C. F. M.

NEW YORK   CHICAGO   TORONTO

Fleming H. Revell Company

LONDON   AND   EDINBURGH

Republished, 1970
Scholarly Press, 22929 Industrial Drive East
St. Clair Shores, Michigan 48080

Standard Book Number 403-00252-4
Library of Congress Catalog Card Number: 70-107165

This edition is printed on a high-quality,
acid-free paper that meets specification
requirements for fine book paper referred
to as "300-year" paper

DEDICATION

To all, of whatsoever church or nation, who with love for the Lord Jesus Christ are trying to give His Gospel to Japan, I dedicate this book.

Differing as we do upon so many points, it is easy for us to see what we deem defects in one another's belief and practice; but if He to whose pure eyes all men must seem so imperfect " is not ashamed to call them brethren " whom He is sanctifying, let us not withhold the name from any that love and follow Him.

May He prosper our work so far as it is in accord with His truth.

May He overrule our mistakes.

May His Kingdom come to Japan.

May He grant that we, whose notes have now too much of discord, may all at last find ourselves in harmony as we join with the ten thousand times ten thousand and the thousands of thousands in singing:

" Worthy is the Lamb that hath been slain to receive the power, and riches, and wisdom, and might, and honour, and glory, and blessing."

PREFACE

IN this volume and one dealing with Protestant Missions in Japan the attempt has been made to write impartially concerning the three great divisions of the Christian Church. Probably, however, complete success has not been attained, for a writer is unconsciously affected by his own prejudices. I will not deny that certain doctrines and practices of the Roman and Greek Churches seem to me gravely erroneous. Members of those churches have the same opinion of what I believe and do. It will be well, however, for all of us to remember that Christ rebuked His disciples for unworthy feelings against those who, though not walking with them, yet cast out demons in His name. If we belong to the Church Universal, we must recognise some degree of fellowship with all followers of Christ and must acknowledge their work for Him as a part of that in which we are engaged. The great missionary to the Gentiles wrote to those that by emphasising differences were in danger of cutting themselves off from joy in the labours of persons not belonging to their own party: " All things are yours; whether Paul, or Apollos, or Cephas . . . all are yours and ye are Christ's." While writing of Xavier, Fernandez, Takayama Ukon, Petitjean, and Dominic Senemon; of Archbishop Nicolai and those of his converts who were so earnest in giving the Gospel to their countrymen; I have said: " Yes, if I am Christ's, these men too are mine. I ought to rejoice in what they have accomplished in His name." I am sorry for any person claiming to be a Christian who can read of Verbeck, and Sawayama, and Neesima without a desire to claim them as his brethren. We see defects in others. Alas! is our own work so perfect that we can point the finger of scorn at theirs? Even the

5

best workers upon God's temple have sometimes intermingled grass, hay, stubble with the gold, silver, and precious stones; but we may well take heed lest we become so occupied with criticising the former that we cannot rejoice in the strength and beauty of the latter.

Notwithstanding what has just been said, the honest historian cannot conceal the faults of those concerning whom he writes. Cromwell's face must be painted with the wart. The artist need not, however, write beneath the picture: " Please notice especially the wart," and so I have not specifically drawn attention to what seem unfortunate features in the methods of any Christian workers, but have simply told the facts, usually in the words of the workers themselves or in those used by writers belonging to the same communion.

It will, after all, be evident to the reader that this book has been written by a Protestant. This will explain why some matters that occupy considerable space in such writers as Charlevoix receive but slight notice here; why, for instance, little is said of the miracles ascribed to Xavier and his successors. Even the diction will be found to have something of a Protestant tinge. I am aware that the term *Roman* Catholic is displeasing to some members of the Church to which it is applied. As a rule, it is desirable to speak of a religious body by the name of its own preference; but I trust that in this case the failure to do so will not be regarded as a discourtesy. Some that do not acknowledge the supremacy of the Bishop of Rome make or desire to make the word " Catholic " the title of their own division of Christianity, and the recognised name of one of the leading denominations in Japan is Seikokwai or Holy Catholic Church. Such facts seem to make necessary the use in this book of the term Roman Catholic. The name Greek Orthodox has been chosen as conveying to many readers a clearer idea than would that of Holy Orthodox Church.

Those acquainted with the Japanese language may criticise my way of writing some words. I have omitted the marks that designate long vowels, because they are misleading to the general reader and because it is difficult to secure such accurate proof-reading as would en-

sure against mistakes. Again, though Japanese nouns
have usually no distinction of number, it has seemed best
for the sake of clearness to use such plurals as *daimyos,*
etc.

As many bibliographical lists have been published,
there is no necessity for mentioning all of the books consulted in the preparation of this volume. For the early
missions, chief reliance has been placed on Charlevoix,
Crasset, Steichen's " The Christian Daimyo," Cros's " St.
François de Xavier," Murdoch and Yamagata's " History of Japan," and papers in the Transactions of the
Asiatic Society of Japan. Special obligation is acknowledged to Murdoch and Yamagata's work for its help in
connecting events narrated by European writers with
those found in Japanese records. In several cases its
translations have been adopted in this book. The intensely interesting work of Abbé Marnas, " La Religion
de Jésus Ressuscitée au Japon," and the letters of Mgr.
Forcade published under the title, " Le Premier Missionnaire du Japon au XIXe Siècle," have been the chief
sources of information concerning the earlier years of
the modern Roman Catholic missions. For more recent
years I have depended on the " Annals of the Propagation of the Faith," the reports of the *Société des Missions Étrangères,* and various periodicals.

The first part of a history of the Greek Orthodox
Mission has been published in the Japanese language under the title " *Nippon Seikyo Dendo Shi.*" In English,
there is nothing available except a few articles in magazines; and I am informed by Archbishop Nicolai that,
even in the Russian language, little has been published
concerning the mission of which he is the head.

A considerable portion of what is found in this book
was used in the Hyde Lectures on Foreign Missions,
given at Andover Theological Seminary in December,
1908.

CONTENTS

PART I

THE ROMAN CATHOLIC MISSIONS

CONTENTS

PART II

THE GREEK ORTHODOX MISSION

PART I
ROMAN CATHOLIC MISSIONS

I

THE CALL TO JAPAN

THE first attempt to carry the Gospel to Japan was made by Christopher Columbus.

Nearly two centuries before the discoverer of America set out upon his memorable voyage, a Venetian merchant, who had recently been taken captive in a naval battle, was confined in a prison of Genoa, the city that afterwards became the birthplace of Columbus. The prisoner, who had spent many years in travelling through distant lands, was wont to relieve the tedium of confinement by telling his companions about the many strange things he had seen and heard. Among those that listened to his stories was a prisoner from Pisa, a man who had already written a few books and who saw that these tales furnished e cellent material for another. It was at his request that Marco Polo, the Venetian merchant, dictated the narrative that gave to Europeans much more knowledge of the Far East than they had before possessed. One day he spoke as follows of a country which he himself had not visited, but of which he had often heard during his sojourn at the court of Kublai Khan:

"Zipangu is an island towards the east in the high seas, fifteen hundred miles distant from the Continent, and a very great island it is. The people are white, civilised, and well-favoured. They are idolaters and are dependent on nobody. And I can tell you, the quantity of gold they have is endless; for they find it in their own island, and the king does not allow it to be exported. Moreover, few merchants visit the country, because it is so far from the mainland, and thus it comes to pass that their gold is abundant beyond all measure.

13

" I will tell you a wonderful thing about the palace of the lord of that island. You must know that he hath a great palace which is entirely roofed with fine gold, just as our churches are roofed with lead, insomuch that it would scarcely be possible to estimate its value. Moreover, all the pavement of the palace and the floors of its chambers are entirely of gold, in plates like slabs of stone, a good two fingers thick ; and the windows also are of gold, so that altogether the richness of this palace is past all bounds and all belief. They have also pearls in abundance, which are of a rose colour, but fine, big, and round, and quite as valuable as the white ones.

. . . .

" Now you must know that the idols of Cathay and of Manzi and of this island are all of the same class. And of this island as well as elsewhere, there be some of the idols that have the head of an ox, some have the head of a pig, some of a dog, some of a sheep, and some of divers other kinds. And some of them have four heads, whilst some have three, one growing out of either shoulder. There are also some that have four hands, some ten, some a thousand. And they do put more faith in those idols that have a thousand hands than in any of the others. And when any Christian asks them why they make their idols in so many different guises and not all alike, they reply that just so their forefathers were wont to have them made, and just so they will leave them to their children, and these to after generations, and so they will be handed down for ever. And you must understand that the deeds ascribed to these idols are such a parcel of deviltries as it is best not to tell." (*Yule's Translation.*)

It has been doubted whether Columbus had read Marco Polo's book before he started upon his voyage of discovery. One reason for supposing he had done so is that in the Biblioteca Colombina at Seville is a copy of the first Latin printed edition (1485) with notes in what is thought to be his handwriting. At all events, it was only through Polo that information concerning Japan had reached Europe; and thus, either directly or indirectly, he had an important part in exciting the zeal of Columbus for his great undertaking. Since Zipangu was the most eastern of all the lands described by the Venetian, Columbus believed that it would be the first one reached in sailing westward from Europe. The gold with which it was said to abound did not furnish the sole incentive for seeking the island : Columbus hoped to extend the blessings of Christianity to this and other lands that he might discover. When he came to write an account of his expedition, he said in the prologue addressed to his royal patrons:

" The Grand Khan of the Mongols and his predecessors had many times sent to Rome asking that doctors of our holy faith be sent to instruct them. The Holy Father had never provided these teachers; and thus many people perished while believing in their idols and imbibing the doctrines of perdition. Therefore Your Highnesses, as Catholic Christians and princes, lovers and promoters of the holy Catholic faith, and enemies of the sect of Mahomet as of all idolatries and heresies, determined to send me, Christopher Columbus, to the said parts of India that I might see the said princes with their people and lands, might discover the nature and disposition of all, and might devise means to be taken for their conversion to our holy faith."

Thus we see that, whatever other considerations may have had weight with Columbus, the missionary motive was professedly, and we may believe actually, the most prominent in his mind and in that of his patrons.

The people of the regions reached on the first voyage showed so many signs of poverty that Columbus could not consider them the inhabitants of Zipangu. They possessed, however, some gold ornaments, and the signs made by them when asked the place from which these were obtained nourished the hope that the land of golden palaces was not far away.

Six of the natives whom Columbus brought back, and whom he supposed to be Asiatics, were baptised with great ceremony at Barcelona; King Ferdinand, Queen Isabella, and Prince John acting as sponsors. The Pope appointed a Benedictine monk to be vicar apostolic in the newly discovered lands, and eleven members of the same order accompanied Columbus on his second voyage. The queen gave into their care some sacred vessels and vestments taken from her own chapel. Although the opinion of Columbus that Cuba was Cathay gained acceptance, Zipangu was believed to be near that land and so was doubtless included in the thought of those who made these provisions for the extension of their religion to the regions beyond the western ocean.

It was half a century later when Europeans really reached Japan. Though it is not certainly known who were the first to do this, the honour is usually ascribed to some Portuguese mariners, who in 1542 were driven thither from the Chinese coast by a storm. Mendez Pinto, in an account of his travels, that he prepared near the close of his life, claimed the discovery for himself and his companions; but there are many reasons for doubting the truth of his statements.

To Francis Xavier * was given the privilege of leading the first company of missionaries to Japan. The place that this remarkable man holds in ecclesiastical history as the "Apostle to Japan" justifies a somewhat extended notice of his life. He was born at the castle of Xavier in Navarre, April 7, 1506. At the age of eighteen he entered the University of Paris, where he became acquainted with Ignatius Loyola. He was one of the six who united in forming the Society of Jesus. War and other obstacles having interfered with the original plans of these associates, who had hoped to go to the Holy Land in order to attempt the conversion of the Mohammedans, they spent some time in Italy, teaching, preaching, working in hospitals, and completing the organisation of their society. In addition to their former vows of chastity and poverty, they now took that of obedience, binding themselves to perform whatsoever the reigning pontiff might command. They held themselves ready to go forth among Turks, heathen, or heretics, as he should direct, and this they were to do without hesitation or delay, as also without question, condition, or reward.

The King of Portugal applied to the Jesuits for missionaries who should seek the conversion of the nations that had lately been conquered in India. At first Rodriguez and Bobadilla were selected for this service; but

---

* The best life of Xavier in English is that of H. J. Coleridge (London, 1886). It is largely made up of Xavier's letters. It will be seen, however, that the extracts from the letters contained in the present book sometimes differ very much from Coleridge's translation. This is because much use has been made of Cros's "Saint François de Xavier, Sa Vie et Ses Lettres" (Paris and Toulouse, 1900). Cros has made a careful study of existing manuscripts and has thus freed the letters from the amplifications and changes introduced by editors and translators.

the sudden illness of the latter made it impossible for him to go at once. Loyola, who was also ill, called Xavier to his bedside, and in the name of the Pope commanded him to set out the next day for Portugal in order to make arrangements for the mission. Rodriguez had already started, and Xavier was to follow in the company of the Portuguese ambassador. The few hours at his disposal gave him barely time to repair his worn garments, say farewell to his friends, and receive the Pope's blessing.*

Rodriguez (who is not to be confounded with others of the same name who afterwards went to Japan) finally remained in Portugal; but Xavier with two other Jesuits proceeded to Goa, which was reached May 6, 1542. In this city, the capital of the Portuguese possessions, he began those missionary labours that have made his name famous. Two classes of people claimed his attention—the Europeans and the natives. It would be hard to say which had sunk lower in the scale of morals. He visited patients in the hospital, preached to the Portuguese, distributed alms, and gave much time to the instruction of children. It was hard for him to remain quiet long in one place, and he visited various parts of India, besides many of the Spice Islands. One of his letters describes his methods of preaching to those natives who were nominally Christians. He says:

" Their native language is the Malabar; mine, the Basque. They do not understand mine nor I theirs. Accordingly I brought together the wisest among them and sought out some men who knew both tongues. After that, in numerous sessions and with great labour, we wrote out the forms of prayer; first, that of the Sign of the Cross accompanied with the Confession of the Three Persons of the Trinity; then the Creed, the Commandments, the Pater Noster, Ave Maria, Salve Regina, and the Confiteor; translating all from Latin into the Malabar language. I learned these formulas by heart, and then, a bell in my hand, I went out collecting all whom I could, children and adults, in the place where I was staying. Two times a day for a month I taught them the prayers. What the children learned they were to teach (it soon

* The story that on his way to Portugal Xavier would not turn a little aside from the direct road in order to bid his mother farewell is happily proved incorrect by Cros, who shows that the mother had died eleven years before.

became a regular institution) to their fathers and mothers, to all the people in their houses, and to their neighbours. Sundays I assembled all the inhabitants of the place, men and women, old and young, to say the prayers in their own language. They manifested great pleasure in this exercise. They came very gladly and forthwith recited aloud the Creed in their own tongue, commencing with the confession of one only God in three Persons. First I uttered the words, and all followed. At the close of this recitation of the Creed, I repeated it myself alone, article by article, stopping after each one. I made them observe that to be a Christian meant nothing else than firmly and without hesitation to believe the twelve articles. Then, since they declared themselves to be Christians, I demanded concerning each article if they firmly believed it, at which the men and women, old and young, with their hands crossed upon their breasts, would always answer, ' Yes.' "

After describing how he taught the prayers and Commandments, Xavier continued:

" In the country where I now am the multitude of those who become converts to the faith of Jesus Christ is so great that my arms often grow weary with baptising, and I am unable to speak any longer . . . I have baptised a whole village in a day."

So much has been written about the success of Xavier's work in India that a reader of his letters is surprised to find that he was greatly disappointed over the results. In 1548 he wrote to a fellow-worker urging him to baptise as many children as possible, for, asked he, " Do you not see that few Indians, white or black, will go to paradise, if one excepts the children of fourteen years and under who die in ignorance of evil? " The next year he wrote to Loyola:

" The experience that I have of these countries shows me clearly that there is no possible hope of perpetuating the Society here by means of the native Indians. Christianity itself will survive only so long as we remain and live here—we who have already come or those whom you shall send."

In a letter to Rodriguez he said:

" From the experience I have had I see only one way and means by which the service of our Lord can be greatly promoted in India. It is this. Whoever may be governor of India, let the King give him a letter of introduction saying, ' In India there are none of the ministers of religion (here the King should mention the Society of Jesus first of all) on whom I so much depend as I do upon you for the extension in those countries of the faith of Jesus Christ, and therefore I command you to make the Island of Ceylon Christian and to cause the Christian community of Cape Comorin to increase. . . . Let him say to the governors, ' I swear that unless you clear my conscience by making many Christians in India, I will cause you on your return to Lisbon to be arrested and put in irons. You will remain long years in prison and I will confiscate all your property.' Let the King talk thus to the governors. Let him then give his orders, and let all disobedience and neglect be severely punished. Then there will be many Christians gained in this country; but there will not be in any other way."

These and many similar expressions showing how much Xavier depended upon political power for the promotion of religious ends, help us to see why he and his successors, on going to Japan, sought with so much earnestness the conversion of the Shogun and the feudal lords.

It was while Xavier was feeling so discouraged over the condition of affairs in India and considering whether he should go elsewhere, that his thoughts were turned toward Japan. He was in Malacca when there came to him a young Japanese who in Xavier's letters is called Anjiro.* The main features of this man's story may best be told by giving the letter which he wrote November 29, 1548, to the Society of Jesus:

" Paul of Japan sends to Father Ignatius and to other Fathers and Brothers of the Society of Jesus the peace, grace, and love of Jesus Christ that He may be glorified and the holy faith extended.

" It had pleased Him who chose me from my mother's womb (coming, as He did, to seek wandering and lost sheep) not to forget me who was so far separate from Himself, but to bring me out from the darkness, leading me into the light and to a place of safety through the faith of Jesus Christ, the Restorer of our souls. . . . How this favour of the Lord came to me I wish to relate in order that He may be blessed and praised.

* There have been various conjectures about the Japanese form of this name. Valegnani, writing about 1600, says, " His true name was Yajiro." Froez says that he was about thirty-six years old when he came to Goa.

"While yet in my native country of Japan and still an in-
fidel, it came to pass that for certain reasons I slew a man. To
escape arrest, I fled by night to a Buddhist monastery. While
I was there, a Portuguese vessel came to the city. One Alonzo
Vaz, whom I had formerly known, happened to be on board.
As soon as he learned what had happened to me, he invited
me to sail with him from Japan. His departure was delayed,
and fearing lest I should incur further risk, he gave me a letter
of recommendation to a friend who was staying in the same
port. In the darkness of the night I mistook the vessel and
gave the letter to George Alvarez instead of Ferdinand Alvarez,
to whom it was addressed. The former, however, received
me in the kindest manner and offered to take me to Father
Francis, with whom he was intimately acquainted. From what
was told me about Father Francis and his works I conceived
a strong desire to be with him.

"Setting sail we came to Malacca. On the voyage George
Alvarez had taught me what it is to be a Christian so that I
was already somewhat inclined to receive baptism. My desire
for this kept increasing day by day, and I should quickly have
become a Christian on this first visit to Malacca if the vicar
in that city would have baptised me. He asked me who I
was and in what condition I lived. I informed him that I
was married and expected to go back to my home. Thereupon
he refused baptism, saying that if I received it I could not
return to be the husband of a pagan woman. Therefore, when
the monsoon favourable for sailing to Japan commenced to
blow, I embarked on a vessel bound for China where I could
avail myself at the proper time of a ship going to Japan.

"Setting sail from China to Japan (a seven or eight days
journey, or two hundred leagues) we came within about twenty
leagues of the coast of my country. While in sight of it we
were overtaken by a violent tempest; the wind blowing from
the land and so against us. The weather was so thick that we
did not know where we were. This lasted four days and nights.
Every one was in terrible distress and cried for mercy. It was
finally necessary to return to the Chinese port from which we
had set out.

"That storm, which thus brought me back to China, gave
me cause for reflection. Moreover my desire to be a Christian
and to be instructed in the faith had never left me. I was in
doubt what I ought to do. Then I met the Portuguese, Alonzo
Vaz, who in my own country had first encouraged me to go
to Malacca. He was much surprised when he heard how I had
left Malacca and had been driven back to China by the tempest.
As he was then about sailing to Malacca, he asked me to accompany him. An honourable man named Lorenzo Botelho
united with him in urging me to go. 'Return to Malacca,' said
he, 'I believe that you will find Father Francis there. From
Malacca you will go to the College of St. Paul at Goa in

India. There you will be instructed in the faith and afterwards some one of the Fathers will go with you to Japan.'

"This advice seemed good and I set forth with joy. On
coming to Malacca, I at once met George Alvarez, who hastened
to bring me to Father Francis. We found him in a church
where he was conducting a marriage service. George Alvarez
introduced me and told him my history. The great joy with
which Father Francis looked on me and welcomed me was
sufficient to show that all things had been brought about by
God's providence. The further I go, the more fully do I understand this. Already the mere sight of Father Francis had given
me satisfaction and comfort. I was able to talk with him, for
I could understand a little of what was said in Portuguese and
could also speak some words.

"The Father at once told me to go to the College of St.
Paul in company with George Alvarez, who was setting out
for Goa. Father Francis was going to visit the Christians of
Cape Comorin and proceed from there to Goa. He did not
delay on the way, for hardly had I arrived in the beginning of
March, 1548, at the College of St. Paul when he came, only
four or five days after me. Great was my joy at seeing him.
Indeed, from the first moment that I had seen him, I was conscious of a holy emotion which inspired in my heart the desire
to be in his service and never to leave him.

"While in the college I gained such a knowledge of the faith
that I was baptised in May of that year on the Day of Pentecost.
On the same day was also baptised my servant, whom I had
brought from Japan and who is now here with me.

"I hope that God, the Creator of all things, and Jesus Christ
who was crucified for our redemption will cause all that has
happened to redound to their glory and to the propagation of
the faith. The special mercies that I have received from
the Lord convince me of the truth of Christianity; while
further witness is given by many proofs and by the quiet and
peace which filled my soul. May God in His mercy grant that I
may not be ungrateful for such benefits nor for the intelligence,
memory, and persistency with which the Fathers of the College
say He has endowed me. They are astonished at the impression
the things of God make upon me, that in so short a time I have
learned to read and write so well and that I have been able to
understand such exalted doctrines, and that I have learned
by heart the Gospel of Matthew, which I have written in Japanese characters and divided into sections so as to remember it
the better. Your Reverences will find specimens of the Japanese
characters and writing enclosed with this letter.

"For the love of our Lord, obtain for me by your prayers
that He who has given me so much will not allow the gifts to
remain without fruit, but that all may redound to His praise and
glory.

"Pray too that our Lord will aid Father Francis, who is

preparing for the voyage to Japan; also that I may have the courage to give my life a thousand times, if necessary, for the love of God. For this I greatly need the powerful aid of Father Ignatius, Father Antonio Gomez, and other members of the Society of Jesus. Let them constantly recommend me to God's favour, for I hope in our Lord that He will gain for Himself much fruit in Japan, and that before I die I shall see a college of the Society established there for the glory of Jesus Christ and the propagation of the faith. Amen.

" Goa, Nov. 29, 1548.

"Your servant in Jesus Christ,

" Paul of the Holy Faith (a Japanese)." *

The name " Paul of the Holy Faith " was received by him at baptism, this being the designation of the College at Goa. His servant took the name Anthony. A third Japanese, who had likewise been sent by Xavier from Malacca to Goa, was baptised as John.

It was in reply to Xavier's question, " If I went to Japan, would the people become Christians? " that Anjiro made his famous reply, " My people would not immediately become Christians; but they would first ask you a multitude of questions, weighing carefully your answers and your claims. Above all, they would observe whether your conduct agreed with your words. If you should satisfy them on these points—by suitable replies to their inquiries and by a life above reproach—then, as soon as the matter was known and fully examined, the king [daimyo], the nobles, and the educated people would become Christians. Six months would suffice; for the nation is one that always follows the guidance of reason."

In January, 1549, Xavier wrote to Paul: " In the space of eight months he has learned to read, write, and speak Portuguese." At one time he was heard sighing and exclaiming: " Oh, unhappy people of Japan, who adore the creatures that God made to be your servants! " When Xavier asked, " Paul, why do you talk thus? " the answer was, " I was thinking of my countrymen who adore the sun and moon, whereas those luminaries are servants to the men who know the Lord Jesus. They were made

---

*In the main I have followed Cros's version of the letter, supplying from other sources one section which he abbreviated.

to illumine the day and night in order that by their light we might serve God upon the earth and glorify His Son, Jesus Christ."

The fervent, restless spirit of Xavier was moved with an earnest desire to carry Christianity to Japan. No sooner did he broach the subject to his friends than he was assailed by a multitude of objections. He was told that there was so much work to be done in the Portuguese colonies that he could not be spared. In reply, he pointed to other Jesuits who had already come to India, and to the fact that more were expected. When the dangers of the undertaking were portrayed, he asked if the servants of God ought to be less willing than the merchants to run risks. In one of his letters he says, after writing of the dangers from tempests, shoals, and pirates: " It is doing well if two out of four vessels make the journey in safety; but were I certain of finding myself in greater perils than those already experienced, I would not give up going to Japan, so strong is the impression on my mind and so great hope do I have in God that I shall see our holy religion propagated there."

Xavier chose Father Cosmo Torres and Brother Juan Fernandez to accompany him in his new undertaking. The former was a Spanish priest who had been on board a ship that touched at the Moluccas while Xavier was sojourning in those islands. Being greatly impressed by what he saw of Xavier and his work, he would gladly have remained with him; but for some reason it was necessary for him to go to Goa, where for a time he served as a parish priest before being admitted into the Society of Jesus. Juan Fernandez had been a rich silk merchant of Cordova. His business led him to Lisbon, and there he was one day invited by a friend to attend a service of the Jesuits, where it was said he could hear the sweetest music to which he had ever listened. On going to the church, Juan found a gathering of over two hundred men belonging to a fraternity that met every week for devotion and penance. After a sermon the lights were extinguished, while the men with tears and groans for their sins began to scourge their bared backs and to beg divine pardon. The young merchant was so much moved by these proceedings that he at once sought out Father Rodriguez and asked to be received into the Society as a lay-brother. Rodriguez, in doubt whether the young man had sufficient of the spirit of self-renunciation, asked whether, as a proof of sincerity, he was willing, richly dressed as he was, to ride on a donkey through the chief street of Lisbon with his face toward the animal's tail. As Fernandez gladly met the test, he was soon afterwards received into the Society. Xavier wished to have him enter the priesthood before sailing to Japan; but Fernandez begged permission to remain in his humbler position as a lay brother.

Xavier's fame has unduly eclipsed that of his companions. If to him belongs the honour of planning the mission and inspiring them with zeal to enter upon it, they were the ones who did the more solid work. They remained in Japan the rest of their lives, learned the language of its people, and laid the foundations of the Roman Catholic Church in that land. Fernandez proved the most apt of the company in acquiring the Japanese language and in reaching the hearts of the people. Father Torres once said concerning him: "Very little would be accomplished in Japan if we should lose Brother Juan Fernandez."

In addition to the three Jesuits and the three Japanese, there were two servants who accompanied them from Goa. One was a native of Malabar, by the name of Amador, and the other was a Chinese named Manuel. The little company went first to Malacca, where they hoped to find some vessel that would take them to their destination. There they received intelligence that gave them much encouragement to believe that God was preparing the Japanese people to welcome them. A letter written from Malacca by Xavier says:

"On our arrival we were given many items of news from Japan. There had come letters from Portuguese merchants who were in that country. They informed me that a great lord in those islands desired to be a Christian and had despatched an ambassador to the Governor of India asking that some Fathers be sent to teach him our religion. They also wrote that in one place visited by the Portuguese traders the lord of the land had given them an abandoned house for their lodging. It was one that the people of the country did not wish to occupy, because, as they said, it was haunted by an evil spirit. The Portuguese established themselves there, but soon they felt something pulling at their clothes. When they looked around to find who was doing this, they could see nothing. This caused them much alarm. Among them was a boy, who one night commenced to cry out aloud. The Portuguese all arose and ran to him with their weapons, thinking that they were being attacked. When they asked the boy the reason of his cries, he replied that a vision had frightened him and made him call out. After this the boy set up many crosses about the house, and nothing more occurred to alarm the Portuguese. The men of the town had heard the boy's cries and they asked an explanation. It was given to them, and it was then that the lord of the place told the merchants that the house was haunted. He asked them if they knew any way of driving out the evil spirit; whereupon they replied that there was nothing better than the sign of the holy cross. As the Portuguese had placed crosses inside and outside their house, the Japanese began to do the same thing to theirs." *

No Portuguese ship was ready for the voyage to Japan, a circumstance that Paul attributed to God's special providence, since, as he said: " If my countrymen should see on the one hand Master Francis preaching the holy law of God, and at the same time should also see the Christian merchants doing contrary to the same law, they would form their judgment of it rather from the deeds of the merchants than from the words of the preacher, and would ask Master Francis how could it be that the Christians look forward to the good things of heaven after death if they live now as if there were no goods but those of this world. I thank God that no European enters Japan along with Francis."

The implication in this last statement is not exact, for, in addition to the two other missionaries, Xavier was accompanied on this voyage by a Portuguese named Domingo Diaz, of whom we know almost nothing, except that Xavier describes him as " a very great friend of mine."

Being unwilling to delay, the party embarked on a junk belonging to a Chinese corsair. The Commandant

* Cros, vol. i., p. 460. Editors of Xavier's letters have considerably amplified this story, as may be seen in Coleridge, vol. ii., p. 177.

of Malacca tried to make their journey less disagreeable by providing a variety of supplies. To these he added many valuable articles that could be used as gifts for gaining the good will of the Japanese rulers.

The following extract is from an account that Xavier wrote of the voyage:

" A hundred leagues from Malacca on our way towards China, we touched at an island where our people provided themselves with tillers and other pieces of timber that were needed in preparation for the great storms of those Chinese waters. After this, they made many sacrifices to their idol, held a feast in its honour, worshipped many times, and then by casting lots inquired from it whether or not we should have a good wind. The reply was that the weather would be favourable and that it was not necessary to wait longer. The anchors were weighed and we set sail. All were in good spirits; the pagans putting trust in their idol, which with much ceremony they had installed in the stern of the ship, where they surrounded it with lighted candles and burned incense before it; while our trust was in God, the Creator of heaven and earth, and in Jesus Christ, His Son, for whose love and in whose service we had come to preach our holy faith.

" After a while the heathen again cast lots, asking the idol if our ship would return from Japan to Malacca. The reply was that the ship would reach Japan, but would not come back to Malacca. This had the effect of deterring them from going to Japan. They decided to winter in China and wait there until the next year. Judge by this how annoying it was for us to be on a voyage where the question of proceeding or not was left to the decision of a demon and his followers; for, in fact, those that commanded the ship did only what the demon through these lots ordered them to do.

" Going on our way, we came off the coast of a country called Cochin-China, a little before reaching China but not far from it, when two disasters befell us on the same day. It was the eve of the feast of St. Mary Magdalene. The sea was high and very boisterous. The ship's sink had carelessly been left open. As the Chinese Manuel, our companion, was passing near it, the violent rolling of the ship caused him to stumble and fall in. We thought he would be dead from such a fall and because the sink was full of water; but God did not permit him to die. For a long time he was head downward with more than half of his body submerged. With much trouble we drew him out insensible, and he suffered many days from a severe wound on the head, but it pleased our Lord to restore him to health.

" We had just finished dressing Manuel's wounds when the

storm made the vessel give a great pitch, thus throwing the pilot's daughter into the sea. The violence of the tempest was such that we were unable to rescue the girl, who was drowned close by the ship in sight of her father and of us all. It was pitiable to hear the groaning and wailing of the poor pagans during the day and night that followed; pitiable too to see the misery of their souls. They passed the time in making constant sacrifices or feasts to their idol, slaying many birds and offering food and drink. The lots that they cast were to find out the reason for the girl's death. The answer was that, if our Manuel had died when he tumbled into the sink of the ship, the girl would not have fallen into the sea."

After the storm had subsided the boat proceeded to Canton. It was only with great difficulty that the captain was dissuaded from remaining in that port. Finally he consented to go to another city, but just as they reached its harbour, where they expected to spend the winter, since the assertion was made that the season for sailing to Japan was nearly past, a boat came out to warn them that the port was infested with pirates. This so frightened the captain that he would have turned back to Canton had it not been that the wind was adverse, while it was favourable for going to Japan, whither they therefore directed their course. It thus came to pass that on August 15, 1549, they reached Kagoshima, the largest city in Paul's native province of Satsuma. The journey from Malacca had occupied only seven weeks.

II

FRANCIS XAVIER IN JAPAN

1549-1551

IN order that the events to be described in the following chapters may be better understood, it will be well to pause at this point in order to consider some of the political, social, and religious conditions of Japan at the time when Xavier and his companions reached its shores.

From ancient times the country had been divided into sixty-six provinces. Though the names by which these were designated have continued in use until the present day, the territories of the feudal lords were seldom coterminous with these divisions. In some cases a daimyo possessed several provinces, while in others a single province was divided between two or more of these barons. Xavier and his associates applied the name of "king" to these feudal lords; and there was much to justify the nomenclature, for many of them were practically sovereigns within their own estates, having little occasion to concern themselves about any person who might claim superiority over them.

The nominal ruler of the whole country was the Mikado, to whom alone the name of Emperor could properly be applied. Since A. D. 793, the Imperial residence had been in Kyoto. As the Japanese designation for a capital is "*miyako*," we find this word under various forms of spelling (most commonly "Meaco") used in older European books as though it were the name of the city. The Emperor possessed but little real authority at the time when Xavier came to Japan. Since the twelfth century the power had been in the hands of military rulers who obtained for themselves the title Sei-i Tai-Shogun, or Barbarian-Expelling Great-General. The

28

name Shogun, originally applied to all generals, came in time to be restricted in common use to the holder of the longer title. He nominally held his commission from the Emperor; but, as different families gained military ascendency, they were able to assert their claims to the office, which in practice became hereditary except as one family succeeded in supplanting another, thus setting up a new dynasty of rulers. The distinction between nominal and real power did not stop at this point. It often happened that a vassal of the Shogun would hold such a position towards him as the Shogun held towards the Emperor. These regents took care that their nominal superiors were kept as mere puppets, unable to assert themselves or to take any active part in public affairs. Children, only four or five years old, were made emperors or shoguns, were surrounded in their palaces with everything that tended to make them effeminate, and then, as they neared the age when there was any possibility of their becoming dangerous, were set aside for other children.

The Imperial power was at its lowest ebb under the shoguns of the Ashikaga family, whose rule began in 1338. As the revenues were chiefly absorbed during this period by the shogunate, the Emperor and the court nobles were ill provided with means for supporting their dignity. In one case the coronation ceremony was for lack of money postponed twenty-two years, and was finally made possible only by a contribution from the head of one of the Buddhist temples. The body of one Emperor lay unburied for forty days because a sum of money equal to about two thousand dollars could not be collected for the expenses of the funeral.

This period was marked by a succession of civil conflicts. Ashikaga Takauji, the first of his line, after failing to gain possession of the occupant of the throne, set up another person as Emperor and obtained from him the appointment as Shogun. For half a century there were two lines of rival claimants to the Imperial power; one supported by Ashikaga remaining in Kyoto, while the other dwelt in the mountains of Yamato. Dissensions afterwards arose in the Ashikaga family itself; or rather, those among its vassals who desired to gain the office of Prime Minister upheld different members of the house as claimants of the shogunate. At one time there were five of these rival shoguns.

As a result of the wars between the factions, Kyoto and the neighbouring provinces were greatly impoverished. Japanese historians say that the capital was filled with mountains of the slain, while the rivers ran with blood. Great conflagrations left behind them heaps of blackened ruins. Many of the people fled to the mountains for safety. Gardens and fields were left without cultivation. Famine and pestilence added their horrors to those of war; while an unusual number of typhoons and earthquakes seemed to show that nature was ready by the use of its most stupendous forces to help men in their work of destruction. Kyoto was still disturbed by civil strife at the time the missionaries began their labours in Japan; and twenty-four years later the Ashikaga family was brushed aside by a militant daimyo named Nobunaga.

The lack of a strong central government had left the feudal lords in the provinces free to fight among themselves as they might please. Those that were strong added the lands of weaker lords to their own. On the other hand, a retainer left in charge of some outlying castle might shake off allegiance to his former daimyo, becoming an independent lord or perhaps inducing others to help him in an attempt to supplant his former master. There was not the great separation between classes that afterwards made the soldiers so distinct from the farmers and artisans. Men were needed for attack and defence; whoever was able and willing to fight could easily find military employment. Some of the most powerful lords cherished ambitions for extending their influence over the whole country. To accomplish this, each schemed how he might gradually make his way towards Kyoto, where, by obtaining possession of Shogun and Emperor, he could become the real ruler of the land. It was finally from one of the small daimiates that there arose a warrior who was able to accomplish more than others had done. This was Oda Nobunaga, who in

1549—the year Xavier reached Japan—succeeded to his
father's estates in the province of Owari. The history
of the early missions in Japan synchronises with that
of the process by which the government became centralised; a movement begun by Nobunaga, greatly advanced
by Hideyoshi, and brought to completion by the early
Tokugawa rulers.

The early religion of the Japanese was Shinto. The
name signifies the Way of the Superior Beings. It combined nature-worship with reverence for ancestors.
Buddhism entered the country from Korea about the
middle of the sixth century. At first its progress was
but slow. Gradually, however, it became the leading
religion of the land, its success being in large part due to
the promulgation of the theory that the beings hitherto
worshipped by the Japanese were incarnations of Buddhist saints. Though the two religions became combined
in such a way that the mass of the people made little distinction between them, the Buddhist elements in the ad-
mixture exerted the greater influence upon the religious
thought and life of the nation. Some of the temples became very wealthy and powerful. The priests often
took an active part in political and even in military movements. The monasteries were in many cases strong fortresses whose inmates were better trained in the use of
the sword than in the ceremonies of worship. Often
the monks of two opposing sects engaged in active war-
fare, attacking and burning each other's temples. They
also took sides with rival claimants to the shogunate
and other offices. Those that had their headquarters on
Mt. Hiei, an eminence overlooking Kyoto, were specially
noted for their turbulence. Sometimes, when displeased
at action taken in the name of the Emperor, they would
march down from the mountain, those in the front ranks
carrying the sacred cars on their shoulders, while others
clad in full armour followed after them. On arriving
at the gates of the palace, they would demand in the
name of religion that their protests be heard. Petitions
backed by such a display of force were not to be lightly
dismissed. In the eleventh century the Emperor Shira-

kawa, who after a nominal abdication of imperial power still wielded it with a vigour shown by few of those who have ruled Japan, once said to a flatterer who praised his achievements: " There are three things that I have never succeeded in controlling—the throw of the dice, the flooded waters of the Kamo River, and the monks of Mt. Hiei." Kyoto was often burned, pillaged, and filled with bloodshed through the contests that these turbulent priests waged with other sects or with their political enemies.

Buddhism was at the height of its influence at the period with which we have to do. Murdoch writes: " It is no exaggeration to say that at the date of the first arrival of Europeans in Japan the greatest political power in the empire was that of the Buddhist priest-hood." As a natural consequence, those that desired power for themselves were ready to welcome whatever seemed likely to weaken that of Buddhism. This is doubtless the chief reason why Nobunaga showed such favour to the missionaries; and it had much to do with the readiness of many feudal lords to receive into their territories the men whom they hoped to utilise as instruments for diminishing the arrogance of the Buddhist priests. Yet it must be remembered that some daimyos were devoted Buddhists and that the custom of having their younger sons enter the priesthood greatly increased the political power of the monasteries.

Kagoshima, the port at which Xavier landed, was in the territories of the Daimyo Shimazu Takahisa. He and Otomo Yoshishige of Bungo, from whose port Xavier was to sail when he returned to India, were the most powerful lords in the island of Kyushu.

A letter written by Xavier shows that his reception in Japan was such as greatly encouraged him. In it he says:

" We have been received by the Governor (*Capitan*) of the city and by the Commandant (*Alcayde*) * with much kindness and friendship, as we have also been by all the people. They

* Cros thinks that this person was in command of the castle of Ichiku, which was afterwards visited by Xavier on his way to Hirado. It was about twenty miles from Kagoshima.

are much surprised to see priests from the land of the Portuguese. Far from thinking it strange that Paul has become a Christian, they greatly approve what he has done. All of them, whether relatives or strangers, have congratulated him on having gone to India and there beholding things which have never been seen in Japan. The Duke of the country has himself congratulated Paul, receiving him with honour and asking many questions upon the manners and the power of the Portuguese. To the great satisfaction of the Duke, Paul has given a full account of all these things. This Duke lives five leagues from Kagoshima. When Paul went to speak with him, he carried a very sacred picture that we had brought from India. It represented Our Lady holding in her arms the Child Jesus. The Duke was so delighted at seeing it that he knelt before the picture of Our Lord and Our Lady, reverencing them with great respect and ordering all his attendants to do the same.* Then the painting was shown to his mother, who looked upon it with the greatest pleasure. Paul returned to Kagoshima, where we reside, and a few days later there came a gentleman whom the Duke's mother had sent with orders to have the picture copied. More than one thing was lacking for doing this, and so the plan was abandoned. The same lady also asked that she might be given in writing an account of the Christian faith. Paul devoted several days to the task, and wrote to some length upon the subject in his own language.

"Believe me and give thanks to God; the way is open for carrying out your desires. If we knew how to speak, we should ere this have reaped much fruit. Paul has been so active preaching day and night to a great number of his kinsmen and friends that through his efforts his mother, his daughter, many other relatives, both men and women, and also many friends have already become Christians.

"No one is surprised in this country if a person becomes a Christian. Since most people can read and write, they quickly learn the prayers. May our Lord be pleased to give us the tongue with which to speak of divine things, for then by His grace and favour we shall produce much fruit. At present we are like statues in the midst of the people. They talk and have much to say concerning us, while we, being ignorant of the language, remain silent. We are reduced to the necessity of making ourselves little children and learning to talk."

Xavier with the help of Paul prepared an account of the principal Christian doctrines. This he wrote out in Roman characters for his own use in order that he might read it before the people. In the processes connected

---

* Probably they merely assumed the respectful posture usually taken by the Japanese when looking at objects of art.

with Xavier's canonisation the claim was made that he was endowed, sometimes at least, with miraculous power to use languages that he had never learned. Fourteen witnesses were found who testified that he spoke the languages of the countries visited by him, as freely and elegantly as though he had been born in those lands; that not infrequently men of different nations hearing him at the same time could all understand his meaning; and that when he first came to Japan " he preached without an interpreter, partly in Spanish, partly in Latin, partly in Portuguese, with a few Japanese words intermingled, and was understood by all as if he had spoken in the native language of each."

It hardly needs to be said that Xavier's letters contain no references to such marvels. On the contrary, there are several passages that show his inability to speak readily to the people. Besides using Paul and afterwards Fernandez as interpreters, much of his work was done by reading or repeating from memory the words of what he calls his " semi-Japanese volume."

It had been Xavier's desire to go directly to Kyoto; but in the letter from which quotations have already been made he says that the winds made this impossible and that it would be necessary for him to wait five months before they would be favourable. Meanwhile the Lord of Satsuma gave permission for the teaching of Christianity in his domains and for its acceptance by any of his subjects. The first converts, as we have seen, were in Paul's family, and after them came a young fisherman to whom the name Bernard was given. He afterwards accompanied Xavier in his travels through Japan and went with him to India.

Xavier hoped that many of the Japanese might be induced to go to Goa and that the college in that city would fit them to return as evangelists to their own people. He wrote to some of the Jesuits:

" Do your best at the college to instruct and train the Chinese and Japanese boys, above all watching over their souls. Let them learn to read, write, and speak Portuguese so that they may be interpreters for the Fathers who, if it so pleases God, shall before many years come to Japan and China. It does not

seem to me that there can be any other land yet discovered
where so much fruit will be garnered as in this, nor that the
Society can be elsewhere so perpetuated as in China and
Japan. . . . . .
  " Should there come to Goa two bonzes who go this year to
Malacca, do all you can to have them welcomed into the houses
of the Portuguese. Show them much attention. Manifest to
them as much love as I did to Paul when I was in Goa. This
is a people which wishes to be led only by love; therefore put
away all severity in dealing with the Japanese."

Another letter stated that the bonzes would be accompanied by several other persons. Xavier also informed the Commandant of Malacca that many Japanese
were on the way thither, being influenced by Paul's
praise of the Europeans, and he added: " Take care
that they be received in the houses of rich Portuguese
where there shall be nothing lacking in what makes up
honourable hospitality, so that the Japanese may return
to confirm concerning the Portuguese all the good that
Paul has been able to report."
A letter written June 24, 1550, by Father Perez, who
was then in Malacca, tells us that the ship bearing the
first news from Xavier had arrived in April. It further
says:

" In the ship came four Japanese. They were well received
in the house of a Chinese Christian; and many of the Portuguese of the city frequently invited them to their houses. They
often came to see us also, and we instructed them in the doctrines of our holy faith, so that they gladly received baptism
on Ascension Day. . . . Three of the new Christians have returned to Japan; the fourth remains here."

When Xavier had been two months in Kagoshima, he
learned that a Portuguese ship had come from China to
Hirado, a port in the northwestern part of Kyushu. Although he was suffering from a fever, he set out at once
for that city, accompanied by a young Japanese who
served as an interpreter. After about a month's absence
he returned to Kagoshima.*   Here he resumed his former

_____
* Cros, vol. ii., p. 55. Most of Xavier's biographers do not
mention this journey, of which we learn through Father Froez,
who wrote in 1586 and had good opportunities for learning the
facts. It seems strange that Xavier himself does not speak of

method of teaching. One of the first Japanese believers admitted to the priesthood afterwards wrote that he had been informed by the Christians of Kagoshima that when Xavier was there he " went twice a day to the terrace in front of a Buddhist monastery and there taught the people by reading to them from a book he had prepared."

Xavier frequently visited the monasteries themselves. The abbot of one belonging to the Zen sect was, according to Xavier, named Ninjit. He became very friendly with the missionary and often discussed religious questions with him. This bonze did not have a very high opinion of his associates, for when Xavier once found the monks engaged in the ceremony of meditation as practised by the Zen sect and asked what they were doing, Ninjit replied: " Some are reckoning up how much money they have gained from their parishioners, others are trying to think how they can manage to dress well and have good food, while the rest are thinking of the pleasures in which they wish to engage. Not one thinks upon any matter of importance."

Though Xavier writes that Ninjit was then eighty years old, he was still alive twelve or thirteen years later when Kagoshima was visited by Brother Almeida, to whom he said: " I wished to know all that Father Francis came to preach in Japan; but, for lack of an interpreter, I was not able to understand. Though I should like to be baptised before I die, my position, my

it in the long letter dated November 5, 1549, which contains the account of the voyage to Japan and the early experiences in Kagoshima. However, there are other omissions that are equally inexplicable. Xavier does not tell us how he found opportunity to forward this and other letters of the same date. Father Cros, extending somewhat the "two months" at Kagoshima, supposes that the letter, which was evidently written by piecemeal, was finished and dated just before Xavier set out for Hirado and that the four Japanese who were to go in the Portuguese ship to Malacca followed him more slowly. Another question to which we find no answer is why Xavier delayed so long in carrying out his desire to go to Kyoto. To say nothing of the possibility of going by land, as he finally did, the more than a year spent in Kagoshima must have brought a favourable season for navigation.

dignity, and the veneration in which I am held prevent me." Afterwards he and the abbot of another temple, who had also known Xavier, asked to be baptised in secret; but Almeida refused to grant their request.

In September, 1550, the three missionaries, accompanied by Amador, Manuel, and Bernard, left Kagoshima and went to Hirado. The reason, as given by Xavier, was the opposition to their work shown by the Buddhist priests, who urged the Daimyo to put a stop to the teaching of doctrines that would turn the people from their former beliefs. The "History of the Japanese Church"* written at Macao in 1634, says the bonzes saw that the progress of the Gospel would cause the ruin of their monasteries, and so they decided to drive away the missionaries. They told the people not to listen to the foreigners, and circulated various rumours concerning them, such as that they ate human flesh. To increase suspicion, they threw blood-stained rags about the house occupied by the missionaries. The bonzes succeeded in getting the Daimyo to issue an edict forbidding under penalty of death that any one should in future become a Christian. He did not, however, persecute those that had already received baptism. Father Valegnani and the author of the history just mentioned say that the Daimyo became less favourable to the missionaries when he found that he could not make them his instruments for inducing the Portuguese ships to come to Kagoshima instead of to Hirado.

Anjiro was left to care for the little company of about one hundred and fifty baptised persons in Kagoshima. Five months after the departure of the missionaries, he was so persecuted by the bonzes that he fled to China. Sad to relate, this first Japanese convert and evangelist proved to be like many after him whose course has been a disappointment to their teachers. "Driven by misfortune," says Froez, "he became a *bafan* along the coasts of China. A *bafan* is nothing more nor less than a pirate who joins to deeds of violence at sea similar deeds on shore, thus inflicting loss upon fishermen and

* This has not been printed, but is often quoted by Cros.

other people that live there. He was slain while engaged in one of these piratical expeditions." *

On the way to Hirado Xavier stopped twelve days at
the castle of Ichiku. Very likely it was not the first
time he had been there. A retainer of its commandant
had already been baptised under the name of Michael;
and it was probably on the present visit that the commandant's wife, his eldest son, who was then about five
years old, and several of his vassals were baptised.
Froez tells us that before Xavier continued on his journey Michael asked that something efficacious for the healing of disease be given him, as the country was without
physicians and medicines. Xavier therefore presented
him with an image of Mary and a scourge. In giving
him the image Xavier said: "My son Michael, here
is a medicine for souls. Adore the image of the Holy
Virgin, and when you wish to obtain forgiveness for
your sins, kneel before it and ask Our Lady to obtain
pardon through her Divine Son." In presenting the
scourge, he said: "This, my son Michael, is for the
health of your body. If any one, Christian or pagan,
suffers from fever, you must give him or he must give
himself three light blows with this scourge, while he
invokes the very sacred names of Jesus and Mary. In
this way the sick will be healed." During the remaining
fourteen or fifteen years of Michael's life invalids were
constantly coming to him from different parts of the
country, being drawn by reports of the benefits that
others had received from the remedy. Michael was so
careful to observe Xavier's directions that he would
never allow more than the prescribed number of blows
to be given, asserting that otherwise the disease would
be augmented.

Xavier taught Michael how to baptise infants and
adults. He also gave him manuscripts in Japanese
which contained a life of Christ, the Seven Penitential
Psalms, some prayers, and a calendar. He told the
Christians to meet on Sundays and feast-days that they
might read the life of Christ and engage in worship;
while on Fridays they were to repeat the Penitential

* Cros, " S. François de Xavier," vol. ii., p. 96.

Psalms. For amulets he gave them some little silk bags, each of which contained either the Creed or the names of Jesus and Mary.

Twelve years later, when Almeida visited Ichiku, he found that Michael was the leader of a company of Christians numbering about seventy. He still kept the scourge and told how by its use the wife of the commandant had been healed of a severe ailment. Every week the Christians of the castle held a meeting in which each gave himself three blows with the scourge. The commandant had not been baptised. He said to Almeida: " Had I not been convinced that your religion is true, I should not have allowed my wife and children to accept it. I adore no God but the One worshipped by you and in all my needs I look to Him for help. Out of regard for the Daimyo I do not yet announce my faith; but I hope that hereafter God will make it possible for me to do so and that I shall have my lord's permission to declare myself a Christian."

On reaching Hirado the missionaries were saluted with a salvo of artillery from the Portuguese ships that were lying in the harbour. They were also furnished with an escort of honour when they went to meet the Daimyo. In one of Xavier's letters he wrote concerning Hirado: " The lord of that country received us with much affection and kindness. In a few days about a hundred persons became Christians, thanks to what was preached to them by Brother Juan Fernandez, who already knew how to speak passably well, and to the book translated into the Japanese language, which we read to them."

Xavier remained in Hirado only ten days. He desired to push on towards Kyoto, where he hoped to effect the conversion of the Emperor. Leaving Cosmo Torres and the two servants in Hirado, he with Fernandez and Bernard continued their journey. They went most of the way on foot, their shoulders laden with the few things they needed to take with them. Many were the difficulties that they met. Sometimes they were refused shelter at the inns. In many places they were rudely treated by the people. The children hooted at them and pelted them with stones.

Fernandez says that while in Kagoshima the missionaries had been reproved by the bonzes for eating meat and fish; therefore on this journey, when these articles of diet were served at the inns, Xavier would explain to those who might be about him that it was perfectly proper to use such things, which God had supplied for the needs of men; but after taking a very small piece in order to enforce his words by his example, he made his meal entirely of rice and vegetables.*

At Hakata the missionaries visited a large temple of the Zen sect, whose priests received them with great pleasure as persons who had come from India, the cradle of Buddhism. Before leaving them, Xavier, as we are told by Fernandez, reproved the abbot and priests in the severest terms for the abominable vice of sodomy which prevailed among them. He also reproached them because on the one hand they told the people that there was no future life and on the other exhorted them to bring in behalf of their dead friends offerings which the bonzes used for their own benefit. His hearers were astonished that a stranger should reprimand them so vigorously, though some of them only laughed at his words.

In a few days the travellers reached Yamaguchi, a city in the southwestern part of the largest of the Japanese islands. Here they met the Daimyo, who, after asking many questions about India and Europe, expressed a desire to know the nature of the religion they had come to teach. Accordingly Fernandez read from their book the account of the Creation and an explanation of the Commandments. When the Daimyo heard the condemnation of sodomy, a vice to which he himself was addicted, his countenance showed that he was much excited, and the officer who had arranged for the interview made a sign to the missionaries that they should

* Cros, vol. ii., p. 102. In one of the letters written before reaching Japan, Xavier says that they had been told that the Japanese would be offended if they saw the missionaries eating animal food, and so to avoid offence they determined to refrain from it. Apparently they had not strictly adhered to this resolution.

withdraw: "As for me," wrote Fernandez, "I was afraid that the King would have our heads cut off."

"The next day," continues Fernandez, "without waiting for any order or permission of the King, Father Francis decided that we should preach in the streets of Yamaguchi. This we did in the following manner. We stood at the crossings where the people were abundant. I first read from the book an account of the creation of the world. Then in a loud voice I spoke of the great sins committed by the Japanese, dwelling principally on three things: First they forgot God, the Creator and the all-powerful One, who made and preserves them. Instead of Him they adored wood, stone, and inanimate things, through them worshipping the devil, who is the enemy of God and men. In the second place, they give themselves up to the abominations of Sodom; and at this point I exposed the shame and baseness of sin, speaking of the chastisements with which the world has been afflicted because of it. The third sin was that of the women, who, to spare themselves the trouble of bringing up children, slay their offspring at birth or even before, an act that proves them guilty of horrible cruelty and inhumanity. While I was thus preaching, Father Francis at my side engaged in prayer, asking God to bless my words to those that listened.

"Thus we continued preaching every day until there did not remain in that great city a street-crossing where we had not made public addresses. We also spoke in the house of gentlemen [fidalgos] who invited us, some of them for the sake of killing time, some because they wished to hear something new, and others that they might make fun of us. Some showed us either affection or pity, while others gave evident signs of despising us. Among these gentlemen was one who had, as I think, brought us to his house only for his amusement or pastime. While I was reading to him the story of the fall of the angels, how Lucifer for his pride was cast down from heaven to hell, and how those that are haughty will meet a like fate, since they will be delivered up to the demons with whom they must suffer eternal punishment, he began to show his contempt for what I was reading. Father Francis at once chided him, saying: 'However powerful you may be, if you do not humble yourself and weep for your sins, God will know how to subdue you by the torments of hell.' As the man drew nearer to us expressing his scorn for the Father and his words, Father Francis was inflamed with zeal and his face was all aglow as he said: 'Beware! unless you humble yourself, you will suffer these torments.' Thereupon we left him. As we were going from his house the Father said to me: 'I am sorry for that gentleman. The more powerful these persons are, the less they profit from God's mercies.'"

It is evident that no fear of consequences held Xavier back from speaking plainly to his hearers. Moreover, when he was aware that men of high rank were using impolite forms of speech towards him, he told Fernandez: " Thee-and-thou them just as they do me." * Fernandez says that in obeying this direction he always trembled lest his head would be struck off, but Xavier reproved him, saying that, in order to gain the respect of the Japanese, they must show that they had no fear of death.

Xavier wrote as follows of the way they were ridiculed by the rabble:

" Whenever we went through the streets of the city, we were followed by a company of boys drawn from the lowest dregs of the populace who laughed at us and mocked us with such words as: ' There go the men who tell us that we must embrace the law of God in order to be saved, because we cannot be rescued from destruction except by the Maker of all things and by His Son! There go the men who declare that it is wicked to have more than one wife."

The missionaries remained about two months in Yamaguchi and then finding, as Xavier writes, that the results of their labour were small, they started the last of December on their way towards Kyoto. The weather seemed very severe to persons that had lived in India and had spent the previous winter in the comparatively mild climate of Kagoshima. Sometimes they had to ford rivers where the icy water was waist-deep. They were ignorant of the roads, and the country was in a confused state owing to the civil wars. In one place through which they passed, an influential man who became interested in the travellers gave them a letter to a friend in the city of Sakai asking him to help them on their way. When they presented this letter, the person to whom it was addressed entertained them hospitably and made arrangements by which they joined the train of a nobleman who was on his way to the capital, now only about forty miles distant. It was a great advan-

* In the French of Father Cros, " *Tutoyez-les comme ils me tutoient.*"

tage to be in such a company, since it afforded them protection from evil-disposed persons along the road.

Xavier and his companions reached Kyoto in January, a month when the winds, sweeping down from snow-covered mountains north of the city, are cold and piercing. Five years previously, war and conflagrations had made a large part of the city almost a desert. There had been a succession of civil strifes, in which the warlike monks of Mt. Hiei had taken an active part. The court-nobles and many other inhabitants had moved elsewhere. The missionaries had a letter to a gentleman who sent them to the residence of his son-in-law, eighteen or twenty leagues distant.* From there they soon returned to Kyoto where Xavier tried to obtain an audience with the Mikado. Those to whom he applied asked whether he had brought any presents. He answered that these had been left in Hirado, whence they could quickly be procured if permission was given him to present them in person to the Mikado. This reply was not deemed satisfactory, and it may be doubted whether in any case an audience could have been procured. Xavier became convinced that the most powerful person in Japan at that time was the Lord of Yamaguchi. Since there seemed to be little hope of accomplishing anything in the capital, he departed after having spent only eleven days in the city.

Such is the account given by Fernandez. Xavier himself wrote:

"Arriving in Meaco, we passed some days making an attempt to have an interview with the King in order to demand permission to publish the Divine Law in his kingdom; but in this we failed, and since we did not find among the people any disposition to listen to the proclamation of the Gospel, wars or other obstacles standing in the way, we returned to Yamaguchi."

Retracing their way to Sakai, Xavier and his companions went from there to Hirado by sea. They found

* This statement is taken by Cros from the unprinted history by Froez. It might be thought a misplacement of the account of the gentleman in Sakai to whom Xavier took a letter were it not that the latter is mentioned in the same history.

that in the four months of their absence a number of persons had been baptised by Torres, who was now left to continue his work while the others soon set out again for Yamaguchi. Increased acquaintance with the Japanese had shown Xavier that both the rich and the poor were inclined to despise a person that was not well dressed. He therefore abandoned the garb of poverty and procured from the Portuguese merchants richer garments than he had hitherto worn. He took with him the letters and presents that had been furnished by the Viceroy of India and the Bishop of Goa. These would have gone to either the Mikado or the Shogun if circumstances had been more favourable in Kyoto. As it was, they were given to the Lord of Yamaguchi, who in return sent a large sum of silver to Xavier. The latter at once returned this, saying that a more acceptable gift would be permission to preach the Gospel.

Xavier also gave the Daimyo a large and beautifully bound copy of the Bible, telling him that in this book was written the whole of the Sacred Law that the missionaries had come to proclaim. Verbal permission for teaching was at once granted, and four months later public notices were posted throughout the city proclaiming that the missionaries were at liberty to preach Christianity and the people to believe it. Moreover, the Daimyo presented the missionaries with a piece of land that had belonged to a Buddhist monastery.

At the Daimyo's residence Xavier met several Buddhist priests belonging to the Shingon sect. As they listened to his explanation of the attributes of God, they professed to find a great resemblance between his views and what they themselves taught concerning Dainichi, that one of the so-called Buddhist Trinity who is the personification of wisdom and purity. They said to him: "We differ in language and customs, but in reality the law taught by you and by us is one and the same." They invited him to their temples and in other ways showed themselves very friendly, apparently hoping to profit by the favour which he enjoyed with the Daimyo. Xavier set himself to learn what he could about this Dainichi. Froez says:

" In frequent conversations with the bonzes he sounded their beliefs so far as his slight acquaintance with the language enabled him to do so. He especially asked them about the three divine Persons and the relations that existed between them, about the incarnation of the Second Person, and about the mystery of redemption through the Cross. The bonzes had no knowledge at all of such doctrines and ridiculed them as fables. On discovering this and also learning their abominable practices, Xavier recognized that their specious doctrines and the words in which these were disguised were the work of the devil. He ordered Juan Fernandez to preach through the streets that men ought not to adore Dainichi nor to consider him as a god; that, on the contrary, they should recognise that the teaching of the Shingon sect, like that of the others, was only an invention of devils and a tissue of falsehoods."

It is not strange that Xavier soon ceased to be a welcome guest at the temples nor that the bonzes did their best to counteract his influence.

In accordance with the permission that had been granted for the public proclamation of Christianity, Xavier was accustomed to go out twice a day for this purpose. Standing at a street-corner or sitting on the curb of the public well, he would read from his book and endeavour to explain its meaning to the people that gathered about him. Most of the preaching, however, was done by Fernandez. Though many persons were ready to praise the new doctrine, none were willing to become its adherents until after the occurrence of an incident that brought about the first conversion. As Fernandez was speaking to a large company of people, a man edged his way through the crowd and, pretending that he was about to whisper something in the preacher's ear, bent forward and spat upon his cheek. The crowd laughed at this exploit and looked to see how the foreigner would treat such an insult. With admirable self-control Fernandez, without pausing in his address or even turning to look at his assailant, quietly wiped his face with a handkerchief and went on as calmly as though nothing unusual had occurred. The spectators were greatly impressed. One prominent man who had been an avowed enemy of Christianity reasoned thus to himself: " A religion that enables its followers to practise such virtue must surely be divine." At the close of the sermon he followed Fernandez home and declared that the words and the behaviour of the preacher had convinced him of the truth of Christianity. He was the first in the city to be baptised, and his example had a great influence upon others.

It was in Yamaguchi that Xavier is said by his biographers to have made a remarkable exhibition of miraculous powers:

"As he was often surrounded by many who hoped to puzzle him by their incessant and contradictory questions—such as the essence of the deity, the creation of the world, the secrets of nature, the malice of the devils, the immortality of the soul, the eternity of rewards and punishments; others again were questions of mere curiosity as to the motion of the heavenly bodies, the causes of eclipses, thunder, lightning, the rainbow, and other equally dissimilar subjects,—he with one and the same answer solved these multifarious doubts, God so transforming the words, either in his mouth or in the ears of his auditors, that each one seemed to hear the answer required by his own special question." *

Those that credit such marvels will not be surprised to learn that "in after years, when other missionaries succeeded him in Japan, the people complained that they did not answer questions as immediately as the first teacher of Christianity they had seen."†

Though Xavier's letters narrate no such wonders, they do speak of the many questions that were addressed to him. In asking for new missionaries he says:

"They will be annoyed more than can well be imagined. At all hours of the day and into the night they will be beset with visits and questions. They will be invited to prominent houses where no excuse can be found for staying away. They will have no time for prayer or thought or meditation. In the beginning especially, they will not be able to say daily mass. The answering of questions will occupy so much of their time that they will hardly find leisure for reciting the office, for eating, or for sleeping."

The missionaries were much encouraged by their success in Yamaguchi. Xavier wrote: "In two months,

---

* Bartoli and Maffei, Eng. Ed., p. 388.
† Coleridge, vol. ii., p. 302.

at least five hundred persons have become Christians and the number is daily increasing." Among the early converts was a young man, totally blind in one eye and having but little use of the other, who made a living as a story-teller and musician. He is said to have had a keen mind, as was shown by the kind of questions he addressed to the missionaries. Convinced by their answers, he was baptised and received the name of Lawrence. This man was afterwards admitted into the Society of Jesus as a lay brother. He became a very effective worker and in the remaining thirty years of his life was the means of procuring many conversions.

A report having reached Xavier that a Portuguese vessel had come to the province of Bungo on the east coast of Kyushu, he sent on the first of September, 1551, to get information concerning it. The messenger brought back letters from the Portuguese merchants and also one from Otomo Yoshishige, the Lord of Bungo, asking him to come to Funai, his capital. This daimyo, then only twenty-three years old, was to have an important place in the history of the Japanese Church. One of the first, perhaps the very first foreign ship to visit Japan had come to Bungo nine or ten years before, and it is said that his entreaties were what prevented its confiscation by his father. This made the youth very popular with the Portuguese. One of those who came on that ship remained three years in Bungo and taught him many things about Europe. When the young man became Daimyo, he did his best to attract merchants to his ports, recognising the great advantages that would come from foreign trade. It seems probable that the letter which had come to Malacca two years before asking for missionaries was from Yoshishige.

Xavier summoned Torres to come to Yamaguchi, while he himself set out for Bungo accompanied by Bernard and three other Christians. They were enthusiastically ·welcomed by the Daimyo and the Portuguese. Among the latter was the famous Mendez Pinto, who describes the ceremonies connected with Xavier's introduction to the Daimyo, besides recounting many other incidents alleged to have occurred during the stay in Bungo. Among other things he gives a full report of a discussion that Xavier is said to have had with a famous Buddhist priest. Unfortunately it is impossible to put much reliance on this and other improbable stories narrated by Pinto in connection with this visit.

Xavier accepted the invitation of the Portuguese captain to take passage with him to India. Affairs connected with the Society's work in that country are said to have made his presence desirable; but in his own letter the only reasons given for the decision to return are that he desired to meet the associates from whom he had been so long separated, to find new workers for Japan, and to provide many things that were needed by the labourers there. In the same letter he speaks of his decision to attempt work in China. He had met many Chinese in Japan and considered them as belonging to a superior race. Moreover, the relations of the two countries were such that he thought the acceptance of Christianity by the Chinese would ensure its victory in Japan.

The ship sailed from Bungo November 20, 1551. Xavier therefore had spent twenty-seven months in Japan. He was accompanied on the return voyage by Bernard and another convert named Matthew. The latter died the next year in Goa. Bernard proceeded to Europe, was admitted as a lay brother to the Society of Jesus, and died a few years later in its college at Coimbra, Portugal.

The Lord of Bungo sent by the same ship an envoy to the Viceroy of India asking for an alliance with the Portuguese. He also requested that more missionaries be sent to teach his people and said: "They will reside at Funai near me, and I will show them greater favour than the other kings of Japan possibly can." The envoy became a Christian while on the voyage. The next year he returned to Japan.

After reaching India, Xavier busied himself over matters connected with the conduct of the Society, selected missionaries to be sent to Japan, and made arrangements for his own journey to China. Setting out at last for the latter country, he in due time reached Chang-chuang

(Sanchian), an island which was at that time the place
for trade between the Chinese and the Portuguese. It
was his hope that some of the native merchants might
be induced to convey him secretly to the mainland.
The Portuguese, who feared that such an attempt might
lead the Chinese to withdraw permission for trade, tried
to dissuade him from his purpose. While trying to sur-
mount the obstacles they put in his way, he was struck
down with fever and died November 27, 1552.*

The accounts given by the Jesuits assert that Xavier's
coffin was filled with quicklime in order that the flesh
might be quickly consumed, leaving the bones to be
taken to India; but in February, when the coffin was
opened, it was found that the body and even the clothes
remained intact. When a slight cut was made in the
flesh, the blood flowed freely. The body was taken to
Malacca and ultimately to Goa. It is affirmed that many
miracles have been wrought in connection with it. At
Goa, every twelfth year, there is a great festival at which
the faithful are allowed to gaze on the hands and feet
of the saint. Those who saw the body in 1890 said that
it no longer retained the fresh appearance it formerly
had, but that the skin had become dry like that of a
mummy. One Roman Catholic missionary in India, in
endeavouring to account for the change, wrote: " It is
my humble opinion that the desiccation of the holy relic
began at the moment when the Jesuits were expelled
from Goa." †

Whatever we may think of these stories and of the
reverence shown for the body, we must recognise that
Xavier yet lives through the influence that he has exerted upon his own church and to some extent upon
others. He did more perhaps than any other man of
modern times to arouse the missionary zeal of Roman
Catholics. He was indeed far from being a model missionary. He did not exhibit that persistence in one line
of effort that is needed to secure the best results. In

* The date is usually given as December 2. The reasons for
considering the one in the text correct may be found in Cros,
vol. ii., p. 55.
†_Missions Catholiques_, February 27, 1891.

India, he relied too much on the power of the government for advancing the interests of religion. He even desired to have a military expedition sent to aid a person who promised to be a Christian if he were set up as a native ruler. Having obtained authority over the pearl fisheries at Tutocorin, Xavier ordered that certain persons should not be allowed to share in them because they had been so disobedient to him that they deserved the name of renegades. He urged the King of Portugal to set up the Inquisition in India.* Such facts show that had he remained in Japan he would doubtless have approved the methods by which afterwards some of the converted daimyos forced their subjects to accept Christianity. All of this, however, is little more than to say that in such matters Xavier was a man of his own age. We must not judge even the progressive men of the past by the standards of to-day. We cannot expect them to surpass their contemporaries in every particular. If some of Xavier's methods, such as the speedy baptism of multitudes who knew hardly anything of the real meaning of Christianity, seem to us unwise, we must remember that he was treading unbeaten paths. They that undertake a new work must frequently make mistakes. They cannot profit by the experiences of others. In missionary methods men of the present day ought to be wiser than those that have gone before them.

Whatever may have been Xavier's faults, he was fitted to be a leader of men. He was a pioneer who, like Livingstone, opened the way for others. An enthusiast himself, he was able to inspire his followers with enthusiasm. There was in him something that to a wonderful degree called out the love of those who came under his influence, making them willing to work or to suffer with him and for him. Many whose religious views differ greatly from his can sympathise with his earnest devotion to Christ; Romanists, Protestants, and Eastern Christians alike finding in the hymn which is ascribed to Xavier an expression of their own deepest thoughts:

* For proofs of the above statements drawn from Xavier's letters see Cros, vol. i., pp. 275, 279, sq.; vol. ii., p. 508.

"O God, Thou art the object of my love,
Not for the hopes of endless joys above,
Not for the fear of endless pains below
Which those who love Thee not must undergo.
For me and such as me Thou once didst bear
The ignominious cross, the nails, the spear;
A thorny crown transpierced Thy sacred brow;
What bloody sweats from every member flow!
For me in torture Thou resign'dst Thy breath,
Nailed to the cross, and sav'dst me by Thy death.
Say, can those sufferings fail my heart to move?
What but Thyself can now deserve my love?
Such as then was and is Thy love to me,
Such is, and shall be still, my love to Thee.
Thy love, O Jesus, may I ever sing,
O God of love, kind Parent, dearest King."

(Translated by Dryden.) *

* Though this hymn was one of Xavier's favourites, the probability is that he was not, as formerly supposed, its author

III

WORK OF THE EARLY MISSIONARIES

1551-1570

WHILE Xavier was in Bungo he received letters from Torres and Fernandez telling him of events in Yamaguchi. Immediately after his departure from that city the bonzes forced their way into the house where the missionaries dwelt, and began to make sport of them and their teachings. There also came for several successive days a number of the gentlemen and scholars of the city to propound various questions concerning the Christian religion. Fernandez sent to Xavier a list of these queries and of the answers that Torres made through him as interpreter. The questions were as follows:—

Of what material did God create human souls?

What is the shape of the soul, and what is its colour?

If the soul is without colour, is it then nothing at all?

What is God and where is He?

Has God a body?

When the soul leaves the body, does it see God?

Why cannot a man see God?

If the soul is not corporeal, is it God?

What are devils?

Why do devils cause so much evil to men?

It is not true that all which God created is good; for did He not create that proud and rebellious spirit, Lucifer?

If God desires the salvation of men, why does He permit the devil to do them so much evil?

If God wishes to save men, why has He made them so that they seem to be set upon doing or desiring evil?

If God wishes that all men should attain to glory, why has He made the road to its attainment so difficult?

As hell is in the center of the earth, then, when the devils come to tempt us, do they escape from their torments?

If, as you say, the devils are in torment wherever they are, why was a special place created for punishing them?

By what road can devils come to us from the center of the earth?

If God wishes to save men, why has He been so slow in giving us a knowledge of His Law?

There are some men so devoid of intelligence that they cannot attain to a knowledge of their Creator. What will become of such persons?

The Buddhist priests did their best to excite the people against the missionaries. Many were the stories that they invented for this purpose. Among other things they declared that they had seen a demon causing lightning to fall upon the Daimyo's mansion because of his relations with foreigners.

A civil strife that broke out at the end of September, 1551, though it had no direct connection with religious matters, increased the danger of the missionaries' position. A revolt was raised against the Daimyo, who, after an attempt at flight, committed suicide. For eight days the city was a scene of confusion and bloodshed. At the beginning of the trouble an influential gentleman of the city invited the foreigners to take shelter in his house. On the way thither they met several armed bands and heard people shouting: "Let us slay those men from India, since they are the cause of the evils that have come upon us." Their protector decided that they would be safer in a Buddhist monastery to whose funds he was a leading contributor. He accordingly sent them thither, and though the bonzes were at first inclined to refuse them admittance, saying: "You are devils and it is you who have brought all these calamities upon the land," they finally yielded and gave them shelter for two days. After this, the missionaries returned to the house of their protector, who concealed them until danger was over.

Those who had brought about the revolution now persuaded the brother of Otomo Yoshishige to take the place of the daimyo against whom they had rebelled. The new ruler, like his brother, was friendly to foreigners. Xavier in one of his letters says:

"Before I left Japan, the King of Bungo promised the Portuguese and myself that he would omit nothing which would induce his brother, the King of Yamaguchi, to treat Father Torres and Brother Fernandez with all favour; and the King of Yamaguchi, who had hardly entered into possession of his estates, promised for himself that he would do this."

As one result of this latter promise, a Buddhist monastery in Yamaguchi was soon afterwards given to the missionaries. The deed, of which a facsimile has been preserved, was to the following effect:

"With respect to Daijoji in Yamaguchi, Agata, Yoshiki Department, Province of Suwo. This deed witnesses that I have given permission to the priests that have come to this country from the western regions, in accordance with their request and desire that they may found a monastery and house in order to develop the law of Buddha." *

After his return to India, Xavier sent Father Balthazar Gago, together with Brothers Edward de Sylva and Peter d'Alcaceva to reinforce the mission in Japan. They reached Kagoshima in August, 1552, and proceeded to Funai, where they delivered the letters and presents that had been sent to Yoshishige by the Viceroy of India. On learning of their arrival, Torres sent Fernandez to act as their interpreter and to accompany them to Yamaguchi. The next Christmas was celebrated in that city with great pomp, and several persons who had become converts were invited to meet with the missionaries for a conference. Among other results of their deliberations was a decision that the Christians should engage in works of charity. One reason for doing this was to disprove the charge made by the Buddhist priests, who said that those who became Christians were influenced by the desire to escape from the necessity of making contributions to the temples. It was therefore ordered that

* The above translation by Sir Ernest Satow is from vol. vii. of Transactions of the Asiatic Society of Japan, where may be found a reproduction of the facsimile.

a box for the reception of alms be placed at the entrance of the building that was used for worship. The administration of the contributions was assigned to men whose rank and probity made them honoured by the people of the city.

Soon after this meeting, Gago and Fernandez went to reside in Funai; Sylva and Lawrence remained in Yamaguchi to assist Torres; while Alcaceva, bearing letters and presents from the Daimyo of Bungo to the Viceroy of India, soon returned to Goa in order to report the state of affairs in Japan and to ask for more missionaries.

For some time Funai and Yamaguchi remained the centres of Christian work. Naito, the Governor of Yamaguchi, was among those that early received baptism. His example was followed by many other prominent persons. Two Buddhist priests of Kyoto, moved by curiosity to see the foreigners and by a desire to enter into a discussion with them, came to Yamaguchi. One day, while Father Torres was addressing the people, these priests began to ask questions. The missionary replied and then continued his discourse, in which he had occasion to refer to the Apostle Paul. " Who is this Paul of whom you speak?" asked one of the priests. Thereupon Torres gave an extended account of the Apostle's life. Hardly had he finished when the questioner called out: " I, too, will be a Christian. As I have hitherto imitated Saul the persecutor, I desire henceforth to be like Paul the Apostle." His companion also declared his decision to be a Christian. The two men were soon baptised and received the names Paul and Barnabas. Both became earnest evangelists, going about the neighbouring towns and villages in order to proclaim their new faith.

In Funai the Buddhist priests, after vain attempts to make the people believe their calumnies against the missionaries, began to claim that Christianity differed from Buddhism only in certain external matters that were of little importance. The missionaries set themselves earnestly to the task of disproving such assertions by showing the radical differences between the two religions.

A revolt that arose against Otomo Yoshishige was thought to have been instigated by the Buddhists, and it threatened to interfere seriously with the progress of Christianity. The Daimyo was besieged in one of his strongholds. He did not know whom he could trust or what was the real strength of the opposition against him. Fernandez at considerable risk made his way to the castle, where he was able to report the real state of affairs. This act, together with the loyalty of the Christians, increased the favour with which Yoshishige regarded the missionaries.

Another revolt at Yamaguchi proved disastrous to Yoshishige's brother and to the church in that city. The number of converts there had reached about two thousand in the year 1556, when the opponents of the new Daimyo attacked the city and set it on fire. Three weeks later, it was reported that the enemy was approaching for another attack. The converts persuaded Torres, the only missionary then in Yamaguchi, to take refuge in Bungo. Soon after this, the Daimyo was slain. Many of the Christians lost their lives. For the next eighteen years the church of Yamaguchi was left without any resident priest, and it never again attained that degree of prosperity that its early history seemed to promise.

Alcaceva's efforts in India to obtain more missionaries for Japan were successful. Even the Provincial of the Jesuits, Melchior Nugnez, decided to be one of the number. He was helped to this decision by a conversation with Mendez Pinto, who, in telling him about Xavier's work in Japan, exclaimed: " Father Nugnez, you are the man who ought to go to that country. Gladly would I accompany you thither. How happy should I be if God graciously permitted me to give my life for the glory of His holy name! " The Provincial, who doubted whether Pinto was in earnest, began to speak of some objections. Pinto declared that his desire to go was so great that no difficulties could hold him back. Moreover, he announced that, after sending some gifts to relatives in Portugal, he would devote the rest of his fortune to the expenses of the proposed expedition to Japan and to the establishment of a seminary in Yamaguchi. This enthusiasm was so contagious that Nugnez, after consulting his associates and the Viceroy, decided that it was his duty to go to Japan with Pinto, who was now appointed the Viceroy's ambassador to the Daimyo—or King, as the Portuguese considered him—of Bungo.* With them went Father Gaspar Vilela and some seminarists. They set sail early in 1554, but were obliged to winter in Malacca. The next year, unfavourable winds detained them in China, where Nugnez received a letter from Loyola saying that a provincial ought not to go to regions so distant that he could not quickly return to his appointed place. Letters also came from Goa urging him to come back. He was about to follow these injunctions when a Portuguese merchant came from Japan with reports that again inflamed his zeal. Moreover, he received a letter from the Daimyo of Hirado, who had heard that Nugnez was on his way to Japan and therefore urged him to come to that city. The Daimyo doubtless thought that the residence there of the Provincial would help to draw the Portuguese merchants. In asking Nugnez to come to him, he referred to the previous visits of Xavier and other missionaries, saying that many of his leading retainers, as well as some members of his own family, had been baptised, and he declared that he himself was almost ready to become a Christian.

Nugnez decided to go forward. The winds were such

* The night before Nugnez started from Goa, he and others were in the chapel renewing the vows of their order. Pinto was also present, and the Jesuits were surprised to hear his voice joining with theirs as they pledged themselves to chastity, obedience, and poverty. When some one would have stopped him, Nugnez made a sign that he should be allowed to proceed. This he did and also added another vow by which he consecrated himself and all his wealth to the use of the mission. At the close, the Provincial signified his acceptance of the profession; but, as Pinto was the envoy of the Viceroy, it was decided that he should make no change in his dress until he had finished his official business. Though Pinto gave large sums for the work in Japan, his zeal for a religious life soon grew cool. It was found advisable to release him from his vows and he returned to India with Nugnez.

that, instead of proceeding to Hirado, the captain found it advisable to land on the coast of Bungo, which they reached in July, 1556. The missionaries were received with great honour by Yoshishige. Using Fernandez as interpreter, Nugnez had a long interview with this lord, who declared that he was convinced of the truth of Christianity. When he was urged to receive baptism and thus make a public declaration of his faith, he said that this was for the time being impossible, as there were in his domains many rebellious spirits who would take advantage of such action on his part and would join the Buddhist priests in seeking his overthrow.

Illness prevented Nugnez from going to Hirado and necessitated his speedy return to India. Before his departure he admitted to the Society of Jesuits two of the seminarists that had accompanied him to Japan, and also Louis Almeida, a Portuguese gentleman about thirty years of age, who had come to India and afterwards to Japan, hoping that by trade or by the practice of medicine, which he had studied, he might be able to repair his damaged fortunes. Just as he was about to return to Portugal, Father Gago had persuaded him to undertake the Spiritual Exercises of Loyola, and as a result of this he decided to give himself wholly to the service of God. Before his admission to the Society, he devoted five thousand crowns, which he had brought with him for trade, to the establishment at Funai of a hospital for lepers and of an asylum for children whose parents were too poor to provide for their support. He was led to found this asylum because he learned that the Japanese women often killed their new-born babes in order to avoid the expense of rearing them. The Daimyo, to whom Almeida appealed for help against this iniquitous custom, promised to provide nurses to care for the children.* Almeida was the first of the noble

* A letter written in 1576 by Father Cabral shows that, though these works of charity may have recommended Christianity to some persons, yet with others they became stumbling-blocks because for a long time the ranks of believers were chiefly recruited from the poor and from those who had been healed of loathsome diseases.

Others were unwilling to profess a religion whose acceptance line of medical missionaries in Japan. The reputation that he gained for his skill in healing disease, the charity that he manifested for those in poverty or distress, and his indefatigable efforts for the spread of the Gospel, made him one of the most successful of the Jesuit labourers.

The persistency with which the Daimyo of Hirado continued to ask for missionaries inspired the hope that he might be more ready than Yoshishige to become an open adherent of Christianity. Early in 1557, Gago, Fernandez, and Paul, the converted Buddhist priest, were sent to Hirado by Torres, whom Nugnez had made Superior. Although they did not find the Daimyo in so teachable a state of mind as they had hoped, the favourable reception that he gave them opened the way by which they were able to attain much success among his subjects. One of the early converts was Koteda Saemonnojo, a brother of the Daimyo, and acting under him as ruler of two neighbouring islands named Takashima and Ikutsukishima. At baptism he took the name Anthony. Under the designation " Prince Anthony " he occupies a prominent place in the letters and reports of the Jesuits. From the first he was very zealous in seeking the conversion of his own subjects. At his invitation the missionaries visited the islands. " The Prince's example drew abundance after it, and his zeal more; for he changed from a prince into an apostle by exhorting his people himself to leave their superstition, and standing godfather to all that would receive holy baptism. He had no greater pleasure in the world than to see them pull down idols out of the temples and houses, and burn, and throw them into the sea." *

With such encouragement it is not strange that adherents to the new religion increased so rapidly that in less than two months there were said to be fourteen hun-

seemed to classify them with such persons. The Annual Letter of the Jesuits for 1579, written soon after the baptism of Yoshishige, says that hitherto the converts had been almost entirely confined to the poor and those that had come to the hospital, one result being that non-believers despised Christianity as being the religion of the indigent and diseased.

* Crasset, Eng. Trans., vol. i., p. 158.

dred Christians in Anthony's estates. For their use he built several churches. In the absence of priests, the meetings held were chiefly for mutual encouragement and for the instruction of children. In the city of Hirado also there were many baptisms, and two churches were erected.

Ere long the number of workers was reduced by the illness of Paul. Feeling that he had not much longer to live, he begged to be taken back to Father Torres in order that he might receive the last sacrament from the same hand that had baptised him. This request was granted, and he died soon after reaching Funai.

Father Vilela was sent to take the place of Paul and of Gago, who had gone in 1557 to Hakata in Chikuzen, a province that had lately come into the possession of Otomo Yoshishige. Vilela was delighted with what he found in his new field of labour. It seemed to him that he had never seen so much religious fervour. All the neophytes, he said, were like catechists, trying to teach others what they themselves had learned. Vilela's own energy had much to do with this exhibition of zeal. He sent out one of the Brothers through the streets to ring a bell, chant prayers, and attract the children to church. The boys were organised in bands that paraded the streets singing Christian hymns, and they were told to repeat to their parents what was taught them in the church.

One morning the Christians were much excited to find that in the night a cross at whose foot they had been accustomed to pray had been removed. This was asserted to be the work of Buddhist priests, who had chosen three of their number to uproot the hated symbol of Christianity. As the story was afterwards told, speedy punishment fell upon those that had committed the sacrilege; for two of them at once fell into a quarrel that ended in their slaying each other, while the third mysteriously disappeared, nothing being heard of him until a demon that had taken possession of a young man confessed to being the spirit of the person who had thrown down the cross and who was now suffering punishment for the evil deed.

On seeing what had been done, the more impetuous of the believers set fire to a Buddhist monastery. They also dragged out the idols from a neighbouring temple, burning some of them and casting others into the sea. The priests hastened to the Daimyo, demanding not only that the Christians be punished, but that Vilela, the foreigner that was causing this trouble, should be driven out of the country. On the other hand, Anthony came to the defence of the missionary, asking if it was right to send away so summarily a religious teacher who had come at the Daimyo's own invitation, to whom protection had been promised, and who had committed no wrong. He declared that though the Daimyo's subjects had been forbidden to annoy the foreigners, the bonzes had circulated calumnies concerning them and had been the first movers in the present acts of violence.

The Daimyo replied by speaking of the difficult position in which he was placed. As the Daimyo of Bungo was about to make war upon him, it was imperative that there should be no division among his subjects; but the Buddhist priests were now threatening to stir up an insurrection. He urged that in view of the coming conflict it would be better for the missionary to withdraw, as he would be suspected of being an emissary of the Lord of Bungo. Moreover, a temporary withdrawal would be for the best interests of Christianity, since it would give an opportunity for the present excitement to cool down.

Convinced by these arguments, Anthony advised Vilela to leave the province for a while. At the same time a letter from Yoshishige urged the missionary to return to him. He accordingly set out at once for Funai. It is said that in his short stop at Hirado he had baptised thirteen hundred persons and converted three temples into Christian churches.

The believers in Hirado were now exposed to great trials, and it was from their number that the first Japanese martyr came. Another cross had been erected in the suburbs of the city. Thither processions of the Christians went every morning and evening, while at other times guards were stationed to preserve it from insult.

Among the Christians was the maid-servant of an unbelieving master who said that he would kill her if she persisted in going to the cross for worship. Unhindered by his threats, she continued her devotions until one morning, as she was returning from the cross, she was met by her master, who drew his sword and cut off her head. The Christians took up the body and buried it with great solemnity, exhorting one another to imitate the woman's example by remaining faithful unto death.

It has been mentioned that shortly before Vilela went to Hirado, Gago had removed to Hakata, the chief city of Chikuzen. He was accompanied by Brother Perreyra, one of the young Portuguese whom Nugnez had recently admitted to the Society of Jesus. They had not been there very long when the city was besieged by its former possessors, who were striving to recover the territories that had been seized by Otomo Yoshishige. At first a vigorous defence was made, but it is said that the Buddhist priests, who were very averse to being under a lord favourable to Christianity, opened the gates to the enemy. Fernandez, who happened to be in Hakata at the beginning of the siege, had been sent away by Gago in charge of some Christian children that served as acolytes. The other two Jesuits and Sylvester, a Christian who had accompanied them from Hirado, escaped by night to a ship that was anchored about two leagues from the city. When the captain learned that Hakata had been taken and that the refugees were the preachers who had been sent by Yoshishige, he took from them the church ornaments and other things they had brought with them, at the same time threatening them with death. Sylvester was told that he was free to depart, but he refused to leave the missionaries. After four days the captain reported to the Governor of Hakata that he had the foreigners in his charge. A force of soldiers that was sent to take them over quarrelled with the captain concerning the plunder and stripped from the missionaries the few clothes that had been left them. On arriving at Hakata, the captives were kept for several days in a dungeon beneath the ramparts. A Christian of high rank finally obtained permission to take them under his care. He also paid money for the ransom of Gago and the children, as their attempt to escape had been unsuccessful. For three months the missionaries lived in daily expectation that orders would be given for their execution; but at the end of that time they were led outside of the city and told that they might depart. They reached Funai only a short time before the arrival of Vilela.

It was not long before the missionaries thus assembled at Funai began to scatter once more. Mention has already been made of Mt. Hiei, a stronghold of Buddhism in the vicinity of Kyoto. The head priest of one of its temples had sent a letter to Father Torres expressing an earnest desire to see him. The writer said that only his own great age kept him from making the journey to Bungo, and he hoped that Torres, who had travelled from the ends of the earth to preach his religion to the Japanese, would be willing to come to Mt. Hiei in order to instruct a person earnestly desirous to know the truth. Xavier in his letters had written much about what he called the three great universities of Japan—Mt. Hiei, Koya, and Ashikaga,—urging that missionaries should be sent who had the ability to cope with their learned men, secure their conversion, and thus gain their help in Christianising Japan. The priest's letter seemed to open the way for entrance to the first of these schools.

Torres, who was unable to go at that time, forwarded to the priest a written statement of the principal Christian doctrines, and soon after he sent Vilela to give further instruction. In company with Brother Lawrence and another Japanese Christian, Vilela went by sea to Sakai and thence by land to Sakamoto, a village on the shores of Lake Biwa and at the foot of Mt. Hiei. There he learned that the priest who had sent the letter to Torres was no longer living. His successor professed considerable interest in what he heard from Vilela and advised him to ascend the mountain in order to visit the chief prelate. The missionary found, however, that it was impossible to get access to this dignitary. He therefore went to Kyoto. There with his companions he at first spent ten days in fasting, prayer, and penance, as a preparation for the work upon which they were entering. Then, with his head shaved after the manner of the bonzes and wearing robes like theirs, but carrying a crucifix in his hand, he went into the streets and began to preach. The capital was at that time enjoying a period of tranquillity, and the people flocked about the stranger to hear what he had to say. His peculiar manners and inaccurate use of the language made him an object of ridicule. Ere long, however, "through Otomo's favours and letters," and, strangely enough, "under the conduct of a Buddhist priest, one of the most respected men in the city," he obtained an interview with the Shogun, who received him with great favour and as a mark of honour drank out of the same cup with him. Moreover, the Shogun assigned him a house, favourably situated, where he was visited by many prominent citizens, some of whom invited him to their own mansions. It was not long before a person who is described as "one of the chief men" of the neighbouring city of Yamashina was baptised together with ten of his friends.

The enmity of the Buddhist priests was quickly aroused. In addition to denouncing the teaching of the preachers, they circulated all sorts of evil reports concerning them, saying among other things that they ate human flesh and that the bones of children had been found in their dwelling. Their landlord was induced to turn them out, so that they were forced to take shelter in a dilapidated building, where they were the object of insults from crowds of ill-disposed men and children who came to annoy them.* In some way, however, Vilela had gained the favour of Miyoshi, one of the Shogun's ministers. Thus it came about that proclamations permitting the missionaries to preach were posted

* Some writers have asserted that in the early days of intercourse with Europeans the Japanese showed no trace of antiforeign feeling and that Buddhists were guiltless of persecution until taught by the example that was set by the Christian missionaries and their converts. It will, however, be remembered that when Xavier was on his journey to Kyoto he was hooted by the children and pelted with stones; while the events above narrated unite with what happened in Yamaguchi, Bungo, and

throughout the city. This for a time put a stop to the opposition of the priests. Some of them even became believers. A great sensation was caused by the conversion of one of their number who had a great reputation for scholarship. It is said that among the writings adorning the walls of his room were sentences that seemed to show that by the light of nature he had attained to a knowledge of some of the truths held by Christians. One writing spoke of a God without beginning or end; another showed the dependence of the human heart on a Supreme Being who rules its movements. With an air of self-sufficiency this priest had come for an interview with Vilela; but after listening for some time to the latter's words, he suddenly called out: " I am a Christian. Baptise me." The news of his conversion spread abroad and fifteen other priests soon followed his example. Among them was one of upright life and austere manners who had vowed to devote his whole life to gratuitously teaching the Buddhist scripture known as Hokke-kyo. He told Vilela that a few years previously he had dreamed that priests came from India to teach the true way of salvation, and the very next day he learned of Xavier's arrival in Yamaguchi.

These conversions led to a new outbreak of hostility. It is charged against the Buddhist priests that they used bribes to induce the Governor of Kyoto to drive the preachers from the city. While he was seeking some pretext for doing what they desired, Miyoshi, who had learned of the plot, induced Vilela to withdraw for the time being to one of the minister's castles a few miles distant. Vilela consented, but afterwards, fearing that his act might be interpreted as a cowardly flight from danger, he returned to Kyoto, where he preached with as much boldness as ever. Miyoshi then caused a new edict to be issued which forbade any interference with the Christian teachers.

other places to show that, ere Christianity had gained sufficient strength to persecute, its followers were themselves the object of attack. The history of the Nichiren sect furnishes a proof that long before Christianity reached Japan, Buddhism knew how to persecute those whom it regarded as heretics.

It is interesting to know that Vilela's rebukes of the immorality that prevailed in the Buddhist priesthood so stirred the followers of the Nichiren sect that they demanded a reform, deposing the abbot of one of their monasteries because he kept concubines, showed a mercenary spirit, and disregarded the Buddhist prohibition of animal food.

The number of missionaries at Funai was further reduced by the departure of Father Gago. He had at first been a very zealous worker and the instrument for many conversions. Not long after his return from Hakata it was noticed that he seemed greatly changed. He had lost his interest in evangelistic labours. He who had once thought nothing too difficult was now abashed by slight obstacles. He finally declared that his physical infirmities made it impossible for him to remain in Japan. Torres, who judged that one in this state of mind would be of no help to the work, consented to his departure, and he sailed from Bungo in October, 1561.

At this time the churches of Japan were reckoned as five in number—those of Funai, Kyoto, Yamaguchi, Hakata, and Hirado. These were in correspondence with one another, sending letters by which each gave intelligence concerning itself and exhorted the others to faithfulness. Father Torres, who had oversight of all, was in Funai, while Father Vilela was in Kyoto; but the departure of Father Gago left no ordained priests who could be put in charge of the churches in the other cities. Brother Almeida, however, set out in June to visit Hakata and Hirado. In the former city he baptised seventy persons, among whom was a Buddhist priest from Yamaguchi. Continuing his journey to the islands that belonged to the estates of Anthony Koteda, he found that all the inhabitants of Takashima were Christians with the exception of eight, and these were being taught by a converted bonze. They were soon baptised by Almeida. In Ikutsukishima there were said to be eight hundred Christians.

About the close of the year 1561, the captain of a Portuguese ship which had anchored at Kagoshima came to Bungo with some of his crew in order that they might make their confessions to Father Torres. They brought a letter from the Lord of Satsuma, who asked that some missionary might come to carry on the work that had been begun by Xavier. In this as in some other cases, the suspicion naturally arises that the desire to attract commerce to his port was the underlying motive in the mind of the writer of this letter. However that may be, Almeida was directed to go at once to Satsuma. He was gladly welcomed by the Christians of that province who had been left so long without instruction. Mention has already been made of his visit to the castle of Ichiku and of his interview in Kagoshima with the priests who had known Xavier. The Daimyo prepared a letter to be carried by the Portuguese captain to the Provincial of the Jesuits in India. Besides speaking of his admiration for the Christian religion and his desire to have it taught to his people, he was careful to call attention to the fact that the excellent harbour of Kagoshima afforded fine opportunities for European merchants.

While Almeida was in Kagoshima, Father Torres received letters from Sumitada, the Lord of the small principality of Omura in the western part of the island of Kyushu. The former Daimyo of Omura, who died in 1550, had left as his heir a son born of a concubine. For some reason the leading vassals were disinclined to receive this person as their lord and thus it came about that Sumitada, son of the Daimyo of the neighbouring fief of Arima, was adopted by the house of Omura as its head. He now desired to further the interests of his people by inducing foreign merchants to visit his ports. Following the advice of one of his retainers, he sought to make use of the missionaries for accomplishing his purpose. Charlevoix states that a book composed by Vilela had come into the hands of Sumitada and proved so convincing that he desired to meet one of the missionaries in order to confer with him about becoming a Christian; though, in order to conceal this purpose from his counsellors, he spoke to them only about the advantages of attracting foreign commerce.

In his letter to Torres he asked that the latter would use his influence for bringing the Portuguese merchants to Omura.   Among other inducements he promised that the foreigners might have for ten years, free from all taxes and duties, the use of the port of Yokoseura and the surrounding land within a radius of two leagues. No persons would be permitted to reside there without previously obtaining the consent of the Jesuits, for whom a residence would be built and a sufficient subsidy given to provide for its maintenance.

Torres at once recalled Almeida from Kagoshima and sent him to complete the arrangements at Omura, while he himself went to consult the Portuguese merchants at Hirado.   As a result of his representations, a ship that was lying in the harbour hoisted anchor and prepared to sail to Yokoseura, the captain announcing that he did not care to trade any longer in a place where Christians were subjected to persecution.   The Daimyo attempted to prevent by force the departure of the vessel, but his attack was repulsed by the Portuguese, who proceeded to the new port.   Torres and Fernandez also hastened to Omura, where they met Sumitada, who assured them that it was his desire not to fall at all behind Otomo Yoshishige in his treatment of the missionaries and their converts.   Yokoseura, which had been only a little village, quickly grew to be a flourishing town.   The Portuguese merchants made it their chief port, and the favour shown to Christianity caused many Japanese believers from other places to remove thither.   Sumitada himself had a residence there.   In 1563 he was baptised and took the name of Bartholomew.   He thus became the first of the Christian daimyos.   Twenty-five of his leading retainers were baptised at the same time.

The morning after his baptism, Sumitada set forth to aid his elder brother Yoshisada, now the Daimyo of Arima, in a war that had broken out between the latter and the Daimyo of Saga.   Hitherto it had been the custom for a daimyo before entering upon a campaign to worship at the shrine of the Goddess of War.   Sumitada therefore marched with his troops to the temple, entered it with his body-guards, and then to the surprise of all beholders ordered that the image of the goddess be overthrown and dragged by a rope to the courtyard, where with his sword he struck off its head. The temple was then burned and a cross erected on its site. Sumitada, who had been much impressed by the story of Constantine as related to him by Torres, had figures of the cross inscribed on his armour and on the standards of his army. The successful outcome of the campaign he regarded as due to the special favour of God.

Sumitada advised his brother to open the port of Kochinotsu to the Portuguese on the same terms that had been granted in the case of Yokoseura. Almeida went to visit the city and in less than a month baptised two hundred and sixty persons, including the Governor and his family. He also visited the city of Shimabara, where he found that a company of believers had been gathered by one of the Japanese evangelists.

The religious zeal manifested by Sumitada aroused the opposition of the bonzes and gave occasion for several of his leading retainers to plot for his destruction. Not only had he caused some of the temples to be transformed into churches, but instead of burning incense before the ancestral tablets of the family into which he had been adopted, he threw them all, including that of his predecessor, into the fire. His enemies made the most of what they regarded as an insult to their former lord, whose bastard son, Takaaki, they now recalled. They had already obtained promises of assistance from the Daimyos of Hirado and Saga. The former made a sudden attack upon Omura, while the latter invaded Arima in order to prevent its Daimyo from going to his brother's aid. This was in August, 1564. The two cities of Yokoseura and Omura fell into the hands of the enemy and were set on fire. Sumitada with a small band of faithful retainers had taken refuge in the castle of Omura, where he was besieged by his former subjects, while the fleet sent from Hirado prevented any help from reaching him by sea. The rebels sent him word that they would return to their allegiance if he would renounce Christianity and banish it from his domains, a proposition to which he refused to listen. At the same time his brother was being hard pressed by his foes; but when the ex-Daimyo of Arima learned that his two sons were in such great danger, he took the field, drove the enemy from Arima, and then advanced to the help of Omura. He succeeded in establishing communication with Sumitada, who on October 4, 1564, made a sally just as his father's troops advanced from the other side upon the besiegers, who were utterly routed. At the same time a severe storm destroyed most of the boats that had come from Hirado.

Sumitada, triumphant over his foes, became more zealous than ever for the promotion of the religion that had excited their opposition. He put to death two of his retainers who in going over to the enemy had renounced Christianity, for he said that he could never trust persons who had thus broken promises made to God. Other revolts kept his territories in a confused state for several years, but more and more his enemies and those of his faith were subdued until Omura became outwardly almost entirely a Christian state.

Though the ex-Daimyo of Arima had hastened to the relief of his sons when they were in danger, he was very much opposed to Christianity, which he regarded as the chief cause of the misfortunes that had come upon them. His ill-will greatly increased the difficulties under which the missionaries laboured. Yokoseura was in ruins and its inhabitants scattered. When Torres visited Shimabara he found that its governor, though personally inclined to be friendly, had been forbidden to have anything to do with him. He therefore withdrew to Takase in the province of Higo, which was then in the possession of Otomo Yoshishige. While he was there Almeida also came, accompanying De Sylva, whose health was so broken that he died soon after his arrival.

The number of missionaries was however increased about this time by the coming of Father Louis Froez, Father Jean Baptiste Monts, and Brother Jacques Gonzalez. Froez was sent to assist Fernandez in the islands belonging to Anthony. A letter written by a Portuguese merchant and quoted by Crasset gives the following account of the earnestness of the Christians in those islands:

"I am confident that the Holy Ghost must live in the two islands of Takashima and Itsukishima belonging to Don Anthony, for none but those who see it with their eyes can imagine the innocency and fervour of these persons after living so many years in idolatry. I never saw any Christians like those at Takashima; they will not suffer a heathen to stay even one night amongst them. Every Friday throughout the year, whilst the Father says litanies, both great and little, old and young, fathers and children, torment themselves so cruelly with smart disciplines that it would even force tears from the very rocks to see them. Most of the men and women creep on their knees to a cross on a little hill where Christians are interred. To see them at their prayers you would take them for the most perfect European religious, and very few surpass them in austerities and fasts."

While Froez was in Takashima two Portuguese ships, soon to be followed by a third, approached Hirado. Froez sent a letter to their captains asking them not to enter the harbour without first getting from the Daimyo a promise that he would cease oppressing the Christians. Accordingly, when the Japanese officials went on board urging that the ships put into Hirado, they were told that this could not be done until the assent of Father Froez had been gained. The Daimyo, in his anxiety to secure the profitable trade, sent to the missionary making excuses for his former misdeeds and promising amendment. In accordance with a second letter from Froez, the ships now entered the port; but the captains refused to land any goods until authorisation had been given for the missionaries to live in Hirado and for a church to be erected at the expense of the Portuguese merchants. The Daimyo, while ready to make promises, was so slow in keeping them that Froez went out in a shallop to intercept the third vessel, whose commander agreed to remain outside the harbour until all was satisfactorily settled. The Daimyo finally yielded to the demands made upon him, and the third ship anchored beside the others.

As this last vessel had brought three new workers to the mission, Torres now redistributed the forces at his disposal. Two of the new arrivals, Fathers Jean Cabral

and Melchior de Figueredo, were assigned respectively
to Takashima and Kochinotsu, the latter port being
chosen by Torres for his own residence. A third Father,
named Balthazar d'Acosta, remained at Hirado with
Fernandez. De Monts went to Bungo, while Froez and
Almeida were sent to aid Vilela in Kyoto; but on the
way thither Almeida was attacked by illness which led
him to return to Kyushu. There were two other European Brothers (Gonzalez and Sanchez), besides four
Japanese Brothers (Lawrence, Damien, Austin, and
Melchior), and these were to be used in different places
as necessity might arise.

While the events related were taking place in Kyushu,
remarkable progress was made in Kyoto and its vicinity.
Vilela had been directed by Torres to begin work in
Sakai, whither he went in August, 1561. Though he
found the character of its people such that after two
years he declared that there was no hope of a speedy
harvest, he had considered it advisable to remain there
because of the civil strife that during most of that time
convulsed Kyoto and the neighbouring country. After
peace had been restored, he returned to the capital
(1563). Following the plan previously adopted in
Hirado, he set the young people to work proclaiming
Christian doctrines and denouncing the Buddhist priests.
For the same purpose he had some of the brightest boys
from the orphanage in Bungo sent to his aid.

The bonzes presented to Matsunaga, who was Minister of Justice and a vassal of Miyoshi, a document in
which they urged that an edict be issued against the
foreign religion. Matsunaga replied that before con-
senting to any such action it would be necessary to
make a careful examination of the new doctrines to
see if they were as bad as the bonzes asserted. He
therefore appointed two persons of high rank to take
this matter in charge. Vilela and the Japanese evangelists found it advisable to withdraw once more to Sakai;
but a Christian of Kyoto named Jacques, who had business with the Minister of Justice, was met by one of the
commissioners and questioned about his faith. Though

not possessed of much education, Jacques was able to explain his belief so well that the commissioner soon declared himself convinced that Christianity was true and asked him to send for Vilela to come and give fuller instruction. The missionary wished to set out at once in response to this summons; but his friends, fearing some plot, had Lawrence go in his place. Soon word came from the evangelist that it was even better than Jacques had reported, for the other commissioner was also ready to declare his belief in Christianity. Vilela therefore went to Kyoto, where he at once baptised the two new converts and also a relative of Miyoshi by the name of Shirai, who commanded the castle of Sangajima in the province of Kawachi. Not long after this, Vilela visited the estates of Shirai, whose son and sixty retainers, besides five hundred of the common people, were baptised.

Another important conversion was that of Takayama, the commander of the castle of Takatsuki about halfway between Kyoto and Osaka. It is said that he was a man of considerable erudition and that he had expressed confidence in his ability to refute the doctrines of the Christians so as to make even the foreign priest acknowledge that his religion was false. He therefore went to hear Vilela preach and at the end of the sermon entered into a discussion that resulted in his own confession that all his arguments had been overthrown. Soon after this he was baptised (taking the name Dario) together with his wife and his son, then fourteen years old, who afterwards became the most famous of the Japanese Christians, Takayama Ukon, or as he is called in the accounts of the Jesuits, Justo Ucondono.

From the first, the elder Takayama showed a great zeal in urging others to become Christians. It was largely through his influence that many men of high rank were baptised, among them being Naito, the Daimyo of Kameoka in the province of Tamba.

It was while Christianity was making such rapid progress that Father Froez reached Kyoto about the close of January, 1565. In February came the day which by the Japanese calendar was the beginning of the new year. On that day officials and men of high rank were expected to pay their respects to the Shogun. Vilela took this occasion for having his new associates presented at court. They took with them several gifts such as had been found adapted to the tastes of the Japanese. The Shogun showed such marked signs of favour to his foreign guests as to increase their reputation among the gentlemen of the court, leading these to press more eagerly than before to hear Vilela's sermons. Many of them expressed a desire for baptism.

Suddenly, just when it seemed as though the capital and surrounding regions were on the point of being completely won to Christianity, the work was interrupted by political disturbances. In the summer of 1565 the Shogun was murdered. The members of his family, with the exception of one younger brother who had become a priest, were also put to death, and all persons that had been closely attached to the Shogun were driven from Kyoto. Among those expelled were the missionaries, who thus had to suffer for the favours they had received from the murdered prince and his adherents. The Buddhist priests were quick to improve the opportunity. After failing in an endeavour to have the missionaries slain, they procured from the Emperor an edict prohibiting Christianity as an abominable religion. For three years the Jesuits were unable to reside in Kyoto.

It is not necessary here to give an account of the succession of conflicts that during the next few years were carried on between the different parties that were contending for political power. The Christians were divided in their allegiance. In following their feudal lords they often found themselves fighting against their brethren in the faith. At the close of the year 1565, two contending armies were encamped near Sakai. Father Froez sent invitations to the Christians on each side, asking them to come into the city for the celebration of Christmas. Accordingly large numbers of them came on the preceding evening, spent the hours until twelve o'clock in preparation for the sacrament, and then attended the midnight mass. They next went to the house of the missionaries, where they ate together, and at daybreak, after asking one another's pardon for what might come from the necessities of the coming conflict, they returned to their respective camps.

The outcome of the civil wars was such as to bring the real power into the hands of the noted General Nobunaga, although Yoshiaki, the younger brother of the murdered Shogun, was made the nominal successor to the office. Nobunaga had no great respect for Buddhism, nor love for its priests. In erecting a new palace for the Shogun he did not hesitate to tear down a monastery that was on the land he wished to use, and it is said that he went so far as to demolish idols in order to obtain the stone of which they were made. The priests soon saw that they could expect no help from him in shutting out their new rivals.

Takayama's brother and overlord, Wada Koremasa, had taken an important part in Nobunaga's campaign for making Yoshiaki shogun. He therefore had considerable influence with both the nominal and the real possessor of power. Though he had not been baptised, he was considered a catechumen and he became the protector of the Christians. He soon secured permission for the missionaries to return to Kyoto. Vilela had gone to Bungo, but Wada sent his brother Takayama to escort Froez from Sakai to Kyoto. Here the missionary was led into the presence of Nobunaga, who received him with marked distinction. At a second interview that Froez had with Nobunaga, a noted priest named Nichijo was present and Nobunaga took the opportunity to draw the representatives of the two religions into a discussion. When the debate turned upon the question of immortality, the champion of Buddhism, who had become very much excited, seized a sword and rushed upon Brother Lawrence, shouting that he would cut off his head so that it might be seen whether any soul remained after the death of the body. Wada and Hideyoshi, who were also present, were obliged to seize and disarm Nichijo.

Nobunaga gave written permission for Froez to reside in the city and to re-occupy the church building. This church was to have the same exemption from taxation that was granted to Buddhist temples, while it was to be free from the requirement by which under certain circumstances the temples were obliged to lodge soldiers. All persons were forbidden to molest the missionary or to prevent other people from attending his services.

The bonzes now had recourse to the Emperor, who was easily induced to aid them. He sent one of his nobles to remonstrate with Nobunaga for failing to consult with the source of all authority in the land before giving such great privileges to the teachers of doctrines that were subversive of everything that had hitherto been held sacred. According to Japanese writers, Nobunaga then entreated the Emperor to approve what had been done, and finally succeeded in having his request granted. This is probably a mere euphemism for saying that Nobunaga paid no heed to the Imperial messenger, and that the Emperor was unable to prevent whatever the powerful general had made up his mind to do.

Nobunaga returned to his own estates in Mino, leaving Wada as his representative in Kyoto. The priest Nichijo caused a rumour to be spread abroad that he had obtained the Emperor's permission to have Father Froez put to death. Wada at once sent out notice that, if any attempt were made upon the foreigner's life, the whole section of the city in which the latter lived would be held responsible and would be destroyed.

The next year, however, Nichijo had gained so much favour with Nobunaga that he was made a councillor of the Shogun. He took advantage of a temporary absence of Wada to renew his efforts against Christianity. Wada wrote to Father Froez advising him to go to Mino and have an interview with Nobunaga. In order that this might be secured, he gave the missionary a letter to Shibata, one of Nobunaga's generals. In accordance with this advice, Froez set out with Lawrence. Their reception was so favourable that they returned bearing documents which made it certain that neither Emperor nor Shogun would venture to issue orders for their banishment.

It was now Nichijo's turn to visit Nobunaga that he might bring accusations against Wada. The particular incident on which he chiefly relied for supporting his charges had arisen from Wada's great zeal in protecting the Christians. Two young men of the military class had snatched a religious medal from a Christian woman while she was at prayer in Wada's own mansion. He at once caused the chief offender to be beheaded and the other to be banished. Such a severe punishment for what was perhaps done only in sport very much excited Wada's enemies, and Nichijo made the most of it as a proof that the interests of the country were being made secondary to those of the Christian religion. Nobunaga, yielding to the words of the crafty priest, dismissed Wada from his office and confiscated a part of his lands. Great was the joy of the enemies of Christianity at Wada's downfall, since this opened the way for attacking those whom he had protected. Their triumph was short-lived. Nobunaga, on returning to Kyoto, expressed a desire to see Wada. The latter came before him with shaven head and mean clothes, as was appropriate for a person in disgrace. Nobunaga, regretting his dismissal of one who had been so good a warrior and officer, appointed him governor once more and made the restoration to favour more conspicuous by walking with him through the principal streets of the city. Nichijo, on the other hand, was deposed, and it was only the Emperor's intercession that saved the priest from death.

It was not long after this that Wada had an opportunity to requite the renewed confidence shown by his lord. In 1570, Nobunaga, while accompanied by a small escort, fell into an ambuscade of his enemies. It was Wada's bravery that prevented utter defeat and capture. Wada himself was severely wounded, so that he had to withdraw for a time from active duties. Much of this enforced leisure he used for receiving Christian instruction. He had already asked Froez to come and baptise him, when an attack upon his territories made him hasten to their defence, although his wounds were not yet healed. In the battle that followed he was slain. His brother Takayama then became master of the estates in Takatsuki and five years later gave them over to his son, who was then twenty-two years old.

It is time to turn back and see what had been happening in Kyushu. Although the desire to secure trade with the Portuguese had led the Daimyo of Hirado to grant the missionaries and their converts some privileges, he had no love for their religion. His eldest son and some of his principal retainers knew that they were in no danger of displeasing him by their open hostility to Christianity. Anthony Koteda was the object of much suspicion, which was increased by an intercepted letter in which Sumitada congratulated him on the success with which he was working to extend the Kingdom of Christ in his territories. Four men who brought this letter were put to death.*

Some religious objects that had been brought from India for the adornment of the church in Hirado, had been seized by the unbelievers, and so came into the hands of one of the officials. He exposed a picture of the Virgin Mary to the mockery of the people after he had plucked out the eyes and otherwise disfigured it. The missionaries complained of this insult to their religion. As the Daimyo seemed disinclined to take up the matter, D'Acosta made use of means such as had formerly proved effective. By his request the Portuguese vessels held aloof from Hirado. After a while the Daimyo sent out a number of his warboats towards a ship that was seen on its way to a rival port, ordering them to make it come to Hirado or else to sink it. The attack was repulsed, many of the men from Hirado being slain.

In June, 1567, Juan Fernandez, who had come to Japan with Xavier, died at the age of forty-two. As he was not a priest, but only a lay brother, he occupies a less prominent place in the accounts of the Jesuits than does Xavier's other companion, Father Torres; but what is told of him encourages the opinion that no one deserves so much as he to be called the founder of the early

* We have little information about the later years of Anthony Koteda. This and other blanks in the history of the early missions may be partly because of the failures of letters sent from Japan to reach their destination. Anthony died a Christian death in 1582. Some of his descendants were prominent Christians.

Japanese Church. He was more successful than Xavier and Torres in learning the language. It is said, indeed, that Japanese became the only language that he commonly used, so that even in his death agony his prayers were in that tongue. He composed several books for the use of the Christians.

A few miles southwest from Hirado are the Goto Islands.* In 1564 their ruler invited the missionaries to visit him, but it was not until 1568 that Brothers Almeida and Lawrence were able to respond to the call. They were lodged in the mansion of the Daimyo, whose family and chief retainers came to receive instruction. Just at that time the Daimyo became dangerously ill, whereupon the bonzes declared that this was a punishment sent upon him for introducing the foreign religion into his territories. Their arguments were considered to be sufficiently answered when the remedies prescribed by Almeida effected a remarkable cure. This was asserted to be a sign that heaven approved of what had been done. Shortly after this, however, a disastrous conflagration destroyed a large part of the city and at the same time the Daimyo began to suffer from a tumour on his hand. Almeida's medical skill relieved the latter trouble, but the loss resulting from the fire left the balance of accounts so unfavourable for the Jesuits that the people joined with the bonzes in demanding their expulsion. The Daimyo held out for a time, and there were some baptisms. Finally, however, Almeida and Lawrence withdrew. Two years later, the son of the Daimyo was secretly baptised with his wife and some of his vassals. The father, who at first seemed to approve this action, was afterwards led by the enemies of Christianity to make vain efforts for inducing the son to give up his faith, or at least to pretend that he had done so. He issued edicts against the Christians and was preparing to take active measures against them, when the son demanded that, if martyrs were to be made, he should be the first to suffer. The Daimyo finally assured the Chris-

* It is convenient to retain the name used in European books, although it is redundant; the word Goto meaning " Five Islands."

tians that they would be left in peace. He died a few years later, while the enemies of Christianity were still' seeking a favourable opportunity to move against it. The son, on succeeding to the estates, showed great earnestness in trying to secure the conversion of all his subjects. It is said that in the churches he would never tolerate any distinctions of rank, he himself sitting among the common people.*

In 1566 the Lord of Shiki, on the island of Amakusa, was baptised with some of his vassals. When, however, he saw that his profession of Christianity did not help him to attract Portuguese traders to his ports, he lost interest in his new religion and began a persecution that led many of those who had followed him in receiving baptism to imitate him also in his apostasy.

Amakusa was divided among five petty lords under the suzerainty of Otomo Yoshishige. In 1568 one of these, the Daimyo of Hondo, asked that missionaries visit him. Warned by what had happened in Shiki, Almeida consented to go only on the conditions that there should be given written authorisation for him to preach; that for the first few days the Daimyo should by his own attendance on the services set a good example to his people; that, if the Christian doctrine was found good, one of the Daimyo's children should receive baptism as a guarantee that others could safely do so; and that the Daimyo should build a church.

These conditions were accepted. Hardly had the work of evangelisation begun when a revolt excited by the bonzes assumed such dimensions that Yoshishige had to send troops for the restoration of order. When the rebels had submitted, the Daimyo of Hondo was baptised (1570). Soon afterwards the rebellion broke out anew, and at length he issued an edict by which he banished the bonzes. He also warned the merchants who had assisted them by their contributions that they must either be converted or leave his territories.

* Christianity continued to flourish in the Goto Islands until this Daimyo died in 1579, leaving a minor son as his successor. During the regency that followed, the believers were severely persecuted, so that many of them took refuge in Nagasaki.

In Omura Christianity was constantly gaining a stronger foothold. In place of Yokoseura, which had been destroyed at the time of the rebellion, another place was chosen as the port for foreign commerce, and soon what had been a little fishing village grew into the important city of Nagasaki. The Daimyo furnished funds for the erection of a church, which was dedicated in 1568.

Father Torres, the last of the little company of missionaries who first brought Christianity to Japan, died October 12, 1570, at the age of seventy-four. Shortly before this, Father Cabral had come to take his place as Vice-Provincial. A congregation of the Jesuits in Japan was summoned, all of them being present except Father Froez. As a result of the conference a re-arrangement of the Fathers was made as follows: the new names here appearing being those of persons that had lately arrived in the country:

De Monts in Bungo,   Lopes in Kochinotsu,
Acosta in Hirado,   Figueredo in Omura,
Valegnani in Goto,   Froez and Organtin in Kyoto.

Father Vilela's health was so impaired that he needed a change. He was therefore sent to India that he might report on the state of the mission and urge that more workers be sent. He died that same year shortly after reaching Malacca.

IV

RAPID GROWTH OF THE CHURCH

1571-1582

IT has already been noted that Nobunaga had no love for the Buddhist priests. His anger had been especially excited against those of Mt. Hiei because on several occasions they had rendered aid to his enemies. He therefore determined upon their destruction. When he disclosed the plan to his generals, they were inclined to remonstrate against an attack upon temples which since the building of Kyoto had been considered a protection against demons and had been held in such honour by Emperor and people. Nobunaga insisted that the priests were little better than a band of traitors who were bringing evil upon their country. Their religious professions, he said, ought not to protect them; for they lived in constant violation of the precepts of Buddha, eating fish and keeping concubines. He declared that it was time these hypocrites and rebels were destroyed. In pursuance of this policy, Nobunaga's soldiers forced their way up the steep sides of the mountain, set fire to the buildings, and put to death every person they could find —priests, servants, concubines, and children. This event occurred September 29, 1571.

The temples of Mt. Hiei belonged to the Tendai sect. Three years later Nobunaga attacked the great monastery in Osaka, belonging to the Shin sect, which had also assisted his enemies. The so-called monastery was in fact one of the strongest fortresses in the land. Nobunaga failed in this attempt to take it, as he also did in subsequent sieges. It was not until 1580 that, by making use of the Emperor's intercession, he persuaded the abbot to surrender the castle and receive in exchange for it land and revenues in other places.

The Nichiren sect also suffered at Nobunaga's hands. It had consented to let him decide a long-standing quarrel between itself and the Jodo sect. He would do this only upon condition that the leaders of the losing side should be decapitated. Representatives of the two sects came to his castle at Azuchi and there held a famous discussion which resulted in the defeat of the Nichiren advocates. Not only did they pay the prescribed penalty, but other prominent priests were banished, while the temples were crippled by large financial demands that were made upon them.

Nobunaga's dislike of the Buddhist priests made him the more ready to favour a religion whose success would help to undermine their power. In one of the letters that were sent by the missionaries as reports of their work it was said of him:

" This man seems to have been chosen by God to open and prepare the way for our Holy Faith, without understanding what he is doing, because he not only has little respect for the *Kami* and the *Hotoke*,* whom the Japanese worship with such devotion, but he is furthermore the capital enemy and persecutor of the bonzes, inasmuch as among the various sects many are rich and powerful, and lords of great fortresses and rich territories, and by their opposition they have put him into great straits. . . . On the other hand, in proportion to the intensity of his enmity to the bonzes and their sects is his good will towards our Fathers who preach the law of God, whence he has shown them so many favours that his subjects are amazed and unable to divine what he is aiming at in this."

During Nobunaga's life the Christian religion made rapid progress in the central provinces of Japan. It was somewhat impeded, however, by difficulties arising from the civil conflicts of that period. The Shogun Yoshiaki, who grew tired of the constraint under which he was kept, joined with several daimyos in a plot for over-throwing Nobunaga. Among those siding with the Shogun was Naito, the Christian Daimyo of Kameoka in the province of Tamba. He marched to Kyoto with two thousand warriors whose banners bore the figure of the Cross, while on his own helmet the name " Jesus " was

* *Kami* is the name of the Shinto deities. The *Hotoke* are the saints worshipped by Buddhists.

inscribed in golden letters. This uprising, which occurred in 1573, was unsuccessful. Yoshiaki was driven from Kyoto, though the title of Shogun was never formally taken from him. Nobunaga did not choose to allow the appointment of any one else and preferred to hold the real power himself under the title of Naidaijin, Minister of the Interior. Naito was replaced by a non-Christian daimyo.

In 1577 a large church edifice was completed in Kyoto. Money for its erection had been contributed by Christians of different provinces and some had come from non-believers. The Buddhist priests so exerted themselves in the attempt to prevent its completion that the Governor of the city was at last forced to threaten them with punishment if they persisted in their efforts. He himself contributed both money and materials.

A revolt that arose against Nobunaga in 1579, had among its leaders Araki, the suzerain of Takayama Ukon. The latter had now become the Lord of Takatsuki. Nobunaga besieged the castle of Takatsuki and sent word to Ukon that unless it were surrendered, all of the Christians in the vicinity of Kyoto, including the missionaries, would be put to death. Ukon, who knew that Nobunaga would not hesitate to carry out his threat, sent a messenger to seek advice from Father Organtin, who was then in Kyoto. Nobunaga had been urging Organtin to use his influence in procuring Ukon's submission; and doubtless, as is stated in Japanese accounts of the affair, he used both threats and promises to make the missionary serve him. Organtin was permitted to enter the besieged castle, where he urged the wisdom of yielding. It was not easy for Ukon to accept this advice. His sister and his eldest son had been put as pledges of fealty in the hands of Araki; his mother and wife, in alarm at the thought of the probable fate of the hostages, begged him not to yield; and his father was opposed to surrender. Ukon finally decided that he would give himself up to Nobunaga, but would not surrender the castle. Having shaved his head and put on the dress of a religious recluse, he went with Organtin into the presence of Nobunaga, who received him back into favour. Meanwhile his father secured the safety of the hostages by promising Araki that he would defend the castle. He was soon obliged to yield to the superior force of the besiegers. Through his son's intercession the sentence of death, at first pronounced against him, was commuted into banishment to the province of Echizen. This proved not wholly disadvantageous to the Christian cause, for he and his wife, on reaching the place of their exile, were such zealous teachers of Christianity that they prepared the way for the missionaries to visit the province. Takayama Ukon was left in possession of Takatsuki.

It was the custom of the Christians to have great reunions in Kyoto and other places. One is mentioned as having been held in 1581, at Takatsuki, which was attended by fifteen thousand believers. In addition to religious exercises, which included an imposing procession, there were feasts and various kinds of games for the amusement of the people. One great attraction was a negro, whom the missionaries had brought from Africa. A report of this strange being reached Nobunaga, and at his request Father Organtin brought the negro to his palace. Nobunaga suspected some trickery, tried to see if the black colour could be washed off, and had the man stripped to see if it extended over the whole body. The missionaries permitted him to keep the negro as his own slave.

As Nobunaga wished to be near the capital and at the same time not too far from his ancestral estates, he began in 1568 to build a new city at Azuchi on the eastern shore of Lake Biwa. In 1576 he made this his chief residence. The Jesuits describe in glowing terms the magnificence of his palace and the splendid entertainments that were given in it. They say that at one time a hundred thousand persons came as invited guests. Nobunaga had declared his unwillingness to have any other temple in the city than the one where his own image was to be installed in the place of chief honour. He, however, presented Organtin with land for the erection of a residence and a church. The Christians were quick to take advantage of this gift. Takayama Ukon furnished much of the necessary timber and also a large number of workmen to assist in the erection of the buildings. A school was also built that the children of the leading families might be taught the sciences and European languages. When this was opened, Nobunaga visited it and manifested much interest in its work. He also frequently invited the missionaries to come to his palace, where he questioned them about their religion and about affairs in Europe. His father-in-law was baptised, while his eldest son showed much interest in Christianity, and even told Organtin that he would gladly become its follower if it were not that it was beyond his power to keep the commandment against adultery. It was felt by the missionaries that many others were held back by the same difficulty. The Annual Letter for 1852, said:

"If sensuality did not pervert their intellect, most of these lords would already be Christians; but the observance of this precept seems so hard to them that it makes their conversion difficult, so that many of them confidently allege that if the Fathers were a little broader with them in this commandment, they would at once become Christians. Among these lords the eldest son and successor of Nobunaga has discussed this three or four times with a Brother, wishing to persuade him that the Fathers should not proceed with such rigour in this matter, maintaining that if they did relax their rigour a great number of lords would forthwith be reduced to our Faith, and that so much was frequently said in the Court. Wherefore the said prince asserted that it would be doing greater service to God to dispense with this sixth [seventh by the usual Protestant reckoning] commandment, and thus make so many converts than to ruin all hopes of their conversion by our rigour in this precept, affirming that if it were dispensed with he himself would be the first to receive baptism."

Many Japanese have thought that Nobunaga became a Christian; but the letters of the Jesuits make it plain that, notwithstanding all the favours he showed to Christianity and the interest he sometimes manifested in its doctrines, their hopes for his conversion were not realised. June 22, 1582, he was slain at Kyoto by the treachery of Akechi, one of his own generals. Retainers and servants who ran to his assistance were also put to death, the only one to escape being the negro slave, who found refuge with the missionaries. When Hideyoshi, who had been Nobunaga's leading general, learned what had been done, he at once marched against the traitor, who, after his army had been defeated, took refuge in flight, but was beaten to death by some peasants whom he had asked to help him escape. Hideyoshi, though not without opposition, soon succeeded to the power that had been wielded by Nobunaga.

In Kyushu the Daimyo of Isahaya, a brother-in-law of Sumitada, having failed in his attempts to induce the latter to return to the Buddhist faith, became, in 1573, the head of a coalition against him. The Daimyo of Hirado was easily won to the plan. The Daimyo of Arima, who had failed to attract the Portuguese to his port of Kochinotsu, suspected that Sumitada had been secretly working against him, and so he became a third member of the league. Some of the castles in Sumitada's territory were commanded by persons so little in sympathy with their master that they treacherously delivered these into the hands of the enemy. The city of Omura was easily taken by the Daimyo of Ishahaya, who then attempted to surprise a neighbouring castle in which Sumitada was living. The latter, who had only fifteen retainers with him, knew nothing of what was happening until he saw the enemy approach. To conceal his desperate condition by giving the appearance of having more soldiers, he caused all the women in the castle to be dressed in armour. In a short time thirty Christian knights managed to force their way through the besiegers and came to his assistance. Others followed until the increase in numbers enabled him to overcome his enemies.

Sumitada now resolved to make his domains wholly Christian. When his knights and priests came to do him homage at the beginning of a new year, he spoke of the great blessing he had received from God and pleaded so earnestly that all of them, whether from interest or from policy, promised to study Christianity. Cabral, the Vice-Provincial, tells us that a Jesuit Father and a Brother "accompanied by a strong guard, but yet not without danger of their lives, went about causing the churches of the Gentiles with their idols to be thrown to the ground,

while three Japanese Christians went preaching the law
of God everywhere.   Those of us who were in the neighbouring kingdoms all withdrew therefrom to work in this
abundant harvest, and in the space of seven months
twenty thousand persons were baptised, as were the
bonzes of about sixty monasteries with the exception of
a few who left this State."

The Daimyo of Arima had been led, after his defeat,
to think more favourably of Christianity.   He was baptised in 1576.   So earnest was he in propagating his new
religion, and so ready were his subjects to follow the
example and exhortations of their lord, that, although he
died the next year, there were said to have been at that
time twenty thousand Christians in his domains.   His son
on succeeding to power issued an edict in which he
ordered the missionaries to depart and all of his Christian subjects to recant.   Many of his people were as
quick to obey the commands of the new ruler as they
had been to follow the wishes of his predecessor.   Others
threatened to emigrate rather than give up their faith.
Fears that they might do this, and hopes fostered by
Father Valegnani that the foreign merchants would frequent his port, probably had much influence in leading
the young Daimyo to change his policy.   Valegnani also
acted as mediator in persuading the Daimyo of Saga to
desist from military movements against Arima.   One of
his arguments may be surmised by Charlevoix's statement that the Portuguese " had promised at the instiga-
tion of Valegnani to serve Arima with their munitions
and even with their persons."   After some delay the
Daimyo of Arima was baptised in 1580, he being at that
time twenty years old.   He took the name of Protasius.
He built churches, established a college for young men of
high rank, and also built schools where instruction was
given not only in Christian doctrine, but also in Portuguese, Latin, and such European arts as painting, clock-
making, the carving of images, and the construction of
organs.

Though Otomo Yoshishige, the Daimyo of Bungo, had
gladly listened to the teaching of Xavier and other missionaries, had erected at Funai a splendid building that

included a church, a residence, and a hospital, and in other ways had favoured the work of the Jesuits, he for many years was unwilling to declare himself a Christian. He professed a great desire to arrive at certitude in religious matters. While ever ready to listen to the Christian doctrine, he sent to Kyoto for Buddhist priests of the Zen sect, which was considered the most philosophical in Japan. After a while he dismissed them, saying that their teaching was inferior to that of the Christians. The missionaries believed that unwillingness to put away immoral practices was what kept him from conversion. He had many concubines and frequently added to their number. His legitimate wife was a strong Buddhist. The Jesuits describe her as a monster of wickedness, and in their letters often refer to her under the nickname of Jezebel. Her second son was being educated for the priesthood. A splendid and richly endowed monastery had been prepared for him, but when the time came for his removal thither, the boy, who was only fourteen years old, declared that he would not go, but wished to be a Christian. Notwithstanding the mother's opposition, Yoshishige gave his assent, and the boy, taking the name Sebastian, was baptised in December, 1575. The young convert soon showed his zeal by going with some of his companions into the city and breaking off the heads of a number of idols. When the bonzes complained of this conduct, the Daimyo upheld his son's act.

Among those that were led by the boy's example to declare themselves Christians was Chikatora, the adopted son of Sebastian's maternal uncle. The Daimyo's wife, who had failed to hold back her own son from accepting the religion she hated, seemed likely to be more successful in the case of her nephew, for she had the assistance of the father, who shut up the young man in a castle, so as to keep him away from the Christians. The relatives even begged Father Cabral to warn Chikatora that he ought not to oppose his father. The missionary did write a letter advising him not to seek baptism for a while, but to be obedient to his father so far as he could do this without offending his own conscience.

Chikatora's conduct was so pleasing to his father and

to Jezebel that he was given more liberty; but at last the means by which they sought to alienate him from Christianity were such—some say recourse was had to magic, others that he was surrounded by temptations to licentiousness—that he ran away to the house of Cabral, begging to receive baptism, and the rite was administered April 24, 1577.

Yoshishige's wife tried to stir up the people to attack the missionaries, whereupon the Daimyo declared that any one molesting them would be severely punished. In other matters Jezebel's conduct was so displeasing that he finally divorced her. He then married another woman who was a catechumen, put away his concubines, and at last (August 28, 1578) was baptised together with his new wife. He was then forty-eight years old. In memory of Xavier, his first teacher of Christianity, he took the name Francis. At this time he was one of the most powerful lords in Japan, five of the nine provinces in Kyushu being subject to him. He decided to abdicate in favour of his eldest son, Yoshimune, a man of weak character, who, though numbered among the catechumens, long wavered between allegiance to Christianity and opposition to it.

The divorced wife of Yoshishige exerted all her influence to induce Yoshimune to favour the Buddhists. Her brother at one time seemed likely to succeed in securing the adoption of his proposal that the foreigners be slain, the churches destroyed, and Christianity proscribed. Yoshishige, however, still retained enough influence to prevent such action. At times, when military affairs or the exigencies of State required a stronger leader than the son, he resumed the actual administration of the government. He showed as much zeal against Buddhism as Jezebel against Christianity. In the Annual Letters of the Jesuits there are several passages describing his acts, of which the following are specimens:

"He captured a very strong place where was one of the chief temples and the most frequented in these parts, which had around it three thousand houses of the bonzes; and he at once gave orders to burn all the houses. The venerable temple was turned into ashes."

"The destruction of the monasteries in this kingdom proceeds.

Their revenues are given to the soldiers. The bonzes are quitting their robes. Some marry, some go to the wars or to seek elsewhere their fortunes."

Doubtless the division of sentiment among the people, fostered in part by religious dissensions, had much to do with the misfortunes that came upon the Otomo family. Four of the five provinces that Yoshimune had received from his father were soon lost. Nothing was left but Bungo, and that was in a rebellious condition.

The Daimyo of Satsuma, son of the one that had been in power when Xavier came to Japan, was among those who had been asking for missionaries. The Annual Letter for 1582 is doubtless right in its surmise of his motives when it says: "The King of Satsuma, desiring that the Portuguese ships should go to his ports, and judging that if there were churches and Christians in his lands the Portuguese would be more readily induced to go there, treated of this matter with the Father Visitor and the Vice-Provincial." In this as in other cases the Jesuits were not so dull that they could not see how the attempt was being made to utilise them; but at the same time they were too wise to neglect the opportunities that were thus afforded. Almeida made a second visit to Kagoshima to arrange for complying with the invitation. The Buddhist priests were once more aroused. It is said that they persuaded the Daimyo to order all his chief retainers to make a solemn promise never to become Christians, or allow their subordinates to do so. One prominent person who argued against this proposition was murdered, and the opposition to the foreigners was so strong that the Daimyo was obliged to tell Almeida that it was inadvisable to proceed with the negotiations.

In the Annual Letter of 1582 the condition of Christianity in Japan at the close of the preceding year was thus described:

"The number of all the Christians in Japan according to the Father Visitor's information amounts to 150,000, a little more or less, of whom many are nobles, since besides the Kings of Bungo, Arima, and Omura, there are also many lords of different lands who, together with their relatives and vassals, are Christians, The majority of these live in Kyushu on the lands of Arima, Omura, Hirado, and Amakusa, where, with the others in the lands of Goto, there are 115,000 Christians. In the kingdom of Bungo there are 10,000; in the Kyoto district, with those scattered in the home provinces and Yamaguchi, there are 25,000. The churches we have in those kingdoms where there are Christians, between great and small, are two hundred in number."

There had arisen a marked difference of opinion among the missionaries concerning the education that should be given to Japanese evangelists. Father Cabral, the Vice-Provincial, feared that the haughty spirit of the Japanese would lead them, if instructed in Western sciences, to despise their European teachers. Hence he desired to have them taught only so much as would enable them to occupy lower positions as helpers of the missionaries. On the other hand, Father Valegnani, who had come as Visitor General, favoured a more liberal policy, which led him to establish a college in Funai. Cabral's opposition was so strong that the Visitor found it advisable to send him to China and transfer his office to Father Coelho.

A few months before the assassination of Nobunaga, the ex-Daimyo of Bungo united with the Daimyos of Omura and Arima in sending an embassy to Europe. It is probable that the first suggestion of this came from the Jesuits, who desired on the one hand to arouse missionary enthusiasm in Europe and on the other to impress the envoys with the splendour of European cities and the power of the Church, so that their report might make the Japanese more ready to accept the religion of Western lands. Doubtless also the Japanese at that time, as has been true in later years, were desirous of learning through their own countrymen the truth concerning foreign lands and to use for their own benefit whatever of good might be brought back by those who had travelled abroad. We have already seen from Xavier's letters how an envoy had been sent from Bungo to the Portuguese colonies in India; the next step was to have Europe itself visited. Yoshishige selected as his representative a grand-nephew named Mancio Ito; the

Daimyos of Omura and Arima sent a nephew of the former named Michael Chijiwa; to these were added two young men of high rank named Julian Nakaura and Martin Hara. Each of these persons was about sixteen years old. Probably those in whose names they went looked upon them less as envoys of state than as young men sent abroad for education; but in Europe they were received in such a way as would have befitted men holding the former position. Father Valegnani did indeed request that the courts to which they might go should not show them too much honour, since he feared that they might be puffed up with an undue sense of their own importance. This warning had little effect. Since the Jesuits in their letters had applied the title "king" to the daimyos, the young men coming in the names of these lords were treated as royal ambassadors.

They set out in a Portuguese ship that sailed from Nagasaki February 22, 1582. On reaching Goa, Father Valegnani, who was in charge of the party, found that he had been appointed Provincial in the Indies. He therefore turned over the care of the young men to Fathers James Mesquita and Nuñez Rodriguez. Owing to long delays at Macao, Cochin, and Goa, it was not until August 10, 1584, that the envoys reached Lisbon. At Macao they had been hailed with salvos of artillery, and in Goa the Viceroy had given them a splendid reception, hung chains of gold about their necks, presented them with three thousand crowns, and expended two thousand ducats in fitting up the quarters they were to occupy in the ship that took them on their way. This was but a prelude to what they were to experience in Europe. Their arrival in Lisbon and their slow progress to Rome were marked by a succession of magnificent fêtes. At the court of the Spanish King, Philip II., they were entertained as though they were royal princes. They spent three days in the Escurial and then went to the college of the Jesuits in Madrid, where they were visited by the King, the nobles, and the foreign ambassadors. Similar honours were shown them at Pisa by the Grand Duke of Tuscany; but the height of all was their reception at Rome. While they were yet two days' journey from the city, they were met by a troop of cavalry sent by Pope Gregory XIII. to escort them to the house of the Jesuits, where they were welcomed by Aquiviva, the General of the Order. As they were supposed to be still *incogniti,* their public entrance to the city did not occur until three days later, March 23, 1585. The Pope had held a consistory to decide upon what ceremonies would be appropriate. According to Crasset, Gregory by the advice of the cardinals ordered that the envoys " should be received publicly in the Royal Hall as ambassadors of crowned heads, and commanded that every one should give them the honour due to persons of that character, chiefly seeing this redounded to the honour of the Holy See, to the edification of the Church of Japan, and confusion of heretics."

On the morning of the public reception, the Japanese visitors were taken in the carriage of the Spanish ambassador to the Vineyard of Julius III., outside the city walls. There a procession was formed having at its head the troopers, the Swiss Guards, and the attendants of the cardinals. Next came carriages conveying ambassadors of France, Spain, Venice, and many other states, and followed by a mounted escort of nobles and papal officials. After these rode the Japanese themselves, clad in the ceremonial dress of their own land and wearing richly decorated swords. Mancio Ito, as representative of Otomo, came first, riding between two archbishops; while Michael Chijiwa and Martin Hara were each accompanied by two bishops. They were followed by Father Mesquita, who served as interpreter. Julian Nakaura was prevented by illness from taking part in the ceremonies. Many Roman nobles and gentlemen, riding on horseback, brought up the rear of the procession. As it entered the city by the Porta del Popolo and made its way towards the Vatican, the ringing of bells, the sounding of trumpets, and the booming of the cannon of St. Angelo united with the acclamation of the people to do honour to the visitors. When the Japanese were ushered into the Palace, they fell at the feet of the Pope, who was so moved with emotion that his eyes filled with tears as he raised the young men and tenderly embraced them. The letters that had been sent by their daimyos were then read. Translations of these documents are given by Crasset. Yoshishige's letter will serve as a specimen.

" To him that ought to be honoured on earth as holding the place of the King of Heaven, the most high and most holy Pope.

" After craving assistance of God my sovereign Lord, I made bold to write to your Holiness with a most profound humility. The Lord and Governor of heaven and earth, who holds under His empire the sun, moon, and stars, hath been pleased to dart a beam of His light upon me, at that time buried in most profound ignorance and darkness, and discovering the treasures of His mercy to the inhabitants of these countries. He sent about four and thirty years ago into these kingdoms the Fathers of the Society of Jesus, who sowed the word of God in men's hearts, and it pleased His divine bounty to let part of it fall on mine, a signal favour which I attribute with many others to your merit, most holy Father, and to the prayers of all Christian people. Had not I been quite broken with old age and infirmities, and otherwise prevented with grievances of war, I would have come myself in person to visit your holy places, and rendered you obedience, and after kissing your feet I would have set them very devoutly on my head and humbly begged of your Holiness to have made with your hand the sign of the Cross on my heart; but being prevented for the above reasons, I had thought of deputing in my place Don Jerome, my nephew, son to the King of Hyuga, but being at this present far from home, and withal the Father Visitor pressing to be gone, I substituted in his room Don Mancio, his cousin-german. Your Holiness holding the place of God on earth will oblige me and all the Christians in these parts if you will please to favour us with a continuance of your wonted kindness and protection. I received by the Father Visitor the reliquary which your Holiness was pleased to send me, and set it with great respect on my head. Neither tongue nor mouth can express how much I think myself obliged to your Holiness. I will make an end of my letter, for the Father Visitor and Don Mancio will give your Holiness a full account concerning either myself or my kingdom. I render you with all my heart a perfect submission of judgment and affection. I wrote this letter with a mighty dread and fear the eleventh of January, from the nativity of Our Lord 1582.

He that lays himself at the most
sacred feet of your Holiness
Francis, King of Bungo."

After the letters had been read, an "address of obedience" was made in behalf of the ambassadors by

Father Gonsalez, a Portuguese Jesuit, in which the reasons for their coming were set forth. A reply was made in the name of Gregory, and the ceremony closed by the ambassadors' kneeling again to kiss the feet of the Pope.

A papal medal issued in connection with this embassy bore the inscription: "AB REGIBUS IAPONIOR. PRIMA AD ROMAN. PONT. LEGATIO ET OBE-DIENTIA." [First Legation and Act of Obedience from the Kings of the Japanese to the Roman Pontiffs.] If this medal and the contents of the letters were known in Japan, they were well fitted to give rise to the suspicion which afterwards grew so strong that the missionaries and their followers were trying to deliver the country into the hands of foreign rulers.

It was only eighteen days after the ambassadors arrived at Rome that Pope Gregory XIII. died. They assisted at his funeral and at the coronation of Sixtus V. The new Pope made them Knights of the Golden Spur. Cardinals, princes, and the representatives of other countries were present at the ceremony of their investiture, the ambassadors of France and Venice performing the office of putting on the golden spurs. A still higher honour was shown when the Pope issued a brief authorising them to take part in consistories, a privilege that was usually accorded only to sovereigns. From the Senate of Rome they received the title of Roman Citizens and Patricians, each of the diplomas being " sealed with a great seal of gold as broad as one's hand, near a finger thick."

Several other cities of Italy were visited by the ambassadors,* who then went back to Spain. Philip II. fitted up a ship for them at his own expense and added rich presents to the many that they had already received. They embarked at Lisbon, April 30, 1586, for their return voyage. Calms and a long stay at Mozambique so hindered them that it was not until May 29, 1587, that they reached Goa. Here they were detained ten

---

* A facsimile of a document written by the ambassadors when in Venice is given in Trans. As. Soc. Jap., vol. xviii.

months longer, and then, accompanied by Valegnani, who was appointed the Viceroy's envoy to Japan, they proceeded on their way, reaching Nagasaki July 27, 1590, to find that great changes affecting the interests of Christianity had taken place during the eight years of their absence.

V

HIDEYOSHI AND HIS EDICTS AGAINST CHRISTIANITY

1583-1598

TOYOTOMI HIDEYOSHI,who succeeded in gaining for himself the power formerly possessed by Nobunaga, seemed at first to regard the Christians with much favour. According to some Japanese writers, he believed that the foreign religion was a source of danger, and so he was only waiting for a favourable opportunity to drive the missionaries from the land. However this may have been, it was worth while to secure the good will of the Christian lords and warriors. Among these Takayama Ukon held a prominent place. In 1583 Konishi Yukinaga, who became commander of Hideyoshi's fleet, was converted through Takayama's influence. Under the name Augustine, which he took at baptism, he has frequent mention in the letters of the Jesuits. They give him the title of Grand Admiral. In connection with the expedition to Korea he holds a prominent place in Japanese history. Another conversion occurring at about the same time as Konishi's was that of Kuroda Yoshitaka, whom the Jesuits term the General of the Cavalry. In their accounts he is called Simon Kondera. The governors of the important cities of Osaka and Sakai were Christians, as were also the officers whom the missionaries call the Secretary of State and the Grand Treasurer. Several daimyos and other men of high rank were either baptised believers or students of Christianity. Magdalen, the secretary of Hideyoshi's wife, and Jane Onogi, wife of the Daimyo of Fukuchiyama and considered the best poetess of that time, held important places among the ladies in Hideyoshi's court.

As soon as Hideyoshi's power over central Japan had become thoroughly established, he made a redistribution of the lands. Takayama Ukon was removed from Takatsuki to Akashi, in the province of Harima, where he was in receipt of larger revenues. Most of his retainers followed him thither. On arriving in his new possessions he gave notice to the Buddhist priests that they must remove all their idols from the land. When they saw that their attempts to resist this order were vain, they put the images on boats and sailed with them to Osaka, which Hideyoshi had made his headquarters. Here they appealed to Hideyoshi's mother, a devout Buddhist, and got her to intercede in their behalf; but it was all in vain, for Hideyoshi refused to interfere, saying that Takayama was free to rule his own territory as he pleased and that, if the priests did not know what to do with their idols, they would better drown them in the sea or use them for firewood. The report of this reply encouraged Takayama to go on in his efforts to make his fief wholly Christian.

After Nobunaga's assassination, Akechi and his followers had pillaged the palace at Azuchi. The establishment of the Jesuits had also been ravaged either by the soldiers or by the populace. The seminary with thirty of the pupils was therefore removed to Takatsuki. One of the missionaries wrote at this time in the following enthusiastic terms concerning the students:

" These youths progress greatly in virtue and in letters, and are of such good parts that what is learned in three years in the schools of Europe they easily master in four months. Already some of them begin to show themselves adapted for preaching and for confuting the falsity of the bonzes, with great hope of notable service to the Lord."

On Takayama's transfer to Akashi, it was decided to remove the school to Osaka. Hideyoshi gave land near his castle for the erection of the school and a church, he himself going in person with Father Organtin to select a suitable site.

A conversion that attracted much attention about this time was that of Imaoji Dosan, Hideyoshi's physician, a man who had been educated in the best schools of

Japan and China, and who was the most celebrated practitioner in the country. Father Figueredo had occasion to consult this physician. Dosan, surprised to see a person of so great age whose general health seemed so good, asked him how he had preserved his strength. The Father replied that from childhood he had lived an abstemious life, had subdued his body by labour, and above all had learned the secret of contentment so well that, even though the ailment which brought him to seek advice should cut short his days, he would not be troubled thereby, since this would introduce him to a life incomparably better than the present and one that had the great advantage of being endless. Dosan, who did not believe in the immortality of the soul, began to argue and to ask questions which received such answers as finally led him to put himself under the Father's instruction with the result that after a while he received baptism. His pupils, said to number eight hundred, were also baptised, while many other persons were led to say: "If such a wise man as this believes the Christian doctrines, they must be true."

In May, 1586, Father Coelho, the Vice-Provincial, accompanied by eight Jesuits and a number of Japanese Christians, was received at the Osaka Castle by Hideyoshi, who the previous year had been made Kwambaku, or Regent, thus attaining the highest office open to a subject of the Emperor.* In a familiar conversation with the missionaries he was remarkably frank in telling his plans for the future. Father Froez, who was present, says:

"He told us how he was resolved to divide the southern kingdoms, minishing somewhat of the state of all the lords there, and how he would destroy and ruin with a great army every one of them who refused to obey him. This lord evinced such liveliness in his countenance and such frankness as he uttered these words that we could perceive without the least doubt that he had not a shadow of suspicion of us. He also added that in the

* This office could be held only by members of the Fujiwara family; but Hideyoshi had no great trouble in procuring genealogical tables that established his kinship and placed him among the nobility. The Shogunate was a military office and nominally upon a lower plane.

46332

division of Japan he wished to give Justo Ucondono (Takayama)
and Ryusa, the father of Augustine (Konishi), who were present, the kingdom of Hizen, leaving the port of Nagasaki to the
Church, and for that letters patent would be issued,—but this,
it was to be understood, was to be after he had thoroughly settled
the affairs of Japan and taken hostages, because he wished to do
everything in such a way that the Fathers should not be hated by
the lords of Hizen. And he wished them further to understand
that he made that donation to them on his own initiative and not
at the instance of others. . . .

" He also said that he had reached the point of subjugating all
Japan; whence his mind was not set upon the future acquisition
of more kingdoms or more wealth in it, since he had enough, but
solely upon immortalising himself with the name and fame of
his power; in order to do which he was resolved to reduce the
affairs of Japan to order and to place them on a stable basis;
and, this done, to entrust them to his brother Minodono, while
he himself should pass to the conquest of Korea and China, for
which enterprise he was issuing orders for the sawing of planks
to make two thousand vessels in which to transport his army.
And for himself he wished nothing from the Fathers except that
through them he should get two great and well-equipped ships
from the Portuguese, whom he would pay liberally for everything, giving the very best wages to their officers; and if he met
his death in that undertaking, he did not mind, inasmuch as it
would be said that he was the first lord of Japan who had ventured on such an enterprise; and if he succeeded and the Chinese
rendered obedience to him, he would not deprive them of their
country or remain in it himself, because he only wished them to
recognise him for their lord; and that he would build churches
in all parts, commanding all to become Christians and to embrace our Holy Law."

A few days after this Hideyoshi gave the missionaries
a patent in which he granted them permission to preach
in his states, exempted their establishments from the
necessity of lodging soldiers, and released Japanese members of the Society from certain obligations to their
feudal lords. He signed and sealed two copies of the
document, expressing his wish that one should be sent
to Europe in order to show Christian kings how much
he favoured their religion.

The progress of events in Kyushu helped on Hideyoshi's plans for that island. The Otomos of Bungo
had been so much weakened that the strife for supremacy among the daimyos was chiefly confined to those
of Satsuma and Hizen. There were constant wars, into

whose particulars it will not be necessary for us to enter. In 1586 Bungo was invaded by Satsuma. It is said that with the latter's army came many Buddhist monks, who delighted in the opportunity that was afforded them to destroy Christian churches. The missionaries, forced to flee, escaped to Shimonoseki and Yamaguchi.

In these straits Otomo Yoshishige went to Osaka and begged Hideyoshi to intervene. Nothing could have been more pleasing to the latter. The first generals whom he sent to oppose the forces of Satsuma were defeated. Funai was captured and Yoshimune fled to Nakatsu in the province of Buzen. Kuroda, who hastened thither, reproved the young man for his evil deeds and urged him to become a Christian. As a result of this exhortation, Yoshimune was baptised April 27, 1587, together with his wife, three children, and several retainers. He took the name of Constantine. Soon after this, Satsuma was driven back. Partly by force of arms and partly by diplomacy Hideyoshi succeeded in making all the daimyos of Kyushu submit to him. He then made a re-distribution of the territory. To Otomo Yoshimune was left only part of the province of Bungo. The Christian lords of Amakusa and Omura were not disturbed, while Arima recovered a part of the territory that had been taken by Satsuma. To Konishi was given the southern part of Higo and he was made a sort of supervisor over the whole of Kyushu. Kuroda was rewarded with a large part of Buzen. One of the Mori family, who had been converted through Kuroda's influence and who now married a daughter of Yoshishige, was given a fief in Chikugo. Another Christian received estates in Hyuga. Thus a considerable part of Kyushu came under the rule of Christian daimyos. It must have seemed to the missionaries that Hideyoshi had made a good beginning in carrying out the promises given to the Vice-Provincial.

It was about this time that the Christians of Kyushu lost the two men who had hitherto been their most illustrious leaders. Omura Sumitada died May 24, 1587, at the age of fifty-five; while a fortnight later followed the death of Otomo Yoshishige, who was fifty-eight years old. During the last part of his life Yoshishige had shown much zeal in the observance of religious ceremonies. Crasset says of him:

" He lived eighteen years after his baptism in piety and devotion, more like a perfect religious man than a worldly prince. He began his conversion by afflicting his weak and infirm body with cruel and continual penances. He fasted several days in the week, disciplined himself daily, and frequently too in public, to repair (as he used to say) the scandal he had given by his loose and libertine life. . . . . He confessed and communicated five or six times a week. He recited his rosary daily on his knees, and over and above, another pair of beads with his domestics. . . . Every year he retired for eight or ten days to make the Spiritual Exercises. . . . Though he was naturally of a warlike disposition, yet after the unction of grace had penetrated into his heart he never waged war but in his own defence, and the fruit he reaped by it was extirpation of idolatry and the establishment of the Christian religion. This was his pleasure and glory above all other conquests. He hunted the bonzes like savage beasts and, in a word, took singular satisfaction in exterminating them out of the land."

While Hideyoshi was in the city of Hakata, the Vice-Provincial went thither to present his congratulations on the recent victories. The Regent, who appeared as friendly as he had formerly been in Osaka, promised to give him land in Hakata and assured him that he would always protect the Christian religion. How great then was the consternation of the missionaries when, in a single night, Hideyoshi's attitude towards them was entirely altered and an edict was issued in which they were ordered to leave Japan within twenty days.

What was the cause of this sudden change? As has already been noted, some Japanese historians state that Hideyoshi from the first was opposed to Christianity and had been waiting some good opportunity to declare his enmity. Another or an additional explanation given by some is thus expressed in the " History of the Empire of Japan," prepared by the Japanese Department of Education for the Columbian Exposition of 1893:

" When Hideyoshi in the course of his campaign against Shimazu reached Hakata, the Christian priests showed such an arrogant demeanour that Hideyoshi, enraged by their conduct, ordered that they should leave Japan by a certain day and prohibited the people from embracing Christianity."

Mr. Murdoch calls attention to Hideyoshi's custom of using outbursts of simulated fury to conceal his deep designs, and holds that Hideyoshi did not wish to extirpate Christianity, but only to reduce it to the position of a serviceable political tool. This led him to take active steps against Takayama, whom he regarded as too much under the control of the foreigners, while Konishi and Kuroda, as men that could be trusted, were left undisturbed.

Roman Catholic historians say that several causes united to arouse the enmity of Hideyoshi. The first was the evil conduct of the European merchants, most of whom gave themselves up to such debauchery as made the Japanese despise a religion that had so little good effect on the lives of its adherents. Thus Hideyoshi was led to think that the missionaries could not believe that the religion they taught was a help to virtue. He one day dropped the remark that he greatly feared the upright conduct of the missionaries themselves was nothing more than a mask of hypocrisy used to conceal the plans of the Europeans to gain possession of Japan.

A second cause of distrust is said to have arisen in connection with an unusually large Portuguese ship that came to Hirado. Hideyoshi, who was thinking of having some vessels built in European style, asked Father Coelho to induce the captain to bring this ship to Hakata. The captain came in a small vessel, alleging that the shoals outside the harbour did not give sufficient water for the larger one. Hideyoshi spent three hours with Father Coelho and the captain on board the small boat, apparently satisfied with the excuse and pleased with the entertainment offered him; but it was afterwards thought that he suspected the merchants and missionaries had some secret reason for not wishing to accede to his request.

Most stress is laid by the Jesuits upon Hideyoshi's anger at the obstacle which Christianity offered to his own debaucheries. According to their account, a man named Yakuin, who had formerly been a Buddhist priest, had now become the procurer for Hideyoshi's licentious pleasures. Some Christian maidens of Arima, whom he urged to go to Hakata, rejected his offers with so much contempt that he returned baffled and angry. He arrived on the evening after Hideyoshi's visit to the Portuguese ship. The Regent was still making merry with some wine that he had received from the captain. When Yakuin told his adventures and declared that the Christians had treated him with such insolence and violence that he had been glad to escape with his life, Hideyoshi roared out that he would cut the throats of all the Christian women of Arima. Then Yakuin joined with others that were present in declaiming against the foreign religion whose followers, they alleged, were preparing to join the Portuguese in overthrowing Hideyoshi. There was even the pretence of disclosing a plot already formed for this purpose, with Takayama Ukon for its leader.

Hideyoshi was quick to take action. In the middle of the night Father Coelho, who had remained on the ship where the Regent had just shown himself so gracious, was aroused from his sleep and called on deck. A voice from the shore commanded him in very impolite language to come at once to land in order to receive a communication from Hideyoshi. The message proved to be a demand for answers to the following questions: " Why do you force the Japanese to become Christians? Why do you make your followers destroy the temples? Why do you persecute the Buddhist priests? Why do you violate Japanese customs by eating meat? Who has given the Portuguese permission to buy Japanese and carry them as slaves to India? " Shortly afterwards another messenger arrived, read an order that had just been issued for the banishment of Takayama, and departed without saying anything more.

The Vice-Provincial was overwhelmed with astonishment. He at once set to work at the preparation of a long letter in answer to the questions that had been asked. In it he said that Hideyoshi himself had given permission for the preaching of Christianity; that since this religion taught the existence of only one God, it was to be expected that those who followed it would renounce all idols and seek to overthrow the buildings in which they were enshrined, although the missionaries had never taken part in destroying temples except so far as the daimyos approved; that while it was not to be supposed that teachers of two religions so different as Buddhism and Christianity could work in harmony, the Jesuits had never maltreated the bonzes; that, although the missionaries according to the customs of their own country had eaten meat when entertained by the Portuguese merchants, they were willing to abstain from it hereafter; and that they were not accountable for the conduct of the merchants, whom they had often reproved for their traffic in slaves, an evil that could easily be prevented if Hideyoshi would prohibit the daimyos and others from selling captives and criminals to the foreigners.

The next morning (July 25, 1587) the following edict was published:

"Having learned from our faithful counsellors that foreign religious teachers have come into our estates, where they preach a law contrary to that of Japan, and that they have even had the audacity to destroy temples dedicated to our *Kami* and *Hotoke;* although this outrage merits the most extreme punishment, wishing nevertheless to show them mercy, we order that under pain of death they quit Japan within twenty days. During that space of time no harm nor hurt will be done them, but at the expiration of that term, we order that if any of them be found in our states, they shall be seized and punished as the greatest criminals. As for the Portuguese merchants, we permit them to enter our ports, there to continue their accustomed trade, and to remain in our estates provided our affairs need this; but we forbid them to bring any foreign religious teachers into the country, under the penalty of the confiscation of their ships and goods."

Orders were sent to Takayama Ukon, who was encamped near Hakata, that he must give up his fief in Akashi and go into exile. For some time he dwelt on an island belonging to Konishi's estate. He was then ordered to remove with his family to Kanazawa in the

province of Kaga. The daimyo of that place received
him as a retainer, giving him a revenue that enabled
him to support the faithful vassals that followed him
into exile.

Coelho hoped to avert the threatened disaster by making a show of submission. As no ship was ready to
sail to the Indies, he succeeded in having the time permitted to elapse before the departure of the missionaries
changed from twenty days to six months. In response
to his summons, all but two of the European missionaries assembled in Hirado for a conference. There were
then in Japan forty Fathers and seventy-three Brothers,
forty-seven of the latter being Japanese. It was decided that for the present it was advisable to refrain
from all open exercise of their ministry. While awaiting the time set for leaving Japan, they accepted the
asylums offered by the Christian daimyos of Kyushu.

There were still many conversions to comfort the
hearts of the missionaries in these dark days. Among
the prominent persons baptised was a nephew of Hideyoshi's wife. Another was the wife of Hosokawa,*
a daimyo whose possessions were in the province of
Tango. She had first learned of Christianity by hearing her husband's account of Takayama's vain attempt
to convert him. Hosokawa went with Hideyoshi to
Kyushu, leaving his wife at Osaka and giving strict
orders that she was not to go out from his mansion in
that city. She, however, was so desirous to hear the
preaching of the Christians that she managed to elude
the guards and went with a few attendants to the church,
where she was much impressed with the decorations and
especially with an image of Christ that stood over the
altar. The meaning of the emblems was explained to
her by Father Cespedes. Afterwards she heard a sermon by a Japanese Brother who, at its close, answered
many questions that she propounded. She and her companions then asked for baptism. As she declined to
give her name, it was thought that she might be one
of Hideyoshi's concubines, and the missionary was there-

---

* She was the daughter of the Akechi who put Nobunaga to
death.

fore unwilling to grant her request. Meanwhile the guards at her mansion had become aware of her absence. When at last they discovered her in the church, they sent a litter to bring her home. After this she daily sent to Father Cespedes a trustworthy maid, with some attendants, to receive his instruction and then report it to her. Ere long this maid and sixteen of her companions were baptised in the church, but their mistress found it impossible to leave the house. When news came of Hideyoshi's edict for the expulsion of the Jesuits, her fear that the opportunity to receive baptism would be lost led her to devise a plan for going to the church by night. This was discouraged by the missionary, who gave the above-mentioned maid such instructions as enabled her to perform the rite. The character of the lady, who took the name Grace, is highly praised by the Jesuits. When her husband returned, his anger at what had been done led him to treat her for a while with great severity.

Of quite a different nature were the conversions forced upon the people of three cities that in the recent conflicts had come into the possession of the Daimyo of Arima. He ordered all to become Christians, and it is said that two thousand of them were baptised in the year 1587. He also aided one of his relatives to regain certain territories on receiving his promise that the inhabitants should be made Christians.

Though the Daimyo of Hirado destroyed several churches and overthrew the crosses that had been erected in the cemeteries, the only feudal lord that was led by Hideyoshi's edict to engage in active persecution of the Christians was Otomo Yoshimune. It was represented to him that as a baptised follower of the foreign religion he was likely to be treated in the same way that Takayama had been. Alarmed at this danger and pushed on by " Jezebel " and her brother, he refused to shelter the missionaries any longer, and issued orders to his subjects of such a nature that obedience on the part of Christians would have been equivalent to apostasy. Two of his retainers who refused to obey were put to death, as were also the wife, two children, and a servant of one of them; but this did not suffice to shake the constancy of others.*

Yoshimune's brother, sister, stepmother, and some of his leading retainers set the example of disregarding his orders. A certain noble lady appeared in his presence with a rosary hanging from her neck. When Yoshimune, who had lately gone before Hideyoshi displaying ostentatiously a Buddhist emblem, asked how she dared to wear this badge of Christianity, she replied: "Sir, we ought to value the presents received from our lords. Since you yourself not very long ago presented me with this rosary, I show my appreciation of your gift by wearing it where all may see it." It was probably fear of an uprising of the Christians that prevented Yoshimune from pressing measures against them.

Meanwhile, Father Coelho was endeavouring through the intercession of powerful friends to secure a withdrawal of the edict. All his efforts were vain. The six months of respite quickly passed away, and a Portuguese vessel was ready to set sail. The Vice-Provincial induced the captain to declare that the ship was so full of merchandise that he could not take many passengers. Only three Jesuits embarked, and they were Brothers who intended to go to India for ordination and then return to Japan. Though the captain sent messengers to Hideyoshi bearing excuses and gifts, the latter was so angry at the disregard for his commands that he destroyed the residences of the Jesuits in Osaka, Sakai, and Kyoto, together with twenty-two churches. Led probably by the suspicion that the foreigners were conspiring with the Japanese Christians, he somewhere about this time took Nagasaki away from the Daimyo of Omura, making it one of the imperial cities, such as were directly under his own control.†

* In a catalogue of Japanese martyrs, eight are mentioned as preceding these of Bungo. Five were martyred at Hirado in 1557, one at Amakusa in 1568, and two in Hizen in 1574.

† A history of Nagasaki published in 1902 says that about 1573 the man who owned the territory where the city was built had been obliged to borrow money to pay his share of Omura's military expenditures. He obtained the funds he needed from the Portuguese upon security of his land. When he failed to pay the

On learning of Hideyoshi's anger, the Vice-Provincial called the Jesuits to Arima for another conference. It was decided that it would be better for all to assume a secular dress, to scatter more widely than before, and to avoid everything that would call attention to themselves. The Christian daimyos were ready as ever to furnish them refuge. Arima sheltered seventy, Omura twelve, Amakusa nine, Bungo five; while four remained in Hirado and two went to Kurume in Chikugo. As the separation of his islands from the main part of Kyushu made John of Amakusa feel more free to do as he liked, he insisted that the churches should not be closed and that as formerly the bells should be rung to call believers to the religious services. A display of independence in other matters soon brought him into trouble. He had declared that he was under no obligation to assist in the construction of a castle that Konishi, his suzerain, was erecting. Afterwards he disregarded Hideyoshi's orders that he come and give an explanation of such conduct. Hideyoshi therefore commanded Konishi to join with others in punishing him. He was soon forced to surrender to Konishi, who, after re-

debt and removed to another place to escape his creditors, they appealed to the Daimyo of Omura, saying that the money they had lent was not their own but had been entrusted to them by the Jesuits, to whom it had been contributed for missionary purposes. Hence, either the debt should be paid or the Jesuits should be put in possession of the land. Omura was not able to pay the money, and finally by the advice of Arima the land was given over to the missionaries, who governed it to suit themselves. The inhabitants, who were much displeased, awaited an opportunity to shake off the foreign yoke. In 1587 they appealed to Hideyoshi. After examining into the matter he declared that it was shameful to have Japanese territory ruled by foreign priests. He therefore made the land national property. The ancient records do not say what was done to settle the debt; but a fine was laid on each inhabitant for having allowed the evil to continue so long without informing the central Government, and it may be that the money thus secured was used to satisfy the claim of the Portuguese. Afterwards the fine was remitted. Tradition says that the people made some arrangement with the Christians for settling up the matter.

Could the facts underlying this story be sifted out, they might help to explain Hideyoshi's action against the Jesuits in 1587.

buking him for disloyalty, spared his life and even allowed him to retain his castle (December, 1589).
Konishi also placed Christian governors over several
other strongholds in the Amakusa archipelago.

News of Hideyoshi's opposition to the Jesuits reached
Goa while the ambassadors who had been sent to
Europe were tarrying in that city on their return journey. Following a suggestion sent by Father Coelho, the
Portuguese Viceroy appointed Father Valegnani his envoy who should go to Japan for the purpose of expressing thanks for past favours shown to the Portuguese,
and to request a continuance of the former relations.
It was hoped that by going in this official position
Valegnani could gain access to Hideyoshi, and it was
believed that according to Japanese custom the admission of one of the Jesuits to the Regent's presence would
be considered as equivalent to a revocation of the edict
for their banishment.

Valegnani and the ambassadors tarried for some time
in Macao. This gave opportunity for sending a letter
to Hideyoshi asking if the envoy would be received.
As the reply was favourable, the journey was continued
so that in July, 1590, they reached Nagasaki, where they
were joyfully welcomed by the Christians. Hideyoshi's
attention was occupied with a military expedition and
the illness of Valegnani caused further delay, so that
it was not until January, 1591, that the envoy and the
Japanese ambassadors set out toward Kyoto, where
Hideyoshi then had his headquarters. Accompanied by
a number of Portuguese, they made their way to Mu-
rotsu in the province of Harima. The deaths of
Hideyoshi's son and half-brother caused a delay of two
months to be made at this place, where Takayama Ukon
and many other prominent Christians came to confer with Valegnani. Among the visitors was Otomo
Yoshimune, who had previously sent a letter asking that
his great sin in persecuting the Christians be forgiven.
Many daimyos that were on the way to pay their respects to Hideyoshi came to hear from the ambassadors
an account of what they had seen in Europe.

Various difficulties which at one time made it seem

likely that Hideyoshi would withdraw his assent for an audience having been overcome, the envoy and his associates finally entered Kyoto with that display and splendour in which both Portuguese and Japanese delighted. This was considered the more necessary because some of the courtiers were endeavouring to persuade the Regent that the embassy was not genuine, but only a trick of the Jesuits. At the head of the procession two Indians led a richly caparisoned horse that the Viceroy had sent as a present to Hideyoshi. Two pages preceded Mancio Ito and his associates, who wore the robes of black velvet trimmed with gold lace that they had received from the Pope. Valegnani and two other missionaries were carried in litters, and the rear of the procession was brought up by the Portuguese merchants "in so rich attire that they might have appeared before the greatest monarch in the world." Hideyoshi did his part to honour the occasion by a display of luxury and by bestowing rich gifts on his visitors. After the formal ceremonies were concluded, he spent some time in familiar conversation with them. He gave Valegnani permission to remain in either Kyoto, Osaka, or Nagasaki, until return presents for the Viceroy of India had been prepared. He himself was about leaving Kyoto for a short visit to his native town.

During Hideyoshi's absence, the missionaries and their companions were visited by large numbers of people who were interested in examining the maps, terrestrial globes, clocks, musical instruments, and other curiosities that had been brought. The Japanese ambassadors did their best to describe the wonders of Europe in such a way as to impress their auditors with a sense of the prosperity of Christian lands and the glories of the Roman Church. At this time, too, So Yoshitomo, the Daimyo of Tsushima, who promised that he would make his whole island Christian, was baptised, but in secret from fear of irritating Hideyoshi.

On the Regent's return to Kyoto, Valegnani took leave of him and went to Nagasaki. He then accompanied the ambassadors as they returned to their homes carrying the gifts that had been sent to their daimyos and making a report of the way they had fulfilled their mission. When all was over, the four young men made known the resolution taken while in Europe that they would renounce the world and seek admission to the Society of Jesus. Resisting the opposition of some of their relatives, they entered the seminary at Amakusa for study preparatory to taking upon themselves the vows of the order. In due time they entered the Society, though Chijiwa afterwards left it.

The two Governors of Nagasaki now caused such representations to reach Hideyoshi as were calculated to renew his suspicions concerning the missionaries. The explanation of their action that is given by the Jesuits is that these officials felt aggrieved because they had been omitted in the distribution of presents brought by Valegnani and also because they had not been given the honour of presenting him at court. However this may be, they informed Hideyoshi that the missionaries had paid no attention to his order for leaving the country and that since the coming of Valegnani they were openly holding religious services and baptising many converts. Arguments were also advanced to show that the professed embassy from India was only a trick for keeping the foreign priests in Japan. It was not difficult to arouse the suspicions of Hideyoshi, who now threatened to have the missionaries put to death. When rumours of the impending danger reached Valegnani, he at first proposed that all the Jesuits should withdraw to some island off the coast of China and there await better times. As the Christian daimyos opposed this proposition, it was finally decided that most of the missionaries should go to Amakusa, where they would attract less attention. Owing to this change, Amakusa became the centre of Japanese Christianity. Here were the leading schools and here was set up a printing press from which, in the coming years, were issued not only religious books but also a Latin-Portuguese-Japanese dictionary and a Latin Grammar in Japanese.

At about this time Kuroda induced one of the Governors of Kyoto to exert his influence in favour of the missionaries. Rodriguez had remained in Kyoto at

Hideyoshi's request, and the Governor seconded his shrewd suggestion that, if there were doubts about the genuineness of Valegnani's mission, the Jesuits who had accompanied him might be retained as hostages until there had been time to communicate with the Viceroy. As this plan was adopted, there were left in Nagasaki several priests who were under no necessity to disguise themselves. The same Governor induced Hideyoshi to revise the letter that he had intended to send to the Viceroy. It had been written in a haughty tone and accused the missionaries of many evil deeds. The letter as finally sent was without these charges and, as the following extract shows, the objections urged against the work of the Jesuits were substantially the same as Japanese have brought against Christianity in modern times:

" With respect to religious matters, Japan is the realm of the *Kami*, that is to say of *Shin* [the Chinese word for *Kami*, the deities of Shinto], which are the origin of all things; the good order of the government which has been established here from the beginning depends on the exact observance of the laws on which it is founded, and whose authors are the *Kami* themselves. They cannot be deviated from without involving the disappearance of the difference which ought to subsist between sovereign and subject, and of the subordination of wives to husbands, of children to fathers, of vassals to lords, and of servants to their masters. In a word, these laws are necessary for the maintenance of good order at home and of tranquillity abroad. The Fathers of the Company, as they are called, have come to these islands to teach another religion here; but as that of the *Kami* is too surely founded to be abolished, this new law can only serve to introduce into Japan a diversity of cults prejudicial to the welfare of the State. It is for this reason that by Edict I have forbidden foreign doctors to continue preaching their doctrine. I have even ordered them to leave Japan and I am resolved no longer to allow any one to come here to spread new opinions. I nevertheless desire that trade between you and us should always be on the same footing as before."

It was not until October, 1592, that Valegnani set out on his return to India. Meanwhile, the attention of Hideyoshi and of the Japanese was being taken up with the expedition against Korea. Many Christian warriors took a prominent part in this enterprise. Hideyoshi, who in giving over the title of Kwambaku to

his nephew had taken that of Taiko by which he has
since been commonly known, did not himself go to
Korea as he had at first planned to do. The command
of the two most important divisions of the army was
given to Konishi Yukinaga, the Christian, and to his
rival, Kato Kiyomasa, who hated the foreign religion.
In order that each might feel himself equally honoured
with the other, and perhaps for the purpose of increasing their emulation, the Taiko gave orders that their
divisions should take turns in leading the vanguard of
the army. In Konishi's division were four Christian
daimyos, and a large number of the eighteen thousand
soldiers were also Christians.* They left Japan in
May, 1592. The earliest successes were won by Konishi. Later honours, so far as honours could come from
a war that in its motives and final outcome was little to
Japan's credit, were somewhat equally divided between
the two leaders, Japanese historians giving the greater
praise to Kato.

It will not be necessary to describe the progress of
this war, which lasted until the death of Hideyoshi in
1598. In 1594, Father Cespedes and a Japanese helper
went by Konishi's invitation to Korea, where they not
only cared for the spiritual welfare of the Christian
soldiers but also gained many new converts. They remained in Korea, however, only two months. Kato
while on a furlough in Japan tried to convince Hideyoshi
that Konishi was engaged in a conspiracy by which
he intended to make his followers all Christians and then
lead them back to take part in a movement for overthrowing the Taiko's power. Hideyoshi, who had always been suspicious of Christianity, gave a ready ear
to these accusations or, at least, pretended to do so.

---

* It has been supposed by some writers that one of Hideyoshi's
objects in the war with Korea was to get rid of the Christian
leaders. If Konishi and his fellow-believers were slain, an end
would be put to the trouble feared from them; if they were victorious, they could be rewarded by lands in Korea, and Japan
would be free from their presence. There is little reason for
thinking that such considerations had much to do with the de
cision to undertake the war or with the prominent position that
was given to Konishi.

Konishi, on hearing what was being done, sent away Father Cespedes and soon after went to Kyoto, where he was able to re-establish confidence in his loyalty.

About the year 1590, John de Solis, a Spanish merchant who came to Nagasaki, considered that he was unjustly treated by the Portuguese traders. He was also angry with the Jesuits because they had sided against him in the controversy. At about the same time an apostate Christian named Harada, who had formerly been to the Philippines, managed to get access to Hideyoshi and suggested that it would be easy for the latter to bring those islands under his sway. Accordingly the Taiko, in 1591, sent a letter to the Spanish Governor demanding that tribute be paid to himself as suzerain. As Valegnani learned that this letter was to be sent, he wrote to the Jesuits in Manila informing them of what was being done. It was feared that the Governor in his indignation would write in such a way as would excite Hideyoshi's wrath against all foreigners, and the Jesuits therefore urged that the affair be so managed as not to prejudice the work of the missionaries.

The Governor sent to Japan one of his officials together with Father Cobo, a Dominican, with orders to tell Hideyoshi that a letter bearing his name had lately been received, but its contents were such as could be most easily explained by supposing that the document was a forgery. The two messengers landed at Kagoshima, where they found De Solis superintending the building of a ship in which he intended to leave the country. Seeing an opportunity to repay the Portuguese and Jesuits for their treatment of him, he went with the messengers to Hideyoshi. Harada served as interpreter. It is asserted that he took advantage of his position to translate the words of the Spaniard so as to signify that the Governor was not averse to Hideyoshi's proposal, while on the other hand he put the Spaniards in good humour by an equally free rendering of what was said to them. De Solis's charges against the Portuguese were then presented. He said that they acted as though they were the lords of Nagasaki, that they prevented merchants of other countries from trading, that they treated the Japanese with cruelty, and that it was they who had kept the missionaries in Japan after Hideyoshi's orders of banishment. As a consequence of these denunciations the Taiko appointed a young man named Terasawa to be Governor of Nagasaki, ordering him to have the churches and other buildings of the Jesuits torn down, and to examine carefully into the conduct of the Portuguese merchants. Hideyoshi had a second letter written to the Governor of the Philippines in even more arrogant terms than the first.

The missionaries hidden in different parts of the country were in constant danger of being discovered by Hideyoshi's officials, who were travelling through the provinces to obtain supplies for the Korean expedition and to make out lists of able-bodied men. At one time a certain person had learned the names and hiding-places of all the priests; but they were able by means of bribes to induce him to keep silence. Those concealed in Nagasaki were in great peril, because a charge that the Christians were providing themselves with arms led to an order that every house in the city should be searched.

There began to be considerable anxiety among the Japanese lest news of the destruction of the religious establishments in Nagasaki should lead the Portuguese merchants to give up coming thither to trade. Among the upper classes had arisen a craze for Western ideas, which was even more intense than those which in modern times have swept over the land. European dress became common; crucifixes and rosaries being worn as a part thereof. It is said that the Kwambaku and even Hideyoshi himself followed the custom of wearing these religious ornaments. Some of the fashionable people carried their imitation of the Portuguese to the extent of repeating Paternosters and Ave Marias. Such was the demand for foreign goods that it would have been regarded as a grave misfortune if the Great Ship sent annually from Macao to Nagasaki should fail to come. As it was now overdue, people began grumbling at Hideyoshi for having offended the Portuguese. Terasawa, as the one responsible for carrying out the

Taiko's orders, had to bear more unpopularity than was his due. This led him to suggest to Hideyoshi that steps should be taken to conciliate the foreigners. He also made advances to the Vice-Provincial, suggesting ways in which the priests ought to conduct themselves so as to regain favour. It was in accordance with his advice that when the Great Ship arrived Father Paez went with the captain to pay his respects to Hideyoshi under the pretence that he had just arrived in the country. Terasawa told Hideyoshi that the Portuguese were anxious to have the large church at Nagasaki rebuilt and to have ten resident priests to conduct its services. Consent was given and the church was quickly erected. This arrangement took away the need for concealment on the part of missionaries living in Nagasaki.

It is hard to believe that Hideyoshi did not know that Paez was no new arrival in Japan or that he was not well-informed concerning what the missionaries were doing. Indeed, many things in his conduct seem to show that he was not opposed to Christianity so long as it could be kept in subjection. When Konishi's father, who was the Governor of Sakai, died, Hideyoshi said to another son who was appointed his successor: "Remember that you are a Christian, and take heed to perform the duties of your office with the care and fidelity that your religion inculcates." Thousands of converts were made between the issuing of the edict in 1587 and the death of Hideyoshi in 1598. Many people of high rank were baptised, and though in many cases the rite was performed in secret, it is not likely that what had been done could long remain unknown to the rulers of a country where the art of espionage was so well developed. Among the secret baptisms was that of Terasawa in 1595. Other noted converts were the lords of Gifu, Aizu, Obi, and Ina. Many converts of high rank were made by Father Organtin, whom Hideyoshi had permitted to reside in Kyoto upon the conditions that he should have no church and should not perform the rite of baptism. The second of these restrictions appears to have been lightly regarded, or it may be that the letter of the prohibition was observed by having

the actual baptisms administered by others. Father
Organtin had qualities that enabled him to gain many
friends among the noble and wealthy families. He
won to Christianity the man that was reputed to be the
richest merchant of Kyoto. Organtin also understood
how to inspire others with missionary zeal. A converted priest, six blind men of high rank, and Hideyoshi's
master of the tea ceremony, are mentioned as being
specially successful in winning members of noble
families.

The last part of Hideyoshi's rule was marked by a
new persecution, whose immediate object was not the
Jesuits but the members of another religious order.
In connection with this and subsequent events it is
necessary to speak of the rivalry that existed between
the religious orders and between the traders of different countries. We have seen that at first the Portuguese
were the only Europeans who engaged in trade with
Japan. In 1580, Philip II. of Spain became also King
of Portugal. One article in the agreement made at that
time was that to Portugal should be reserved the monopoly of commerce with Japan. In 1585, Pope Gregory
XIII. issued a brief forbidding under pain of major
excommunication that any but Jesuits should teach
Christianity, administer sacraments, or perform any other
ecclesiastical function in Japan except as special permission might be given by the Pope. Philip II. sent a
copy of this brief to the Viceroy of India, enjoining him
to see that it was strictly observed.

The Spanish merchants that had established themselves in the Philippines had long been turning their
eyes towards Japan. They very naturally thought that
if missionaries holding such relations to them as the
Jesuits did to the Portuguese could get a footing in the
land it would help toward the establishment of commercial relations. Hence it was that, as we have seen, a
member of the Dominican order was sent in company
with the Governor's envoy to inquire the meaning of
Hideyoshi's letter and to see if an opening could not
be found for trade. Both of these messengers were lost

at sea on their return voyage. Harada, the rascally interpreter, had gone to the Philippines on another vessel, and he took advantage of this opportunity to pretend that he was Hideyoshi's ambassador and that his credentials were on the ship that was wrecked. A paper that he presented declared that Hideyoshi desired trade and also wished that there might be sent some Franciscan monks, since he had learned that that order was highly reputed for sanctity and devotion. The friars were the first to whom this document was shown and they were so delighted with the prospect opening before them that they helped to quiet any suspicions that the Governor had concerning Harada. It was decided that another official, together with Father Pierre Baptiste and three other Franciscans, should be sent to inquire the contents of the Taiko's letter that had been lost at sea. They reached Japan in June, 1593. Hideyoshi graciously received them and the presents they brought, but said he must insist upon being recognised as ruler of the Philippines. Father Baptiste, who apparently served as spokesman for the envoys, said that the Governor of the Philippines could not give his assent to this claim without first consulting the King of Spain, and he asked that the Spaniards be permitted to engage in trade until a reply could be received. Meanwhile, he and his companions were willing to remain as hostages. Hideyoshi consented to this arrangement, but imposed the condition that the envoys should not attempt to teach their religion to the Japanese. They chose to remain in Kyoto, but requested that they be given a residence in the suburbs, since, as monks accustomed to a quiet life, they found it unpleasant to live among people of the world. As their petition was granted, they at once proceeded to build a chapel where, in October, 1594, they began to say mass in the presence of Japanese Christians. Though the friendly Governor of Kyoto and many of the believers told them that they were running great risks of exciting Hideyoshi's anger, they paid little heed to such warnings. They were joined very soon by three more of their order, who came bringing a message from the Governor of the Philippines to the effect that he could not acknowledge Hideyoshi as his sovereign. Whether owing to the skilful way in which the refusal was expressed or to the promises of favourable commerce that were made, Hideyoshi showed no special resentment, but allowed these Franciscans to remain with the others. They now opened houses in Osaka and Nagasaki. They also became bolder in their preaching. When the Jesuits called their attention to the Pope's brief, they said they had done nothing contrary to its decrees; for it was not as missionaries but as ambassadors that they had come, and it could never have been the Pope's intention to prevent the clergy from performing the functions of their ministry wherever they might be. Probably they also used an argument that is found in books upholding their action on the ground that Sixtus V. in 1586 had issued a bull authorising the Franciscans to labour in the Philippines and other lands of the East Indies. It is claimed that this as a later decree repealed the prohibition of Gregory XIII.

The Jesuits were naturally very much irritated by what they considered an intrusion on territory reserved to them. They realised, too, that the course pursued by the Franciscans in openly disregarding the orders of Hideyoshi was likely to lead to more active measures against Christianity. In fact, after the Franciscans began work in Nagasaki, the officials of that city issued orders threatening punishment to any who attended mass; and in other ways they so interfered with the Franciscans that the latter decided to return to their brethren in Kyoto. There they did not hesitate, even before the Japanese Christians, to accuse the Jesuits of having been the means of putting an end to their labours in Nagasaki. A letter of Father Organtin tells of the great sorrow it gave him " to behold the best-founded hopes of soon seeing Christianity dominant in the empire vanish by reason of this fatal dissension."

The Jesuits had long desired to have a bishop appointed for Japan. The first to whom the Pope turned was so loath to leave his work in Africa that he was excused from taking the office, and two others that were successively chosen died on their journey to Japan. The next one appointed was Father Pierre Martinez, who arrived in Nagasaki August 13, 1596. Though the Christians did not venture to make in public so full a display of their joy as they would have liked to do, the Bishop on landing was met by the clergy in their robes and was preceded by crosses and banners as he was escorted to the church.

According to the stories preserved among the Japanese and by them repeated to Kaempfer, this Bishop and his successors acted in an arrogant way, being " carried about in stately chairs, mimicking the pomp of the Pope and his cardinals at Rome," and thus helping to increase the ill-feeling against Christianity. Soon after his arrival in Japan, so it was said, he " met upon the road one of the Councillors of State on his way to court. The haughty prelate would not order his chair to be stopped in order to alight and to pay his respects to this great man, as is usual in this country, but without taking any notice of him, nay indeed, without showing him so much as common marks of civility, he very contemptibly bid his men carry him by. . . . This great man, exasperated at so signal an affront, thenceforward bore a mortal hatred to the Portuguese, and in the height of his just resentment made his complaints to the Emperor [Taiko] himself." Father Steichen in " The Christian Daimyo " doubts this story, declaring that the Bishop " was not, any more than any bonze of the lowest position, obliged by Japanese custom to descend from his litter under such circumstances;" * that as bearer of despatches from the Viceroy of India he would be released from such a necessity, had it otherwise existed; and that the honour with which he was treated by Hideyoshi during the year of his stay in

---

* Whatever force the other arguments may have, those who remember that persons were expected to kneel beside the road when a daimyo's train passed, and that in 1862 one foreigner was killed and others attacked for not dismounting from their horses at such a time, will not think it unlikely that, when the feeling against missionaries was so strong, resentment would be felt against one who was thought to show lack of respect to a person of high rank.

Japan shows that he had not incurred the Taiko's disapproval.

Bishop Martinez had indeed followed the example of Valegnani by coming with political as well as religious functions. While he was at Goa on his outward journey, Valegnani had arrived there with the letters in which, among other things, Hideyoshi asked whether that priest was in truth an official envoy. The Viceroy now entrusted his answer and many rich presents to the new Bishop, hoping thus to pave the way for him to gain the good will of Hideyoshi for both the missionaries and the merchants. While their official relations may have helped Valegnani, Martinez, and the Franciscans to get a foothold in Japan, it is easy to see that they would also tend to strengthen the growing suspicion that the missionaries were all emissaries of foreign governments and that their labours had some political object in view.

In July, 1596, the *San Felipe,* a Spanish galleon that was on its way from Manila to Mexico, was driven by a storm to Urado in the province of Tosa. Among its passengers were six priests. The local officers declared that by the laws of Japan the vessel should be confiscated. The captain sent two of the ship's officers and two Franciscans to ask the Taiko's permission to refit the galleon and proceed upon the voyage. These messengers had orders to do nothing except by the advice of Father Baptiste, the Commissary of the Franciscans. The Daimyo of Tosa, who professed to be friendly, had recommended them to the favour of an official named Masuda, who deceived them and advised Hideyoshi to have the vessel seized. The Jesuits assert that when this treachery was discovered an appeal was made by the Spaniards to Bishop Martinez, Father Rodriguez, and Father Organtin, all of whom were in Kyoto, where they possessed much influence. They accordingly did all they could, but it was now too late to effect anything. Masuda was sent to take possession of the wreck and its rich lading. In an endeavour to deter the Japanese from their purpose, the pilot declared that the King of Spain would certainly take vengeance upon those that so wronged his subjects. To prove to them the extent of that monarch's power, a map was spread out so as to show that he ruled not only over Spain and Portugal, but also over the Philippines, Mexico, Peru, and other lands. When Masuda asked how it had been possible to get such great possessions, the pilot replied: "The kings of Spain begin by sending out teachers of our religion, and when these have made sufficient progress in gaining the hearts of the people, troops are despatched who unite with the new Christians in bringing about the conquest of the desired territory." Whether the pilot hoped that his words would serve to excite suspicion only against the Jesuits and their Portuguese allies, or whether he was the forerunner of the many haters of all missionary work, who delight in disparaging the preaching of Christianity, it is certain that the remark had great influence upon Hideyoshi, to whom it was reported. Not only do European historians consider it one of the chief causes of the persecution that immediately followed, but Japanese accounts of the early missions describe the Spanish policy in terms almost identical with those used by the pilot.

An account of the confiscation of the ship that was printed in the Philippine Islands and sent to Europe held the Jesuits and their Portuguese partisans responsible for the misfortunes of the Spaniards. It declared that Bishop Martinez joined with others in petitioning Hideyoshi to drive the Franciscans from the land, and that they spared neither accusations nor promises in the attempt to induce him to do this, one of their assertions being that the Spaniards, instead of being driven to the land by a tempest, had intentionally come to Japan for the purpose of stirring up a revolt. This account went on to say that Hideyoshi, greatly scandalised at the baseness of the Jesuits, declared that the Franciscans were holy men whose virtues their rivals would do well to imitate. Nevertheless, the Bishop succeeded in exciting his desire to gain possession of the Spaniards' goods.

At about this time other attempts to arouse opposition against the Jesuits took the form of memorials, one addressed to the King of Spain and another to the Pope. The former made the surprising statements that, although it had been in the power of the Jesuits to have the daimyos of Kyushu recognise the Governor of the Philippines as their suzerain, they had been so lacking in loyalty to the King of Spain and Portugal as to invite Hideyoshi to Kyushu; that the missionaries themselves possessed estates that on the death of Hideyoshi they could render tributary to any ruler whom they wished; that they had thirty thousand armed men in their employ; and that of the Japanese who had professed Christianity all but six had abandoned the faith.

The other memorial, which was presented to the Pope in March, 1598, said that it was not hatred of Christianity but fear of the excessive power of the Jesuits that led Hideyoshi to oppose their teaching; that the Jesuits alone were proscribed, while the Franciscans had been treated with honour and given liberty to preach the Gospel, which they did with so much success as to lead back many that had apostatised; and that Valegnani when in Japan had appeared in court with an equipage not becoming a priest, for he wore pontifical garments, had a mitre on his head, and was followed by two hundred men in livery.

The Jesuits, aware of these attacks, took means for defending themselves; but ere either the charges or the defence could have reached Europe, both Jesuits and Franciscans were feeling the force of Hideyoshi's wrath. No sooner had the Taiko been informed of what the Spanish pilot had said than he took action. On the evening of December 9, 1596, the establishments of the Franciscans and Jesuits in Kyoto and Osaka were surrounded by guards. The governors of the two cities were ordered to draw up lists of persons who were in the habit of frequenting the churches. In a few days three Franciscan Fathers (Baptiste, Aguirre, and Blanco), three Franciscan Brothers (Las Casas, Parilha, and Garcia), Paul Miki, who was a lay brother of the Society of Jesus, two other Japanese who were novices preparing to enter the same Society, and fifteen persons in the employ of the missionaries were arrested. In the last group were boys only twelve, thirteen, and fifteen years of age. The Jesuit missionaries were left unmolested. There is reason to think that Hideyoshi did not care to have any harm come to the latter at this time. He is reported to have said to one of the officials in Kyoto that it was his desire to have only the priests from the Philippines apprehended. Apparently his irritation at the unwillingness of the Governor of those islands to acknowledge him as suzerain, as well as the suspicions aroused by the words of the Spanish pilot, led him to order the arrests. It is said that the setting of the guards about the establishments of the Jesuits and the apprehension of some of their Japanese followers came from a misunderstanding of his commands.

There was great excitement among the Christians, who at first thought that all of them would be arrested. Either to share in the glory of martyrdom or to exert their influence in favour of their brethren, many prominent believers, such as Takayama Ukon and the son of the Governor of Kyoto, hastened to the capital. A letter of Father Organtin represents the Christians of all ranks as being ready to lay down their lives for the Faith.

The prisoners that had been arrested in Osaka were taken to Kyoto. There Organtin tried to obtain the release of the three Jesuits on the ground that they were held contrary to Hideyoshi's wishes. The Governor declared that, though he would be glad to free them, he could not do so without consulting Hideyoshi; and this, by calling attention to the Jesuits, might lead to more arrests.

On the third of January, 1597, the twenty-four prisoners were led through the streets of Kyoto to the northern part of the city, where the executioner cut off portions of their ears. They were then put on carts, three in each cart, and drawn through the city in order to expose them to the derision of the populace. Before each cart was suspended a placard which said in substance: "The Taiko has condemned these men to die because, though coming from the Philippine Islands as ambassadors, they have disobeyed his commands by preaching the Christian religion. Therefore, they and the Japanese that have become their followers shall be crucified in Nagasaki."

The next day they were put on pack-horses and sent to Osaka. They were led through the principal streets of that city and Sakai, after which they were taken by land to Nagasaki. Everywhere they were subjected to the insults of the people, although in some places through which they passed the Christians came to speak words of cheer and exhorted them to be faithful unto death. By this protracted journey, which took over two months, a large part of the country was warned of the danger of following the foreign religion, while the place of execution was evidently chosen with the thought of having the Portuguese report to the people of Christian lands that missionaries could come to Japan only at peril of their lives.

The prisoners had at first numbered twenty-four: there were twenty-six when they reached Nagasaki. Father Organtin had sent two persons to follow after the captives in order to minister so far as possible to their necessities. On being discovered by the guards, these persons confessed that they were Christians, and accordingly, they were added to the others. An attempt was made in Nagasaki to secure their release; but the officials in that city feared trouble for themselves if they failed to execute all who had been delivered into their hands.

Father Baptiste had sent a letter to the Jesuits of Nagasaki asking that, if possible, arrangements be made for administering the sacraments to the prisoners. All that the officials would grant was that Father Paez might go to one of the towns through which the captives would pass and there shrive Miki and his two companions. Paez received the vows of the two latter, thus admitting them into the Society. Father Rodriguez, who had come to Nagasaki, managed to gain access to the prisoners and to administer the sacraments to some of them. As Terasawa, the Governor of Nagasaki, who had been secretly baptised, was absent at this time, the care of the execution came upon his brother Hasaburo. He as a boy had been a playmate of Paul Miki, and for years he had seen nothing of him until he met him among the captives that he must put to death.

There were fears that the Christians of Nagasaki might seek to rescue their fellow-believers. The prisoners were not brought into the city until the day (February 5, 1597) that they were to die, and then, instead of being taken to the usual execution-ground, they were led to a hill whose approaches could be easily guarded by men with muskets and spears. Death was by crucifixion, a method of punishment said to have been unknown among the Japanese until they heard of it in connection with Christianity. It afterwards became a common form of executing those guilty of heinous crimes. As it was practised by the Japanese, the victim was tied by ropes to a cross and, instead of being left to suffer for a long time, his body was pierced with a spear that was first thrust from the right side upwards towards the left shoulder and then from the left side towards the right shoulder. Thus the heart was usually pierced, causing instant death. It may be that this use of the spear was borrowed from representations that had been seen of the crucifixion of Christ.

After the martys had been bound to the crosses, some of them, especially Paul Miki, addressed the crowd of Christians and others who were pressing up as near as possible to them. Fathers Paez and Rodriguez had obtained permission to remain with the sufferers. Two Franciscans in disguise were in the crowd that stood outside the cordon of soldiers. When at last the execution was over, the Christians, unmindful of the blows that the guards bestowed upon them, pressed forward through the lines to dip kerchiefs in the blood of the martyrs or to obtain shreds of their clothing.

In after times various stories were told of bright lights that shone over the martyrs, of the bodies that did not suffer corruption in the two months that they were left on the crosses, of blood that remained in a liquid state, and of a dumb woman who received the power of speech when she kissed Father Baptiste's cross. Two witnesses declared that ere the bodies were removed they saw Father Baptiste celebrating mass in the church, assisted by one of the martyred children. Amazed at this, they went to the execution-ground, where the cross of the Father seemed to be empty. The guards told them that the body often vanished and after a short absence returned to its place. These and other alleged marvels constituted a part of what was considered essential for justifying the canonisation of those who are now known as the Twenty-Six Martyrs, for it was not long ere steps were taken towards having them enrolled among the saints of the Roman Catholic Church. A brief issued September 14, 1627, by Pope Urban VIII. authorised the Franciscans to say the office and mass of the six priests and seventeen laymen connected with their order, and another issued the next day gave permission for the Jesuits to honour their martyrs in the same way. The canonisation to which this beatification formed a necessary prelude was long delayed; the chief reason, it is said, being the great expense involved. In March, 1862, Pius IX. pronounced the decree of canonisation, the imposing ceremonies connected therewith being performed the next June.

Soon after the arrest of the Franciscans, Hideyoshi issued a new edict in which he forbade any daimyo to become a Christian. He also directed that all the missionaries should be assembled at Nagasaki and at the first opportunity sent out of the country. He made an exception of Father Rodriguez, whom he used as an interpreter, of Father Organtin, and of a few others who were allowed to remain for the benefit of the Portuguese. Three or four Franciscans were at once deported.

There were now one hundred and twenty-five Jesuits left in Japan, of whom forty-six were priests. Terasawa, the Governor of Nagasaki, was still absent; but the Deputy Governor continued to demand that Father Gomez, who was then Vice-Provincial, should send these people out of the country. Gomez, after interposing all possible objections, thought it necessary to make a show of yielding. Though some of the missionaries remained in their places of concealment, most of them came to Nagasaki as though they were getting ready for their departure to Macao. The last vessel of that year weighed anchor in October, 1597. According to Charlevoix, " All the bridge seemed to be filled with Jesuits, although there were only a few students with their professors, two sick priests, and some catechists. The others were Portuguese disguised as Jesuits, and by this innocent stratagem, which had doubtless been concerted with Terasawa, Father Gomez saved his mission; but inasmuch as, in spite of the wise precautions he had taken to prevent the *religieux* from being discovered, it might happen that such a misfortune would overtake some of them, he caused the report to be spread that all of them had not had time to reach the port before the departure of the ship, and that he would profit by the first opportunity to make them embark."

Rumours that Hideyoshi was soon coming to Kyushu made the officials think it wise to enforce the edicts against the Christians. Early in 1598, one hundred and thirty-seven churches, the college in Amakusa, the seminary in Arima, and many residences of the Jesuits were destroyed. In some places the Christians were subjected to severe persecution. Those missionaries that did not succeed in concealing themselves were brought to Nagasaki for deportation.

Bishop Martinez died in 1598 while on his way to India, and in August of the same year his successor, Mgr. Çerqueira, arrived in Japan. One of the first acts of the new Bishop was to call together the leading missionaries for a consultation upon the question of slaves. The Portuguese merchants had been in the habit of purchasing prisoners of war and criminals, who were sold by the feudal lords, sometimes as slaves, sometimes as servants for a limited number of years. Bishop Martinez at first had issued licenses for this trade, but had afterwards prohibited it under pain of a fine, major excommunication, and the loss of the slaves thus bought. The new Bishop now asked advice as to the policy that he should pursue. The conference was unanimous in its opinion that he ought to renew the prohibition made by his predecessor, and to abstain scrupulously from giving any of the Portuguese licenses to buy or take away from

Japan persons purchased either as slaves or under the name of servants bound for a certain number of years. He ought also to urge the King of Spain to renew and enforce laws concerning the liberty of the Japanese that had formerly been published by King Sebastian of Portugal. The report of this conference shows that the trade had been attended by terrible evils.*

It was feared that Hideyoshi would be aroused to renewed activity against Christianity by an incident that happened about this time. Among the Franciscans that had escaped arrest in 1596, was one named Jerome de Jésus. Great efforts had been made to find him. According to one account, he was finally apprehended and sent to Manila; others say he had gone there of his own accord. However this may have been, in June, 1598, he, with another of his order, took passage from the Philippines in a Japanese vessel, whose crew betrayed them to the officials of Nagasaki. The Franciscans were arrested, but Jerome's knowledge of the country enabled him to escape. The Vice-Provincial of the Jesuits sent a messenger to Terasawa begging him not to have this reported to Hideyoshi. Terasawa accordingly sent his officers orders to keep the affair secret, but to put forth every effort for recapturing the fugitive. Enemies of the Jesuits hint that the latter had a part in securing the original arrest of the Franciscans and would have been glad to hear that Jerome had been again apprehended.

Immediate danger of increased persecution was removed by the death September 16, 1598, of Hideyoshi. He was undoubtedly one of the shrewdest statesmen Japan has ever produced. A recent writer † goes so far as to call him " the greatest man Japan has ever seen," and also, " the greatest statesman of the century, whether in Japan or in Europe." Whatever his talents, there was much clay mingled with the iron; and it is not a cause for wonder that in the letters of the missionaries and in the histories founded upon them much em-

* The report may be found in Pagés, " Histoire de la Religion Chrétienne au Japon," vol. ii., p. 70.
† Murdoch, " History of Japan," pp. 301, 386.

phasis is laid on the weak points in his character. In ecclesiastical history he will be remembered as a persecutor, and yet it should not be forgotten that throughout most of the time that he was in authority the teachers of a foreign religion were left unmolested, that he held some of them, as Organtin and Rodriguez, in high esteem, and that he appointed to important offices those that were recognised as leaders among the Christians. It is not strange that, seeing the splendour of some of the religious ceremonies and the honour shown by the believers to their teachers,* he feared lest Christianity would succeed to the political and even to the military power that had been held by some of the Buddhist sects ere they had been crushed by Nobunaga and himself.†

We may at first be inclined to smile at the suspicions aroused by the unfortunate remark of the Spanish pilot; yet the mere fact that within a hundred years the Spanish kings had gained possession of much of America and India as well as of the Philippines and other islands, might well give cause for apprehension. Hideyoshi knew that messengers had been sent by the Christian daimyos of Kyushu to greet the King of Spain, and to bow at the feet of the Pope. Had he been acquainted with what European rulers and the Popes had done in connection with new countries, his fears would not have been lessened. Pope Martin V., about 1418, had granted to the King of Portugal all the territories that might be discovered by his navigators between Cape Bodajor and India. This grant was afterwards confirmed by Eugene

* Charlevoix, writing of the welcome extended to new missionaries in 1568, says: "Some prostrated themselves and even stretched themselves on the ground in the places where the missionaries were to pass, hoping to be trodden upon by the feet of those whose steps the Scripture says are full of charm; and, what ought to pass for a miracle of humility in a people so proud, a missionary never appeared in a street without all the Christians he met, even to persons of the highest rank, assuming a respectful posture. The Annual Letter of 1582 says of Takayama Ukon that in his intercourse with the Fathers he seemed more like a servant than so great a lord."

† In 1584 Hideyoshi destroyed the powerful monastery of Negoro, after fifteen thousand of its monks had been defeated in an armed attack that they made upon Osaka.

IV.   Similar concessions were made to the Spaniards for any discoveries they might make in sailing westward. In 1479 the rulers of Spain and Portugal had agreed that each would respect what had been granted to the other by these papal decrees.   In 1493 Pope Alexander VI. issued his famous Bull of Demarcation, authorising Spain, on condition of planting the Catholic Church, to take possession of all lands that lie beyond the meridian drawn one hundred leagues west of the Azores, so far as these lands were not already subject to Christian powers.   Though Portugal was not mentioned, it was understood that she could have all lying east of that meridian.   Of Càbral, who was sent out from Portugal towards India in 1500, it has been said: " The sum of his instructions was to begin with preaching, and, if that failed, to proceed to the sharp determination of the sword." *

The history of Spain at that time abounds with examples of this vicious linking together of religion and the power of the sword.   The civil and ecclesiastical counsellors drew up a form of proclamation to be used by the invaders of new provinces in America.   In case the rulers and people hesitated to acknowledge allegiance to Spain and to the Church, the invader was to give this warning: " If you refuse; by the help of God we shall enter with force into your land, and shall make war against you in all ways and manners that we can, and subject you to the yoke and obedience of the Church and of their Highnesses; we shall take you and your wives and your children and make slaves of them, and sell and dispose of them as their Highnesses may command; and we shall take away your goods, and do you all the mischief and damage that we can, as to vassals who do not obey and refuse to receive their lord; and we protest that the deaths and losses that shall accrue from this are your own fault." †

Another proof that Hideyoshi's fears were not altogether foolish may be found in the fact that in 1575, twenty years before the ambassadors came to Japan from

---

* Quoted in Encyc. Brit., *sub* India.
† Helps, " Spanish Conquest in America," vol. i., p. 8.

the Philippines, Captain Maldonado had sent from the same islands a report in which he asked that five hundred soldiers be sent from Spain in order that he might attempt the conquest of Loochoo and Japan.

The remembrance that Philip II. of Spain died only three days before Hideyoshi, may suggest a comparison between the two men and lead us to ask what would have happened if conditions had been reversed so that Japanese teachers of Buddhism had attempted to carry their religion to Spain and had pursued the methods that were used by the Jesuit and Franciscan missionaries. One man's errors do not excuse those of another; but a comparison of Hideyoshi and Philip may at least help to soften our condemnation of the former, who, whatever his faults, does not deserve to have his name placed high in the list of those who in the sixteenth century were noted for religious intolerance.

VI

INCREASED PERSECUTION UNDER IEYASU

1598-1616

HIDEYOSHI, shortly before his death, had appointed a board of five Regents, with Tokugawa Ieyasu at their head. Under their direction was another board of five Ministers. To these last was committed the care of Hideyoshi's son, Hideyori, who was then six years old. Ieyasu, who was born in 1542, had served under both Nobunaga and Hideyoshi. His original territories had been in the provinces of Mikawa and Totomi; but in the re-distribution of fiefs made by Hideyoshi he had been transferred to the provinces lying about the Bay of Yedo. He made Yedo his capital, building there a castle that became the centre of the great city that quickly grew up around it.

One of the first acts of the new government was to recall the army from Korea. This brought back to Japan some of the men who were recognised leaders among the Christians. The missionaries saw many reasons for believing that a new era of prosperity was about to dawn. Ieyasu's desire for foreign trade made him ready to favour Christianity, or at least to shut his eyes to the fact that the edict of Hideyoshi, though unrepealed, was not being enforced. The daimyos were allowed to treat the Christians in their own territories as they thought best.

Jerome de Jésus, the Franciscan that had escaped from prison, was arrested in December, 1598, and brought before Ieyasu, who, after hearing his story, said to him: "Do not fear. Henceforth make no attempt to conceal yourself, and do not lay aside your ecclesiastical dress, for I wish you well. Every year the Spaniards in their voyages to Mexico pass very near my estates in Eastern Japan. I wish they would visit my ports to obtain supplies, trade with my people, and teach them how to develop the silver mines. In order that ere I die I may carry out my wishes in this matter, I desire that you will show me how it can be done." Jerome suggested that he ask the Governor of the Philippines to send pilots, who by making soundings and surveying the coasts could render navigation safer. Ieyasu accordingly sent a messenger to make his desires known to the Governor; but since just at this time a number of ships and men had been sent from Manila to aid the King of Cambodia in his war with Siam, the Governor could do nothing except offer encouragement that on their return he might be able to accede to Ieyasu's requests.

Jerome for a while was given lodgings in Ieyasu's own mansion in Kyoto. He was then allowed to go to Yedo, where he built a church in which he celebrated the first mass on the Day of Pentecost in 1599. Afterwards he was sent by Ieyasu to Manila that he might help in securing success for a second envoy to the Governor.

The missionaries soon came out from their hiding-places. The churches that had been destroyed in Arima and Omura were rebuilt. Organtin re-established the houses of the Jesuits in Kyoto and Osaka. New residences were built in Yamaguchi and Hiroshima. Bishop Çerqueira says that in two years the number of baptisms amounted to seventy thousand.

There were, however, some drawbacks. Terasawa was now opposed to the faith into which he had been secretly baptised, and on returning from Korea he annoyed the missionaries to such an extent that in March, 1599, Bishop Çerqueira removed, with several members of the Society and thirty seminary students, to Amakusa. While Terasawa was on a visit to Kyoto he sent an order to his deputy that Japanese Christians should not be allowed to attend services in the church. Father Rodriguez was at once sent to Kyoto, where he succeeded in inducing Terasawa to revoke this order, and also received assurance from Ieyasu that the Christians would not be disturbed.

More serious trouble arose in Hirado. The Daimyo had recently died. The one who succeeded him was in Kyoto and sent back word to his son that all the people must be forced to take part in the Buddhist rites performed in honour of his predecessor. The son was also ordered to repudiate his wife, a daughter of Sumitada, unless she was willing to give up the Christian religion. She stood firm and sent for her brother, the Daimyo of Omura, to take her home; but her husband, unwilling to give her up, promised to leave her undisturbed in her faith. Several of the leading retainers, with their families and many other Christians, fled by night to Nagasaki, where they were sheltered by the missionaries. The Daimyo was so alarmed by this action, which was being imitated by others, that he sent orders to have none of the Christians molested.

In the year 1600 fourteen new Jesuit missionaries came to Japan. This brought the whole number of those connected with the Society, the Japanese included, to one hundred and nine. They were divided among six central and twenty-four subordinate residences. Many of the churches that had been torn down were now rebuilt, and new ones were erected. Several charitable institutions were also established. Konishi, since his return from Korea, had been very active in religious and philanthropic endeavours. It is said that in the year 1600 there were thirteen thousand baptisms in his daimiate. His nephew showed his zeal by declaring that all the Buddhist priests in the district under his care must become Christians or leave the country. Six of them chose the former of these alternatives. Konishi himself established a leper hospital in Osaka and appropriated annual rents worth one hundred *koku* of rice for the support of foundlings. He also bought a piece of land in Sakai to be used for a church, a missionary residence, and a cemetery.

The hopes of what might in the future be done by this powerful patron of the Church were doomed to disappointment. It was soon evident that Ieyasu was trying to gain the supreme political authority for himself, and a movement against him had for its leader Ishida, who had shown much favour to the Christians. He induced

Konishi to join him. * The battle of Sekigahara, October 21, 1600, resulted in the utter defeat of the confederates and made Ieyasu the real ruler of Japan. Although he treated most of his enemies with clemency, Ishida and Konishi were condemned to death. They were beheaded at Kyoto in the dry bed of the Kamo River, and their heads were exposed on the principal bridge of the city. The Christians bore Konishi's body to the residence of the Jesuits for the performance of funeral rites. In his robe was found a letter addressed to his wife and children, in which he expressed his trust in God and exhorted them to remain firm in the faith. Four other Christian lords were deprived of their fiefs.

Fear of being involved in Konishi's ruin led So, the Daimyo of Tsushima, to repudiate his wife, who was Konishi's daughter. This meant also his rejection of Christianity. The divorced wife hastened to seek advice from Bishop Çerqueira, who procured shelter for her in the nunnery at Nagasaki, where with sad heart, separated from her children, she spent the remaining years of her life.

It will be remembered that, while Konishi's possessions had been in the southern part of Higo, the northern half of the province was held by his rival, Kato Kiyomasa, a strong Buddhist. When the civil war broke out, Kato, as a supporter of Ieyasu, laid siege to Konishi's castle in Udo. Among those shut up in this stronghold were two Jesuit Fathers, three Brothers, and some Catechists. According to Japanese accounts, after Kato learned the result of the battle of Sekigahara, he had letters attached to arrows and shot into the castle, giving information of what had happened and calling on the defenders to surrender; but the missionaries induced the soldiers to burn these letters without reading them. The Jesuit accounts say that Kato wrote letters to the two priests, urging them

* Kuroda was a zealous supporter of Ieyasu. Charlevoix asserts that the same was true of the daimyos of Arima and Omura; but in fact they seemed inclined to hold a neutral position until after Ieyasu's victory was assured. Oda Hidenobu (grandson of Nobunaga), the Christian Lord of Gifu, was among Ieyasu's foes.

to prevent useless slaughter by persuading the leaders to submit. He also wrote to the Vice-Provincial in Nagasaki, asking him to use his influence to the same end. The Jesuits replied that, as religious teachers and foreigners, they had no right to interfere in matters of this kind. It was soon evident to the besieged that further resistance was useless, and on Kato's promising to spare the lives of all except Konishi's brother, the castle was surrendered. The missionaries were sent to Nagasaki after they had been held for some time as prisoners.

Otomo Yoshimune, who had taken advantage of the civil strife to make an effort for the recovery of his former estates, was also condemned to death, but through the intercession of Kuroda his sentence was commuted into one of exile. Afterwards he was allowed to go to Kyoto, where he lived in destitution except as Father Organtin procured help for him. He professed repentance for his backslidings, and in 1605 he died.

Early in the contests, those that acted in the name of Hideyoshi's son Hideyori seized as hostages the wives and children of many of Ieyasu's supporters. The soldiers came to the Osaka residence of Hosokawa, the romantic baptism of whose wife Grace has already been narrated. The steward of the mansion hastened to her, saying that Hosokawa, apprehensive of what might happen, had left orders that he should put her to death rather than allow her to fall into the hands of the enemy. She at once placed her two daughters in the care of a trustworthy woman that they might be taken to the residence of the Jesuits, and then she knelt before the steward. After he had performed his sad service, he set fire to the house and joined with the other servants in committing *harakiri*. Grace is said to have been a very talented as well as a devout woman. In order to write letters to the missionaries she had learned to read and write Portuguese, having no foreign instruction but depending on an alphabet and a few manuscripts received from her brother. She was greatly beloved by her husband. Though he was not a Christian, he caused Father Organtin the next year to conduct solemn funeral rites in her behalf, and at the close of the ceremonies gave a large sum of gold to be used for the poor.

Reference has been made to the Brief of Gregory XIII. that had confined to Jesuits the privilege of preaching the Gospel in Japan. December 12, 1600, Pope Clement VIII., yielding to the request of Philip III., published a Bull that allowed other orders to engage in this work upon the condition that they went under the Portuguese flag and by way of Goa. This was not wholly satisfactory to those that desired a removal of the old restrictions, and we shall find that they paid little heed to the conditions, thus giving occasion for bitter dissensions that did much to hinder the progress of Christianity.

The same year saw the first coming of men from other nations, who were in time to be powerful rivals of the Spanish and Portuguese. It was in April, 1600, that the first Dutch ship came to Japan. Moreover it brought as its pilot an Englishman, Will Adams, who holds an important place in the history of Japan's relations with Western lands. A consideration of the state of affairs in Europe at that time will suffice to show that there was likely to be little love lost between the newcomers and their predecessors; while the Jesuits could not but be apprehensive that the advent of Protestants might be even more dangerous than that of rival orders.

Of a fleet of five ships that had sailed together from Holland, all but one had fallen out by the way, and this one met with severe storms and various disasters, until at last it anchored off the coast of Bungo. Of the twenty-four men on board, only seven were able to stand, and six died within a few days. In the main they were kindly treated by the people of Bungo, notwithstanding that the Portuguese tried to excite suspicion against them. In a letter from Adams to his wife he says:

"After wee had beene there fiue or sixe dayes, came a Portugall Jesuite, with other Portugals, who reported of vs that we were pirats, and were not in the way of marchandizing. Which report caused the gouernours and commonpeeple to thinke euill of vs: in such manner that we looked alwayes when we should be set vpon crosses: which is the execution in this land for theeury and some other crimes. Thus daily more and more the Portugalls increased the justices and people against vs."

After a while Adams with one of his shipmates was taken to Osaka, where they were brought before Ieyasu.

" He viewed me well, and seemed to be wonderfull fauorable. He made many signes vnto me, some of which I vnderstood, and some I did not. In the end, there came one that could speake Portuges. By him, the king demanded of me of what land I was, and what mooued vs to come to his land, beeing so farre off. I shewed vnto him the name of our countrey, and that our land had long sought out the East Indies and desired friendship with all kings and potentates in way of marchandize, hauing in our land diuerse commodities, which these lands had not; and also to buy such merchandizes in this land, which our country had not. Then he asked whethre our countrey had warres? I answered him yea, with the Spaniards and Portugals, beeing in peace with all other nations. Further, he asked me, in what I did beleeue? I said, in God, that made heauen and earth. He asked me diuerse other questions of things of religions, and many other things."

In another letter Adams wrote:

" The Iesuites and the Portingalls gaue many euidences against me and the rest to the Emperour [Ieyasu], that wee were theeues and robbers of all nations, and were we suffered to liue, it should be ageinst the profit of his Highnes, and the land; for no nation should come there without robbing; his Highness iustice being executed, the rest of our nation without doubt should feare and not come here any more: thus dayly making axcess to the Emperour, and procuring friendes to hasten my death. But God that is always merciful at need, shewed mercy unto vs, and would not suffer them to haue their willes of vs. In the end, the Emperour gave them aunswer that we as yet had not doen to him nor to none o fhis lande any harme or damage: therefore against Reason and Iustice to put vs to death. If our countrey had warres the one with the other, that was no cause that he should put vs to death: with which they were out of hart, that their cruell pretence failed them."

Adams spent the remainder of his life in Japan, where he was " in such favour with two emperors as never was any Christian in those parts of the world." Ieyasu relied not a little on his advice concerning matters connected with foreign trade. He taught the Japanese how to construct ships in the European style, and was also a source of information concerning various sciences. He helped to open the way for Dutch and English commerce. Pagés says that in 1605, when one of the Jesuits visited Yedo, where " still dwelt the Englishman Adams and many Hollanders who were his companions," the missionary, in behalf of the Bishop, offered them a safe-conduct for going to Nagasaki, and from there wherever they wished.* "In fact, it was feared that these heretics might scatter the seeds of evil among the people. The offer was declined by Adams, who alleged as a reason that the Shogun would never consent to his departure. The Father did all he could for the conversion of these unfortunate men, but he found them rebellious and confirmed in their error."

Adams probably did not hesitate to say things derogatory to the missionaries. He is said to have told Ieyasu that the Roman Catholic priests had been driven out of Protestant countries. This led Ieyasu to exclaim: " Why should I tolerate those that are not endured by European rulers? " Richard Cocks, who became the manager of the English factory in Hirado, wrote in 1614 about a friar who had a long argument with Adams, and for the purpose of convincing him offered to perform a miracle by walking on the sea. The affair was well advertised, so that thousands of people came to behold the event. The friar stepped out boldly into the water and would have drowned, had not one of the Hollanders saved him. He afterwards reproved Adams for lack of faith, saying: " Had you only believed, I should have been able to do it." He was afterwards obliged " for very shame " to leave the country and went to Manila, where the Bishop imprisoned him for his rash attempt that had brought dishonour upon the Church. Charlevoix, who also relates the incident, is inclined, as a Jesuit, to make merry over the discomfiture of this fanatic, who belonged to another order.

* " Offrit de la part de l'évêque, à lui et aux siens, un sauf-conduit pour aller à Nagasaki, et de la, où ils voudraient." " Hist. de la Rel. Chrét. au Japon," vol. i., p. 114. One wonders how the Bishop had authority to make such an offer.

In 1601, Father Rodriguez, who had been sent by his superior to solicit Ieyasu's protection for the Christians, induced him to send an order to Terasawa, the apostate Governor of Nagasaki, that he should not annoy the missionaries or their followers. Two official patents, issued at the same time, authorised the Fathers to reside in Kyoto, Osaka, and Nagasaki. Before this, Terasawa had brought accusations against the Daimyos of Omura and Arima, because they openly professed Christianity and were erecting many churches, and Ieyasu had commissioned him to destroy the buildings and send the missionaries to Nagasaki. As the accused daimyos were at Ieyasu's court, they quickly learned of what had been done, and sent word to the Father Visitor advising him to tear down the churches himself, so as to prevent their profanation. Hardly had he begun to do this, when a messenger came with the welcome intelligence that the daimyos had been able to get Ieyasu's consent to their remaining Christians, and so there was no longer any reason for demolishing the churches. In fact, Terasawa had at this time fallen somewhat into disfavour. According to Pagés, one of the Governor's servants had purchased goods for Ieyasu without at all consulting Father Rodriguez, as it had been the custom to do. Since the goods did not prove satisfactory, the servant tried to throw the blame upon Rodriguez and the Portuguese merchants. An investigation that followed led Ieyasu to issue a patent providing that thereafter all purchases should be made through the missionaries and without Terasawa's assistance. Warned by this event that it was unwise for him to be on bad terms with the missionaries, Terasawa sought to win their friendship and promised that in Amakusa, which now belonged to him, he would receive them and favour their work. The next year, when he built a new castle in Amakusa, he gave land in its vicinity for a church and also paid for its erection.

Soon after Kato Kiyomasa came into possession of the territory formerly belonging to Konishi, he commenced to persecute the Christians. Having banished the missionaries, he ordered the leading retainers to sign a document in which Christianity was renounced. Many were weak enough to yield, while some allowed others to sign in their behalf. The goods of those that remained faithful were confiscated, and they were forbidden to leave the daimiate as some others had done immediately after their former master's fall. Driven from their houses, they built huts for themselves in the fields and forests. Other people were forbidden to rent houses to them or sell them food. The Bishop and other Jesuits sent letters to comfort the afflicted Christians, and one missionary managed to reach them in disguise.

The persecution was kept up until the middle of 1602, when Kato, apparently moved by fear that his acts would be censured by Ieyasu, permitted those who desired to do so to depart from his domains. The most of them went to Nagasaki, where the Jesuits gave them shelter and provided for their necessities. We shall soon see that no long time elapsed ere still more bitter persecution arose in Higo.

Father Moralez, the prior of a Dominican convent in Manila, had asked some Christians who formed part of the crew of a Japanese vessel visiting that port, if there would be an opening for his order in their country. As their reply was favourable, he wrote a letter to the Daimyo of Satsuma offering to send missionaries. In due time a ship came from Satsuma bearing a letter that invited the missionaries to come and promised them a favourable reception. The merchants of Manila were desirous of having closer commercial relations with Japan. One of the early acts of a new Governor of the Philippines had been to give what was in the main a favourable response to a second envoy who had been sent by Ieyasu, though to his request for shipwrights the reply was made that the consent of the King of Spain must be obtained before any could be sent. The ecclesiastical and secular councils having been summoned to consider what ought to be done regarding the letter that had now come from Satsuma, they were agreed that " for the sake of the propagation of the Christian faith and for the service of the King of Spain " missionaries of dif-

ferent orders ought to go to Japan. The particular field
that each society should occupy was also decided.

In accordance with these plans, several missionaries set
out in 1602. The Dominicans sent Father Moralez as
Vicar Provincial, with four others of his order, to
Satsuma. Apparently they went on the Japanese ship
last mentioned; and in accordance with the orders given
to the captain by the Daimyo, they were landed on an
island named Koshiki, where a Buddhist temple, from
which the priests had been removed, was assigned for
their temporary abode. In a few days they were summoned to the Daimyo's capital. The favour with which
they were received awakened the opposition of the Buddhist priests, who demanded the expulsion of the foreigners. While the Daimyo did not yield to this demand,
he became less cordial, disregarded his promise to give
land to the missionaries, and failed to provide them with
a due supply of the necessities of life. After waiting
three months and seeing no improvement in his attitude
towards them, they went back to the island of Koshiki.

The Franciscans, who were nine in number, went at
once to pay their respects to Ieyasu, taking with them a
letter and presents from the Governor of the Philippines.
Ieyasu at first showed that the substitution of so many
religious teachers for the ship carpenters that he had
requested was far from pleasing to him. He soon, however, resumed his good humour, and on the whole they
had little reason to complain of the treatment they received. Four of them went to Yedo, where, by his permission, they built near the church that was already there
a monastery and a hospital. The others remained in
Kyoto, where they also built a monastery.

Two Augustinians landed at Hirado and soon after
went to Bungo, where, in accordance with permission received from Ieyasu, they built a church and a residence.

Thus, notwithstanding the monopoly once granted to
the Jesuits, three other great orders had come to share
their labours, their triumphs, and their sorrows. Little
attention was paid to the conditions under which the
Pope had finally assented to their coming; for, as has
been seen, they sailed directly from the Spanish colony

without taking the trouble of going first to Goa. Petitions had been sent to Rome asking that the restrictions
be removed, and it was claimed that the Pope had given so
much encouragement to believe this would be done that
the missionaries were justified in utilising the present opportunities. The Jesuits were very much incensed at this
disregard of the papal mandates.* During the following
years a bitter conflict raged between them and the other
orders, especially the Franciscans. Each side tried
in various ways to get the advantage over the other, and
the letters written to Europe abounded with charges and
counter-charges. These contentions had not a little to
do with the increasing distrust excited among the Japanese against the missionaries. The division extended to
the native Christians and did not cease with the expulsion
of the foreigners. Two and a half centuries later, when
descendants of these Christians were discovered in
Kyushu, it was found that they were still divided into
groups having to some extent different religious vocabu-
laries, paying homage to different saints, and suspicious
of each other.

A report written in January, 1603, by Bishop Çerqueira
shows something of the methods of the Jesuits and the
condition of the work at that time. It says:

" In every daimiate where a body of Christians is found, there
is a principal house or college with its rector. There are also
other residences distributed among the villages. The Fathers
in these residences are not only visited annually by the rectors,
but they usually assemble a few days every two months in the
principal house, where they confer concerning their spiritual
progress and the care of souls. Each residence has usually a
church of a size proportionate to the population. In these

* In the Appendix to Pagés's " Religion Chrétienne au Japon,"
pp. 14-28, is given a letter written in 1602 by the Bishop of Japan
to the Vice-Provincial of the Jesuits in Manila. It criticises the
action of the other orders in coming to Japan and declares that
the invitations they had received from different places had been
dictated only by the desire to utilise them as a means for attracting
foreign commerce. The Bishop asks that the letter be shown to
the Governor, who is urged to forbid the coming of other missionaries from the Philippines and to recall those already in
Japan.

churches reside certain tonsured men called *Kambos,* who are held in great esteem among the Christians. They are charged with preserving good order and propriety, with giving doctrinal instruction to children, and with reading spiritual books to the people on Sundays and feastdays if there is no Father, Brother, or *Dogique* to preach. It is also the duty of the *Kambos* to visit the sick, to summon the Fathers for the confessions of such persons, to inform the Fathers about all disorders and about the temporal or spiritual needs of the Christians, and especially to baptise children in danger of death, when there is not time to call a Father. They help in burials and in other necessary offices for the good of souls. The Fathers likewise support in the seminaries, as also in other houses and in the residences, a considerable number of *Dogiques* (as the native pupils are called). These are much esteemed in Japan and are held in high honour because they have renounced the world in order to serve our Lord in the Church. These *Dogiques* are clad in long robes and live as *religieux.* In general, they all learn the method of catechising and are trained to preach, so that they may go into the villages when the Fathers and Brothers are absent. They chant the office in chorus and form a choir to aid in the celebration of mass, having learned for that purpose the full chant, the musical chant, and how to play the organ. There is already a large number of organs that have been made by the *Dogiques* themselves, as also harpsichords, viols, and other instruments. These on occasion help to give solemnity to worship. The presence of these *Dogiques* and *Kambos* supplies to a noteworthy extent the insufficiency of workers felt by the Fathers, and the Christian community finds itself greatly helped by them. I have elsewhere stated that, as shown by the appended reports, the number of Fathers and Brothers of the Society is one hundred and twenty-six; that of the *Dogiques* exceeds two hundred and eighty-four; and that of the *Kambos,* one hundred and seventy. Thus all the workers supported by the Society and helping in the conversion of this people amount to more than five hundred and seventy persons, not to mention the servants and the labourers for carrying baggage and performing other services, who live in the houses and residences. Such persons are numerous, for the Japanese by the customs of the country have their employment defined ; each must perform work in accordance with his condition, and the labour of servants cannot be taken by the *Dogiques.* Hence, in fact, the Society usually supports more than nine hundred persons.

" I have stated that the Fathers in the residences are constantly making circuits among the villages in order to instruct the Christians and to administer the sacraments. In the midst of a thousand difficulties and trials they busy themselves night and day with the confessions of the sick, travelling through rain and snow as well as through excessive heat, and going with great zeal to places two or three leagues from their residences. I have found that among the *Dogiques* a large number learn Latin so that they may be more helpful in these ministrations and also in order that they may become Brothers or Seminarists. Great numbers of them have been received into the Society under these last titles. I myself have brought together many of these *Dogiques*. I keep them in my house, where they study theological themes in order to become clerics. Others learn painting and the art of engraving on wood so as to make pictures or blocks for printing in European as well as in Japanese characters, which is a great help for this church. I have found the churches very well provided with paintings in oil or distemper, which the *Dogiques* know how to execute marvellously well, many of them being excellent artists. The Fathers distribute a great number of pictures in water colours and of engravings. This helps arouse the devotion of the Christians. As reported by the Rector of Nagasaki, Latin and Japanese books have been published, a great number of European books and various spiritual treatises having been translated and printed in Japanese characters. I have personally seen and examined some of these books, and have given permission for printing them. Afterwards they are distributed by the same Fathers, to the very great benefit of the Christians.

" All of these things are not accomplished without costing the Fathers a large sum. I have made proof of this and have actually seen the expenditures that the Fathers make to erect and adorn the great number of churches under their care. In fact, the Japanese are usually poor and are oppressed by their lords, so that, although they contribute by means of their own labour as well as by gifts of timber and other materials used in the construction of churches, the expense in silver and commodities for paying the carpenters or supplying artisans and labourers falls entirely upon the Fathers. Notwithstanding that all the churches, like most other buildings in Japan, are constructed of wood, and that their size is proportioned to the localities where they are situated, the expense amounts to a large sum. In small villages the cost of a church is ten, fifteen, or even thirty cruzades; and in other places fifty, eighty, or one hundred. For the churches of the principal cities one hundred, eight hundred, or one thousand cruzades are spent. In the city of Nagasaki three thousand were spent, although in fact the greater part of this sum has been realised from the alms of the Christians in that city, as is noted in the report of the Rector of Nagasaki. Churches like those of Nagasaki, Arima, and Omura are not and could not be built without the permission of the lord of the country nor without his providing at least a part of the funds. This is stated in the reports of the Rectors of Arima and Omura. Moreover, as all the churches are of wood, it follows that they are easily destroyed and annihilated by fires, persecutions, and wars. . . . . I find, nevertheless, that at the present time, that is, at the beginning of 1603, the Fathers of the Society possess in

Japan two colleges—that of Nagasaki and that of Arima—; a
house of probation in the place called 'All Saints'; two seminaries—a great one in Arima and a smaller one in Nagasaki—;
and independently of these establishments, twenty-one residences
where Fathers are domiciled in different provinces; with more
than one hundred and eighty churches, as reports presented to
me declare. As to the number of Christians; before the war
of 1600 and when the lands of Augustine, Simon Findecan, and
other Christian lords were in their primitive condition, it may
have reached three hundred thousand.* . . . Meanwhile, as
a result of the war and the re-distribution of fiefs, all the Christian communities have suffered great loss. The Christians have
scattered among the different provinces; some have apostatised
because of the pressure of their gentile lords; and others are dispersed among the gentiles without constituting a company or a
religious family."

In 1603 Ieyasu took the decisive step of having himself appointed Shogun. This rank had not been taken by
Nobunaga or Hideyoshi; indeed Ieyasu was the only one
of the trio who was a descendant of the Minamoto
family, to which custom prescribed the limitation of the
honour. By this step he placed himself above Hideyori,
whom he left in possession of the strong castle of Osaka
with a large revenue to be derived from three provinces.

Though Hideyoshi's edicts against Christianity had
never been repealed, the new Shogun showed no inclination to have them enforced. Indeed, he himself gave
financial aid to the missionaries. The only regular
source of support for the Jesuits was in the subsidies sent
by the Pope and the Spanish King. Often these were
deficient or their payment was delayed. That of the
King had fallen into arrears. These subsidies were sent
by way of Macao, where with the Pope's approval the
money was invested in merchandise that formed part of
the cargo brought by the Great Ship that annually sailed
from that port to Japan. Sometimes the failure of the
vessel to complete the voyage caused the missionaries

---

* It will be noticed that this number is much below what is
given in the extravagant statements of many books. Bishop Çerqueira says the reports show that, exclusive of unrepentant
apostates and of scattered believers living in places where they
were without pastoral oversight, the Christians at the time he
wrote numbered about two hundred thousand.

great trouble. It was thus in the year 1603, when it was captured by the Dutch. This misfortune came at a time when the care of the exiles from Higo was increasing the burdens of the missionaries. As a consequence, they were obliged to dismiss some of their pupils and to retrench expenses in other ways. On hearing of their distress, Ieyasu sent them a gift of three hundred and fifty taels and offered to lend them five thousand more until the arrival of the next annual ship.

In August, 1603, Father Bermeo, the newly appointed Commissary of the Franciscans, reached Japan and at once wrote a letter to Bishop Çerqueira enclosing communications from the Archbishop of Manila and from others in the Philippines, including the Vice-Provincial of the Jesuits. In his reply, the Bishop with courteous but plain words rebuked the zeal that led to disregard of the papal prohibitions. He said that his conscience compelled him to refuse the Franciscans permission to exercise their ministry in Japan, for he could not admit them as labourers in that vineyard until they proved that they had proper authorisation for doing what the Popes had forbidden.* In utter disregard for his authority, the Franciscans proceeded to establish new residences in Osaka and Sakai, while at Kyoto a Japanese Christian, in fulfilment of a vow, built for them a monastery and a church.

Meanwhile the Dominicans, on the island of Koshiki, were living in great destitution. On hearing of their devotion and austerities, the Daimyo offered to assign to them the revenues of a small village. They replied that the rules of their order did not permit the acceptance of such a gift. They consented, however, to use for a time a boat with twelve oarsmen that he put at their disposal for conveying them to and from the mainland of Kyushu, whither they frequently went for evangelistic work. He afterwards gave them permission to build a church and a residence in the city of Kyodomari.

Persecution was renewed in Higo. It is asserted that Kato Kiyomasa at first gave orders for the execution of all his officers who were Christians, but was led to desist

* This letter is given by Pagés, vol. ii., p. 33.

by the thought that such an act would excite horror and
might enable the Christians, who were numerous in
Ieyasu's court, to bring about his downfall. As he had
done before with those who had been Konishi's leading
retainers, so now he did with many others, confiscating
their goods and driving them from their homes. In
October, 1603, he visited several cities, coming first to
Yatsushiro, where he gave the officers charge to do all
they could to make the Christians apostatise. In November, all the under-officials were ordered to appear before
a famous bonze who had been invited to the city that he
might superintend a ceremony that implied an acceptance
of Buddhism by all that took part in it. Some who had
been numbered among the Christians shared in the exercises, but fourteen refused. Afterwards these yielded,
with the exception of two, John Minami and Simon
Takeda. The former of these had shown less bravery
two years before when, in order to save his own life and
the lives of his family, he had signed the promise to renounce Christianity, a weakness of which he soon repented. Takeda's name had also been signed to the
paper; but this was done without his consent by a friend
who wished to protect him. At this time, therefore, their
sentences declared that, since they continued to adhere to
Christianity after having abjured it, they with their
families were condemned to die. Orders were given that
the two men should be sent to Kumamoto for execution,
while the members of their families should be put to
death in Yatsushiro. The officer that was charged with
the duty of carrying out these orders was a very intimate
friend of Takeda and, wishing to save him from the disgrace of a public execution, obtained permission that he
also should suffer in Yatsushiro. He did his best to induce Takeda to abjure his faith and even offered to con-
nive at his escape. The execution took place in Takeda's
own house. An account, perhaps somewhat embellished,
is given of the way in which the sentence was carried out.
December 9, 1603, a little after midnight, an executioner
came bringing to Takeda a letter in which his friend
told him that he must be beheaded that night. When
Takeda had finished reading the missive, he thanked the

bearer, and after kneeling a few minutes before a picture of Christ, went to awaken his mother, Joanna, and his wife, Inez. They prepared for him the bath that it was customary for the Japanese to take under such circumstances. After writing a few letters, Simon entered the bath and, on coming out, he clothed himself in his richest garments. He then said farewell to his mother, wife, and servants. From these last he asked pardon for any wrong that he might have done them, gave each of them a present, and exhorted those that were Christians to stand firm in the faith. Three catechists who resided in the city had been called to assist him in his preparations for death. They, the two women, and the Christian servants, joined with him in repeating the General Confession, three Paternosters, and three Aves. To his wife he then said: " The hour for separation has come. I go before you and thus show the road by which you also should reach Paradise. I will pray to God for you. I hope that ere long you will follow in my footsteps." He repeated such words several times, although he was not aware that the wife had also been condemned to death.

The little company marched in solemn procession to the room chosen for the execution. At the head was one of the catechists bearing a crucifix, while the two others carried lighted candles. The martyr followed, holding the hands of his wife and mother. Then came the executioner with three attendants, and last of all, the household servants.

Arrived at the place where he was to die, Takeda first prostrated himself before an image of Christ and then took the appointed seat on the mats. Opposite him was the catechist with the crucifix, and on each side was one of those that held the candles. The three women sat a little behind him. Once more they repeated the Confession, the Paternosters, and the Aves. As they finished their devotions, a soldier, who had previously denied the faith, came in to pay his respects to the martyr, who obtained from him a promise of repentance. After Takeda had given his reliquary to Joanna and his chaplet to Inez, he loosened his robe and bent forward to receive the fatal blow. As the head fell upon the mats, one of the catechists, following the form that Japanese etiquette prescribes for taking up anything deserving of honour, raised it reverently as though about to put it on his own head. The mother then placed her hand caressingly on the severed head, saying: " Oh, my fortunate son, you have been deemed worthy to give your life for God's service. How blessed am I, sinful woman though I am, that I should be the mother of a martyr and that I can offer as a sacrifice this my only son, for whom during these many years I have so lovingly cared." The wife also venerated the relic as though it were a sacred object, showing herself no less heroic than her mother-in-law.

In accordance with Kato's orders, the head was sent to Kumamoto that it might be exposed in a public place beside that of John Minami. The body was buried in Yatsushiro, but soon after was transferred to Nagasaki, that it might be placed in the church of the Jesuits.

Later in the day of Takeda's martyrdom, the two women, together with the wife and adopted son of Minami, were taken to the execution ground and there crucified. The corpses were left hanging on the crosses for a whole year in order that they might serve as a warning to the Christians. For some time, however, the believers were left unmolested, except that the three catechists were thrown into prison. The executioner who had beheaded Simon and superintended the crucifixion of the women, had been so much moved by their conduct that he soon after went to Nagasaki to ask that the missionaries would teach him the religion that enabled its followers to meet death with such joy and courage. On the day of his baptism he presented to the Bishop the sword with which Takeda had been beheaded. On his return to Yatsushiro, attempts were made to bring him back to his former religion. The next year he was banished and went to Nagasaki, whence a little later he removed to Siam.

An investigation of the complaints brought by the merchants of Kyoto against the quality of goods received from the Portuguese led in 1604 to the disgrace of Terasawa, the Governor of Nagasaki. He was replaced

by a commission of five persons who were all Christians.
Terasawa now changed the policy that he had recently
adopted in Amakusa. He destroyed all but two of the
churches, exiled some of his Christian retainers, confiscated their goods, and in other ways showed his
hatred of their religion, until at last the fear that volun-
tary exile would seriously weaken his forces led him to
desist.

In the suburbs of Nagasaki there had sprung up a new
and flourishing settlement. In 1604 Ieyasu annexed it
to the Imperial city, thus seriously lessening the revenues
of Omura, to which it had previously belonged. The
Daimyo considered that in some way the Jesuits were
responsible for the change, and he took his revenge by
apostatising.

In 1605 Ieyasu, then sixty-three years old, caused his
son, Hidetada, twenty-six years of age, to be appointed
Shogun in his place. His purpose was evidently to secure the office in the Tokugawa family. Ieyasu kept the
real power in his own hands until his death eleven years
later (1616). He caused a new castle to be built at
Shizuoka, which he made his chief residence, though he
often went to Kyoto, Osaka, and Yedo. This last city
was the residence of the Shogun, and there too the daimyos built mansions in which they spent part of each
year, while during their visits to their own domains their
wives and children remained in Yedo as hostages. It will
be seen that this was a great step towards establishing
the centralised system that for the next two and a half
centuries gave such power to the Tokugawa Shoguns.

For some time neither the nominal Shogun nor the
actual possessor of power showed any inclination to annoy the Christians. The missionaries that from time to
time obtained audiences with them were graciously received. The erection of churches and hospitals was permitted. Some of Ieyasu's own retainers publicly professed their belief in Christianity. In 1606, it is true, at
the request of Yodogimi, Hideyori's mother, who was
disturbed by the baptism of some of her relatives, the
following edict was published:

"His Highness, having learned that several persons have embraced the doctrines and the religion of the Fathers, is exceedingly displeased at this infraction of the edicts. His Highness makes it known that he enjoins his servants, the nobles, and the ladies of the Household to observe the preceding law, and declares that in future the said servants and vassals must take great pains not to embrace the religion of the Fathers. Those that have accepted it must adopt another religion in its place."

It was evident, however, that there was no serious intention to enforce this order, which was issued merely to satisfy Yodogimi.

When, in 1606, Bishop Çerqueira went in ecclesiastical dress to pay his respects to Ieyasu, the latter also put on his ceremonial robes to show due honour to his guest, who was permitted to have his litter carried to the interior of the palace, a privilege usually reserved for lords of the highest rank. The next year Father Paez, the Vice-Provincial of the Jesuits, went with five others to Shizuoka. They were well received by Ieyasu and invited by him to visit the newly discovered silver mines in Izu. Hidetada also welcomed them in Yedo. On his journey back to Nagasaki, Paez waited upon Hideyori, thus giving great pleasure to Yodogimi, who from this time became less opposed to Christianity. In after years the missionaries frequently received subsidies from her.

The missionaries were gradually extending their operations into remote provinces and the number of believers was increasing in all parts of the country, except where persecutions carried on by a few daimyos were causing defection and exile, or where the apostasy of feudal lords that had once been numbered among the Christians influenced their followers to return to the old religions.

The scientific and mechanical knowledge possessed by the missionaries helped them to gain the esteem of the upper classes. Hidetada asked that one of the Jesuits who understood clock-making might reside in Yedo. Feudal lords and other visitors to Kyoto were eager to see the astronomical instruments that showed the movements of the earth and planets. The missionaries improved the opportunities that were thus afforded for throwing ridicule upon the fanciful cosmogony taught by the Buddhists. The visitors, on seeing so much knowledge concerning mathematical and astronomical subjects, were more inclined to give respectful attention to what was said concerning religion. Even the Mikado asked the missionaries to come to his Palace and exhibit their wonderful instruments.

Ieyasu was more interested in commerce than in science. The favour he showed the missionaries was due to the belief that through them he could retain and increase foreign trade. Yet, as we have seen, he did not wish that this commerce should be monopolised by the Portuguese. He had tried to foster that with the Philippines. It was not merely for the sake of trade, however, that Ieyasu sought to have relations with the Spaniards. As has already been stated, he had asked for shipwrights and for experts who could help him to develop the mines that he had recently opened. The eagerness once shown by the Spaniards to share the profitable trade of the Portuguese had so far abated that they did not avail themselves of these opportunities. One reason may have been that their attention was being more drawn at that time towards the Spice Islands. Moreover, their experiences with the Japanese did not incline them to be very favourable to the nation. The *San Felipe,* driven on the coast of Tosa in 1596, had been confiscated, as has already been related. In 1602 another storm-tossed ship, seeking refuge in a harbour of the same province, was surrounded by guard-boats and escaped only by opening fire upon them. Though Ieyasu issued orders that such ships should thereafter be free from molestation, the merchants could not quickly forget these experiences. Many Japanese had gone to the Philippines, where they gained the reputation of being turbulent disturbers of the peace. In a despatch sent to the Spanish Governor in 1605, Ieyasu asked that these people should not be allowed to return to Japan. They were said to number fifteen thousand, and that same year they had been engaged in a quarrel with the Spaniards, which was kept from becoming serious by the intervention of a priest. In 1608 the Japanese residing in Manila engaged in a riot that had to be put down by force of arms.

The Spaniards feared that the Japanese, if taught how to build European ships, would use these in piratical or military movements against the Philippines.

Two ships sent out by the Dutch East India Company reached Japan in July, 1609, and the kindness that the Daimyo of Hirado had shown to the Hollanders, who had been Will Adams's companions, was now requited by having that city chosen as the place for a new factory that was established by their countrymen.

Not quite two months after the arrival of the Dutch, two Spanish vessels on their way from Manila to Mexico were wrecked, one on the coast of Bungo, the other on the coast of Awa, about forty miles from Yedo. Among the passengers saved from the latter was Don Rodrigo Vivero, who had just finished a short term of service as acting Governor of the Philippines. Being taken to Yedo and afterwards to Shizuoka, he was treated with great honour by both Hidetada and Ieyasu. He took the opportunity to present three requests:

1. That Christian priests of different orders who came to Japan should be protected and have the free use of their houses and churches.

2. That an alliance between the Shogun and the King of Spain be confirmed.

3. That, as an attestation to this alliance, the Hollanders should be expelled, since they were the sworn enemies of the Spaniards, and the worst kind of pirates.

Ieyasu assented to the first two propositions; but, while thanking Vivero for making him acquainted with the true character of the Hollanders, he declared that he could not now withdraw the permission he had given for their residence in Japan. He offered to let Vivero have for his conveyance to Mexico one of the vessels that Adams had built in European style, and asked him to get the King of Spain to send out fifty experienced mining engineers who could teach the Japanese the best methods of working mines and extracting precious metals from the ore.

Vivero said that, before deciding what to do, he wished to visit Bungo and see if the vessel that had been driven ashore there could not be made seaworthy. Apparently he found it injured beyond repair, for he soon returned to take the ship built by Adams. He now proposed to Ieyasu that, if miners were sent from Spain, one-half of the metals extracted should belong to them, one-fourth to Ieyasu, and one-fourth to the King of Spain. The King should be allowed to have his agents in Japan to look after his interests in the mine, and these might bring with them members of different religious orders, who should be permitted to have churches and to conduct public services. Furthermore, Spanish ships coming to Japan should be protected from harm. If the King wished to construct war vessels or merchant ships in any of the ports of Japan, or if munitions of war or provisions were wanted for the Spanish fortresses in the East, the King's agents should be permitted to superintend operations and to make purchases at current prices. If an ambassador should be sent to Japan, he should be received with all the honours due to one who represented so great a monarch. A treaty incorporating these points was concluded July 4, 1610. Ieyasu, however, refused to grant the repeated request for the expulsion of the Hollanders.

To show his sincerity, Ieyasu decided that he would send an ambassador bearing rich presents to King Philip and to the Viceroy of New Spain. In response to his request that Vivero would choose one of the missionaries to be the ambassador, Father Munoz was selected. The despatches and presents were put in the care of Vivero himself, to whom were also given four thousand ducats for fitting up the vessel in which he and Munoz set sail, August 1, 1610.

Meanwhile the relations with the Portuguese were becoming more strained. A Japanese vessel on its return voyage from Cambodia wintered in Macao. A quarrel that arose between its crew and the Portuguese developed into a fight in which many were wounded and some killed. Pessoa, the Portuguese Governor, quelled the disturbance and made the Japanese sign a document in which they acknowledged that the blame lay entirely with them. On returning to their own land, they made loud complaints that they had been treated with great injustice. The next January (1610) Pessoa came to Nagasaki in command of the annual ship, *La Madre de Dios*. Ieyasu sent orders to the Daimyo of Arima that he should seize the vessel and take Pessoa, alive or dead. The ship was therefore surrounded by a flotilla of boats carrying more than twelve hundred men. For three days a fierce fight was carried on. Finally Pessoa set fire to the magazine. The vessel, with a cargo valued at a million ducats, sank beneath the waves, and the few Portuguese who were not destroyed with the ship were massacred. As this disaster brought to the Jesuits the loss of their subsidy for two years, they were in such great financial straits that they were obliged to close their seminary and also to send home the pupils that were being educated in the residences of the missionaries.

The Portuguese in Macao were in consternation when news of this event reached them. They finally decided to send an embassy to Ieyasu carrying rich presents, offering excuses for what had been done at Macao, requesting that trade might be continued, and asking that compensation should be given for the loss of their ship and cargo. Ieyasu was not inclined to do much more than accept the gifts. He gave no definite answer to the requests. He felt more independent of the Portuguese merchants because of other channels of trade that were being opened. The Dutch had promised to send ships every year, and though a defeat of the fleet of which they formed a part prevented the coming of those that were due in 1610, one reached Hirado in July, 1611, about a month before the embassy from Macao met Ieyasu. Another embassy came from Manila, and moreover a vessel had just arrived from New Spain bringing the Viceroy's ambassador, Nuño de Sotomayor, to return thanks for the favours shown to Vivero and to present a new set of proposals as follows:

1. That Spaniards be allowed to build in Japan such ships and as many as they might desire.
2. That their pilots should be permitted to survey the coasts and harbours of Japan.

3. That the Shogun should prohibit the trade of the Hollanders, in which case the King of Spain would send men-of-war to Japan to burn their ships.

4. That when Spanish vessels came to Japan they should not be subjected to search and should be free to sell their goods to whomsoever they pleased.

Spanish pride came in collision with that of the Japanese and made the conduct of this last ambassador displeasing to Ieyasu. Sotomayor was told that he must kneel on both knees while in the presence of Ieyasu and remain with hands and head to the floor until bidden to rise. To this he objected and was finally allowed to follow the etiquette of Spain. Three friars were with the ambassador during the interview. Whenever they spoke to him, he made a low obeisance in order to show the respect that he had for their holy office. He says that this made a great impression on Ieyasu and his counsellors.

On St. John's day the ambassador with his escort attended mass; his object, as he says, being both to honour the saint and to give the Japanese an example of attendance at church and of respect for the priesthood. On his way to the convent where the service was held he was met by the powerful Daimyo of Oshiu, Date Masamune, whose name will appear later in this history. As soon as Date saw the ambassador he dismounted and sent a messenger to ask that the Spanish soldiers would discharge their firearms, as he wished to see and hear them. When this was done, many of the horses in the Daimyo's train were so frightened that they threw their riders, much to the amusement of the onlookers. Afterwards, at the elevation of the Host, there was another discharge of musketry and the royal standard was lowered at the foot of the altar.*

With the exception of that concerning the Hollanders, the requests presented by Sotomayor were granted. When in accordance with the second of these the Span-

* Nuttal, "Early Historical Relations between Mexico and Japan."

iards came the next year (1612) and began to make soundings along the coast, Ieyasu's suspicions were aroused. Will Adams was his trusted authority in all matters concerning European customs and it is probable that, when his advice was asked, he replied, as is asserted by Roman Catholic historians, that, since in the West it would be considered an act of hostility for one nation to take soundings in the harbours of another, there was good reason to suppose that the Spaniards had designs upon Japan, the missionaries (one of whom, Sotelo, had come with Sotomayor and was now on the ship engaged in the surveys) being emissaries of the King and employed to seduce the people from their rightful allegiance. Since Spaniards and Portuguese were subjects of the same monarch, care should be taken to guard against the machinations of each.

An end was put to the survey and the captain of the ship was told that, though merchants would still be welcomed, no more missionaries were to be brought to Japan. It was at this time that Ieyasu began to take active measures in opposition to Christianity. Before describing these it will be well to retrace our steps in order to consider the conditions of the churches from 1605 to 1612. Pagés gives the number of Christians at the former date as 750,000; but it will be remembered that Bishop Çerqueira in 1603 put the number of Christians under pastoral care at 200,000. The adult baptisms administered by the Jesuits in 1605 numbered 5,430; in 1606, 7,950; in 1607, 7,000; and after that until the general persecution arose, such baptisms averaged about 4,000 a year. There are no reliable statistics for the other orders.

The daimyos were allowed to deal as they pleased with the Christians in their own domains. Kato Kiyomasa in Higo and Mori in the western part of Hondo were the most severe in their measures. No missionaries were permitted to enter their territories openly, and many ways were found for annoying those Christians that would not give up their faith. In a few cases those that stood firm were put to death.

In 1608 the baptism of a prominent man in Satsuma

aroused the active opposition of the Buddhist priests against the Dominicans. The Daimyo, to whom the priests appealed, was already vexed that the presence of the missionaries had not brought any ships from Manila to his ports. He told Father Moralez, the Superior, that Ieyasu was complaining because none of the Dominicans had gone to pay their respects to him, and he urged that some one be sent at once. Accordingly Moralez set out for Kyoto, where he was well received by Ieyasu. In his absence the Daimyo issued orders that the Christians must give up their faith. They were also told that they must not carry any food to the missionaries, and these were prohibited from leaving their residences.   For some time the only means the latter had for communicating with the outside world was by means of a leper, who on account of his disease could go back and forth without exciting suspicion. When Moralez returned the next spring, he and his associates were ordered to leave Satsuma. He at once dismantled the church and, taking with him the inmates of the leper hospital, sought shelter in Nagasaki.

Nagasaki, which Pagés describes as being " all Christian and governed by the Bishop," was still the headquarters of the Jesuits. The merchants that came thither from all parts of the country carried back to their homes Christian books and reports of what they had heard and seen in the churches. The presence of many exiles who had been driven by persecution from their own homes greatly increased the burden of the missionaries, especially when their supplies were cut short by the delay of the annual ship from Macao. The Japanese Christians, however, showed themselves very charitable and ready to do what they could for their brethren in distress. Pagés praises them for being also so " very charitable towards the dead " that they would sometimes tear off their clothes in order to pay for the celebration of masses in behalf of departed friends.

In 1611, when news reached Japan that the Pope had two years previously issued a Bull declaring the beatification of Ignatius Loyola, the Jesuits of Nagasaki arranged for a great festival in honour of the founder of their

Society. The Bishop officiated pontifically at a vesper service. The vocal and instrumental music was such that a hearer " might have thought himself in Europe." There was also a solemn procession through the streets of the city. The Bishop, shaded by a canopy, carried a piece of the true Cross and some relics of Loyola. Then came the priests, the lay brothers, and the pupils of the seminary, all chanting psalms to an instrumental accompaniment. The members of various confraternities carried torches ornamented with flowers. The heathen governor of the city was " so much impressed as to declare that, if he had foreseen there was to be such a beautiful ceremony, he would have had the streets decorated and would have ordered a platform to be erected for himself so that he might at leisure contemplate all the marvellous features of the procession." The next day there was a pontifical mass and two panegyrics, one in Japanese and the other in Portuguese.

The possibility of having such a festival shows how strong a position Christianity held in Nagasaki before the breaking out of the persecutions that were soon to desolate the city and to drive out not only the missionaries but also the Portuguese and Spanish merchants who had built up the trade on which its prosperity depended.

It was afterwards believed that the coming troubles were presaged by divine signs sent to strengthen the Christians for the trials they would soon have to endure. Near the close of the year 1611, a neophyte who was hewing the trunk of a tree found a black cross plainly marked upon the white wood. The arms of the cross and the title were of the proper proportion, while the lower part of the figure was shaped like a sword. Many Christians came to see the wonder. It is asserted that one of them who had long been ill was immediately healed by drinking a cup of water in which a chip of the tree had been placed. Other cures were effected in a similar way. When the matter came to the ear of the Bishop, he had the cross brought to Nagasaki, examined into the alleged facts, and then pronounced the cross to be truly miraculous. A public service was held in

which a discourse was preached telling of the discovery
of this cross and the miracles that had been wrought
by it. A procession was formed, headed by the Vice-
Provincial of the Jesuits carrying the sacred object,
while the Bishop, the missionaries, and the principal men
of the city followed after. The cross was exposed on
the altar for the remainder of the day and afterwards
was carefully preserved. A similar cross was found a
few months later in a tree that grew on land connected
with the residence of the Jesuits. Its miraculous character, as in the case of the other, was attested by the
Bishop. According to Roman Catholic histories, similar
crosses were found at various times in different parts
of Japan; and there are frequent references to other
marvels.

The change in Ieyasu's attitude toward Christianity
began to manifest itself in 1612. Mention has already
been made of the way his suspicions were aroused that
year by the soundings that the Spaniards made along
the coast. His displeasure was also excited against a
Christian named Okamoto Daihachi, the secretary of an
officer who was practically Ieyasu's prime minister and
his chief adviser in matters concerning the distribution of territory among the feudal lords. The Daimyo
of Arima, desiring to have certain lands restored to his
domains, had bribed Okamoto to aid him. The secretary pretended to do this and indulged in considerable
sharp practice that finally became known to Ieyasu. The
Daimyo was exiled and afterwards put to death, while
his lands were allowed to remain in the hands of his
son, who had given information against the father.
Okamoto was sentenced to be burned alive. The fact
that both of the offenders were adherents of Christianity
increased the prejudices of Ieyasu against the religion.
He exiled some of the believers and forbade his retainers to become Christians.

Many of the feudal lords imitated the example thus
set before them. In that one year the Jesuits lost eighty-
six churches and residences. Other orders suffered in a
similar way. The Franciscan church in Yedo, though
it had been erected by the express permission of the

Shogun, was destroyed. Itakura, the Shogun's representative in Kyoto, was friendly to the Christians and gave the missionaries permission to remain and to receive believers in their houses. At his request, the Franciscans demolished a church that had been erected without his authorisation. By means of bribes the Jesuits were able to save several of their buildings.

The young Daimyo of Arima openly abjured his faith and ordered his subjects to do the same. Some yielded; others prepared for exile or death. The Jesuit Fathers were kept busily employed in hearing confessions and strengthening the faith of those that might ere long be called upon to suffer. The next year (1613) persecution in Arima became violent. The churches were demolished, the religious teachers driven out, and many Christians sent into exile. More severe measures followed. A prominent believer, previously banished from two other provinces and now resisting all attempts to make him apostatise, was invited to a feast given by a high official. In the midst of the repast a sword was placed before him. Knowing very well what this signified, he raised it respectfully to his head as is done by Japanese when receiving anything worthy of honour, examined it carefully, praised the workmanship, and handed it over to the officer, who at once cut him down. His brother was slain in a similar manner. Afterwards their mother and the two children of the first victim were beheaded.

The Christians organised Confraternities of Martyrdom to strengthen themselves by prayers, exhortations, and austerities. The children, in imitation of their elders, formed societies of their own, and we are told that they often used their scourges until the blood flowed.

The Daimyo put forth every exertion to obtain the apostasy of eight of his principal officers. He even went so far as to quote Scripture in favour of such yielding to the necessity of the times, saying with tears in his eyes that St. Peter had denied his Lord not only once but three times and yet had obtained pardon, and they ought not to be more obstinate than the great Disciple. Five yielded for a time. The other three were condemned to be burned with their families at the stake. Thereupon, four of those that had fallen repented and asked to be included in the condemnation, since they were Christians at heart. As no one would listen to them, they sent a declaration of their faith to the Buddhist priest that had presided at a ceremony in which they called on the name of Amida Buddha. The execution of the others with their wives and children took place October 7, 1613. Those condemned to die were clad in festal robes sent to them by one of the confraternities. Each of the martyrs held in one hand a lighted candle and in the other a rosary; he was attended by two of his fellow-believers. The victims were bound to stakes and surrounded by fagots. The president of the united confraternities erected in sight of the martyrs a large image representing the Saviour bound to the column where He was scourged. All the Christians joined in chanting the Creeds, the Paternoster, and the Ave Maria. When the cords that bound one of the children burned away, he went to his mother, who said to him: "Look up to heaven." He died while still clinging to her. The charred remains of the bodies of the martyrs were taken to Nagasaki for burial in the Jesuits' cemetery.

In most other parts of the country the persecution lagged during 1613. Ieyasu's hesitancy about cutting off commerce with Macao and the Philippines doubtless restrained him from active measures. He and Hidetada received with the usual marks of favour the envoys sent by the Bishop and the Provincial of the Jesuits.

The Franciscans, though they had been driven out from Kyoto the previous year, were left undisturbed in Fushimi and Osaka. The Jesuits were in those cities and also in Kyoto. It is said that the Mikado's aunt, who was the abbess of two Buddhist nunneries, came with her mother and sister to hear them preach, and all three would have asked for baptism had it not been for the restraints put upon them by their position. In Osaka, Hideyori and his mother were showing much favour to the Jesuits.

In August, persecution began in Yedo. Father Sotelo, after the destruction of the Franciscan church a year before, had built a small house and oratory on land connected with the hospital for lepers. There he held services for the benefit of any believers that ventured to attend. This reached the ears of the Shogun, who at once ordered a vigorous search for Christians to be made in Yedo and its suburbs. Those that were discovered, including many lepers from the hospital, were thrown into prison. Twenty-two of them were soon put to death. Sotelo himself was arrested, but was released on the intercession of Date Masamune, a daimyo who possessed large domains in northeastern Japan and who now took the priest to Sendai, his capital.

At this point it will be well to consider one of the most remarkable episodes connected with the political and religious history of this period. Father Sotelo, a Spaniard of noble birth, had come with other Franciscans to Japan in 1608. Four years later he aided Vivero in conducting negotiations with Ieyasu, and he was at first appointed to go as the latter's envoy to Mexico and Spain. Ill health, however, led to his being replaced by Munoz. Sotelo had become intensely interested in plans for promoting commerce with Spain by way of Mexico. He believed that this could be made a great aid to the evangelisation of the Japanese. In 1611, when Sotomayor came as the envoy of the Viceroy of Mexico,* Sotelo again took a prominent part in the negotiations. He was on board the vessel that made soundings along the coast of Japan, and shortly afterward (October 12, 1612), having been intrusted with a letter from Hidetada to the King of Spain, set sail from Uraga with a number of Japanese. The vessel was wrecked the first morning after leaving port, and it was subsequent to this failure that Sotelo established himself in the leper hospital at Yedo.

He had previously become acquainted with the great Sendai Daimyo. Date Masamune was one of the most

* According to Pagés (vol. i., p. 202. See also vol. ii., p. 103), Sotelo came from Mexico with Sotomayor. If this is correct, he may have gone with Vivero as far as that country.

enterprising men of his day. He did much for the
advancement of commerce, agriculture, and forestry.
Extensive canals were planned by him and partly ex-
cavated. As is shown by his statue at Matsushima, he
had only one good eye; but it was commonly said that
he could see more with this one than most persons
could with two. Sotelo, who had managed to get into
his good graces, excited his interest in plans for establishing commercial relations with Mexico and Spain.
According to a Japanese authority, Sotelo wrote a letter to Date proposing that an embassy be sent to these
countries, and the Daimyo promised to furnish the
necessary men and means.* It was probably while these
negotiations were being carried on that Sotelo was arrested and by Date's intercession was soon released.
That the favour was so readily granted may have been
owing to Ieyasu's interest in the project, for we find
that he sent some of his officials to take part in the
preparations. Pagés says that in Europe, Sotelo claimed
to represent the Emperor [Shogun] and that he bore
an "Imperial letter" to the King of Spain; but this
is probably a mistake, or else is to be explained on the
supposition that he had kept the letter entrusted to
him five years before, and at this late date took the opportunity to deliver it.

Sotelo's plans were not regarded with favour by the
Jesuits nor even by his own order. It is asserted that
his superiors had gravely censured him for his unsuccessful attempt in 1612. One reason for this and for
the opposition afterwards encountered by Sotelo was
that trade between Japan and Mexico would be against
the interests of the Philippines and contrary to special
privileges granted to them. Spanish colonies, with the
one exception of that at Manila, were forbidden to trade
with foreign nations, and most of them were also prohibited from trading with one another. All their commerce must be carried on through the port of Seville
in Spain itself. Special privileges given to Manila allowed its merchants to trade with China, Japan, and

* See Meriwether's "Life of Date Masamune" in As. Soc.
Trans., vol. xxi.

the Spanish colonies of America. It is easy to see why they would not look with favour on any plans for direct commerce between Spain and Japan by way of Mexico, while that of Mexico with Japan would be contrary to the Spanish policy, and illegal unless the Spanish King should remove the prohibition, as Sotelo hoped he might be induced to do if the Pope's intercession could be secured. The Franciscans in Japan had come from the Philippines, and their relations with the merchants of those islands account for their opposition to Sotelo.

A letter written in 1615 by Bishop Çerqueira to the General of the Jesuits says: " The Jesuit Fathers here did all they could these last few months to prevent not only the embassy, but also the voyage of Father Sotelo to New Spain. They worked hard, though without success, to get him into their hands and send him to Manila." The reason for this opposition was declared to be that if, as Sotelo desired, a large band of missionaries should come to Date's dominions, " great inconvenience may be expected to come, not only to the Christians, but also to the Franciscans themselves for having taken a prominent part in the business." Moreover, fear was expressed that " should any further mission of the Franciscans or any other order come here, it might greatly excite the King [Ieyasu] against them and against Masamune, whose real object in wishing the mission in his estates would then become too evident. As the King, for reasons we have before given you, is already very suspicious of the Spaniards, he may be led to think there is some ominous alliance between them and Masamune." The Bishop says that he has written to the King of Spain, urging him to use great prudence in connection with the embassy. In addition to the reasons for Çerqueira's opposition that are stated in his letter, there were those that arose from the ill-feeling that existed between the different orders. This would have been greatly increased if the Jesuits had known that the letters to be carried by Sotelo asked for his appointment as bishop for northeastern Japan.

With Sotelo was associated as Date's representative one of his retainers named Hashikura Rokuemon. To their care were committed letters from Date to the Pope, to the King of Spain, and to others. The one addressed to the Pope was as follows:

" I, Idate * Masamune, King of Oshu in the Empire of Japan, while kissing with profound submission and reverence the feet of Pope Paul V., the great, the universal, and the most holy Father of the world, say as a suppliant:

" When Father Louis Sotelo, a monk of the order of St. Francis, came to my kingdom and preached the Christian faith, he visited me. I have learned from him about that religion and he has explained to me many mysteries concerning the rites and ceremonies of the Christians. I have received these teachings into my heart, and upon examining them have seen that they are true and salutary. I would not hesitate to profess them openly if certain affairs had not hindered and invincible reasons prevented my doing so. But, although personally I am for the time being held back, I desire that my subjects at least shall become Christians. That this may be brought about, I beseech Your Holiness to send me monks of the order of St. Francis, called of the Observance. These I especially esteem and reverence. May Your Highness grant to accord to them in abundance licenses, favours, and all else that will contribute to their success. On my part, from the moment they enter my domains, I will never cease to protect them. I will help them by erecting monasteries and in all other possible ways. I likewise earnestly entreat that you will dispose, govern, and institute in my kingdom everything that you judge useful for the propagation of God's holy law, and especially I request that you will designate and appoint some grand prelate,† under whose direction and zeal I doubt not that all the inhabitants will quickly be converted to Christianity. You need not have any anxiety concerning their expenses and revenues, for I wish to assume for myself the whole responsibility and care for seeing that ample provision is made.

" For these reasons I am sending to you Father Louis Sotelo as my ambassador, from whom you will be able to inquire at pleasure concerning my intentions, for he well understands my views upon the above-mentioned matters. I beseech Your Holiness to lend a favourable ear to him and to receive him with honour. He will be accompanied by a noble gentleman of my house by the name of Hashikura Rokuemon, who has likewise been made my ambassador so that the two may go to the very

* This form of the name is said to have been used by Masamune as a special mark of honour to the person addresssed.

† What was intended by Masamune, or rather by Sotelo, who evidently had much to do in deciding the contents of this letter, was that the latter should come back as a bishop or perhaps as an archbishop.

holy Roman Court as bearers of my homage and obedience, and there kiss your sacred feet. If by chance the aforesaid Father Louis Sotelo should die on the voyage, I wish that such other person as he may have designated be admitted to your presence as my ambassador the same as though he were there himself.

"I have also learned that my kingdom is not far from the states of New Spain, which form part of the dominions of Philip, the very powerful King of Spain. Desiring therefore to enter into relations with him and with his Christian states, I wish to enjoy his friendship, which I certainly hope to obtain through the intervention of your authority. I therefore humbly pray that Your Highness will undertake and accomplish this, and so much the more as these states are on the road necessarily to be taken by the monks that will be sent by you into this kingdom.

"Above all pray to Almighty God that I may be able to attain to His friendship. If you know of anything in our country that would be agreeable and acceptable to you, let Your Highness command and we will do all in our power to satisfy your wish. For the present, since they come from a distant country, permit me to offer with reverence and respect a few slight gifts from Japan. For the rest, we rely upon the aforesaid Father Sotelo and Rokuemon, and we ratify all that they arrange and conclude in our name.

"From our city and court of Sendai in the eighteenth year of the Keicho era, the fourth day of the ninth month, that is, October 6, in the year of Salvation 1613.

"Matsudaira Mutsu no Kami, Idate Masamune." *

Attached to the letter addressed to the Spanish King were the following propositions and promises:

"1. I am willing that my people should become Christians. Send me therefore some Fathers who belong to the order of St. Francis. I will treat them kindly.†

"2. Send Fathers every year. In the ships now despatched to Mexico I send some of the products of Japan. Hereafter please send for my use some goods made in your land.

"3. When my ships return, you can send in them people or goods without expense. Should my ships suffer damage, please give my men what is necessary for repairs.

* As. Soc. Trans., vol xxi., contains the Latin of this document taken from a facsimile of the original. Several other documents are given in Latin or in translation. See also some of these documents in Pagés, vol. ii.

† In some versions this article begins with Date's promise to join the Christian church; but since his letters say that there were insuperable obstacles to his doing so at that time, the above version is probably the correct one.

"4. When ships on their way from the Philippines to New Spain come to this land, I will protect those on board. If ships are injured, I will supply whatever is necessary for repairs. In case it is necessary to rebuild the ships, I will take like care to provide what may be needed.

"5. When you wish to build ships in my country, I will supply wood, iron, carpenters, and whatever else is needed.

"6. When ships come here from your country, I will allow them to trade freely and will treat the people kindly.

"7. When Spaniards come here to live, I will give them houses and other things. In case any of them commit a crime, I will refer the matter to their own chief and look to him for punishment of evil-doers.

"8. If the English and Dutch, who are your enemies, come here, I will not honour them. Sotelo will tell you in detail about this.

"9. Having once assented to these articles, our agreement should be perpetual."

Sotelo and Hashikura set sail October 21, 1613, from the small port of Tsukinoura, about forty miles from Sendai. In addition to some seventy persons directly connected with the embassy, there were a number of merchants, who laded the ship with screens, chests of drawers (the *tansu* for which Sendai is still noted), and other articles to be sold in Mexico. Acapulco was reached January 24, 1614, and the ambassadors went on to the city of Mexico, where they were received by the Viceroy with due honour. Sixty-eight of Hashikura's suite were there baptised. It was decided that his own baptism should be postponed until his arrival in Europe. As several months were spent in Mexico, it was not until October that the embassy reached Seville. This, as has been said, was the port through which passed all commerce with the colonies. Moreover, it was the birthplace of Sotelo, and the city received him and his associates with the greatest enthusiasm. In Madrid they were welcomed by the King, and there, February 17, 1615, Hashikura was baptised. Three of his followers expressed a desire to become monks, but "this was opposed for prudential reasons." *

* Pagés (vol. ii., p. 132) quotes from Sotelo's account of the royal reception a letter addressed by Hashikura to King Philip. After stating the religious motives that had furnished one reason for the embassy, Hashikura goes on to say: "The second reason

In the Italian cities the embassy was honoured by a succession of magnificent fêtes. At Rome the ceremonies were similar to those witnessed thirty years before at the coming of the young men from Kyushu; though the Jesuits, by arousing a feeling of suspicion concerning the nature of the new embassy, caused some abatement in the warmth of the welcome. A despatch from the Venetian Ambassador at Rome speaks of Hashikura's reception by the Pope and mentions one speech that would be likely to make trouble if a similar report of it ever reached Ieyasu:

" A Franciscan monk made a very able exposition of the embassy and said that the King [Date] wanted a prelate to instruct him, and also a number of missionaries; that the King, being next in power and dignity to the Emperor [Shogun], would endeavour to supplant him and then would not only declare himself an obedient Christian to the Church of Rome but would afterwards compel all other princes in his country to be the same. Most of the people here in Rome think there are other interests at the bottom of this affair."

Pagés says that the Pope had some thought of appointing an archbishop and four bishops for Japan, and even of conferring on Sotelo the dignity of a cardinal. Such strong influence was brought against this that the Pope finally did not go beyond nominating Sotelo as Bishop of North Japan. It was probably because of the Jesuits and of the letters against Sotelo that came from the Philippines that Philip III. objected to having one of his subjects created bishop before the royal assent had been obtained. He succeeded in having the appointment withdrawn.

is that the King of Oshu, my master, having learned of Your Majesty's grandeur and of the kindness with which you shelter under your wings all those that seek your protection, has desired that I should come in his name to put his person, his kingdom, and all that it includes under Your Majesty's wings, and to proffer his friendship and his services in order that, if now or hereafter any or all of these offers can be of any advantage for Your Majesty's service, he can with zeal and affection carry them into effect."

Meriwether (As. Soc. Trans., vol. xxi., p. 80), quoting from Berchet, reduces this paragraph to a request for a treaty of perpetual friendship.

In 1617 Sotelo and Hashikura, returning towards Japan, reached Acapulco and from there went to Manila, where Sotelo fell into the power of his enemies. In accordance with orders from the Council for the Indies, his papers were taken from him and he was not allowed to proceed to Japan. It was not until 1620 that Hashikura, as will afterwards be related, reached Sendai, where Date was then proving to be anything but a patron of Christianity.

Ieyasu's sixth son, Tadateru, became disaffected with his father and was suspected of having plans for supplanting his brother in the shogunate. It is thought that Date, who was Tadateru's father-in-law, may have had something to do with the plot. If Ieyasu had learned the contents of the Sendai Daimyo's letter to the Pope and what was said at Hashikura's reception, he might well have thought there was need for scrutinising sharply the conduct of his vassal and the work of the missionaries. Date's later attitude toward Christianity may have been dictated in part by a desire to turn away the suspicion that had arisen against him.

Some Japanese books speak of another conspiracy whose discovery had much to do in increasing Ieyasu's suspicions against the Christians. A petty daimyo by the name of Okubo had been made superintendent of the gold and silver mines in the island of Sado. After his death, it was found that he had been guilty of financial irregularities. This led to a close scrutiny of his books and papers. It is alleged that several documents were found that showed that Okubo had been in communication with foreigners and had entered into an arrangement with them by which they would furnish troops to aid in overthrowing the Shogun's power. Tadateru was more or less involved in this affair. The discovery of the plot led to the punishment of several persons, among whom was a brother of Takayama Ukon.

It is easy to see how the different events that have been narrated—such as the soundings made by the Spaniards, the trickery of Okamoto and Okubo (especially if there is any foundation for the story that the latter's fellow-believers were involved in his schemes), and the embassy sent by Date—were likely to make Ieyasu think that the missionaries and their followers ought to be closely watched. He had about him those that were ever ready to fan his suspicions by repeating the old charges and inventing new ones. In a letter written to the Pope by Carvalho, the Jesuit Provincial, he says that the chief reasons leading to the persecution were that the enemies of Christianity had persuaded Ieyasu that it taught its believers to hold in high honour those that disobeyed their feudal lords, and even to worship common criminals. These accusations, he said, were grounded on the veneration shown by the Christians for those who suffered death rather than obey the Lord of Arima when he commanded them to give up their faith, and on the fact that when a professing Christian had been executed for some crime, others knelt upon the ground in order that they might pray for him. When Ieyasu was told that the Christians worshipped criminals, he angrily exclaimed: "A religion teaching such things is devilish!" and gave orders to the Governor of Nagasaki that he should expel all Christian teachers.

The Annual Letter of the Jesuits for 1614, quotes a letter that this Governor wrote to the Rector of Kyoto in which he said: "When Ieyasu heard that some of the Christians had gone to worship a citizen of Nagasaki named Jieobioe, who was executed for violating the law against the purchase of silver bullion, he said that it must be a diabolic religion that led its followers to worship persons executed for crime and also to venerate those that were burned or cut in pieces by order of their lords. Those that teach such a religion must be the most wicked of all men."

It is doubtless true also that the Dutch were only too willing to do their part in inciting Ieyasu to take action against their rivals. There was none too friendly a feeling between the different nations trading with Japan. We have seen how the Portuguese tried to shut out the Spaniards, how the Spaniards urged Ieyasu to drive away the Dutch, and how Will Adams said that the

Spaniards were acting the part of enemies when they sounded the harbours of Japan. It is asserted that in 1611, the Dutch, in translating a letter sent to Ieyasu by Maurice of Nassau, took the liberty of changing its meaning so as to make it accuse the Spanish and Portuguese merchants of being engaged in plots with the missionaries and Japanese Christians.

The rivalry of the merchants found its counterpart in that between the different orders. This could not fail to be a source of weakness, and there are indications that in trying to further the interests of the Portuguese or Spanish traders, with whom they were in close relations, the missionaries increased the amount of suspicion that had arisen against themselves and against the merchants.

Apostates from Christianity were ready to foster the feeling against it. Thomas Araki, a Japanese priest who had been ordained at Rome, returned about 1605 to his own country and declared that while in Madrid he had discovered that Spain was using the missionaries to pave the way for the conquest of Japan. It was largely through his influence that the Daimyo of Omura was led to give up Christianity and become one of its persecutors. Japanese books tell of a native priest from Yatsushiro, Higo, who in 1611 told Ieyasu that the King of Spain every year devoted large sums to sending merchandise into lands as yet unconquered in order to help in gaining converts to Christianity. He declared that the missionaries sent back annual reports telling how many persons they had succeeded in winning, and that valuable goods were distributed among them in proportion to their success in gaining converts. When a sufficient number of the people in any land had been made allies through their religious faith, possession was taken of the country and its precious metals were sent to Spain.

January 27, 1614, Ieyasu issued his celebrated decree against Christianity. After an introduction dealing with Chinese philosophy and Buddhism, it said:

"But Christians have come to Japan, not only sending their merchant vessels to exchange commodities, but also longing to disseminate an evil law and to overthrow right doctrine so that they may change the government of the country and obtain possession of the land. This is the germ of great disaster and must be crushed."

After speaking of the crimes condemned by Buddhism, the decree continues:

" The faction of the missionaries rebel against this dispensation; they disbelieve in the way of the gods, blaspheme the true law, violate rightdoing, and injure the good. If they see a condemned fellow, they run to him with joy, bow down to him, and do him reverence. This, they say, is the essence of their belief. If this is not an evil law, what is it? They truly are the enemies of the gods and of Buddha. If this be not speedily prohibited, the safety of the state will assuredly be hereafter imperilled; and if those who are charged with ordering its affairs do not put a stop to the evil, they will expose themselves to Heaven's rebuke.
" These must be instantly swept out, so that not an inch of soil remains to them in Japan on which to plant their feet, and if they refuse to obey this command, they shall pay the penalty." *

To this decree were appended rules for the guidance of Buddhist priests, who were directed to examine into the orthodoxy of their parishioners. Among these rules are the following:

" Because the Christian law teaches that those who despise death can pass through fire without being burned, or be plunged into water without being drowned, and that those who die by shedding their own blood are saved, the law of the Empire is most strict. Therefore you must examine such as make light of death."
" To those who follow Christianity a daily allowance of seven cash is made from Dattan(?) Land in order to convert the Empire to Christianity. It is an evil law which injures the Country of the Gods. As the persons who follow these doctrines do not observe the law of Buddha, they object to paying contributions to their parish temples and dislike the establishment of the Buddhist law. Such you must examine."
" . . . . By the help of their God, if they look in a mirror, they see the face of a saint; but if they have changed their religion, they appear as dogs."
" Although the parents for generations past may have belonged without the slightest doubt to one of the eight or nine Buddhist sects, it is impossible to be sure that the children may not in their

* A translation of the whole document may be found in As. Soc. Trans., vol. vi., p. 46.

hearts have been persuaded to join the evil law. The temple of
the sect to which they belong must examine them."
    " To every person in the Empire who clearly follows the true
law a sect-certificate, authenticated by a seal, shall be given.
Samurai shall put their seal in the certificate registry of the temple to which they belong. Those who cannot make a seal with
blood shall send a certificate attested by a guarantee." *

The daimyos received notice that they must send to
Nagasaki all the missionaries living in their territories,
that the churches must be destroyed, and that the Christians must be forced to give up their religion. Itakura,
the Shogun's representative in Kyoto, was ordered to
make out a list of the Christians living in that city.
Father De Mattos at once sent his assistants from house
to house that they might encourage the believers to
stand firm. On the other hand, relatives and neighbours were beseeching them to renounce their faith or
at least to conceal it. Though the whole number of believers in Kyoto is asserted to have been more than
seven thousand, only four thousand of these were put
upon the lists, and then, in order that Ieyasu might not
be too much irritated, Itakura, who was friendly to the
Christians, sent him the names of only sixteen hundred.

* The above follows with slight changes Satow's translation in
As. Soc. Trans., vol. vi., pp. 48-50. The " Hekija Kwanken-
roku," from which he takes it, is a collection of historical notes
concerning Christianity which was printed in 1861. It bears a
stamp which signifies that the buying and selling of the book was
prohibited. It appears to have been compiled for the use of
Buddhist temples at a time when the re-opening of Christian
missions suggested the need of renewed efforts for opposing them.
    The custom of having temples vouch for the orthodoxy of their
parishioners was kept up until recent times. The following is a
translation of one of the certificates.
    "This is to certify that Jimbei and his younger brothers,
Monnojo, Gonkichi, and Jinshichi, and their sister Tome, of
Ishigasaki Ward in the city of Hikone, are parishioners of my
temple and belong to the Jodo Sect, as did their ancestors. I
will maintain against all accusers that they do not belong to the
Christian sect, and if they should be examined and condemned
as Christians, I hold myself ready to be condemned as guilty of
the same crime.
                             " Oyo, Priest of Soan Temple.
First month, twelfth year of Kyoho [A. D. 1728]."

In February, the Jesuits in Kyoto were told that they must be taken to Nagasaki in order to be transported to their own countries. There were then fifteen members of the Society in the city, three of whom managed to conceal themselves. The others with some of their followers were put on boats and floated down the canal to Fushimi, where some Franciscans were added to their number. At Osaka they were joined by still others, so that there were seven boatloads, besides the two boatloads of soldiers sent to escort them as they were taken by sea to Nagasaki. There they found other missionaries and Japanese Christians brought from different parts of the country. Among the latter was Takayama Ukon. Since there were no ships ready to sail, their embarkation was delayed until October.

The tribulation through which they were passing ought to have united the hearts of those belonging to different orders; but, strange to say, it was at this time that the dissensions broke out with more virulence than ever. On the twentieth of February, Bishop Çerqueira died. Before his death he had asked Father Carvalho, a Jesuit, to care for the interests of the Church,* and soon after this the seven Japanese secular priests had come to throw themselves at Carvalho's feet asking him to administer the bishopric until some one could be appointed by the Archbishop of Goa. This was not pleasing to the Franciscans and Dominicans, who, in addition to their jealousy of the Jesuits, were moved by a desire to have Japan under the jurisdiction of the Archbishop of Manila. They therefore got the secular priests to act with them, and chose a clerk in minor orders to be their notary for drawing up an act in which they declared the deposition of Carvalho. In his place they elected Father Moralez of the Dominican order. Carvalho was not ready to be set aside in this way. He affixed to the door of the church an edict in which he pronounced a censure against his opponents and excommunicated the notary. Moralez retorted by excommunicating Carvalho. For some reason the Vicar Gen-

* According to Charlevoix, a papal brief had provided that, in case of Çerqueira's death, Carvalho should act in his place.

eral of the Dominicans disapproved of these proceedings and ordered Moralez to desist. The Japanese Christians and the Portuguese residents of Nagasaki became involved in these dissensions, which continued long after the deportation of many that had taken a prominent part in them.

After the missionaries had been sent away from Kyoto, efforts were renewed to secure the apostasy of the Christians who remained. Itakura would gladly have left them in peace, but Okubo Tadachika, Daimyo of Odawara, who was under suspicion of being connected with the alleged plot of the Christians to overthrow Ieyasu and Hidetada, was sent to his assistance. Okubo, who supposed this to be Ieyasu's way of testing his sentiments, made the most of the opportunity to clear himself. He posted a notice in which he said that, as all obstinate Christians were to be burned alive, those unwilling to give up their faith would do well to prepare the stakes to which they must be bound. Many of the Christians followed this order to the letter.

Some women who had taken vows of celibacy were living in a community under the care of Julia Naito, a sister of John Naito, the former Daimyo of Kameoka. Okubo had a number of them tied up in straw sacks, which were suspended on poles and carried through the city in order that the women might be subjected to the derision of the populace.

According to a Japanese account, Okubo destroyed the churches in Kyoto and put some sixty Christians to death. European histories do not mention the executions, but say, what is in accord with the Japanese account, that the persecution, after being carried on for eight or nine days with great vigour, was brought to a sudden end by the recall of Okubo, who was sent into exile. Apparently he had been sent to Kyoto in order that Ieyasu might in his absence gain easy possession of his castle in Odawara.

Nagasaki was still a Christian city. Its officers were little inclined to annoy believers or to put any restraint upon the missionaries, whose numbers were greatly increased by those that had been sent there for deportation. At first it was thought wise to desist from such public religious exercises as would attract attention. After a while, however, a different policy was adopted and the orders began to vie with one another in religious processions. The first of these was arranged about the end of April by the Franciscans. After their Superior had delivered a sermon, he washed and kissed the feet of twelve poor lepers. He then threw off the ecclesiastical robes that he had been wearing over a garment of sackcloth, sprinkled his head with ashes, took a large cross upon his shoulders, and had a boy lead him through the streets by a rope that was fastened about his neck. With him were the other Franciscans, scourging themselves until the blood flowed as they walked along the streets. Among the believers that joined the procession was Murayama Toan, the Deputy Governor.

The Dominicans chose the day of Pentecost for a similar service. Two thousand women dressed in white, but wearing dark veils, led the procession. They had crowns of thorns on their heads, and in their hands carried crucifixes and other sacred emblems. They were followed by eight thousand men who marched three abreast, the one in the middle carrying a lighted candle, while the two others scourged him and themselves. At the end of the procession was a large cross covered with a black veil.

The next day came the Augustinians, and shortly after, the Jesuits. These last exerted themselves to outdo all their predecessors. As a representation of the sufferings that they must be prepared to bear, some of the Christians were tied up in straw sacks, some carried great crosses on their shoulders, some were ranged in companies of eight or ten with their necks compressed between wooden planks, some had the upper part of their bodies enveloped with thorns over which they wore heavy reed mats that pressed the points into their flesh, while still others were bound to crosses and scourged by their companions who walked beside them.

From this time until October there was a constant succession of such spectacles. In some cases they were under the charge of missionaries; often they were arranged by the native Christians. Nagasaki was crowded with believers who came from other places to see the ceremonies and to receive the sacraments before their teachers should be sent out of the country.

The time drew near for deportation. All attempts at inducing Ieyasu to withdraw his orders had been unavailing. The month of October was occupied with many sad ceremonies. The Dominicans uprooted the two large crosses that stood before their cloister and in their cemetery. These with other sacred objects that could not be taken away nor concealed were burned so that they might not be left for the insults of heathen. The Jesuits dug up the relics of martyrs that had been deposited beneath their churches, and had them conveyed to a safe place. Many of the Christians disinterred the bones of their friends and hid them away. This was not a vain precaution, for afterwards, when the persecution became more severe, the Christian cemeteries were desecrated and the remains of those buried in them were insulted.

In some of the churches solemn services were held in which the lamps of the sanctuaries were extinguished and the altars dismantled, while the worshipers looked on with grief at what was being done. " It was like a scene from the Last Judgment."

The embarkation of the exiles took place on the seventh of November. Three small junks, in such poor condition as to be hardly seaworthy, were employed. One of these was sent to Manila. Among those on board were Takayama Ukon and John Naito with their families, Julia Naito with fourteen of her companions, two secular priests, and about thirty members of different orders. The other two vessels were ordered to go to Macao, taking seventy Jesuit priests and a number of Japanese Christians.

Not all of these persons actually left Japan. The Deputy Governor, Murayama Toan,* whose son was one

---

* Murayama Toan apostatised not far from this time. In 1618 a rival official charged him with having connived at the escape

of the secular priests, was probably privy to a plan by which, when the junk bound for Manila had sailed about two leagues and had been freed from the guards, small boats put off from shore and took back two Dominicans, two Franciscans, and the two Japanese priests. Some of the Jesuits also escaped, and the number would have been greater if it had not been that by mistake too few boats were sent. Many of the persons that were carried to Manila and Macao soon found ways of returning disguised as merchants, sailors, or even as slaves. There also remained in concealment a number of missionaries who had not been found at the time their associates were deported. Some of the feudal lords showed little zeal in hunting them up or in taking action against the Christians. One of those in Tamba joined with his son in openly resisting the orders, an act of nullification to which Ieyasu is said " to have shut his eyes."

The exiles that went to Manila were given a magnificent reception. The Governor, the Bishop, members of the religious orders, nay, the whole Christian populace, united in doing them honour. A splendidly decorated galley was sent to meet the junk as it entered the harbour. The booming of cannon and the ringing of bells welcomed the exiles, who were taken in carriages to the cathedral, where a religious service was held. Takayama, the most illustrious of the company, died in February of the next year (1615). His funeral was attended by a great concourse. Many kissed his feet as those of a saint that had suffered much for his faith. The Governor, in the name of the Spanish King, assigned the rents of certain lands to his family. He was buried in the church of the Jesuits. Eleven years later, the body of John Naito was placed beside his. Some of their associates afterwards returned to Japan. The descendants of those that remained, together with those of later exiles, form no inconsiderable element of the mixed population now found in the Philippines.

One of the most active persecutors of the Christians

of his son and with permitting missionaries to reside in Nagasaki. He was deposed from office and the next year was beheaded.

was Hasegawa Sahioe, the chief Governor of Nagasaki. In that city he was somewhat restrained by various privileges that had been granted to the Portuguese, by fear of an insurrection, and by the apprehension that he might be blamed if his acts put an end to foreign commerce. He had for a long time desired to be put in possession of Arima. He had already been given some oversight of the apostate Daimyo of that fief and it was partly because of this that the persecutions there had been particularly severe. He now succeeded in getting that daimyo transferred to Hyuga, while he himself obtained the coveted territory. He determined to purge it from the hated religion. For this purpose he made use of a large force of soldiers from Satsuma and Hizen. He is said to have issued the following directions to his subordinates:

" The Christians desire death in order that they may be honoured as martyrs. Hence it is not desirable to slay them, but rather to prolong their lives, subjecting them to such severe punishments as will finally overcome their resistance. The most effective trial will be to enslave their women, sending the most beautiful of them to the houses of prostitution in Kyoto. If the people will renounce the religion of Christ, they shall be exempted from imposts and other obligations; moreover, Chinese ships will be induced to come to their ports for trade, and this will be for the great enrichment of the country."

As most of the Christians in Arima stood firm, arrests and persecutions soon began. Most of the soldiers that were sent to scour the country had little taste for attacking unarmed men, women, and children. In many cases, they sent warnings before them to the villages so that the inhabitants might escape to the mountains. The men from Satsuma soon reported that they could find no Christians in the section allotted to them. Not all the soldiers, however, were so indulgent. Many Christians were arrested and subjected to torments. Notwithstanding what Hasegawa had said about disappointing the desire of the Christians for martyrdom, he caused a number of them to be put to death.

After personally supervising these proceedings in Arima, Hasegawa returned with his soldiers to Nagasaki, where he threatened that he would compel all the Christians to apostatise. It is asserted that an order from Ieyasu directed him not to cause any check to commerce by taking action before the arrival of the next Great Ship from Macao, and also to be careful not to adopt such methods as would excite the people to revolt. However that may have been, another reason for the temporary cessation of persecution was that Hasegawa and his soldiers were called to take part in Ieyasu's military operations against Hideyori.

The last great struggle, which was to establish the Tokugawa family firmly in the shogunate and to put an end to the hopes that Hideyoshi's son might recover the power his father had wished to bequeath him, was now beginning. Hideyori held the strongly fortified castle of Osaka. Many powerful lords remained faithful to his cause. In various ways Ieyasu had tried to involve him in undertakings that would diminish the treasure inherited from his father, and to increase the difficulties that the young man had found in asserting his claims. At last, when the time seemed propitious, Ieyasu found means for picking a quarrel that opened the way for laying siege to Osaka Castle. After a long struggle and as much through trickery as by good fighting, it was captured June 4, 1615. Hideyori with some of his retainers committed *harakiri* in the innermost citadel, which was then set on fire.

A large proportion of the Christians had been inclined to favour Hideyori. Pagés says that because of the promises he had made, all the inhabitants of Nagasaki desired his triumph. We are not told what these promises were; but among the English and Dutch traders there was apprehension that, if Hideyori were victorious, the Spanish and Portuguese priests would obtain so much power that they themselves as heretics would be driven out of the country. It was believed by many that the missionaries stirred up Hideyori to oppose Ieyasu. Will Adams wrote:

"He mad warres with the Emperour allso by the Jessvits and Ffriers which mad his man Fiddeyat Samma belleeue he should be fauord with mirracles and wounders; but in fyne it proved to the contrari."

One of Hideyori's prominent generals was a Christian named Akashi Morishige, who found that military necessities required the burning of about two hundred temples, including three of the most important in Osaka and Sakai. A son of Takayama Ukon with three hundred of his father's former retainers joined Hideyori's forces, as did sons of John Naito and Otomo Yoshishige, besides many Christian warriors who had been banished from their homes. We are told of six great banners that, in addition to the cross, had representations of Christ or of St. James, the patron saint of Spain. Some even bore ideographs signifying " The Great Protector of Spain." Moreover, five missionaries, together with a Japanese priest, the son of Murayama Toan, were in Hideyori's camp. It is asserted that this priest led a band of four hundred Christian warriors. He was slain; but the foreigners managed with great difficulty to escape. One of them, Father Porro, wrote a vivid description of the destruction of Osaka and of his own adventures. Two of the Christians had persuaded him to leave the castle and had brought him to the mansion of one of Ieyasu's followers, where it was thought he would be safe. While there, he saw the burning of the castle and city. A high wind increased the fury of the flames. The buildings of the mansion where he had found shelter caught fire one by one, so that he was forced to take refuge in a clump of bamboos. While there, he heard the confessions of several Christians and even baptised a new convert. The next morning a company of soldiers came up and threatened him with death. They stripped off most of his clothes, but finally let him go free. Making his way among the ruins of houses and the corpses of the slain, he reached the camp of Date Masamune, who had been among the besiegers. Porro says:

" I was noticed by a soldier who, thinking I might be one of the Fathers, called to me in a very respectful manner, led me to his tent, and said that in the present circumstances he would never consent to my going farther at the very evident risk of my life. I remained with him all that day. On the morrow, which was the fifth of June, my host started for Kyoto, while I, falling once more into extreme peril, took my way toward Masamune. I found this lord on the point of mounting his horse as he started for Kyoto. I explained briefly that I was a foreigner from the city of Nagasaki and that, having found myself in Osaka during the recent occurrences, I had been reduced to the sad condition in which he saw me. I asked that he would generously assist me to go to Morro and from thence to Nagasaki. Masamune replied through a page that he would have acceded to my request gladly and at once if I had not been a Christian."

This reply of Masamune is the more noticeable because it was just at this time that his ambassador Hashikura, after being specially welcomed in Mexico, was about to proceed to Europe, where he represented his master as ready to become the protector of the Christians. After this repulse, Porro passed on through other dangers until he found persons who treated him kindly, gave him clothing, and sent him on his way until he found shelter among believers.

Although many Christians were among the soldiers in Ieyasu's army, it is not strange that the presence among his enemies of religious teachers whose deportation he had ordered, and the prominent display of Christian emblems increased his dislike for the foreign religion. Will Adams wrote:

"The Emperour heering of these jessvets and friers being in the kastell with his ennemis, and still from tym to tym against hym, coummandeth all romische sorte of men to depart out of his countri, thear churches pulld dooun and burned."

There were reports that Hideyori was still alive and that he was being concealed by the Christians. The diary of Richard Cocks, who was in charge of the English factory at Hirado, makes frequent mention of these rumours. He tells of a search that was being made in all parts of Japan " to look out for such as escaped out of the fortress of Osekey when it was burned. Soe that prive enquirie was mad in all howses in Firando [Hirado] what strangers were lodged in eache howse, and true notis thereof geven to the justice. It is thought the padres at Langasaque [Nagasaki] and else where will be narrowly looked after."

During the contests in Osaka the church had a season of calm. There had remained in Japan twenty-nine Jesuits, six Franciscans, six Dominicans, and one Augustinian. Their numbers were increased by the secret return of some of those that had been banished. Disguised in various ways and travelling mostly by night, they went about the country visiting the sick, encouraging the faint-hearted, baptising children, and even gathering new converts. One of the Franciscans, assuming the garb of a soldier and mingling with those of Ieyasu's army, managed to get to Yedo itself. He lodged for a time in the leper hospital, which was kept up under the direction of one of its inmates, who belonged to a distinguished family. This seemed a safe retreat, for the lepers were so avoided by other people that it was unlikely any search would be made among them. He frequently made his way into the city, and for a short time lived in a house belonging to the retainer of a high officer. Finally he was arrested, as were also fifty of the lepers. The hospital itself was destroyed.

This missionary, with ten or twelve of the Christians, was confined in a single room so closely packed that any person wishing to sleep had to support himself by leaning against his neighbour. There were many other prisoners, and these were constantly quarrelling about the amount of space each could have and the length of time he could sleep. In summer it was so hot that objection was made to any person's wearing clothing, because he thus made those near him warmer. The missionary, as a special favour, was allowed to wear a thin garment, though at times he himself found it unendurable. The food was so scanty that many died for lack of nourishment. The Father was kept alive by food that outside Christians bribed the guards to give him. Many prisoners committed suicide. Others were murdered. Frequently the corpses were not removed for seven or eight days. All the prisoners soon became covered with frightful ulcers. In the midst of these horrors, the missionary was at first able to perform religious exercises with his fellow-Christians; but afterwards the prison received a rougher set of men, who

put an end to preaching and the open performance of
any sacred ministry. The missionary remained in the
prison for more than a year, when he was released by
the intercession of one of the Shogun's officers, who desired to conciliate the Spaniards so as to facilitate certain commercial enterprises.

VII

APPARENT EXTIRPATION OF CHRISTIANITY

1616-1715

IEYASU died June 1, 1616. This brought no relief to the Christians, for Hidetada was more
violent against them than his father had ever been.
Will Adams wrote:

"Now this yeear, 1616, the old Emperour died. His son
raigneth in his place, and hee is more hot agaynste the romish rel-
ligion then his ffather wass: for he hath forbidden thorough all
his domynions, on paine of death, none of his subjects to be
romish christiane; which romish seckt to prevent everi wayes that
he maye, he hath forbidden that no stranger merchant shall abid
in any of the great citties."

On the death of Ieyasu, Richard Cocks, the English
agent, thought it best to visit Yedo in order to pay his
respects to the Shogun and to request a continuance of
the commercial privileges hitherto enjoyed by the English. In a letter to the East India Company he wrote:

"The 5th day after I arrived at court our present was deliverd,
and had audience with many favourable words, but could not
get my dispach in above a month after; so that once I thought
we should have lost all our pirivelegese, for the Councell sent
unto us I think above twenty times to know whether the English
nation were Christian or no. I answered we were and that they
knew that before by our Kinges Maties. letter sent to the Emperour his father (and hym selfe), wherein it appeared he was
defender of the Christian faith. 'But,' said they, 'are not the
Jesuists and fryres Christians two?' Unto which I answered they
were, but not such as we were, for all Jesuists and fryres were
banished out of England before I was borne, the English nations
not houlding with the pope nor his doctryne, whose followers
these padres (as they cald them) weare. Yt is strang to see how
often they sent to me about this matter, and in the end gave us
wayning that we did not comenecate, confesse, nor baptiz with

them, for then they should hold us to be all of one sect. Unto
which I replied that their Honours needed not to stand in doubt
of any such matter, for that was not the custom of our nation."

Having at last obtained, as he supposed, documents
giving the desired privileges, Cocks set out on his return to Hirado, when a letter from Kyoto led him to sus-
pect that all might not be as he wished:

"Whereupon I sought one to read over our privelegese, which
with much a do at last I found a *boz* (or pagon prist) which
did it, and was that we were restrayned to have our shiping to
goe to no other place in Japan but Firando, and there to make
sales."

This meant a great restriction of English trade. Cocks
turned back to Yedo and asked that the fuller rights
granted by Ieyasu might be renewed. He "could get
nothing but words." In fact, by that time the Shogun's
Council had issued the following decree:

"Be it strictly instructed that according to the command of
the Premier issued some years ago to the effect that the conversion of the Japanese to Christianity is strictly prohibited,
the lords of all the provinces shall take special care to keep all
people, down to farmers, from joining that religion. Also, as
the black ships, namely the English ships, belong to that religion,
the provincial lords should send any of those ships to Nagasaki
or Hirado, in case they happen to put in to the ports of their
dominions, and no trade shall be carried on therein."

Pagés speaks of an edict issued by the Shogun that forbade the Japanese, under the penalty of being burned
alive, from having any relations with the teachers of
Christianity or their servants. The same penalty was to
be visited on the wives and children of offenders and on
their five nearest neighbours upon each side, unless these
gave information. Daimyos were forbidden to keep
Christians in their service.

Cocks thought that his troubles were partly owing to a
Spaniard who was then in Yedo. Two great ships full
of soldiers and treasure on the way from New Spain to
the Philippines had been driven by contrary winds to
Satsuma, and this man had been sent to pay his respects
to the Shogun. An audience was not given him and in

his vexation at being refused what was granted to the
English he commenced to bring accusations against them
and the Hollanders, saying that they had robbed all the
Chinese junks sailing towards Japan, which was the
reason why few had come that year. It may well be
believed that Cocks would not hesitate to requite the ill
turn done by the Spaniard. He himself wrote, saying:

"Yf they lookt out well about these 2 Spanish shipps arrived
in Xaxma full of men and treasure, they would find that they
were sent of purpose by the King of Spaine, haveing knowledge
of the death of the ould Emperour, thinking som papisticall *tono*
[lord] might rise and rebell and so draw all the papistes to
flock to them and take part, by which meanes they might on a
sudden seaz upon som strong place and keepe it till more suc-
cors came, they not wanting money nor men for thackom-
plishing such a strattigim. Which speeches of myne wrought
so far that the Emperour sent to stay them, and, had not the
great ship cut her cable in the howse so to escape, she had byn
arrested, yet with her hast she left som of her men behind;
and the other shipp being of some three hundred tons was cast
away in a storme and driven on shore, but all the people saved.
So in this sort I crid quittance with the Spaniardes for geveing
out falce reportes of us, yet since verely thought to be true
which I reported of them."

Cocks soon went so far as to suggest to the " Amerall
of the sea " that he " put it into the Emperour's mynd to
make a conquest of the Manillias and drive those small
cre of Spaniards from thence, it being so neare unto
Japon."
With such accusations and counter-accusations made
by the merchants, it is not strange that Hidetada became
more suspicious of foreigners. It did not help matters
when commissioners sent in search of one of Hideyori's
captains who was thought to be concealed in Nagasaki
reported that many missionaries were living there and
in other places. In 1617, when the daimyos went on
New Year's Day to pay their respects to the Shogun,
he took the occasion to administer a severe rebuke to
the Daimyo of Omura. This young man, who had been
baptised in infancy, still regarded Christianity with considerable favour, and his sister was an earnest believer.
He was one of those that had been ordered, in 1614, to
take charge of the deportation of the missionaries. Not-

withstanding his report that he had done what was commanded, there was good reason to think he knew that some of the missionaries remained in his territories or had afterwards returned thither. He was now told that he must atone for his negligence by seeing that all were driven out. Pagés says that he received secret orders to put them to death. Only the first command was known by the Christian officials in Nagasaki, who decided it would be better to send away a few persons in order to make it safer for the others. Accordingly, some of the missionaries were sent in March to Macao, a part of whom very soon found means for returning.

Omura, though he had little liking for persecution, was afraid to disobey the Shogun. He thought that by putting one missionary to death he could frighten the others so that they would flee of their own accord. To his chagrin, the officials, instead of being satisfied with making one arrest, took into custody two of the missionaries, Fathers De l'Assumpcion and Machado, belonging respectively to the Franciscan and Jesuit orders. Omura still hoped he would be permitted to spare their lives. He sent a report of their arrest to Yedo and asked for further orders. The reply soon came that both men must be beheaded.

The letters written by these missionaries while in custody show the spirit in which they met their fate. Machado wrote:

"It is now twelve days that I have been a prisoner. I return a thousand thanks to Our Lord that He has deigned to grant me such great peace that there is nothing in the world I would prefer to my present condition of being a captive for the love of God. I return infinite thanks to His Divine Majesty that from the hour when I was made a prisoner I have not ceased to behold myself stretched upon the cross or bending beneath the edge of the sword. Blessed be the Lord who thus comforts those who for the love of him suffer even the lightest pains. I have never understood the deep meaning of the words of Scripture and the spiritual power they communicate as I have since I found myself in this condition."

The sentence was carried into effect May 21, 1617. Though guards were put about the place where the bodies were buried, the Christians went there in crowds to do honour to the martyrs.

Omura's hope that this execution would terrify the other missionaries was not realised. When Fathers Navarette and Saint-Joseph, Vicars Provincial respectively of the Dominicans and Augustinians, heard of the martyrdoms, they judged that the time had come when they ought to conceal themselves no longer, but go openly to Omura for the sake of strengthening the faith of the Christians and calling apostates to repentance. Their purpose soon became known to the people of Nagasaki. More than three thousand persons followed them out of the city to bid them farewell and to seek their blessing. Spending the first night in the suburbs of Nagasaki, the two missionaries then went slowly on their way, stopping at several places to preach, say mass, and administer the sacraments. In one place they erected an altar in the open air. Crowds gathered about them, listening eagerly to their words and coming afterwards to kneel at their feet for a blessing. Many that had apostatised professed repentance and sought forgiveness.

The two missionaries sent a letter to the Daimyo of Omura, saying that compassion for him and his people led them to come out from their concealment in order that they might urge him to repent of his great sin, and might do all in their power for the conversion of his subjects. This appeal was ineffective. The brave men were at once thrown into prison, whence in a few days they were taken to a small island and beheaded. A catechist who had accompanied Machado suffered with them. To put an end to the honours shown by the Christians to those that died for their faith, Omura had the bodies of the former martyrs disinterred so that, with those of the new victims, they might be weighted with stones and sunk in the sea. The Christian fraternities for a long time tried in vain to find the bodies, but some months afterwards two of them were washed ashore. These were taken to Nagasaki, whence at a later date some of the bones were sent to Manila and Macao as sacred relics.

These events made a great impression upon the believers. Many of those who had shown weakness became ashamed of their cowardice. In Nagasaki the Christians began to engage openly in religious services. The officials hesitated about taking action that would involve so many persons, and they also feared that in the existing state of excitement any attempts at suppression would lead to a riot. Father Moralez, who had become the Superior of the Dominicans, sent two monks to work secretly in Omura; also one of the Franciscans, clad in the dress of his order, went to the city in which the Daimyo lived and there preached openly. After having the joy of converting one of the executioners of De l'Assumpcion, he was thrown into prison, as was also one of the missionaries sent by Moralez.

By the order of the Shogun, Hasegawa Sahioe sent a violent letter to the officials at Nagasaki, giving directions that those persons who had furnished an asylum to Fathers Navarette and Saint-Joseph should be punished. These persons were arrested and soon after were put to death secretly so that there might be no danger of disturbance.

Another martyr that suffered at this time was a high officer of Omura, who had governed the territory during the absence of the Daimyo. It was he who had arrested De l'Assumpcion and presided at the execution of the first martyrs. The contemplation of their bravery led him to accept their religion. He became zealous in seeking to convert others, and especially to lead back those that had apostatised. The Buddhist priests soon procured his arrest and execution. The Daimyo, who wished to terrify the Christians, took pains to have it made known that he had not hesitated to condemn even his favourite officer for becoming an adherent of the proscribed religion.

From time to time missionaries were arrested in different provinces; but with a single exception none were executed between May, 1617, and August, 1622. This one exception was Father Sainte-Marthe, an aged Franciscan. For three years he was a prisoner in Kyoto. Itakura, the Shogun's representative, was little inclined to put him to death, and offered to send him to Mexico. The old man said he did not wish to be set free unless at the same time he was allowed to remain in Japan. He was finally beheaded in August, 1618.

There were many executions of Japanese Christians. The records from this time were crowded with accounts of their sufferings. Nagasaki furnished many of the victims. In that city Hasegawa Gonroku, a nephew of Sahioe, had become Governor. He had a number of persons arrested for sheltering the missionaries and native priests. Their wives and children were taken from them. November 25, 1618, fourteen persons were burned at the stake, among them being children aged ten, seven, and four years, as well as a babe only two months old. The next year another step was taken, and the Portuguese merchants saw among those being burned at the stake one of their own number, Domingo Jorge, who had sheltered two Jesuits. This merchant may have been under suspicion for other reasons. Japanese accounts say that in 1617, a foreign ship was captured by the Dutch. "It belonged to Jorchin [Domingo Jorge]* and brought letters from the Portuguese. When these had been translated by the interpreters in Hirado, it was found that the Southern Barbarians [Spaniards and Portuguese] instigated the Japanese Christians to make a revolt." The sense of one letter was: "As soon as the news arrives that the number of Japanese Christians is sufficient, men-of-war will be sent." Kaempfer mentions two other letters alleged to have been found, one by the Dutch and the other by a Japanese ship, in which the Christians of Japan wrote to the King of Spain the details of a plot for overthrowing the Shogun's government. Most European writers have been inclined to consider these letters, especially the last two, either as never having existed or as having been forged by the Dutch.

Gonroku employed many spies who, under the pretence of becoming converts to Christianity, tried to dis-

*Germ. As. Soc., vol. vii., pt. 1. Another account, however, says Jorchin (or Jojin) was a Japanese. Trans. As. Soc., vol. vi., p. 44,

cover the hiding-places of the missionaries. Bars of
silver had hitherto been exposed to view in the public
square with a notice that they were for the reward of
any one who gave information leading to the arrest of
a thief. To the placard making this promise were now
added the words, " or of a Christian teacher." The
difficulties of concealment became so great that most of
the missionaries left the city to hide in the mountains or
to flee to other parts of the country.

A letter written March, 1620, by Richard Cocks refers
to the destruction of Christian edifices. He had often
wished that the English factory might be removed to
Nagasaki, but this, he says,

" Heretofore was not thought fitt, because then a papist Portin-
gale bishopp lived in the towne and ther was 10 or 12 parish
churches, besids monestaries, all which are now pulled downe
to the grownd this yeare, an end being made thereof; and the
places where all such churches and monestaries weare, with the
churchyords, are all turned into streetes, and all the dead mens
boanes taken out of the ground and cast forth for their frendes
and parentes to bury them where they please. I doe not re-
joyce herin, but wish all Japon were Christians; yet in the
tyme of that bishopp heare were soe many prists and Jesuists
with their partakers that one could not parse the streetes without being by them called Lutranos and herejos [Lutherans and
heretics], which now we are very quiet and non of them dare
open his mouth to speake such a word."

Nagasaki was not the only place where the Christians
were persecuted. In 1619 orders from Yedo, and afterwards a visit of the Shogun himself, led to more active
measures in Kyoto. After leaving the city, the Shogun
learned that a large number of believers was confined
in the prison. Angry at not having been informed of
this, he ordered that all be put to death, without distinction of age or sex. October 7, 1619, the people gathered in crowds to watch the victims as they were carried to the place of execution. Preceded by officers to
clear the way and by criers to announce their crime,
fifty-two martyrs were drawn in carts through the
streets. The first and last carts contained only men;
but nine others were laden with women and children,
the latter carried in their mothers' arms or clinging to

their knees. One child, eight years old, was blind. A woman named Thecla was the mother of five children from three to thirteen years of age. They as well as her husband were to suffer with her that day. From time to time a herald called out: "The Shogun desires and commands that all these persons be put to death because they are Christians;" and then, as though it were the response in an antiphonal service, the martyrs shouted: "It is true; we die for Jesus. Blessed be Jesus!" Crossing one of the bridges over the Kamo River, the procession came to a large open space opposite the temple in which was the great image of Buddha erected by Hideyori in honour of his father. Here had been planted a number of stakes with fagots piled about them in such a way as to leave a little space for the victims, two of whom, placed back to back, were bound to each of the stakes. When Thecla descended from the cart, she was seen to be clothed in a rich garment, as though for a festival.

A great crowd of people had gathered to see the strange sight. The fagots were lighted and through the smoke could be caught glimpses of the mothers trying to quiet the little children held in their arms. One of Thecla's daughters, who was bound near her, was heard calling out: "Mother, I cannot see any more;" and then came the woman's reply: "Invoke the help of Jesus and of Mary." These names uttered by many lips mingled with the cries of frightened children and the groans of the dying, until gradually all such sounds ceased and nothing more was heard but the roaring and crackling of the flames.*

---

* In 1897 a suggestive sight was seen on what I suppose was almost the exact spot where these martyrs suffered. In connection with the funeral of the Empress Dowager, the Japanese Red Cross Society made preparations to care for any persons among the immense crowds viewing the procession who might be injured. Its tents were set up before the Temple of the Great Buddha and almost within the shadow of the Mimizuka, a mound under which were buried the ears of Koreans that had been sent back by Hideyoshi's soldiers to show the number of the enemy they had slain. In strange contrast with the spirit that led to the erection of that mound and with the event

Through the first years of the persecution, the number of missionaries in Japan, instead of being lessened, was gradually increasing. Those sent away soon returned, while others, ready for martyrdom and even desiring it, came from Macao and the Philippines. In 1619, the Jesuits are said to have baptised one thousand eight hundred converts. The next year four Fathers baptised over a thousand persons in northeastern Hondo. One of them went into the island of Yezo (which had been visited by another missionary two years earlier) and found there many believers from the mainland who were eager for his ministrations. At some mines in the interior were two persons who had formerly served as catechists and were now glad to assist him in teaching their fellow-labourers.

The return of Hashikura, Date Masamune's ambassador to Europe, had been long delayed. In 1617, he and Father Sotelo came to Acapulco, where they found a ship belonging to Date. The Sendai Daimyo had sent a second messenger in 1616, to learn what had become of the first, and this may account for the presence of the ship in Mexico. A new governor who was on his way to the Philippines made arrangements to have the ship take him thither, those in charge being willing to do this because they could obtain there a more profitable cargo than was to be found in Mexico. Manila was reached in June of the next year. Here, as already recorded, Sotelo and his papers were seized. He was afterwards sent back to Mexico. For some unknown reason the Japanese also were delayed so that it was August, 1620, when, after his seven years of absence, Hashikura, with a suite now numbering only eleven persons, reached Sendai. According to Pagés he reported to Masamune that the Christian religion was only an

related in the text, there floated over these tents white flags bearing what, though once the most hated emblem in Japan, is now honoured as that of the Red Cross Society, which, though not distinctively Christian, owes it origin to the influence of Him who transformed the cross from a thing of shame into a symbol of love.

empty show. This is in accord with other accounts that represent him as apostatising. A letter written in 1677 by his grandson says that Hashikura, though never a Christian at heart, became one nominally " because otherwise he could not see the Spanish King and get the answer to Masamune's letter."

The return of this ambassador may have increased the suspicion that Masamune was planning an alliance with Spain for the purpose of supplanting the Shogun. His desire to clear himself from such charges is thought to be the reason why at about this time he issued three proclamations. In the first, all those who, in opposition to the Shogun's will, had become Christians were exhorted to return to their former religions. In case of refusal, the goods of the rich were to be confiscated, while the poor were to be put to death. The second proclamation promised honour and rewards to informers. The third ordered the banishment of all Christian teachers who would not renounce their faith. For several years these edicts were not enforced, Masamune turning his blind eye towards the fact that missionaries were residing in Sendai. Indeed, one of his leading vassals was " father of the Christians and the strongest pillar of the church."

Father Zuñiga, an Augustinian monk, had so won the appreciation of his converts that after he had been driven out of Japan they wrote to the Provincial in Manila, asking that he be sent to them once more and promising that in exchange for the living missionary they would send the body of the martyr Saint-Joseph.*

The ship in which Zuñiga sailed, in company with a Dominican named Flores, was captured off the coast of Formosa by an English vessel that belonged to a combined fleet of English and Dutch. The commander of this latter vessel had once been a prisoner of the Inquisition in Seville, and was doubtless very willing to pay off

* " Les chrétiens . . . écriverent à Notre Réverénd P. Provincial, afin de la faire renvoyer, promettant de livrer en échange le saint corps du bienheureux martyr Fray Hernando de San Joseph, qu'ils avaient en leur possession " (Pagés, vol. ii., p. 257).

the debt of vengeance he owed to Spain and Roman Catholicism. The ecclesiastical character of the monks was recognised through the disguises they had assumed, while among their papers were found a letter appointing Zuñiga to be Vicar Provincial, the commission of Flores, and other suspicious documents. The missionaries were therefore sent to Hirado, where they remained in custody of the Dutch. For sixteen months Zuñiga and Flores refused to acknowledge that they were priests. A letter written by Zuñiga says that to the direct questions of a Japanese official, who was sent to examine them, " We replied that we were not Fathers," and shows that they justified themselves for making this statement by the mental interpretation that they were not fathers in the sense of being parents of children.* He adds: " Our reasons for so doing were the necessity common throughout Japan, and the desire not to cause the death of those who had brought us nor to expose a great number of persons to the danger of denying the faith."

Various tortures were inflicted by the Dutch in the vain attempt to extort confessions. The Diary of Richard Cocks, as well as the letters of the missionaries, gives accounts of several examinations that were held before Hasegawa Gonroku. What is remarkable is that Gonroku had formerly known Zuñiga; yet, although many Japanese and Chinese, besides Portuguese and a native of Manila, insisted on the identity, Gonroku declared the proof insufficient. His unwillingness to pronounce judgment gave rise to the doubts mentioned by Cocks, who wrote: " As some say, Gonroku Dono is suspected to be a Christian."

Finally three missionaries of as many different orders were brought from their confinement in the Omura prison to see if they recognised the accused persons. With them came Thomas Araki, the apostate priest, who for some reason, perhaps that he might act as a spy, perhaps because the sincerity of his recantation was doubted, had also been imprisoned at Omura. On arriving at

---

* " *Nous répondimes que nous n'étions pas Péres, intrinsecè filiorum.*" This letter and one by Flores are given in Pagés, vol. ii., pp. 204-215.

Hirado, he took part in some Buddhist ceremonies, and afterwards bore witness that while in Omura he had heard some of his fellow-prisoners assert that one of the captives was a priest named Zuñiga. The missionaries all declared that they had never seen Flores, though all but one of them testified that in former years they had seen the other person at Nagasaki, dressed as a merchant. One of the Japanese officials, an apostate from Christianity, who was doubtless well aware that they knew more than they had told, asked:

"Is it permissible for a monk or a priest to deny being such?"

Father Spinola, one of the Omura prisoners, answered:

"You do not understand the difference between a Christian and a priest. The former ought always to declare himself a Christian; but no one is under obligation to acknowledge that he is a priest."

Thereupon an Englishman that was present said that in his country the Roman Catholic priests constantly denied that they were such and so saved themselves from being executed. Spinola declared this to be a calumny, saying that he himself while in England had acknowledged that he was a Jesuit priest, and that many of his associates had done the same, though it had cost some of them their lives.

At last, the Fathers from Omura, seeing that the proofs were too strong to be resisted, had a private interview with Zuñiga in which they advised him not to deny his identity any longer, for it was improbable that he would be released, and a continuance of the dissimulation was likely to cause scandal. Zuñiga therefore acknowledged before the judge that he was a priest. Flores did not confess until some months later and after an unsuccessful attempt had been made by Father Collado to rescue him from prison. When the Shogun heard of this attempt, he was filled with greater wrath than before against the Christians. His suspicions had been increased by a report that Zuñiga was a natural son of the Spanish King (he was really the son of a former Viceroy of Mexico) and had now come to lead the Christians in delivering over Japan to his father. Gonroku was censured for having been remiss in duty and was ordered to put to death not only Zuñiga, Flores, and the Japanese captain of the boat on which they had been apprehended, but also all the missionaries that were in prison, and the families of those persons who had given them shelter.

The first execution took place in Nagasaki, August 19, 1622. Twelve Japanese, who had been sailors or passengers on the captured ship, were decapitated and their heads were placed before the stakes where Zuñiga, Flores, and the Japanese captain were burned. Three weeks later (September 10, 1622), came what has since been known as the "Great Martyrdom," when thirty persons were beheaded and twenty-five burned. Among the latter were nine foreign priests. The most famous of the number was Father Spinola, a Jesuit of noble birth, and a man of unusual talents. He had been in Japan since 1602. His scholarship had done much to commend him to the Japanese, and at Kyoto he had founded an academy for scientific studies and original investigation. He had been in captivity for nearly four years.

The Omura prisoners were brought the preceding day by boat to a small village, where they were transferred to horses; Spinola, mounted on a sorry-looking white nag, being placed at the head of the procession. To the neck of each captive was attached a rope, whose other end was held by a guard walking beside the horse. Four hundred soldiers acted as an escort. The night was spent at Urakami, the town whence, two hundred and fifty years later, a new persecution sent into exile three thousand descendants of the Christians who now looked with mingled sorrow and exultation on those that were about to attain the glory of martyrdom.

The next morning the procession went on its way, the confessors singing psalms or occasionally speaking a few words to the Christians, who came as near as possible in order to receive their blessing. It was but a short distance to the hill on the outskirts of Nagasaki where the martyrs of 1597 had given up their lives. Here a large space had been enclosed. Inside the paling had been set twenty-five stakes for those that were to be burned. Instead of having the wood placed as near as was usually done, it was put in two long rows seven or eight feet distant from the line of stakes, the object being to prolong the sufferings of the victims. Within the enclosure was also erected a stand for the use of the Governor's deputy and other high officials of Nagasaki and Omura. Thousands of spectators crowded about the fences or stood on the neighboring hills. It had been Gonroku's desire to have the Christians present so that the sufferings of their teachers and fellow-believers might be a warning to them.

The martyrs from Omura had to wait an hour for the arrival of those that came from Nagasaki. While still mounted upon their horses, they confessed one another, sang hymns, and addressed the people that were within hearing. Special mention is made of the discourse of Spinola to the Spaniards and Portuguese. When at last the thirty-three prisoners from Nagasaki arrived, those condemned to be burned were brought to the stakes. Among them was one woman, aged eighty, who had given shelter to a missionary. Those decapitated included several women and children. As before, the severed heads were placed in front of those that were bound to the stakes. Father Spinola chanted the "*Laudate Dominum, omnes gentes*," the other Fathers and Brothers responding, while the children, who were in the crowd outside the enclosure, also joined in the singing. Spinola then addressed a few words to the Governor's deputy. After the fires were lighted, he and the other martyrs continued to speak to the people so long as it was possible for them to do so. Some remained alive for two or three hours. When the flames burned too briskly, the executioners partially quenched them by throwing on water so that death might not too quickly put an end to the agony of the martyrs.

Three Japanese Brothers, belonging to the order of the Jesuits, "disturbed the joy of that day." Almost as soon as they felt the heat of the flames, they began by their contortions and struggles to show how weak they were. Their associates tried in vain to inspire them with courage. At last they broke their bonds, and rushing out from the midst of the flames, begged for mercy. Two of them called upon the name of Buddha, while the third, as though ashamed of his cowardice, returned at once to his stake. Some say that he left it only to remonstrate with the others. None, however, were spared; the executioners thrust the cravens back into the fire and held them there by long poles.

For three days the remains of the martyrs were carefully guarded so that they might not be taken as relics by the Christians, who came in crowds to the outside of the enclosure that they might venerate those who had died for the faith. Finally, the charred remains, the heads and bodies of those that had been decapitated, and the various religious objects that had been found in the houses of those arrested, were thrown with wood and charcoal into pits, where they were burned for two days. The ashes and even the ground that had been soaked with blood were then put into straw sacks and carried out to sea. The sailors, before returning to shore, were made to bathe themselves and to give their boats a thorough washing, so that none of the polluted dust should be brought back to land.

Other executions soon followed at Nagasaki, Omura, Hirado, and other places. The number of those burned or beheaded in 1622 was over one hundred and twenty, including sixteen Fathers and twenty Brothers of the different orders.

Alas! how often does the weakness of men stand out in contrast with their displays of strength. It seems strange to read that at the time when community of suffering ought to have united the hearts of all the missionaries, there was a new display of the dissensions between the societies. September 7, an apostolic inquest, relative to the martyrs of 1597, was opened in Nagasaki. Of the three judges originally appointed, one had gone to Manila, another was among those to be martyred three days later, and the third was Father Collado, the Vicar Provincial of the Dominicans. The places of the first two were supplied by others, and the proceedings, after the interruption caused by the Great Martyrdom, were re-

sumed September 14. Pagés says that many of the
witnesses that had been summoned declined to appear,
those who would have given their life in confession of
their faith not fearing the excommunication that might be
incurred by their disobedience. Apparently these were
the Jesuits, who refused to acknowledge any authority
save that of the Prelate of their Society appointed by the
Metropolitan of the Indies, and who disregarded the
legitimate Bishop, Mgr. Valens, himself a Jesuit, who
was then in Macao. Probably their disinclination to witness was in part because, so far as Europeans were concerned, the glory of the martyrdom belonged to members
of other orders. Some of the meetings of the inquest
were held on board a vessel that was lying in the harbour.
Collado, who took the documents to Rome, also carried
many accusations against the Jesuit missionaries. He
was ably seconded by a letter alleged to have been written
by Father Sotelo, who had finally succeeded in reaching
Japan, where he arrived just after the martyrdom of
Zuñiga and Flores. He had been immediately arrested.
Having been granted his request to be brought before the
Governor of Nagasaki, he said: "I am Father Louis
Sotelo, the same who went to Spain as an ambassador of
Date Masamune. I have now returned with the replies
to his letters. As no shipmaster would give a priest
passage, I assumed a secular dress. Will you kindly announce to the Shogun's Council that I have returned. If
it condemns me to death, I am prepared to submit for the
sake of the religion of Jesus Christ, which I have always
desired to preach in this country." The Governor
promised to send the desired message, but kept Sotelo
confined in the prison at Omura. It is from there that a
letter, which has given rise to much controversy, is said
to have been written by him in 1624. Charlevoix regards it as a forgery. Pagés thinks it is genuine, but
suggests that it may have been somewhat changed when
printed by enemies of the Jesuits.* It charges the latter
with intriguing against Sotelo, with causing scandal by
their evil acts and pernicious doctrines, with annoying

---

*The letter is given by Pagés, vol. ii., p. 137.

the members of other orders, and with being the cause of various evils that hindered the progress of Christianity. Father Cevicos published a reply to this letter and the controversy gave rise to much ill-feeling.

In 1623, Hidetada, following the example set by Ieyasu, had the title of Shogun transferred to his son Iemitsu. The investiture of the new Shogun was made the occasion for re-publishing the laws against Christianity. In that same year between four and five hundred persons were put to death in the immediate possessions of the Tokugawa family. On December 4, a company of fifty persons, including two foreign priests, was led out to a hill near Yedo, where preparation had been made for their execution by burning. One of the number had apostatised while in prison, and though he was led out with the others and bound to the stake, he was set free before the fagots were lighted. It is said that his place was supplied in a way that made a great impression upon all the spectators. After the preparations had been completed, a gentleman of high rank, accompanied by a retinue of servants, came riding up towards the judges. The guards made way for him, supposing that he was the bearer of an official message. Descending from his horse, he went before the chief judge and asked why these men were being put to death in such a cruel way.

"Because they are Christians," was the answer.

"I, too, am a Christian," said the man, "and I demand the privilege of sharing their fate."

The officials were in doubt as to what they ought to do. Finally the Shogun, to whom word was sent, ordered that the man should be added to the number of martyrs. When he was bound to the stake, five of his servants tried to follow him, while from among the spectators, three hundred other persons came to kneel before the judges asking that they, too, be allowed to give up their lives for the sake of Christ. The judges drove them away, and fearing a tumult, hastened to complete the execution. The remains of the victims were left under guard on the place of martyrdom. The third day the

Christians gathered in a crowd and took away whatever they could find. This angered Hidetada, who ordered that all the Christians who could be found should be put to death. Twenty-seven persons were executed. December 29. Thirteen of the number were not Christians, but had received believers into their houses, or as neighbours were held responsible. Eighteen of the victims were children. These had their brains beaten out, were cut in twain, or were otherwise killed in the sight of their parents, before the latter were put to death.

Orders were issued in 1623 and 1624 against the Spaniards in general. All of them were to be sent out of the country. They were forbidden to take with them any Japanese, even their own wives. Moreover, no Japanese Christian was to go abroad for trade, while even unbelievers were not to go to the Philippines, it being feared that they would bring back Christian teachers in their ships. This put an end to all commerce with Manila. In 1622 Hidetada had refused to receive an embassy from the Philippines. A second one that came in 1623, although it was able to report that the Spanish Governor had issued orders forbidding missionaries to go to Japan, and that the Archbishop of Manila had been induced to use his authority to the same end, was sent back with the reply that the Shogun could not consider the embassy as anything more than a device of the missionaries, and that he could never receive the envoys of a country that followed a religion so false and pernicious that he had been compelled to issue a prohibition against it and to exile its teachers. It was added that at first the Spaniards had been welcomed because they came in the name of commerce; but instead of bringing any advantage to the country, they had polluted it with their diabolical religion. While in the harbour of Nagasaki the embassy was closely guarded and subjected to many humiliations. The reason why the prohibitions against the Philippines were more strict than those against Macao, may have been because nine Dominicans, Franciscans, and Augustinians came from the former place in 1623, notwithstanding the Governor's and Archbishop's interdiction of such enterprises. The truth was, whether the Japanese knew it or not, that these dignitaries had yielded to the entreaties of the heads of the three orders in the Philippines "under the condition that the departure should take place in the greatest secrecy." In Macao, the officials were more earnest to keep their commerce from being ruined by the zeal of the missionaries, and this was so well recognised that many Fathers went from there to the Philippines, where they thought the chances for reaching Japan were better.

Further orders of the Shogun declared that any foreign ship coming to Japan must register the names of its crew and passengers. The officers of the ship were to be held responsible for all persons on board. Not only missionaries, but also those that brought them to Japan, were to be burned; the ship and its merchandise to be confiscated.

Date Masamune now began to take a prominent place among the persecuting daimyos. His subordinates were told to make out a list of the Christians. Many of these were imprisoned and some were put to death. Among those arrested was Father Diego de Carvalho, a Jesuit. In February, 1624, he and his companions were led to the bank of a river, stripped of their clothing, and bound to stakes that were placed in a pool of icy-cold water. They were kept there for three hours and then left to sit or lie upon the frozen ground. Two of the Christians soon died, and their bodies, after being cut into small pieces, were thrown into the river. The others were taken back to prison, only to be led forth four days later to the same pool. They were made alternately to stand in the water, which reached to their knees, and to kneel down in it. A cold wind was blowing and ere long a snowstorm set in. As evening approached, the surface of the pool began to freeze over. One by one the sufferers became insensible. Father Carvalho was the last to die. Their bodies were treated as those of their companions had been, though the Christians managed to get possession of the heads of five of the martyrs, including that of Father Carvalho.

In that section of the country known as Dewa, in the

northwestern part of Hondo, one hundred and nine Christians were put to death. Other parts of the country added to the number of the martyrs. Three foreign priests who had been confined in Omura were burned at the stake in August, 1624. One of them was Sotelo, Date's former ambassador.

In 1625 there were still in Japan twenty Jesuit Fathers and four Brothers, besides some members of other orders. Nagasaki was regarded as the safest place in the country. Two of the four Sub-prefects were Christians, as were many of the citizens. There were, however, many defections, and those that remained faithful were subjected to much annoyance. Hasegawa Gonroku ordered that none of the Christians should be allowed to travel by land or sea more than a league from the city. It is evident that this must have caused much hardship to those engaged in trade. When foreign ships came, the citizens were to have no direct communication with them. The persons and goods of all strangers entering the city were to be searched so as to make sure that no Christian books, rosaries, or medals were brought. Portuguese merchants were permitted to lodge only in the houses of non-Christians.

The next year (1626) Hasegawa was replaced by Mizuno Kawachi no Kami. While the former had taken little pleasure in the persecutions that his office compelled him to superintend, his successor was a bitter opponent of Christianity. Almost immediately after his arrival, three foreign priests and six Japanese Christians were burned. Thirteen stakes had been erected, but at the last moment four Portuguese who had been arrested purchased their lives by the denial of their faith. A few days afterwards nine Japanese, who had given the missionaries shelter, were executed.

Near the close of 1626, when Portuguese and Chinese ships came as usual to Nagasaki, the Christians were not allowed to lodge the merchants, to trade with them, to become their servants, or even to converse with them. The Portuguese merchants themselves were treated with much insolence. Their chests were searched, their papers read, and their religious medals thrown into the sea. Two vessels that came from the Philippines were immediately turned back.

Mizuno, who held his office for three years, did his best in that time to exterminate the religion he so hated. Christian artisans were not permitted to ply their trades. Many new forms of torture were introduced. In this, however, Mizuno's powers of invention were not equal to those of Matsukura, the new Lord of Arima. In the latter's territories Christians were made to kneel on hot coals, were suspended by different parts of the body to trees, were branded on cheeks and forehead with the three ideographs that were pronounced *Kirishitan* (Christian), or were plunged into the sea until nearly drowned, when they were drawn out only to have the operation repeated at short intervals. But what was regarded as the most terrible of all torments was to plunge the victim again and again into the sulphur springs of Onsen, whose corrosive waters gave rise to horrible sores. The frightful sounds, the heat, the sulphurous vapours, and the dismal surroundings of these springs have led to their being named " Jigoku," the Buddhist word for Hell. One spring has a temperature of over 200° Fahr.

The missionaries that were in hiding suffered many privations. A letter written in 1626 by Father Couros, says:

" The Christians that had me under their care lost courage and earnestly urged me to take ship at once and hasten to secure my safety. In order to calm them I promised to depart the following night. Meanwhile my host, unknown to the others, had arranged a pit or subterranean cavity twelve palms long by four broad. Neither the rays of the sun nor any other light entered it. That night I, together with my catechist and a servant, crept into it without the knowledge of any person except our host. The nights and days passed by in darkness. The only light I obtained was a little for eating, for reciting the divine office, and for writing certain letters connected with my ministry. Food was passed to us through a concealed opening that was reached by pulling away the straw in an adjoining hut where an old man was at work, and this was opened only for so long a time as was necessary for introducing the food. Every three days the door of the pit was opened for the removal of ordure. The food was very scanty and very poor, for our host feared to make purchases lest he should excite suspicion. I remained thirty-five days in this dungeon, going out only on Holy Saturday, Easter, and the days of the octave, in order to celebrate mass. Afterwards I moved to another pit of the same size that my host's charity had prepared for me. I am still there at this time, namely, the last of September. I have with me the necessary outfit for celebrating mass. Above the pit is a shed where my host keeps his tools. Here there is a small door covered with straw and heaps of matting in such a way as to avert suspicion. I go out at night, arrange my altar, and say mass. Before daybreak I return to the pit with the vestments and other sacred objects." *

A Franciscan missionary arrested in 1627 was unable to destroy a paper that contained a list of the members of his order who remained in Japan. This was forwarded to the Shogun and became the occasion for his ordering a more stringent enforcement of the laws. Mizuno was replaced by Takenaka Uneme, whose reputation for cruelty was so great that many of the Christians, on hearing of the appointment, hastened to escape from Nagasaki before he should arrive. His acts did not belie his reputation. The chronicles of the next few years are largely occupied with details of the methods taken by him and others to exterminate Christianity. The stories of suffering are so terrible that modern readers will prefer to be spared the details of what was endured by those subjected to torture. Very many persons who had been numbered among the believers were unable to stand the test, and promised to give up Christianity. Ere we condemn their weakness, let us think how hard it is for us to endure some comparatively trifling pain, and ask whether we could bear up under the most excruciating tortures that human ingenuity could invent. Let us remember, too, that many of the sufferers had for years been shut off from their religious teachers, that some of them were new converts, and that behind none of them was that kind of strength and training that comes to those whose ancestors for generations have known the Christian religion. Yes, thousands did fall away; but there were others whose faithfulness unto death proved their sincerity and has won for them the admiration of all Christendom.

* Pagés, vol. ii., p. 331.

The missionaries by their words and example helped to sustain the constancy of the believers and even inspired in many a desire for martyrdom like that seen in the early church when Rome tried to crush out Christianity. Of what avail were threats uttered against those that longed to die for their Lord, believing that the more severe the tortures they endured the greater reason was there to rejoice in thought of the reward that awaited them?

The first arrests made by Takenaka were those of thirty-seven men and twenty-seven women, whom he sent to Onsen with directions that they were not to be put to death, but to be tortured until they apostatised, even though years might be required to bring this about. By day and night the corrosive water was poured at intervals upon their bodies. This plan was so successful that sixty of the sufferers yielded. To avoid the inconvenience of sending other persons to so distant a place as Onsen, artificial baths, which proved as efficient as the natural springs, were about this time made in the suburbs of Nagasaki. Takenaka was not satisfied with persecuting the living. Saying that he could not tolerate even dead Christians, he caused their bodies to be dug up from the cemeteries and burned.

After a few months there was a lull in the persecution as though all had been done that the Shogun had ordered. It was afterwards thought that Takenaka's purpose was to make the missionaries less cautious so that he might discover where they were. However this may have been, he was soon able to secure the arrest of three and also of a Japanese Jesuit Father, Ichida Pinto. These were confined in the Omura jail and active persecution was resumed.

The Christians in other parts of Japan were suffering in much the same ways as their brethren in Nagasaki. The missionaries that remained in the country were obliged to keep closely concealed. Not much information concerning their movements has been preserved, as it was difficult for them to send letters. The little knowledge we have of this period is chiefly concerning the sufferings to which the Christians were subjected. The list of martyrs constantly grew longer. How many lost their lives in these persecutions cannot be known.   Many authors have written as though the martyrs were to be reckoned by tens of thousands or even by hundreds of thousands. One writer has given the number as over two millions. Father Cardim's Catalogue, printed in 1646, gives the names of the martyrs from 1557 to 1640; and Murdoch, after carefully checking the list, says that, apart from those perishing in the Shimabara Revolt and those put to death in connection with the Portuguese embassy of 1640, Cardim records only 1420 victims.   Father Steichen in " The Christian Daimyo " reckons that, allowing for omissions and adding those suffering after 1640, the whole number of martyrs may have been about 2000. It may be questioned, however, whether there may not have been many more who lost their lives on account of their faith.   Little account was made in those days of the common people, and such officials as were bitterly opposed to Christianity would not hesitate to brush aside its followers in the humble ranks of life.   Moreover, outside of the persons officially executed, there would be many deaths indirectly caused by the privations of those that were driven from their homes, who were as truly martyrs as if they had perished at the stake or by the sword.

Takenaka, as we have seen, was ready to have a long time spent in securing apostasy.   It would have been particularly pleasing to him if some of the foreign missionaries could have been induced to renounce their faith. Those arrested in 1629 were kept for two years in the jail at Omura.*   In December, 1631, they were taken

* Possibly this delay of two years before taking more vigorous measures against the prisoners was owing in part to negotiations that Takenaka had begun with the Philippines.   Both he and Matsukura had sent envoys to consult about the renewal of commerce.   The Spanish Governor suspected that the real purpose was to spy out the land before making an attack upon it.   Though he received the visitors with a great show of cordiality, he took care to show them the forts, arsenals, and troops, so as to impress them with the military power of the colony.   His suspicions were not unreasonable, for, though he probably did not know it, Matsukura had shortly before this sent a memorial to Yedo asking that he be allowed to invade the Philippines.

to Onsen, together with a Spanish Brother and two
women of mixed Portuguese and Japanese blood.   All
remained firm and were brought to the prison in Nagasaki.   The women were sent to Macao and the men were
burned at the stake in September, 1632.

Hidetada died in 1632.   His son, Iemitsu, carried out
to its completion the policy his father had adopted concerning the Christians.   Under his rule the land was
finally rid of the foreign missionaries and most of their
native helpers.   Thirty-three Jesuits, six Dominicans,
two Franciscans, and two secular priests were put to
death.   In the first year of his rule (1632) the number
of missionaries had been increased by the arrival of
eleven.   One of these was Father Sebastian Vieyra, who
had been appointed Vice-Provincial of the Jesuits and
the deputy of the Bishop.   The latter still remained in
Macao, his failure ever to come to Japan being the cause
of much adverse criticism.   The account of Vieyra's
voyage will serve as an example to show how much some
of the missionaries were willing to endure in order to
reach a land where they knew that almost certain death
awaited them.

Vieyra, who had formerly spent several years in Japan,
had been sent in 1623 to Macao, and from there to Rome,
that he might plead the cause of the Jesuits against their
accusers and create a deeper interest in their work.
Desiring to return to Japan, he went to Manila, where,
by paying an enormous price, he hired a Chinese captain
to give him passage.   Disguised in Chinese costume, he
went on board the junk to find that, instead of being
allowed to remain in what might by courtesy be called
the cabin, he was forced to conceal himself in the hold,
where there was not sufficient light for reading, and the
air was made almost unbearable by the stench of deer-
skins that formed a large part of the cargo.   He remained ten days shut up in this place.   Then he learned
that, contrary to the agreement made with the captain,
there were a Dominican and two Franciscan missionaries
on board.   There were also eleven Japanese from Arima,
who had interest in the cargo.   When the sailors discovered that there were missionaries on the ship, they

wished to return to the Philippines, or to leave on some island the passengers whose presence might be a source of danger to all. The Japanese merchants also desired this, though when Vieyra, recognising in the most hostile of them a man whom he had formerly known and whose confessor he had been, called him by name and reminded him of their former relations, the whole eleven, all of whom were apostate Christians, respectfully saluted the Father and showed a more favourable disposition. Notwithstanding this change, the missionaries would probably have been set ashore on Formosa had not a severe tempest driven them past that island. There are few things like a storm at sea for making men mindful of religious duties, and the frightened apostates, as well as many of the crew, confessed their sins to the priests and sought pardon, promising that if their lives were spared they would take the missionaries to Japan. Both Japanese and Chinese signed a written agreement not to give information against them. As the vessel neared the Goto Islands, the Fathers were concealed in various places so that they might not be discovered by the officials. Vieyra was hidden in a water-tank where he almost died for want of air. The others suffered in similar ways, but felt repaid by their success in getting into Japan undiscovered.

The next year Vieyra was captured, and after spending some time in the prison at Omura, was sent by the Shogun's orders to Yedo. There he was closely questioned by the officials. One of his letters says that they, and a large number of the people who gathered to see him, expressed their conviction that the doctrines as he explained them were true, but the Shogun's dislike of Christianity prevented them from becoming its adherents. Vieyra was asked to write out a synopsis of his belief. He spent nearly fourteen hours in preparing this statement, which was sent to the Shogun. June 6, 1634, he and Father Gomez, with several Japanese, were sent to the *fosse,* as French writers have denominated a form of torture that had recently been invented. By the side of a pit about six feet deep was erected a post with a projecting arm from which the victim was suspended head downwards after he had been bound with cords in such a way as to retard the circulation of the blood. He was lowered into the pit, whose air was sometimes made stiflingly offensive by the presence of offal. In some cases the sufferer was tied up in a sack, one hand being left outside, so that it might be used in making a sign of recantation. After a person had hung for a short time, blood would begin to ooze from his mouth, nose, and ears. It was customary to bleed the temples, so as to prevent too great congestion. It is said that death would not come for two or three days, and in some cases might be delayed for six days. Father Vieyra was alive at the end of three days, though his companions were all dead. The impatience of the executioners to be done with the affair then led them to commit him to the flames.

Less happy was Father Ferreyra, a Jesuit, who the previous year (1633) was sent to the *fosse* in Nagasaki with three other Europeans and four Japanese. Among them was Father Julian Nakaura, one of the four Japanese who went to Rome in the embassy of 1582. All the sufferers remained faithful to the end except Ferreyra, who, after five hours, yielded to the terrible torture and made the sign that showed his readiness to renounce Christianity. Great was the joy of Takenaka. At last he had gained the desired victory over one of the foreign teachers of the hated religion. To the Jesuits this was a sad blow, and it doubtless had much influence, as Takenaka had hoped, in making it easier to secure the apostasy of Japanese Christians. The Roman Catholic historians state that twenty years later Ferreyra repented of his weakness, openly professed his belief in Christianity, and at the age of seventy-four endured, without faltering, the torments of the *fosse* from which he had once shrunk. The proofs of this statement, however, are not so strong as could be desired.

In June, 1635, new orders were sent to all the daimyos that they should completely extirpate Christianity from their domains. Directions a year later to the Governors of Nagasaki included among other specifications the following:

"The sending of Japanese ships to foreign countries is strictly forbidden."

"Japanese must not be sent to other countries. If any try to go secretly, they shall be punished by death, while the ship and crew must be kept in custody, and the matter reported."

"If any Japanese who has resided abroad returns to Japan, he shall be punished by death."

"Rewards to those informing against Christians shall be as follows:—For religious teachers, three hundred or two hundred pieces of silver according to their rank. In other cases, as previously provided."

"Foreigners who propagate the religion of the Fathers, and likewise persons of evil reputation, shall as before be sent to prison in Omura."

"Descendants of the Portuguese* must not be allowed to remain in the country. Any who retain them contrary to the law shall be put to death, and their relatives shall be punished according to the degree of the offence."

The next year the Japanese prepared a small artificial island that was connected with Nagasaki by a bridge. To the narrow limits of this island, which was called Deshima, the Portuguese merchants that came from Macao were confined during their stay in Japan. Kaempfer tells us that by his own measuring he "found the breadth of the island to be of eighty-two common paces, and the main length of two hundred and thirty-six."

The last two survivors of the Dominicans in Japan had been martyred in 1634. The members of the order in the Philippines were earnest in the desire to resume the work for which their brethren had given up their lives. In 1636 four Fathers, one of whom was a Japanese, were selected to make the attempt. The Governor of Manila, on receiving information that a ship had been prepared to take them to Loochoo, had the vessel burned. A second was procured and despatched without attracting the attention of the sentinels that had been put along the coast to guard against such attempts. The Fathers, ac-

* The "Nagasaki Sambyakunen-kan," from which I take these directions, says "Descendants of the Fathers" (*Bateren no shison*), but as afterwards it speaks of two hundred and eighty-seven children of the Portuguese who were sent to Macao, we may suppose that there has been a mistake in copying.

companied by two secular priests, one a Japanese and the other of mixed Spanish and Chinese parentage, reached Loochoo in safety, and after remaining there about a year, were sent as prisoners to Nagasaki, where they were executed. The next year Father Mastrilli, a Jesuit who had managed to enter Japan, met with the same fate.

We now come to what has been known by the Japanese as the "Christian Rebellion." It has also been named the "Shimabara Revolt" from the place where its principal events occurred. Though it may be doubted whether religious considerations held the chief place in causing this outbreak, many of the leaders were Christians, and, as the movement went on, it became more closely associated with Christianity, so that its suppression gave what at the time seemed the death-blow to that religion in Japan.

The peninsula of Shimabara formed a part of the daimiate of Arima, which has held so important a place in our history. It will be remembered that under its Christian daimyos the Buddhist temples were destroyed, many churches were erected, and most of the inhabitants professed the new faith. For a long time Arima was a stronghold of Christianity, and in its schools were educated not only those that became evangelists but also those who painted the pictures, carved the images, and made the various utensils used in the churches.

The apostasy of a later daimyo was followed by that of many of his subjects. Others stood unmoved, and even among those that conformed to the new order of things there must have been many who sympathised with the Christians. When persecutions broke out in different parts of Japan, Nagasaki was for a long time the asylum where believers sought shelter; and when that city became dangerous, the proximity of Arima, together with the fact that a large proportion of its inhabitants was ready to give them succour, caused it to be chosen as a refuge.

Near the peninsula of Shimabara was the island of Amakusa. This, which had at one time been another stronghold of Christianity, was now under the rule of Terasawa, the son of the man by the same name whose defection from Christianity has been previously recorded. He also held Karatsu, in the northern part of Kyushu, and made it his chief residence. The elder Terasawa, who died in 1633, had, after his own defection from Christianity, dealt for the most part leniently with his believing subjects, but in 1629 he had sent to Amakusa as his lieutenant another apostate, with orders to suppress the Christian religion. Among the inhabitants of the island were some of the former retainers of Konishi, who, under the persecutions instituted after the fall of their lord, had left their old homes rather than give up their faith.

The insurrection is often described as an uprising of "farmers." It needs to be remembered, however, that the distinction between the agricultural and the military classes was not then so marked as it afterwards became, and also that some of these farmers were men who had once fought under Konishi and other generals in Korea, but who, having lost employment because of the misfortunes of their lords or on account of their own faith, had been forced to earn a living by the labour of their hands. Such persons would not entirely lose the martial spirit, and, though age had now enfeebled their powers, it is probable that they had taught their children how to use military arms. The number of those in Arima who had formerly been warriors was increased by the fact that when, in 1614, the apostate daimyo was removed to Hyuga, very few of his retainers cared to follow him, even though the failure to do so involved the loss of the revenues they had once enjoyed. On the other hand, three years later, when Matsukura Shigemasu came to take possession of the fief, he, according to the usual custom, brought his vassals with him and so had no occasion to employ those left by his predecessor. Koeckebacker, the Superintendent of the Dutch trading factory at Hirado, wrote of these things as follows:

"The servants of the departed prince were then deprived of their income and obliged by poverty to become farmers in order to procure for their wives and children the necessaries of life. Although thus becoming peasants in name, they were in reality soldiers well acquainted with the use of weapons. The newly arrived Lord, not content herewith, imposed upon them and upon the other farmers more taxes and forced them to raise such a quantity of rice as was impossible for them to do. Those who could not pay the fixed taxes were dressed by his order in a rough straw coat made of a kind of grass with large and broad leaves and called *mino* by the Japanese, such as is used by boatmen and other peasantry as a rain-coat. These mantles were tied round the neck and body, the hands being tightly bound behind their backs with ropes, after which the straw coats were set on fire. They not only received burns, but some were burnt to death; others killed themselves by bumping violently against the ground or drowning themselves. This tragedy is called the 'Mino dance.' This revengeful tyrant, not content with his cruelty, ordered women to be suspended quite naked by the legs, and caused them to be scoffed at in various other ways."

The new Lord of Arima exhibited like cruelty towards those whose only offence was a belief in Christianity. He soon gained the reputation of being the most successful extorter of recantations that Japan had yet seen. His son, Matsukura Shigetsugu, who succeeded him in 1630, imitated his father's virulence against the Christians, but was not so skilful a ruler. He was dissolute and luxurious, so that he exacted from the people heavier taxes than had before been known. It is said that even his own soldiers were so financially burdened that they had to engage in menial labour in order to provide themselves with the necessities of life. Koecke-backer in the letter already quoted said:

" As the present Lord, who resides in Yedo, feels also inclined to follow in the footsteps of his father and forces the farmers to pay more taxes than they are able to do, in such a manner that they languish from hunger, taking only some roots and vegetables for nourishment, the people resolved not to bear any longer the vexations, and to die one single death instead of the many slow deaths to which they were subjected. Some of the principal amongst them have killed with their own hands their wives and children in order not to view any longer the disdain and infamy to which their relatives were subjected."

Evidently everything was ready for revolt if leaders could be found. There is said to have been preserved among the Christians the following prophecy left by one of the missionaries who had been driven from Amakusa about 1612.

" When five times five years have passed, a remarkable youth will appear. Without study he shall of himself know all things, and he shall be famous throughout the land. Then shall the clouds of the east and west shine with a ruddy glow, wistaria flowers shall blossom from the trunks of dead trees. Multitudes shall bear the cross on their helmets, white flags shall float over sea and river, mountain and plain. Then shall come the time for Jesus to be honoured."

In 1637, strange appearances in the sky and unusual blossoms in the gardens seemed to coincide with the signs foretold by this prophecy. Neither was there lacking a person that was thought to answer to the description of the promised deliverer. His name was Masuda Shiro, the son of one of the Christian warriors that had left the province of Higo at the time of the persecution under Kato Kiyomasa. The boy had been brought up in Nagasaki, and it is probable that what he learned there from the missionaries and other foreigners enabled him to astonish the people of Amakusa by a display of wisdom. It was asserted that he could walk upon the sea, make birds fly down from the sky to light on his hand, cause stags to issue from a sea-shell, and perform many other miracles.

Five of the former retainers of Konishi are mentioned as leaders of the movement in Amakusa. They began by holding meetings in which they spoke to the peasants concerning this young man who had come to inaugurate a movement that would result in the firm establishment of Christianity in Japan, China, and India. They promised that those who became his first followers would be given high honour and office in the new kingdom soon to be set up, while all who opposed him would miserably perish.

In the months of November and December, 1637, the agitation gradually assumed a more violent character. In several villages the peasants attacked the public granaries and took possession of the rice that had been collected by the tax-gatherers. By the end of the year five or six thousand men were in arms, the larger part of them besieging the castle of Tomeoka. Terasawa's lieutenant, Miyake Tobei, who had received early warning of the danger, sent to Kusatsu asking for reinforcements. Fifteen hundred men, who attempted to come to his aid, were intercepted by the insurgents and defeated in three successive engagements. A portion of them, however, managed to enter the castle, where they also succeeded in repelling an assault made January 7, 1638, by the insurgents.

In this assault the rebels of Amakusa were assisted by some from Shimabara, for Shiro and his advisers had extended their agitation to that peninsula. News that the peasants were holding meetings reached the officials, who surprised a company of farmers and arrested two of their leaders. As it was supposed that these last would be immediately put to death, their associates came together to perform funeral rites. When an officer attempted to interfere with them, he was torn to pieces by the angry people. This was on the eleventh of December. Word of what had happened was at once sent to other villages. In these, too, the people arose, killing officers and destroying temples. On the twelfth of December, a part of the city of Shimabara was burned, and the insurgents then laid siege to its castle.

When intelligence of these events reached the central government, there was great fear lest the insurrction might become general throughout the land. The Shogun's brother was sent to Sendai that he might be on the watch for any indications of trouble in that region. Other officials were sent to Nagasaki, while Itakura Shigemasa was ordered to put down the insurrection in Amakusa and Shimabara by the help of troops collected from neighbouring daimiates.

As there was little reason to hope that in the absence of artillery the castles of Tomeoka and Shimabara could be taken, Masuda decided to occupy and repair an old deserted castle at Hara, twenty miles from the city of Shimabara. This was situated on a high bluff whose cliffs on three sides descended for a hundred feet perpendicularly to the sea, while the fourth side was partly protected by a swamp. Two deep moats across the narrow ridge of land that led to the bluff formed an important part of its defence. Japanese accounts of the struggle say that twenty thousand men, together with seventeen thousand women and children, gathered in the castle. Dr. Reiss thinks that the whole number could hardly have reached twenty thousand. He supposes that thirty-seven thousand included all that in Shimabara and Amakusa took part in the uprising. All in the castle worked vigorously at strengthening its defences. The movement was now professedly Christian. On the battlements were placed wooden crosses, while flags were marked with the same symbol. The warriors encouraged one another by shouting out the names of Jesus, Mary, and St. James. A letter that at a later date was shot into the camp of the besiegers said:

" For the sake of our people we have now resorted to this castle. No doubt you will think that we have done this for the sake of seizing lands and acquiring houses; but such is by no means the case. It is simply because, as you know, Christianity is not tolerated as a distinct sect. Frequent prohibitions have been published by the Shogun that have greatly distressed us. Some there are among us that consider the hope of future life as of the highest importance. For these there is no escape. Since they will not change their religion, they incur various kinds of severe punishments, being cruelly subjected to shame and extreme suffering until at last, for their devotion to the Lord of Heaven, they are tortured to death. Others, and among them some men of strong will, have been moved by solicitude for their sensitive bodies and through dread of torture have, while hiding their grief, obeyed the will of the Shogun and recanted. While things were in this state, all the people have been moved in an unaccountable and miraculous manner to unite in an uprising. Should we continue to live as hitherto with these laws unrepealed, we must suffer all sorts of fearful punishments. As our bodies are weak and sensitive to pain, we might be led to sin against the infinite Lord of Heaven, and from solicitude for our brief lives incur the loss of what we most value. These things fill us with unbearable grief. Hence we have taken this action. It is not the result of a corrupt doctrine."

Itakura, who had at his disposal a force of over twenty-six thousand men, made an attack upon the castle. The result was a complete failure. None of the insurgents were slain, while Itakura lost six hundred men. A second assault made on the fourteenth of the month was even more disastrous. Though only ninety of the defenders were injured, the attacking force suffered a loss of about five thousand. As Itakura himself was among the slain, Matsudaira Izu no Kami was sent to take his place. It was now seen that these so-called " farmers " possessed much military skill as well as bravery. To overcome them an army of over one hundred thousand warriors was collected. Matsudaira received orders not to allow a single Christian, whether man, woman, or child, to escape. At the same time he was told not to waste unnecessarily the lives of his own soldiers. He therefore determined that for a while he would make no assault on the castle, but would guard its approaches so as to keep the rebels from escaping or obtaining supplies of food. Artificial hills were constructed from which cannon sent frequent shot into the castle, while other cannon were placed on junks that they might fire upon it from the sea. These last accomplished so little that Koeckebacker, the head of the Dutch factory, was " advised " and afterwards commanded to send ships with heavy artillery for taking part in the bombardment. A few years before this, Koeckebacker had made such engagements with the Japanese that he now thought he could not avoid compliance with these orders. He had already sent six cannon, as well as some powder, and, after managing to hurry off two of his three vessels to Formosa, he went with the other, a ship with twenty guns, to help in the reduction of Hara. In fifteen days the Dutch fired four hundred and twenty-six shot. Though Koeckebacker says that the conditions were such as prevented his guns from accomplishing very much, the Japanese were surprised at the accuracy of aim, and the insurgents were compelled to dig cellars in which to take refuge from the cannon-balls. Suddenly the Dutch were told that they might withdraw, the reason given to Koeckebacker being that Matsudaira had pity for them on account of the inconvenience they were occasioned by having their homeward voyage delayed. A more probable reason is that some of the daimyos considered it derogatory to their honour that the aid of foreigners should be thought necessary for suppressing the revolt of a few farmers. Koeckebacker says that the insurgents had shot a letter into the camp of the besiegers asking why, when there were so many brave soldiers in Japan, they had to seek help from the Hollanders.

The rebels had reason to fear treachery. After Itakura's first attack, one of their number, named Yamada, sent word to the besiegers that he and eight hundred others were not real Christians, but had been compelled by popular opinion to take part in the uprising. He therefore proposed a plan by which the besiegers could gain entrance to the castle, promising that in the resulting confusion he would either assassinate Masuda or deliver him into their hands. This plot was discovered, the family of Yamada was put to death, and he was placed in confinement to await the time when the leaders should inflict upon him such punishment as his treachery deserved. When the castle was finally taken, he was found and set free, he being the only person within the fort whose life was spared.

Matsudaira hoped that as the sufferings of hunger began to be felt by those in the castle, others would be found to desert a cause whose helplessness was every day becoming more evident. Notwithstanding that he had been ordered to slay all the Christians, he had a letter shot into the castle promising to those who would surrender themselves that they should have full pardon, if they were not Christians or if they were willing to recant. The letter fell into the hands of the leaders, who at once sent back a reply, saying that, since all in the castle were ready to die for the sake of God, nothing would induce them to give up their faith or to surrender.

The insurgents sustained their courage by religious

exercises and by songs of faith or defiance. One of the latter has been preserved:

" While powder and shot remain, continue to chase the besieging army that is blown away before us like the drifting sand. Hear the dull thud of the enemy's guns: ' Don! Don!' Our arms give back the reply: ' By the blessing of God the Father, I will cut off your heads!' "

A vigorous sortie failed to obtain the provisions that were so much needed. Evidently there could be but one end to such an unequal conflict. The final assault began at noon, April 11, 1638. The insurgents fought desperately until the last. In the absence of ammunition they used stones, billets of wood, kitchen utensils, anything and everything that could be shot from their rude cannon or otherwise employed as a weapon. It was not until the next morning that the besiegers succeeded in taking the castle. They did their best to carry out the grim order for the destruction of old and young. Only one hundred and nine were taken prisoners and they were put to death a few days later. The bodies of the slain were thrown into the sea, but previously the heads had been severed in order that they might be exposed in Nagasaki as a ghastly spectacle to warn all men of the punishment due to rebels. A journal kept by the Dutch in Hirado says that they numbered seventeen thousand. The insurgents were not the only ones punished for the outbreak. Matsukura, whose tyranny had been one of its causes, was ordered to commit *harakiri*. From Terasawa were taken away parts of his territory and revenues. He soon after became insane and took his own life.

This revolt led the Government to put forth all its efforts for the suppression of Christianity. The feudal lords sought more energetically than before to apprehend any believers that might be in their territories. The news of the extermination of those who had fought at Hara in the names of Christ and Mary so disheartened others who had before been numbered among the

Christians that they had little courage to meet the new trials to which they were exposed. Nearly all who remained in the country made at least a pretence of returning to the old religions.*   Yet from time to time, believers were discovered.   In 1639, Father Pedro Cassoui, a Japanese Jesuit, was put to death in the *fosse;* and Father Porro, an Italian Jesuit, was burned alive with all the inhabitants of the village where he was found.   A Japanese manuscript says that in Nagasaki ten per cent. of the Christians detected were retained in prison to be utilised as witnesses in future trials, ten per cent. were assigned (probably as slaves) to informers, and the rest were executed.

Special officers called *Kirishitan bugyo* were appointed to seek out Christians, and various plans were adopted for the detection of those that concealed their faith.   One of the most effective devices was that known as *efumi* (picture-trampling).   It is not certain when this was introduced.   References to it are found as early as 1658.   Suspected persons were ordered to tread upon a cross or upon a picture of Christ.   Those shrinking from the act of irreverence were recognised as followers of the proscribed religion.   In 1669, a copper tablet with a representation of Christ was substituted in Nagasaki for the picture.   Similar ones were afterwards used in other places.   Thunberg, who came to Japan in 1775, says that once a year in Nagasaki, the inspectors assembled the inhabitants of each ward, calling them by name and making them step on the image. Infant children were brought by their mothers and held

* Some of the Christians escaped to Macao, the Philippines, Siam, and other countries.   About 1666, Japanese who had taken refuge in Siam told of three hundred and seventy of their fellow-believers in Japan who had been put to death the previous year.   They said that, although the absence of priests prevented the reception of the sacraments, the fervour of the Christians was ever on the increase.   The Bishop in Siam asked the Japanese to write to their friends at home, assuring them of his sympathy and of his readiness to admit to holy orders any fit for the priesthood who would come to Siam.   *Relatione delle Missione de Vescovi Vicarii*, Rome, 1677, as quoted in Trans. As. Soc., vol. xiii., p. 209.

in such a way that their feet touched the tablet. Thus they were taught from their earliest days to despise and hate the religion that it symbolised. Four days were occupied in this ceremony, and then the plate was carried to the neighbouring villages. Thunberg denies, as others have done, the assertion that the Dutch merchants were obliged to trample on the picture and that they were willing to do it rather than lose their trade.*

In time the Christians adopted various subterfuges for avoiding the tests or for reconciling their consciences to an outward observance of the ceremonies. It is said that in some places the Christians, after trampling on the picture, would wash their feet and then drink the water, returning thanks that they had been permitted to touch the sacred emblem.

One result of the Shimabara Revolt was that the Portuguese, being suspected of having encouraged it, were forbidden to come any more to Japan. In 1639, orders were given that, if a Portuguese ship should come, it must be destroyed and all persons on board be immediately beheaded. Notice was given to the Dutch and Chinese that their ships would be confiscated if any Christian teachers were found upon them. The Dutch were also ordered to give information if they knew of missionaries being brought by the vessels of any other nation.

The Portuguese merchants of Macao, greatly disturbed at the loss of such a profitable trade, finally decided to send to Japan four of the most honourable men of the colony, who should bear rich presents, declare that the Portuguese had no connection with the revolt, and ask that commerce be renewed. It was recognised that those taking part in this expedition were running great risks. In all the churches of the city special religious services were held in their behalf. The envoys, their attendants, and the sailors received the sacraments before starting.

---

* The 'Nagasaki Sambyakunen-kan" (History of Nagasaki for Three Hundred Years), published in 1902, says the Dutch were required to perform the ceremony and continued to do so until 1856.

No one was permitted on the ship who did not have a certificate showing that he had been to the confessional.

The vessel reached Nagasaki July 16, 1640. The Japanese at once surrounded it with guard-boats; removed rudder, sails, and ammunition; and placed the Portuguese under a guard of soldiers until an answer could be received from the report of the affair that was sent to Yedo. When the answer came, it was as follows:

" The crimes committed for many years by these men while promulgating Christianity in disregard of the Shogun's decrees are very numerous and exceedingly grave. Last year the Shogun forbade under the severest penalties that any one should come from Macao to Japan, and he decreed that, in case any vessel should come in disregard of the prohibition, it should be burned, while all the sailors and passengers, without any exception, should be put to death. All these points have been provided for, drawn up in articles, and published in due form. Nevertheless, by coming in this ship, these men have disregarded the decree and have also greatly prevaricated. Moreover, however much they may assert in words that henceforth they will send no teacher of the Christian religion, it is certain that the letters from Macao do not promise this. Since it is solely because of the Christian religion that the Shogun has rigorously forbidden this navigation, and since in the despatches from the Portuguese city the aforesaid promise is not given, it is proved that the whole embassy is only an out-and-out lie. Consequently all persons coming in the ship have merited death, and none ought to be left to report the catastrophe. It is ordered that the ship be burned and that the chiefs of the embassy with all their attendants be put to death, so that the report of this example may reach even to Macao and Europe, and that the whole world may learn to respect the majesty of the Shogun. Nevertheless, we wish that the lowest persons of the crew shall be spared and sent back to Macao. If by any chance or by accident at sea any ship of the Portuguese should come to Japan, let it be known that, no matter at what port a landing is made, all on board to the very last man shall be put to death."

In accordance with this sentence, the four envoys and fifty-seven other persons were beheaded August 3, 1640. The thirteen whose lives were spared witnessed the execution and also the burning of the ship. The next day they were taken to identify the heads of the slain. Near the places where these were exposed tablets had been erected, on one of which was an account of the embassy and the reason for the execution of those connected with it. The second had this inscription:

" Thus is it that hereafter shall be punished with death all those coming to this Empire from Portugal, whether they be ambassadors or common sailors, and even though it be through mistaking the way or because of a tempest that they come; yea, every such person shall perish, even though he be the King of Portugal, or Buddha, or a Japanese God, or the Christians' God Himself; yea, all shall die." *

The survivors were given an opportunity of going back to Macao on a Dutch ship, but not wishing " to be under obligations to those infidels," they preferred to take passage on a fragile craft that after a perilous voyage reached Macao September 20, 1640.

" The whole city," says Pagés, " received their message with the most admirable sentiments, and rendered solemn thanks to God for having made the ambassadors of earth ambassadors to heaven. The families of the slain occupied the places of honour at the festivals. To the sound of church-bells and artillery, the hymn of glory broke forth on the air and carried to the feet of the Almighty the Christian joy of the people together with their resigned and grateful adoration."

Not yet would the Portuguese give up all hope of resuming trade. In December, 1640, their country, having become independent of Spain, installed a king of its own. The envoy sent from Macao to congratulate him on his accession urged him to send an ambassador to Japan. This was done in 1647. As the two vessels that accompanied him refused to give up rudder and arms, a large force of Japanese gathered to guard

* This is as given by Pagés. A more common version reads somewhat as follows: " So long as the sun warms the earth, let no Christian be so bold as to come to Japan; and let all know that if the King of Spain, or the Christians' God, or the great God of all violate this command, he shall pay for it with his head."

them. The ships were finally permitted to depart without injury, but nothing was accomplished by the embassy.

As the English factory had been discontinued, the Dutch were now the only Europeans remaining in Japan. They did not escape suspicion, notwithstanding their attempts to make it plain that their religion was very different from that of the Spanish and Portuguese. In 1640, they came very near getting into serious trouble through having inscribed the Christian date on a new warehouse they erected in Hirado. It may be, as suggested by Kaempfer, that this edifice, being unusually high and built of stone, was suspected of being made as much for a fortress as for a warehouse. Some of the enemies of the Dutch took this occasion for having an official inspection of the factory, turning over all the goods in hope that some religious wares might be found that would serve as an excuse for making an armed attack upon the merchants. Nothing of the kind was discovered, but orders were given that the warehouse bearing the obnoxious inscription should be torn down. The Dutch director had the good sense to comply, and thus a conflict was avoided. The next year the factory was removed to Nagasaki. The Dutch had long desired to gain entrance to this port, but they soon found that, instead of the comparative freedom they had enjoyed in Hirado, they were to be hardly better than prisoners on the little island of Deshima, almost entirely cut off from communication with the Japanese, and hampered by many annoying regulations. Though these varied from time to time, they were in general for the next two centuries very much the same that are described by such writers as Thunberg, Kaempfer, and Siebold. When a Dutch ship arrived, it had to give over its rudder and armament to the Japanese. A list of all persons on board was required, and frequent inspections were made to see that none were absent. Bibles, prayer books, and other objects having connection with the Christian religion were enclosed in a chest to be put in the care of the Japanese, or else hidden where it would escape their notice. All persons who went on shore

were carefully searched to see that they carried no
contraband goods. At one time the captains of ships
were exempt from such inspection. It is said that they
became noted for their corpulency; cloaks and trousers
being made of such immense proportions that they afforded room for a good-sized cargo to be taken to and
from shore in the three visits that were made each day.
Thunberg says that sometimes the captains went so
heavily loaded that they had to be supported under the
arms by sailors who walked at their side. The commander of the vessel in which he came to Japan had
made due preparation to avail himself of this custom;
but to his disgust he found, on reaching Nagasaki, that
new regulations made this convenient method of smug-
gling impossible. Japanese officials held the keys of the
warehouses at Deshima. The gate leading to the bridge
that connected the island with Nagasaki was closely
guarded. No one could pass it without the Governor's
permission. Once or twice a year the prisoners were allowed to take a walk on shore, and embassies were sent
annually to Yedo. No Japanese (except public women)
were allowed to live in the houses of the foreigners, or
even to visit them. For a long time the Dutch were not
allowed to bury their dead on land, but the bodies were
sunk at sea. Shortly before Kaempfer came in 1690,
this rule was relaxed and a burial place on land granted,
though the ground was kept level so that there was nothing to distinguish the location of the graves. The Hollanders were very careful to make it evident that their
religion was not that of the Spanish and Portuguese.
Kaempfer says that they had " to leave off praying
and singing of psalms in public, entirely to avoid the
sign of the cross, the calling upon Christ in the presence of the natives, and all the outward marks of
Christianity."

The Jesuits in Macao were as desirous as the merchants to re-enter Japan. In 1642, ten of their number
decided that the time had come for making an attempt.
Their leader, Father Anthony Rubin, had been appointed
" Visitor of China and Japan." He resolved to go to

the latter of these countries. When his friends protested against such a dangerous and almost hopeless
undertaking, he replied that the duties of his office left
him no choice, for he ought to visit in person the places
for which he had been made responsible. He felt under
a special obligation to seek out Ferreyra, the Jesuit who
had apostatised and who might perhaps be led to
repentance.

It was decided that those joining in the enterprise
should divide into two bands. The first was composed
of Fathers Rubin, Moralez, Capece, Mecinske, and
Francesco Marquez. They were accompanied by three
persons not belonging to the Society, who volunteered
to share the dangers of the expedition. One of these,
De Souza, was a Portuguese; one named Thomas was
a Korean; while the third, named Juan, was a native of
India. The party set out July 5, 1642. All the priests
were disguised as Chinese. Though the pretended destination of their boat was Formosa, it took its passengers
to a small island belonging to the province of Satsuma.
On landing, they knelt down and kissed the ground. It
was not long before they were discovered and taken to
Nagasaki. When brought before the Governor of the
city, they found that the interpreter was the apostate
priest whose recovery had been one object of their coming. Father Rubin, who acted as spokesman, replied to
all questions and also reproved Ferreyra so severely for
his conduct that the apostate was too much ashamed to
remain in the room. The captives were subjected to
various tortures intended to make them give up their
faith.

Several months of imprisonment and torture did not
avail to shake the steadfastness of these brave men.
Finally, in March, 1643, sentence of death was pronounced against them. They were then placed on horseback, with their hands tied behind them and their mouths
so gagged that they could not speak to one another nor
to the people on the street. On their backs was placed
the inscription, " The Shogun condemns these persons
to death for propagating the Christian religion, which
has long been condemned." Led to the place of execu-

tion, they were subjected to the punishment of the *fosse*. It is said that several days elapsed ere death ended their sufferings.

After the news of this martyrdom reached Macao, the second group of Jesuits set out únder the leadership of Father Peter Marquez, who had been appointed Father Rubin's successor. His companions were Fathers Arroyo, Cassola, and Chiara, besides a Japanese Brother named Vieyra. According to Roman Catholic histories, they first went to Loochoo and thence were taken to Yedo, where three of them were put to death, while the others were remanded to a prison in which they soon after died. Japanese accounts, whose general accuracy is undoubted, tell a far different story. According to these, the Jesuits were arrested in 1643, in Chikuzen, the northeastern province of Kyushu. With them were five Japanese catechists. All were sent to Nagasaki and in the following year to Yedo. The six Japanese soon consented to abandon Christianity. The foreigners also, after being put to torture, recanted, repeated an invocation to Buddha, and signed a declaration that there was no deception in their professed apostasy. They were thereafter kept in a prison that was constructed for them in the mansion of Inoue Chikugo no Kami, who was the chief of a commission for the suppression of Christianity. This prison was beside a steep lane that about that time received the name Kirishitan-zaka (Christian Slope) by which it is still known. One of the priests (Arroyo) after a while retracted his denial of Christianity, and soon after this he died. Peter Marquez died in 1657. Cassola and Chiara married Japanese women. To Chiara were transferred the name and swords of a criminal who had suffered capital punishment. Chiara died in 1685, at the age of eighty-four, and was buried at Muryoin, a temple near Kirishitan-zaka, where is still to be seen his grave-stone, the top of which is shaped like the hat worn by a Jesuit missionary. Vieyra died in 1678, aged seventy-nine, and was buried at the same temple. The Japanese records mention the arrest on an island near Chikuzen of a Sicilian priest, who was induced to apostatise. He was confined in the same place with the others, dying there in 1700.*

Five Dominican friars are said to have set forth in 1647 from Manila in the attempt to get into Japan. Little is known about this enterprise, except that it was unsuccessful.

Some attempts were made to reach the Japanese by way of China. Christian books printed in that country were mingled with others carried by the Chinese merchants. These could be read by well-educated Japanese. In 1687, the Shogun's Government published a list of thirty-eight books whose importation was forbidden. Some of them were simply almanacs, which were objectionable because of casual references to Christianity. It is said that the Chinese also sent porcelain decorated with cryptic designs that could be recognised by the initiated as having Christian significance.

The most daring and romantic attempt to enter the country, so far as we have any record, was that made by Father Sidotti, a native of Palermo. He had, even as a boy, become so deeply interested in the history of the missions to Japan that he determined to carry Christianity again to the land where it had once been so prosperous. While preparing for the priesthood he found some books that enabled him to gain a slight

* The accounts of these missionaries were drawn from Japanese sources by Sir Ernest Satow (Trans. As. Soc., vol. vi., pp. 56-62). The records also mention an Annamite Christian named Jikuan, who was also buried at Muryoin. Further notices of Kirishitan-zaka are contained in a paper by J. M. Dixon in Trans. As. Soc., vol. xvi., p. 207, and in an article in the *Toyo Gakugei Zasshi,* No. 83, reproduced in the *Romaji Zasshi,* Nos. 40 and 41. The latter speaks of a Brother from Canton, named John, who was arrested at the same time as Chiara, was imprisoned with him, and died in 1697 (cf. Satow's paper, p. 58). It also says that in 1675 Chiara was ordered to become a Buddhist but refused to do so; also, that his widow died in 1695.

In *The Month* for May, 1905, Rev. Herbert Thurston, after bringing together the reasons that may be adduced for hoping that the Japanese accounts are incorrect, feels obliged to say: "Reviewing, however, the evidence as a whole, it can hardly be doubted that some sort of renunciation of Christianity was extorted from one or more of the Jesuit missionaries by the extremity of their tortures."

knowledge of the language. Better opportunities for study came during a sojourn that he made in the Philippine Islands, where some shipwrecked sailors from Japan were kindly treated by the colonial government and through the rest of their lives were supported at public expense. They entered the Roman Catholic Church.*

In August, 1708, through the favour of the Governor, who fitted out a ship for Sidotti's use, he left Manila, and after a long and tedious voyage drew near the shores of Kyushu, where, on the night of October 12, he had himself put on shore. The ship at once returned to Manila, leaving Sidotti alone, one man against a nation. He had dressed himself in the garb of a Japanese of the military class, even to the two swords thrust into his girdle.

The next morning a charcoal-burner on the way to his work heard some one calling to him. On turning around he saw a tall man who was talking and making signs. The peasant was unable to understand the stranger's words, but thought the gestures signified a desire for water. After bringing some, he hurried away to tell the villagers about the strange man he had seen. He soon returned with two companions and took Sidotti to his house, there giving him food but refusing to accept the gold that was offered in payment. It was not long before the matter became known to the officials, who sent the stranger to Nagasaki.

Sidotti's study of Japanese had not given him ability to speak intelligibly. None of the official interpreters were able to communicate with him. Recourse was then had to the Dutch traders, among whom was found one who knew a little Latin. Through him Sidotti was questioned concerning his country and his reasons for coming to Japan. After being kept for nearly a year

---

* The "Historia General de Philipinas" tells of another party of shipwrecked Japanese in 1753. They were received by the Franciscans living near the place where they were rescued. The sum needed for their maintenance was drawn from a fund that had been gathered by Sidotti for the relief of suffering Chinese and Japanese.

in Nagasaki, he was sent to Kirishitan-zaka in Yedo. Arai Hakuseki, an officer in the Shogun's Government, has left an interesting account of several interviews that he had with Sidotti. Though the latter's Japanese was a medley of badly pronounced provincialisms, Hakuseki says that he gradually became able to understand what the stranger wished to say.

It was December when Sidotti reached Yedo. He was so thinly dressed that warmer clothing was offered to him, a kindness that he refused to accept because, as he was understood to say, his religion did not allow him to receive gifts from unbelievers. At the close of the first interview he said that it gave him sorrow to think he was causing much trouble to the guards, who remained day and night in the cold prison to prevent his escape.

"Surely, there is no need of this," he said, "for it is not likely that, after voluntarily coming thousands of miles in order to reach Japan, I shall now try to run away. Indeed, where could I go? If an attempt to escape is feared, why cannot you securely chain me every night so that the guards will be free to sleep in comfort?"

The other officials were much moved by this thoughtfulness, but Hakuseki said: "This fellow is a liar. In this respect I am much disappointed in him."

Sidotti understood what was said and warmly remonstrated: "There is no more insulting charge than to call a man a liar. Falsehood is forbidden by my religion. From childhood I have never said what is not true. Why do you accuse me of such a sin?"

"Did you not profess sympathy for the guards, who on your account are compelled to endure the severe cold of these winter nights?"

"I did."

"Therefore did I accuse you of deceit. You profess to have sympathy for the guards, and yet you do not hesitate to cause them great anxiety by your refusal to accept warmer clothing. You pain them by this rejection of their kindness."

"I acknowledge," said the priest, "that I made a

mistake. I will accept the clothes; only, I pray you, let them be of cotton and not of silk."

Hakuseki was evidently greatly impressed by Sidotti's character, and enjoyed having long interviews with him, especially since he was thus able to satisfy his curiosity concerning foreign lands. He presented to the Government a report in which he gave the main points of their conversation. An account of what he learned from Sidotti about foreign customs has been preserved. Among other things it contains an outline of Christian doctrine.

In a memorial that Hakuseki sent to the Government he said: "According to my humble opinion, there are but three ways of dealing with the prisoner. These I shall describe as the best, the intermediate, and the worst. The first and best way is to release him and send him home. The intermediate plan is to imprison him for life. The third and worst of all is to kill him at once." In recommending mercy, he said: "The stranger was born in a country where that odious religion prevails. The education that he received has become a second nature to him, and he cannot be blamed for not discerning that his religion is unreasonable and false. He is not personally blameworthy if, at the command of a superior authority, he left his old mother, sixty-eight years of age, and a brother also well advanced in life, that he might come to this land where he was in danger of being put to death and where he has lived for six years among the perils and distresses that have come upon him. The steadfastness of his determination is to be admired. I cannot but wonder at his resoluteness and the persistency of his purpose. To put him to death under these circumstances would be like shedding innocent blood."

He further asserted that humane hearts could not endure to think of having Sidotti confined for the rest of his life in a narrow prison. If those who sent him should learn that he was alive, they would think the prohibitions against foreigners were being relaxed, and so others would be encouraged to come; and on the other hand, if no information concerning his fate reached them, they would send messengers to inquire about him. Hence, the best plan would be to deport him to the Philippines or to China, with a warning that the laws would be rigorously enforced against any others that ventured to come to Japan.

In disregard of Hakuseki's advice, Sidotti was kept a prisoner. In the house where he was confined lived a man named Chosuke and his wife Haru, both of whom had once been employed as Chiara's servants.* Though they were not believers in the forbidden religion, their employment by such a person was considered a sufficient reason for not permitting them to leave the place. When Sidotti had been four or five years in Yedo, these persons confessed to the officials that through his influence they had been converted and that he had baptised them. They said: "When our former master was alive, he secretly taught us his doctrines; but we did not know that in so doing he was acting contrary to the laws of the land. Now in our old age we have seen how this Roman, in disregard of his own life and for the sake of religion, has come many thousand miles to this land where he has been imprisoned; and, loath as we are to lose the little that remains of life, the knowledge of what a fearful thing it is to fall into hell has led us to receive his instruction and become believers. As it would be opposing the goodness of the Government not to acknowledge these things, we make our confession. Whatever the consequences may be to us, we ask that we may be dealt with according to the law."

The two servants were confined in separate rooms and Sidotti was put in chains. He supposed that they would be executed, and as they were within hearing, he often shouted out, urging them to be faithful unto death. Both Sidotti and Chosuke died in 1715.†

* *Romaji Zasshi,* vol. iii., No. 40. Roman Catholic accounts say they had been servants of an apostate Japanese priest.

† The article in the *Gakugei Zasshi* and the *Romaji Zasshi* has a map showing the situation of the graves of Sidotti and of the servants. Apparently the grave supposed by Griffis ("Mikado's Empire," 1st ed., p. 263) to be Sidotti's was that of Hachibei, who was not a Christian but a robber brought from another place that a *samurai* might test a new sword by decapitating him.

The " Annals of the Propagation of the Faith " (Eng. ed., 1849, p. 215), after speaking of Sidotti says: " Subsequently to this an attempt of the same kind was made and the result is not known." Possibly this notice may refer to four mysterious persons who are said to have appeared in Cochin China about the end of the eighteenth century, saying that they were missionaries to Japan. They asked the Vicar Apostolic to give them some sacred vestments, but insisted on the utmost secrecy. Nothing more is known about them.*

Apparently persecution had attained its object and wholly extirpated the religion against which it was directed. So it seemed to Europeans, save as there remained among Roman Catholics a lingering hope, nourished by one or two incidents hereafter to be noted, that some secret believers in Christianity yet remained; so it seemed to the Japanese, except as now and then suspicion arose against the inhabitants of certain villages whose customs had some strange peculiarities. References to the hated religion were not permitted in books, and its very name might have been almost forgotten were it not written so prominently on the public proclamation-boards of every town. As soon as a child could read, he saw upon the boards that the KIRISHITAN JASHU-MON (Evil Sect of Christianity) was strictly prohibited, and when he asked what this meant, he was told by his parents about the wily scheme of the barbarian nations that sought to gain possession of Japan by means of a religion that was a strange compound of foolish doctrines and powerful magic.

Thus the close of this stage in the history of Christianity in Japan left it as a religion that seemed to have been thoroughly defeated and whose very name was enough to excite the derision and hatred of those that heard it.

* " Pulo-Pinang Compendium of Ecclesiastical History," as quoted in " La Relig. de Jésus Ressus. au Japon," vol. i., p. 77.

VIII

JAPANESE TRADITIONS OF THE EARLY
MISSIONS

IF history is that version of a story which has
been able to gain general acceptance, we shall expect to find that what the Japanese have until recently understood to be the history of Christianity in
their country is far different from that which is narrated in European books. During most of the Tokugawa period, all publications containing references to
the hated religion were prohibited. There lingered
among the people various traditions that were sometimes
recorded in manuscripts intended for private circulation.
The following narrative is compiled from several manuscripts of the eighteenth century, and shows what stories
were current among the people.* Owing to the difficulty of identifying names, and the confused state of
the narratives, it is not easy to connect these accounts
with those derived from the letters of the missionaries.
It may be conjectured that " Urugan and Furaten " were
Fathers Organtin and Froez, who, though not the first
to preach in Kyoto, were among the best known of the
missionaries, and for this reason the traditions may have
gathered about their names. Europeans were known
as Southern Barbarians because they approached Japan
from the south.

In some of the family records of the daimyos and in
other manuscripts the name of Xavier is found, and
there are a few other references to the missionaries;
but so far as these documents have been made public,

* Such manuscripts are not very rare. I have three or four,
and others are now reproduced in print. While they differ in
details, all of this class of writings that I have seen have a
general agreement upon the main points of the narrative.

they add but little to our knowledge of events directly connected with the propagation of Christianity.

THE TEMPLE OF THE SOUTHERN BARBARIANS

One day the King of Southern Barbary said to his council: "I am told that far to the east lies a country called Japan and that it abounds in gold, silver, and precious stones. Why should not that land be subjugated and added to my domains?"

"Furnish me with an army," said one of his generals, "and I promise to conquer it for you."

Another general, however, advised caution. "It would be a great mistake," said he, "to make a direct attack upon Japan. Hitherto there have been many attempts to conquer that country. At one time the Mongols went with a vast fleet and a great force of soldiers; but the guardian gods of Japan sent forth a mighty wind that destroyed the ships, so that only three persons escaped with their lives. In my opinion, the best way to make ourselves masters of the land is by means of our religion. Send thither some wise priests who, by healing the sick, giving alms to the poor, and practising magic, shall win the esteem of the people. When a third of the inhabitants have been gained, we can depend upon their helping the army that should then be sent to occupy the country. The Japanese are too brave warriors to be overcome by force of arms, and so you must be content to adopt slow but sure methods."

"What you say seems reasonable," the King said, "but it would require a person of great sagacity to manage such a delicate business as your plan proposes."

"Twenty-five hundred miles west from here," the general replied, "dwell two learned priests named Urugan and Furaten. If you could only induce them to go to Japan, you might rest assured of success."

The King at once sent messengers to call the priests to his palace. In the interview that followed, Urugan said: "The plan proposed is excellent, but we must move cautiously. You should first send out merchants who, by selling cheaply such goods as are pleasing to the Japanese, will gain their good will. On their second voyage I will go with them. Too much haste would spoil everything."

In accordance with this advice, two ships were despatched to Japan. Three priests accompanied the expedition in order to learn the condition of the country and to prepare the way for Urugan. In 1542, these ships reached Funai. While the merchants were selling their goods at less than cost, the priests quietly taught their religion, special advantages in trade being given to those that became converts.

On the second voyage, Urugan accompanied the merchants. He received from the King the following articles to be used as presents to the ruler of Japan:— a telescope with which a man one hundred and eighty miles distant could be clearly seen, a microscope, two hundred tiger-skins, twenty guns, one hundred pounds of aloes-wood, a number of rosaries, and a mosquito-net that would cover a space twelve feet square and yet would fold into a box measuring two inches each way.

These ships reached Nagasaki in 1568. Whenever Urugan and another priest that came with him walked about the streets, crowds flocked to see the strange-looking foreigners. Reports of them spread far and wide, at last reaching Nobunaga, who had a great desire to meet the strangers. As, however, the western provinces had not submitted to him, he feared that any request to have the priests sent to Kyoto would be refused and thus he would be put to shame. He therefore sent a messenger, who pretended to come from the Shogun with orders to the officials of Nagasaki that the barbarians should be forwarded to Kyoto. The supposed command was obeyed; but just before the priests reached the capital they were met by some of Nobunaga's retainers and taken to a temple near his castle.

Urugan was soon invited to an audience. On a raised platform in the reception room of the castle was seated Nobunaga, while below him were the members of his family and his chief retainers. All looked with curiosity on the strange guest. He was over seven feet high, with a small head, red cheeks, round yellow eyes, high nose, long ears, broad lips, wide mouth, and teeth like those of a horse. His words were unintelligible, but sounded like the cooing of a dove. In reply to the question why he had come to Japan, he said:

"In order that I may preach Buddha's law, and I request that you will give me permission to do so freely."

After honourably entertaining the stranger and promising to take his petition into consideration, Nobunaga allowed him to return to the temple. He then called a council of his retainers, to which were also summoned several Buddhist and Confucian scholars that he might have their advice about allowing the barbarians to teach their doctrines. For a time all were silent. Then a learned Buddhist priest said:

"This barbarian is a mean-looking fellow, who is evidently unworthy to be a religious teacher. When the founder of Buddhism vanquished the demons that opposed him, they took refuge in foreign lands, where they continued to practise their magic arts, and it was probably from them that this man received instruction. Since Japan has already received Buddhism in its completeness, it has no need of this new doctrine, which is doubtless heretical."

After a little reflection, Nobunaga said: "I should like to see what would come from his preaching. Buddhism first came to us from a foreign land; and unless we give these strangers a fair chance, we cannot tell but that their doctrine is valuable. If any evil should appear in connection with their teaching, it will then be easy to prohibit it. I shall allow them to preach."

Not only did Nobunaga grant the request of the foreigners, but he also gave them a piece of land in Kyoto for the erection of a church. When this was built, it received the name Eiroku Temple. The Buddhist priests of Mount Hiei were much enraged that this title, which was that of the current era, had been given to the church. When they urged their abbot to protest, he replied:

"There is something about this new temple that I do not understand. What is taught there is apparently heretical. If we wait a little, the thing will probably come to an end of itself.   At present the military power is so much in the ascendency that even Buddhism and the Imperial Court have to submit to its dictation. Should we make any trouble over the name of the temple, the only result would be to excite Nobunaga's anger. It will be better to let the matter rest for a while."

When the priests, who were displeased at the abbot's timidity, came together for a conference, one of their number said:

" The year after the Emperor Kwammu established his capital at Kyoto [A.D. 794], he ordered this temple to be built in order that it might protect his palace from the evil influences that come from the north-east.   He bestowed upon it the name of his era, a distinction such as no other temple has ever enjoyed.   Once, indeed, a temple in Yamato took the name of the era in which it was built, but the priests of our mountain went thither and smashed the tablet on which the title was inscribed. This act of Nobunaga and the barbarians is an insult to the Emperor and to our temple.   We must bestir ourselves to uphold our honour."

Excited by these words, over a thousand priests put on armour beneath their robes, while others brought forth the sacred cars; and all hastened towards the Imperial Palace to make their complaint.   The Emperor, alarmed at the tumult, summoned his council, who advised that Nobunaga be ordered to have the obnoxious title changed. Henceforth the church was to be known as Nambanji (Temple of the Southern Barbarians).

Nobunaga was very angry at this interference of the priests.   His resentment was increased by the aid they gave his enemies, and reached its height a few years later when one of their number attempted to assassinate him.

" Both Buddhist and Shinto priests," he declared, " have gained so much wealth that they give themselves over to luxury and idleness.   They lay up military stores and sometimes take part in battles.   They ought to be shorn of their power."

In accordance with these words he confiscated the lands of many temples; but his chief vengeance was directed against Mount Hiei, whose priests were massacred and the temples burned.

In response to Urugan's request for more missionaries, Furaten came to Japan accompanied by two Brothers, who were skilful physicians. The Temple of the Southern Barbarians was now in a flourishing condition. It was richly ornamented with gold, silver, and precious stones. Rich banners hung from the ceilings. The fragrance of burning incense filled the air and penetrated to the street. The missionaries sent out men to hunt up beggars, widows, orphans, outcasts, and lepers. All such were brought to the temple, where alms were given to the poor and medicine to the sick. To the multitude thus aided the priests said:

"We came here by order of the King of Southern Barbary, a country a hundred times larger than Japan, whose people, being believers in the true God, never suffer from disease. The land produces many medicinal herbs that are used for the benefit of heathen countries. Because you do not believe in the Lord of Heaven, you have been punished by these diseases, and we will show you how much more terrible things await you in the next world."

So saying, they took from its wrapping a large mirror on which they bade their hearers look. The people saw with terror that they were reflected as having the forms of birds or beasts. It added to their fear when they were told that this proved that after death they would become inmates of the hell of animals. One of the Brothers then said to them:

"The only way to escape such a sad fate is to believe in the teaching of the Lord of Heaven. We will not urge you to perform the necessary rites unless you desire to do so. It is for you to choose whether or not you will escape from the threatened evil."

When all begged to receive instruction, they were taught the use of the rosary and were assured that by spending seven days and seven nights in repeating prayers they would be cleansed from their sins and thus fitted for further instruction. At the end of the week they were brought to an inner room that was richly

adorned with gold and pearls.   There also were Urugan
and Furaten clad in golden garments.   The Brother that
introduced the candidates, said:
   " These persons, after being healed of their diseases,
have for a week observed the prescribed ceremonies."
   " Then," said the priest, " let them be shown a proof
of the efficacy of such exercises."
   Accordingly the mirror was once more produced, and
as the candidates crowded about it, they shed tears of
joy when they saw themselves reflected as a company of
radiant saints.   The priest then said:
   " If seven days have wrought so great a change, it
cannot be doubted that constancy in the faith will insure
the attainment of sainthood.   You will now be permitted
to worship the chief Deity of the temple.   Remember,
however, that those who once do this must never let their
faith be shaken, even though their bodies should be
lacerated by swords or tormented on the rack; for it is
only by this God that you can be saved.   There remains
one more rite to be performed before you can engage in
worship."
   Each candidate was now presented with a *kurusu*
(cross?), which was an instrument about two inches
square, made of gold and having a handle eighteen inches
long.   Its surface was studded with nails, making it
resemble a horseradish-grater.   With these instruments
the candidates lacerated their naked bodies, and then they
anointed their hands with the flowing blood before
joining them in the attitude of prayer.
   One of the priests said: " The chief object of Christian worship is Deusu. *   Even the greatest sinner in
the world may, through faith in Deusu, go to heaven.
You must now engage in His worship."
   Urugan then led the way to the " Hall of the Secret
Thing."   At first the interior was so dark that nothing
could be seen.
   " Let all approach and worship," said the priest.
" You must first repeat the prayer that you have been
taught."

   * The Jesuits, dissatisfied with any Japanese word for the
Deity, retained the Latin word *Deus.*

When the candidates had said the prayer about three hundred times, the curtain slowly lifted, so as to admit more and more light, until the radiance was like that of noonday. The worshippers now saw before them an image of Deusu hanging head-downward upon a cross.

"This," explained the priest, "is the image of our Lord and shows how He suffered for us."

The candidates were next taken to the "Hall of Meeting," where was the image of a beautiful woman crowned with gems and holding a child. This was explained to mean that, just as a mother embraces her child, so does God love and care for mankind. The worshippers, joining their blood-stained hands, shed tears of thankful joy.

Those who so desired were permitted, after inscribing their names in a book, to return home. From those who chose to live in the temple several were selected to receive instruction in medicine and magic. Among these were three men, who by their dissolute habits had been reduced to beggary and afflicted with leprosy. They had now been healed, and on embracing the new religion had received the names Hiyan, Kosumo, and Shimon (John, Cosmo, and Simon). Under the disguise of merchants or priests, they went about the country practising magic and saying to the people: "Through the benevolence of the foreign physicians, all diseases are freely healed at the Temple of the Southern Barbarians. Not only are poor patients supported while there, but money is also given to their wives and children. Change your religion and become followers of Deusu."

Thus many poor people were led to the temple. The new religion also began to make considerable headway among the upper classes. At last Nobunaga, becoming apprehensive of evil, said to his officers:

"There are beginning to be bad reports about the foreign temple. Its methods are very peculiar. In Buddhism, contributions are made to the temples; but who ever heard of a temple that gave alms to the people? This new religion is gaining too much influence over men's hearts. I am considering the question whether it would not be better to destroy the temple and send the barbarians home. What is your opinion?"

One of the councillors replied: " There is indeed much reason for apprehension. Christianity is gaining many adherents even among the nobility. Yet, since any movement against the temple might lead to an insurrection, it would be better to conceal your suspicions until a favourable time comes for taking vigorous action."

Nobunaga, who agreed with this view, said: " I made the greatest mistake of my life when I permitted the barbarians to teach their doctrines."

Among the prominent persons that became Christians was Takayama Ukon. A revolt having arisen against Nobunaga, Takayama was about to join the rebels; but Nobunaga said to Urugan:

" You assert that your religion teaches righteousness. How then does it happen that Takayama is about to rebel? Unless this wickedness is prevented, you shall no longer be permitted to preach."

The barbarians therefore said to Takayama: " This insurrection is so sure to fail that it would be folly for you to take part in it. Moreover, such a rebellion is contrary to the precepts of our religion."

As a result of their expostulations, Takayama became a leading supporter of Nobunaga, who was thus led to regard Christianity with renewed favour.

When Hideyoshi came into power he was urged to prohibit the foreign religion. He replied that he did not have time then to give the matter such careful consideration as he hoped to do after his authority was fully established.

In Yodo, a few miles from Kyoto, lived a noted architect named Shuri, who had been put in charge of Hideyoshi's extensive building operations. It seemed to the Christians that by gaining this man to their faith a way might be opened for reaching Hideyoshi himself. Hiyan finally decided upon a method of procedure. Knowing that the architect was seldom at home, he one day just at sunset appeared before the gate of Shuri's house. An attendant was sent in to say that a priest from Kyoto had been belated on his return from the provinces, and being timid about travelling after dark, asked for lodging. Shuri's aged mother, who was in charge of the house, did all that she could for the worthy entertainment of such a guest. The next morning, when he was engaged in his devotions, she thought it strange that he paid no attention to the family shrine, where she had carefully lighted the lamps and the incense. After eating breakfast and re-turning profuse thanks for the hospitality he had re-ceived, Hiyan continued on his way to Kyoto.

A few days later a messenger came to Yodo, bringing some beautiful presents in acknowledgment of the favour shown to the belated priest. Though the old lady tried to decline the gifts, the messenger insisted on leaving them. After this, there frequently came letters and presents.

Not many months afterwards, Hiyan again appeared one afternoon at Shuri's house, where he stopped to pay his respects. As considerable time was spent in conversa-tion, the old lady said it was too late for the priest to go further; and Hiyan readily assented to an invitation to spend the night. In the evening, while talking about vari-ous things, he said to her:

" I do not know to what sect of Buddhism you be-long, but the Christian sect is the only one that insures immediate salvation. You ought to become one of its adherents."

" For sixty years," said she, " I have been a devout fol-lower of Amida. I am now too old to think of making a change."

Hiyan, in trying to convince her of the superiority of Christianity, showed her the magic mirror. Though the lady was greatly troubled at what she saw, she simply said:

" I am too ignorant to judge about these matters; but in Kyoto lives a priest who has hitherto been my instructor. If you will sometime meet him here and convince him that what you say is true, I shall then be ready to accept your teaching."

Hiyan gladly consented, for he supposed the priest was some ignorant fellow that could easily be silenced. In reality, he was a very learned man named Haku. All preliminaries having been arranged, Hiyan appeared on the appointed day in splendid apparel. Two of his serv-ants bore a lacquer box that they placed on the floor beside their master. The people of the neighbourhood came in crowds to see what was going on.

After the contestants had saluted each other, Haku asked: " What is the chief object of your worship? "

" We worship Deusu," replied Hiyan, " a divinity who appeared while yet there was nothing in the universe. He created all things. Though men were at first upright, they fell into sin. Deusu had pity on them and gave a prayer by whose repetition they could be saved. Shaka, Amida, and others worshipped in Japan were only men, and so unable to save others. Because Japan does not follow the religion of Deusu, its streets are filled with beggars and outcasts, while its people are afflicted with grievous diseases. Southern Barbary, because of its religion, has no paupers, robbers, nor invalids. If the teaching of Shaka and Amida is true, let them prove it by punishing me for what I am about to do."

So saying, he took from the box at his side some Buddhist books, which he tore into shreds, ground under his feet, spat upon, and otherwise insulted. Then he cried out:

" Do you see what I have done? That I suffer no harm proves your religion to be false. Forsake it, and enter the true way of salvation."

The astonished bystanders held their breath, wondering what Haku would do; but he quietly asked: " Is that all you have to say? "

" There is much more," replied Hiyan, " that I might add; but this is sufficient for the present."

Haku then said with a derisive laugh: " This deity that you call Deusu appears to be very stupid. Instead of creating men and then being obliged to take so much trouble to save them, it would have been better never to have made them at all. The sacred books make no mention of this Deusu, and so your teaching must be heretical. I am not surprised that you could insult the books with impunity. No punishment is sent to rats and mice that gnaw and defile them; for, being only animals, they know no better. If your teaching is more correct than ours, bring me some proof from the sacred books. Come, show me even one such proof."

Hiyan, knowing his inability to meet this challenge, turned red in the face. At last, he took out the magic mirror, saying as he thrust it before Haku:

" Learn from this your true nature and the fate that awaits you in the future life."

Though Haku saw himself reflected as having the head of a horse, he showed no sign of surprise. Taking a flower from a vase, he held it before the mirror. It also appeared as a horse's head. He then asked for a nearer view of the mirror, and Hiyan, suspecting nothing, allowed Haku to take it in his own hands. The latter suddenly turned it around, and the people saw that Hiyan himself was reflected as having a head like that of a horse.

Haku threw down the mirror with a laugh. " In my youth," he said, " such toys were very common. In the process of manufacture, a picture is drawn with lacquer on the surface of the metal, which is then re-heated and polished. Are you not ashamed to deceive people by such tricks?"

Hiyan hung his head; then crying out: " You are a fool and no fit antagonist for me," he was about to leave the room. Haku caught him by the sleeve; but the impostor, freeing himself from the priest's grasp, fled in the direction of Kyoto.

" I had supposed," said Haku, " that it would be necessary to debate concerning astronomy, geography, and other sciences. Since he had recourse to insulting words and acts, I was forced to answer him according to his folly. His doctrine is surely heretical, and in due time the Government will doubtless prohibit such teaching."

Shuri reported these events to Hideyoshi, who soon after ordered the barbarians to be sent home and their temple to be destroyed. The Japanese believers fled to different parts of the country. Hiyan became a mountain priest and went about seeking opportunities for quietly teaching the barbarian religion. Kosumo and Shimon changed their names and became physicians. They also practised legerdemain, being often invited to furnish amusement at banquets. In 1588, Hideyoshi, happening to hear of their skill, called them to exhibit it before him.

After they had done many strange things, they offered to show the assembled guests anything that might be desired. The court ladies, to whom the choice was left, asked to see Mount Fuji. To this request the magician said:

" We are unable to bring the mountain into this room; but, if the paper windows can be closed for a minute, we will grant your desire."

The windows were closed, and when, after some words of incantation, they were re-opened, the guests saw that the appearance of the garden had wholly changed, and beyond it they could see the beautiful form of the mountain. After other noted places had been shown in the same way, Hideyoshi said:

" Though there are many stories about ghosts, I have never seen one. Can you make a ghost appear?"

" Ghosts do not appear by daylight," answered the magicians; " but if you will wait until evening, you shall see one."

Accordingly, when the evening's feast was concluded, the magicians caused the candles to be extinguished. The full moon was shining brightly; but soon clouds began to float over its surface, while a chill breeze sighed mournfully through the branches of the trees. Finally, from the deep shade of a clump of shrubbery in the garden, there glided forth the form of a woman clad in white, her hair disheveled, and her face turned away from the spectators. All were filled with terror at the apparition. The ladies fled shrieking to the rear of the palace. The ghost drew nearer and could be distinctly seen, notwithstanding that the moon was now completely hidden by dark clouds. The spirit turned its face and fixed its eyes upon Hideyoshi, who carefully scanned the features and then called out:

" Enough! Let there be no more of this!"

" We obey," said the magicians, as they closed the windows. When these were re-opened, the ghost was no longer visible and the moon was once more shining brightly.

The magicians, who had hoped that their skill would win Hideyoshi's approbation, were in great dismay when he ordered them to be cast into prison.   In explaining this to the guests, Hideyoshi said:

" These men are not mere sleight-of-hand performers, but Christians who have hitherto escaped detection.   The ghost was that of a woman whom I loved in my younger days and who was executed for poisoning her rival. Though this happened long ago, these men have in some way gained a knowledge of the affair, and they doubtless expected that I would reward them for letting me see again the woman I once loved."

The two men were found guilty of believing in the barbarian religion, and were crucified.

In the summer of 1615, a great drought prevailed throughout central Japan.   All prayers and incantations proving futile, the despairing farmers saw their fields being parched by heat.   Hiyan, under the disguise of a Buddhist priest, now returned to the neighborhood of Kyoto.   Going to one of the villages, he assured the farmers that he was able to bring the desired rain.   In accordance with his directions, a large heap of brushwood and charcoal was collected and set on fire.   Hiyan then jumped into the midst of the flames, moving about among them unscathed as he repeated his incantations.

Meanwhile a report of what was going on had reached the officials in Kyoto, who hastened to the village and arrested Hiyan as he emerged from the fire.   On being taken to the city, he was asked to what sect he belonged. He named a temple of which he professed to be a priest; but on making inquiry, it was found that the abbot knew nothing of such a person.   He was finally recognised as a Christian by some one who had formerly known him in the Temple of the Southern Barbarians.

A few days later he was led out for execution.   Crowds assembled to witness the spectacle.   The prisoner had hardly been bound to the cross when he suddenly changed to a rat.   Great confusion ensued.   The officers tried to catch the creature.   " There it is!" they shouted; " Step on it!   There it goes!   Kill it!   Kill it!"

In the midst of the excitement, an immense hawk came swooping through the air, grasped the rat in its talons, and flew away.   The wondering people stood gazing into the sky until the bird vanished in the distance.   The officers trembled at the thought that they would be held responsible for the prisoner.   When, however, their report had been given, they were told that, though blameworthy for letting him escape, yet, in view of the fact that he had been re-captured, no punishment would be inflicted upon them.   All were filled with joy at the Government's clemency.

A strict search was now made for other Christians. Those that were found were sewed up in straw sacks, their heads sticking out like those of tortoises, and thus they were piled in heaps upon the dry bed of the river that flows through Kyoto.

At first the sufferers called out: "We have great reason for thanksgiving.   Since we suffer here on earth, we shall be re-born in Paradise.   Make haste to put an end to our lives."

After a while one of the officers said to them: "Why do you not recant?   You have nothing to hope in the present or the future.   We have heard you say that when in trouble you would be nourished with heavenly food; but no one gives you so much as a rice cracknel."

Some near the bottom of the heap, being unable to endure the agony any longer, declared their readiness to renounce Christianity; and these were released.   There still remained fifty or sixty, who called out to the others: "Cowards!   Cowards!"

Those that had recanted replied: "You may say to us what you like.   So long as we are free, we do not care, even though in the future world we should be re-born as cats or mice."

The officers now had three hundred horse-loads of fagots brought and heaped on the sand.   When the Christians were told that they would be burned, they were in great terror and asked permission to recant.   Even at that late hour, they were allowed to go free.

It was commonly reported that these recantations were not genuine.   Accordingly strict orders were issued that priests must annually make investigations in their parishes and give to the people certificates that they were not Christians.   When any believers in the barbarian religion were discovered, they were burned, crucified, or drowned.   Thus the evil was stamped out of the central provinces.   In more distant parts of the land, there continued to be those that secretly adhered to the faith of the Southern Barbarians.   Those of Arima and Amakusa united in the great Shimabara Revolt that resulted in their utter extermination.

IX

LOOCHOO

1844-1853

THOUGH missionaries were unable to enter Japan, the Roman Catholic Church could not forget the land where its efforts had once been crowned with so great success, and where so many martyrs had consecrated the soil by their blood. Many were the prayers that the country which had been the scene of such triumphs and such sufferings might again be opened to the heralds of the Cross. There were indications that some knowledge of Christianity yet remained among the people. In 1820, some Japanese came to Batavia for the purpose of purchasing Christian books.*

In 1826, the Christians of Korea, who were likewise obliged to hide themselves from bitter persecution, learned that the Japanese Shogun had requested their King to send back to him six men, believers in Christianity, who had escaped in a boat to Korea.† In 1831, it was found that twenty Japanese sailors wrecked on the Philippines possessed Christian medals that they seemed to regard with superstitious veneration. When asked the meaning of these objects, they could give no satisfactory reply. All they knew about them was that they had been handed down from their ancestors as objects of devotion. After receiving instruction, seventeen of these men asked for baptism.‡

* " Annals Prop. Faith," English Ed., 1849, p. 215.
† Dallet, " Hist. de l'Eglise de Corée," as quoted in Griffis's " Corea," p. 359.
‡ " La Relig. de Jésus Res.," vol. i., p. 82. Many medals, crucifixes, and images had thus been preserved. It is said that sometimes they were concealed in the family shrines so that, while the worshipper was apparently performing his devotions before

In 1832, Gregory XVI. established the Apostolic
Vicariate of Korea, attaching to it the care of the Loochoo
Islands, which it was thought might prove the most important part of the jurisdiction. The Vicar was enjoined to make every effort to reside there rather than
in Korea, as it was hoped that the islands could be made
the gateway for entering Japan. Mgr. Bruguiere, the
first to hold the office, was inclined to think that a better
way to accomplish the end in view would be through
the Japanese colony that since the time of Hideyoshi
had remained at Fusan in southern Korea. His successor, Mgr. Imbert, favoured the same policy, and en-

ancestral tablets or Buddhist images, his thoughts were fixed
upon the Christian symbol hidden behind them. In other
cases, provision was made for securing adoration of these
objects by those that did not know their meaning. Dr. J. H.
DeForest writes: "I know a farmer's house where a copper
image of the Virgin was kept during all these ages and passed
down from father to son with this solemn injunction: 'In this
little box is a precious charm that, if worshipped unopened, will
bring blessings to all the house; but if the least attempt be made
to open the box, untold curses will fall upon all of you.' Later,
in days of liberty and enlightenment, the farmer ventured to
open the box, and out dropped the image." ("Sunrise in the
Sunrise Kingdom," p. 97.)

It is said that among the personal effects left by Nariaki,
Prince of Mito, who after the coming of Commodore Perry
was the leader of the party opposed to foreigners, were a Bible
and an image of the Virgin, which led some to suppose he had
made a study of Christianity. Others suppose that the book
was the one sealed by his ancestor, the noted author of the
great historical work "Dai Nihonshi," who lived 1628-1700.
"Among his retainers was a Christian believer, who was well
known for his loyalty and bravery. He made no secret of his
faith, and used to carry a banner with a cross upon it. The
prince summoned him to his presence and asked him the reason
of the hope that was in him. In answer thereto the man held out
a Chinese Testament, adding that his whole hope was to be
found therein. Mito read and re-read it with increasing interest.
Finally he shut the book and wrote on its cover: 'Surely this
is a wonderful book, worthy of acceptance. Its effect is to
create in the believer a longing for liberty and freedom for
which the present state of our country is not yet ripe.' He
sealed the book, and wrote upon it: 'Mito Komon forbids this
book to be opened.'" (Nitobe, "Intercourse between the U. S.
and Japan," p. 25.)

deavoured to have a catechist visit the Japanese colonists that he might seek their conversion and learn from them whether anything was left of the ancient church in Japan. As nothing came from this attempt, Mgr. Imbert authorised the agent of the Société des Missions-Étrangères in Macao to send missionaries to Loochoo whenever a good opportunity should come.*

The Opium War in China (1840-1842) opened a new chapter in the history of the Far East. Other nations wished to have a share in the commercial advantages that England was gaining. Admiral Cécille, who was commander of the French fleet in Chinese waters, looked with favour upon the missionaries, not merely because he could use them in carrying out his plans for the extension of French influence, but also from a real interest in their work. He at one time meditated the occupation of some point in the Loochoo Islands, whose position between China and Japan proper made them a suitable place from which to overlook movements in each country. Affairs in China that necessitated his presence caused him to postpone a proposed visit to these islands, Korea, and Japan. In April, 1844, he despatched a corvette under the command of Captain Fornier-Duplan to reconnoitre Loocho. He also requested the Société des Missions-Étrangères to put at his disposal one of its missionaries, who would consent to be left upon the islands in order to study the language so that he might at some future time accompany the Admiral to Japan as interpreter. M. Forcade,† a young missionary who had recently come to Macao, was appointed for this service. He took with him Augustine Ko, a Chinese catechist who, by Admiral Cécille's intervention, had been freed from a prison in Canton, where he had been confined because of his connection with the missionaries.

---

* Cf. "La Relig. de Jés. Res.," vol. i., pp. 78-84, and Launay's "Hist. Gen. de la Société des Missions-Etrangères," vol. iii., p. 202.

† Information concerning M. Forcade may be found in his biography by Marbot, and in a collection of his letters published by the *Missions Catholiques* under the title " Le Premier Missionnaire Catholique du Japon au XIXme Siècle."

The corvette reached Napha, April 28, and was at once boarded by six officials. Two of them could speak a very few words of English. The Chinese language proved the least unsatisfactory means for communicating with them. Upon most subjects they were very reticent. When asked whether in talking among themselves they used the Japanese language or one peculiar to Loochoo, they at first pretended not to understand the question and afterwards gave irrelevant answers. They also made no response to the inquiry where their king resided.

In the interviews that were held with the Loochooan officials during the stay of the corvette at Napha, they tried to make it appear that their country was too poor and unproductive to make it worth the while for Europeans to come there for trade. Every effort was made to keep the French from visiting the city, it being alleged that they would cause great terror to the populace. The officers of the corvette, however, were unwilling to accede to the request that their walks be confined to the seashore. Much to the annoyance of the native officials, they several times pressed forward into the streets of Napha. M. Forcade describes one of the excursions in which he shared. He writes:

"I fell into the hands of a very good police-officer. Hardly had I taken two steps when he offered me his arm, saying:

"'You cannot go there; you cannot go there.'

"'Oh, yes, we can go,' I replied, and taking his arm started along.

"Every minute and at every turn of the road, my guard would say: 'You cannot go there,' to which I invariably replied, 'Oh, yes, we can go.' For three hours, my arm in his, I led him about in the city and in the fields, through all the streets and along all the paths, while the rain was constantly falling upon us; yet not for a single instant did he lose his patience. Though he kept repeating the same refrain, he all the time treated me with respect and kindness.

"Partly to recompense him for his trouble and partly to see what he would do, I tried to make him a present of my umbrella, which he had admired and carried for me. I could not get him to accept it. Desirous, however, of showing in some way how much I appreciated his services, I praised him to an official, apparently his superior, simply saying: 'This is a good fellow and he has taken excellent care of me.' This compliment appeared to embarrass the poor man, for it seems that I had compromised him in the eyes of the other."

Just before going back to the ship, M. Forcade noticed the figure of the cross carved on one of the stones that formed the pavement of the landing-place. He believed that it had been put in that position in order that it might be trodden under foot by every person that disembarked there.

At the first formal interview with the Governor, Captain Fornier-Duplan said that his superior had ordered him to leave at Loochoo the First Imperial Interpreter,* named Forcade, and another interpreter of lower grade, in order that they might become acquainted with the language of the country. The formal despatch in which the Governor replied to the request for the establishment of friendly relations contained the following postscript:

"The Commandant desires that two interpreters should be left here. We have duly considered this request. Never before have foreigners landed on our shores with the intention of remaining. As the country is unhealthy, we very much fear that if these two men dwell here they may contract some illness caused by the unfavourable climate. We beg you to consider how unfortunate this would be."

Fornier-Duplan therefore wrote to the Governor:

"I am glad that you have not declined to receive the interpreters; for, since my orders are to leave them in your country, I should have been obliged to do so, even if you had sent a refusal; though in that case I should have shared in the chagrin this would have caused you. The observations that you make concerning the climate and your anxiety lest the health of the two men should suffer are proofs of your kindness; but, as you know, whenever Frenchmen receive a command, they obey it, even at the risk of their lives. Hence I shall land these men with their effects to-morrow, and I again ask for them your kind attentions."

In accordance with this message, M. Forcade and Augustine Ko were sent ashore on the morning of May 6.

* Though this was in the reign of Louis Philippe, it was considered advisable to speak of him as Emperor, so that it might not be thought that he was inferior to the rulers of China and Japan.

They were taken to Tumai, in the suburbs of Napha, where a Buddhist monastery had been assigned to them for their abode. The corvette sailed away, and M. Forcade was left as the chief actor in a comedy whose ridiculous features he himself could appreciate and vivaciously describe in his letters, though the serious and annoying side of the situation weighed heavily upon his spirit. A large number of officers was installed in the monastery for the purpose, so it was said, of helping the foreigners pass the time pleasantly. Under the show of guarding them from harm, a sharp watch was kept upon every movement. M. Forcade wrote: "By night as by day we could not blow our noses, expectorate, or cough, without seeing ourselves approached by a dozen persons who, in anxious tones, inquired if we felt ill." The foreigners could not take a step in any direction without being followed by some one. It was with difficulty that they could get out of doors for exercise, and then only to the seashore, where they were surrounded by officers carrying bamboo sticks to drive away any people that happened to be there. They had no reason to complain of the food that was provided, for their table was supplied with the best that the country afforded. Apparently the attempt was made to keep them so well contented that they would not care to go outside the walls of the monastery.

After long negotiations M. Forcade obtained the concession that he could have to himself the chamber in which he slept and the little garden upon which it opened. Despairing of obtaining permission to walk elsewhere than on the beach, he determined to take matters into his own hands. Without paying any attention to the clamour of his attendants, he began to take walks upon the roads near the monastery. One day, however, when he directed his steps towards the city, an officer grasped him and prevented him from going further. On his return to the monastery, M. Forcade sent a letter of remonstrance to the Governor, who replied that the laws forbade foreigners walking anywhere except on the seashore, and that Captain Fornier-Duplan had promised that the persons whom he left behind would carefully obey all laws. M. Forcade answered that in giving this assurance of obedience to the ordinary laws of the country it was not intended that the foreigners should be subjected to special regulations or that they should not enjoy such liberty as the captain had insisted upon having for himself. M. Forcade further said that until it was shown that he was in the wrong he should not change his conduct. As nothing further came from the Governor, he resumed his walks and was subjected to no further annoyance than that which came from being accompanied by a crowd of attendants. He then adopted the policy of varying his pace in accordance with circumstances. The larger his escort and the more they beat the people with their poles, the faster would he walk, much to the discomfort of the officials, who did not enjoy such active exercise. After some time they learned the lesson so well that during the last part of his stay in Loochoo he was allowed to go about with only two officers and one servant.

For a long time little progress was made in the study of the language. At first none of the people about M. Forcade would give him instruction, help him to obtain books, or tell him the names of even the most common objects. Finally, however, one of the officials who had become very friendly, commenced to dictate sentences and otherwise assisted him until he had compiled an extensive vocabulary.

Approach to the people was still denied. One day M. Forcade and Augustine took a longer walk than usual into the country, and their attendants resorted to an expedient that had succeeded on former occasions. They professed to be so tired that they could hardly drag one foot after another. They lagged behind, sitting down every few minutes in the hope that the foreigners would take pity on them and go no further. The latter thought the opportunity too good to be lost. Watching their chance, they turned into a side lane and advanced at a quick pace. The people of the villages through which they passed gave kindly salutations and showed no signs of fear. Finally, M. Forcade sat down beside the road, and as the villagers gathered about him he found that he was able, in a stumbling way, to carry on a conversation with them.

On another occasion when he found opportunity to talk to a peasant, an attendant came up and thought he would prove to the Frenchman what had previously been asserted about the attitude of the people. In a tone that implied a demand for an affirmative answer, he asked the countryman: "Is it not true that you farmers are very much alarmed when this person appears in your village?"

"Yes," replied the man, "but it is not because we are afraid of the foreigner. We know that he will do us no harm. The officers and attendants that go with him are the ones that we fear."

From the beginning M. Forcade daily celebrated mass. On the first morning he had hardly uttered the words, "*In nomine Patris,*" when his guards awoke from their slumbers and looked with wonder to see what was being done. Augustine, in accordance with the instructions he had received, said to them in Chinese:

"He is praying to his God. Woe to you if you do not keep quiet. Either go out of the room, or else, if you remain here, kneel down."

That day they remained, but afterwards they left the room every morning at the time of this service, apparently fearing that some evil influence would be exerted upon them.

Near the beginning of the sojourn in Loochoo, one of the officers propounded such questions as encouraged Augustine to talk to him about the existence of a Creator. As some impression seemed to be made upon the man, it was hoped that he might become an earnest seeker for the truth; but for some reason he was soon removed and the foreigners were unable to learn where he had gone. After this, it was almost impossible for them to have conversation on religious matters with any of the attendants. Every time that Augustine broached the subject, his auditors found some excuse for bringing the interview to an end.

It is said that when the Japanese Government learned that a Frenchman was living in Loochoo it was on the point of taking steps for his arrest and execution, but that the Dutch Resident in Nagasaki interposed and prevented any action from being taken.*

M. Forcade waited impatiently for the promised coming of Admiral Cécille. Two years passed by and he had not appeared. Meanwhile two or three English vessels had touched at Napha. April 30, 1846, another ship was seen approaching. As it drew near, M. Forcade was again disappointed to see it display an English flag; neither did it lighten the disappointment when he found that the vessel had brought a Protestant missionary, Dr. Bettelheim. Two days later, however, came the *Sabine* of the French navy. As soon as M. Forcade could obtain a boat, he hastened to the ship. Hardly had he reached the deck when his neck was embraced by the arms of some one who exclaimed: "Once your pupil, now I am to be your co-labourer." The person proved to be M. Leturdu, a fellow-missionary who had been sent to reside in Loochoo. The ship brought a budget of letters to M. Forcade. The first one he opened told him that he had been raised to the episcopate and made Vicar Apostolic of Japan and Loochoo.

After a month's stay in Napha, the *Sabine* proceeded to Port Melville, a little farther to the north, where it was soon joined by two other French ships, on one of which was Admiral Cécille. Considerable time was spent in negotiations with the Loochooan officials, and the fleet then set out for Japan, taking with it M. Forcade and Augustine, while M. Leturdu was left in their place. The ships reached Nagasaki July 29, but remained only two days. The French considered that the treatment re-

---

* The following extract from a modern history gives the Japanese version of the French movements: "In the third month of 1844, a French man-of-war came to Loochoo, sent a letter to the King, and caused a report to be spread abroad that the English were so much offended at the way Japan had closed the country and refused intercourse with other lands that they were about to attack the Empire. Their first movement would be to seize Loochoo. The best way to avoid the threatened evil would be for Loochoo to come under the protection of France. The ship departed, leaving behind it a Frenchman and a Chinese." ("Shin Nihon-shi," vol. i., p. 15).

ceived from the authorities of the port was very overbearing, and so the Admiral, after protesting against
the restrictions that were put upon his movements, sailed
away without going on shore.

While M. Forcade was still with the fleet in China,
M. Adnet, a priest appointed for work in Japan, arrived from France. He was at once sent to join M.
Leturdu, while M. Forcade remained for his episcopal
ordination, which took place at Honkong, February
21, 1847.

The French ship that took M. Adnet to Loochoo
brought back a favourable report of the treatment received by the missionaries. According to promises made
to Admiral Cécille, three persons had been appointed
to teach them the language, the monastery where they
lived had been repaired, and they enjoyed considerable
freedom of movement. Later intelligence, however,
showed that, as soon as the ship had sailed away, the
old restrictions had been renewed, though the missionaries were allowed to retain their teachers. One of
these, who was styled the "chief teacher," was really
the chief spy. Apparently his duties were to note carefully the subjects of conversation and to see that the
other instructors did not become too intimate with their
pupils. When the missionaries went upon the streets,
they were accompanied by guards to keep them from
having any intercourse with the people. Purchases,
however trifling, had to be made through one of the
officers.

If the missionaries attempted to speak to any of their
guards about Christianity, they were met by the reply:
"What you say is very good, but we cannot listen. The
Government does not wish us to do so, and we cannot
disobey without incurring great danger. There was,
however, an old man who had formerly been the head
officer of a small island and who now found occasional
opportunities to converse with the foreigners. One day,
as M. Leturdu was walking on the seashore, the man
made a sign for the missionary to follow him to a retired spot, and there asked him:

"Will you not explain to me who Jesus is?"

M. Leturdu replied to the inquiry and then said:

"It is for the purpose of teaching these things that I have come hither. Do you not wish to hear what we have to say?"

"Yes, yes; but it is dangerous. We cannot do so."

"At least, promise me that every day you will use this prayer: 'Lord, help me to know Thee.' Then, as soon as permission can be gained, come and listen to us."

"I will do so," was the reply.

At one time a man seventy years old came from the northern part of the island for the sole purpose, as he said, of seeing the missionaries. He came into the house, but the presence of a servant put a check upon conversation. After he had gone, the missionaries, in considering his manner, thought that he had wished to speak with them on religious matters. Might he not be a descendant of the Japanese Christians, or else some one whose heart God had touched? They hurried out in search of the visitor, who was not to be found and nothing more could be learned about him. Finally, M. Leturdu resolved to go to the northern part of the island, hoping that he could find him there. The officials did their best to keep him from making this journey. When they saw that their remonstrances were of no avail, they sent word to the villagers along the road, ordering them not to furnish the foreigner with food, nor even to talk with him. When he entered a house, all the people seemed to be struck dumb. When he told them that he would not stir until they spoke to him, it usually was not long before they found their tongues sufficiently to answer his inquiries. He was unable, however, to get any trace of the object of his search.

The Governor of Loochoo sent to the Imperial Commissioner in China many complaints regarding the conduct of the missionaries. Admiral Cécille, to whom these complaints were reported, believed that the interests of missions in China, as well as his own honour, made it advisable to promise that MM. Leturdu and Adnet would soon be removed. When Mgr. Forcade learned of this decision, he was filled with great anxiety. He wrote to the Directors of the Seminary in Paris, urging that they use their influence to have the French Government take the position that the Loochoo Islands were not subject to China and that therefore, the Imperial Commissioner had no right to object to the presence of the missionaries. With China out of the way, he thought it would be possible for some satisfactory arrangement to be made directly with the Loochooan Government. In any case, it was well to gain time, since, thanks to the English, great changes were taking place in the Far East.

Circumstances led to Mgr. Forcade's being requested to go to France that he might explain certain action that had been taken by a French fleet. He was the more willing to go because he would thus have an opportunity to plead for his Mission. He reached Paris in July, 1847. There he found that the only one of the men at the head of affairs who showed any interest in religious work was M. Guizot. "Though a Protestant, it is he whom I have found most Catholic of them all," was Mgr. Forcade's report to the Pope.

It was decided by the Propaganda that it would be best for Mgr. Forcade to reside in Honkong, which was a better place than Loochoo for watching the course of events, so as to take advantage of any opportunities that might facilitate movements upon Japan. The interests of the Roman Catholic Church in this English colony were put in his care.

M. Adnet, who had been in poor health from the time of his arrival in Loochoo, died July 1, 1848. The Loochooans showed at least the outward signs of sympathy. The Prime Minister and also the Governors of Shui and Napha sent letters of condolence to M. Leturdu. The messengers that brought them asked permission to attend the funeral services. This request was readily granted, but when they further expressed a wish to offer sacrifices at the grave, it took some time to make them understand that this would not be acceptable. "To put an end to the matter," wrote M. Leturdu, "I told them that such an act was forbidden by the law of my country. At this they kept silence and made no more remonstrances. I added that, if the officials desired to honour my associate, they could come to the monastery, where I would offer in their name a sacrifice to the Lord of Heaven for the repose of him whose loss we were mourning; but they did not accept this suggestion."

At the funeral, the three officials with a large train of attendants were present. The procession, preceded by a cross, went to a small graveyard by the seashore, where M. Adnet's body was placed near that of a French surgeon, who had been buried there two years before. A cross, ornamented with other Christian symbols, was erected over the grave, and the missionary's name was inscribed upon a stone.

Before the end of the next month, a French corvette came to Napha. Its captain had been told to take away M. Leturdu. In case the latter was unwilling to go, the officials were to be informed that he remained on his own responsibility. Under these circumstances it seemed inadvisable to insist on staying, and the attempt to reach Japan through Loochoo was for the time abandoned.

When Mgr. Forcade arrived in Hongkong he found there two priests, MM. Thomine-Desmazures and Mahon, who had been assigned to Japan. The former had elaborated a plan for reaching the appointed field of labour. It was to go to Saghalien or to the Kurile Islands, and thence to enter Yezo. Since no foreign ships went to those regions, it would be necessary to hire a Chinese junk and for the missionaries to make all the calculations needed in directing its course. M. Thomine had already written to the Director of the Seminary of Foreign Missions asking that funds be sent for hiring the junk as well as for the purchase of a chronometer, compass, sextants, charts, mathematical tables, and other essentials.

M. Leturdu on coming back from Loochoo was convinced that it was useless to attempt anything further there. He wrote to Paris:

"We were carried thither by war-vessels; we have there an official title—that of Interpreters of the King of France; and we are regarded as French officers sent to spy out the land. Is not all this fitted to increase the opinion which all Japanese have had since the former persecutions that missionaries are only spies and emissaries of the countries from which they come? . . . Because of the opposition of the Government it is impossible, humanly speaking, to make a single convert. Even though the King of Loochoo should come to favour us, he could authorise nothing, since it is not he that governs, but the Emperor of Japan through his envoys."

M. Leturdu desired that another attempt to enter Japan should be made; this time not under the protection of cannon, but trusting only in God and the Virgin. He would have the missionaries approach from the north, conceal themselves among the mountains in some place not likely to be visited by police, and then get into communication with persons in the neighbourhood so as to effect their conversion and utilise them as evangelists. This plan, which was similar to that of M. Thomines, failed to gain the approval of Mgr. Forcade, who wrote in one of his letters:

" I know from a trustworthy source that in less than two years a military expedition will be sent to Japan, and I think it will be prejudicial for us to precede it. We might be regarded as its advance-couriers. It is better to know how to wait. When the ports are opened to foreigners, we can enter them. Even though we should be forbidden to advance into the interior, we could, while waiting for better opportunities, seek the conversion of the Japanese about us."

Mgr. Forcade found conditions in Hongkong so unsatisfactory that he was on the point of going with his missionaries to Loochoo, when he met a Japanese who had been shipwrecked a number of years before, and who was now able to converse in English. This man declared that the language used in Loochoo was a corrupt dialect which could not be understood in Japan. This made it seem useless to go again to those islands. The Japanese waif and another who had likewise been shipwrecked were utilised as teachers of the language. The Bishop's ill health made it impossible for him to pursue his studies. M. Mahon, however, was soon busy in preparing a catechism. In January, 1851, the Japanese employed as his teacher was baptised.

In November, 1850, Mgr. Forcade sent a letter to
the Prefect of the Propaganda, in which he said he was
tired of waiting for the Americans or the English to
make any move for opening Japan, and that in the de-
pressing climate of Hongkong he found not only his
physical strength impaired, but also his moral and in-
tellectual forces deteriorating. He asked permission to
have himself landed on the coast of Japan. There he
would attempt no concealment. Wearing his ecclesiastical robes and with the cross suspended from his
neck, he would go to the first house that he saw, or, if
he found himself near Yedo, would proceed directly to
that city. As the Vicar Apostolic of Japan he would
demand that he be led into the presence of the Shogun.
Though it was improbable that he could gain access to
that ruler, he believed that sooner or later he would be
brought before some person of high office to whom,
both by word of mouth and by written documents, he
could present the claims of Christianity, and demand
permission to exercise the ministry entrusted to him.

M. Mahon, to whom also this plan was presented, believed that its conception arose from Mgr. Forcade's
ill health, and that it would be unwise to make any
move upon Japan just before the expected sailing of
the American Expedition. The Bishop's health had indeed been seriously impaired and was but little benefited
by voyages that he made to Singapore, Manila, and
other places. About the close of 1851, he attended a
council of the bishops residing in China, and it was
largely in the hope that a visit to Europe would facilitate
his recovery that the others delegated him to carry a
report of their proceedings to the Propaganda. M.
Marnas hints that the Jesuits were not wholly disin-
terested when they favoured this appointment. As their
Society had been the first to carry Christianity to Japan,
they considered that to them ought to be assigned the
duty of resuming a work that there was reason to believe would soon be possible.* Mgr. Forcade, who decided to sever his connection with the Société des Missions-Étrangères, bestowed on one of the Jesuit Fathers

* "La Relig. de Jés. Res.," vol. i., p. 230.

the title of Vicar General, considering that authorisation for such an appointment had been given him by the Propaganda. It was not his intention, however, to give over all authority to the Jesuits, for he also left to M. Mahon the same title.*

M. Mahon was much perplexed to know what course he ought to pursue. There was much uncertainty about the plans of the Americans; and he did not know whether or not it would be decided at Rome to turn over to the Jesuits the mission that had before been entrusted to the Société des Missions-Etrangères. In 1853, however, M. Colin of the latter Society was chosen as Mgr. Forcade's successor, with the title Prefect Apostolic of Japan. The new appointee died while on the way from Manchuria, where he had been serving as a missionary. He had previously sent letters directing that missionaries be sent once more to Loochoo. We shall see in the next chapter how his plan was carried into effect and how ere long it was possible to enter upon work in Japan itself.

* "La Relig. de Jés. Res.," vol. i., p. 231.

X

THE RESURRECTED CHURCH

1855-1867

THOUGH the United States in 1854 negotiated a treaty with Japan, this and the similar arrangements made by other Western nations did not provide for the residence of foreigners in the country. It was, however, evident that the first breach had been made in the barriers that shut the Japanese away from other peoples and that the time could not be far distant when it would be possible for even religious teachers to enter within the walls. In accordance with the plans made by M. Colin, Messieurs Girard, Furet, and Mermet were sent in February, 1855, to Loochoo, which was again chosen as the point from which to watch the progress of events in Japan. No more cordial welcome was given to them than had been received by their predecessors. On the arrival of the French merchantman that conveyed them to Napha, the captain of the ship said to the officials:

" I have on board certain doctors, men of prayer, who are desirous of obtaining information for themselves and of communicating to you the knowledge that they already possess."

On hearing this, the officials used all sorts of excuses and arguments without being able to turn the Frenchmen from their purpose. On the ship were three other missionaries on their way to Shanghai, and one of them has left us an account of the way in which the landing at Napha was accomplished:

" After having offered up the Holy Sacrifice, M. Girard went on shore with the captain. We were to join them by another road with the luggage and to meet all together at the house of the bonzes formerly occupied by our confrères Messrs. Adnet and Leturdu. At mid-day we were on our way reciting the *Veni Creator* and *Memorare*. Some magistrates of the island came to us on our landing. We shook hands with them cordially, and having exchanged gracious salutations with them, we left these mandarins with our two confrères Messrs. Boyer and Mermet, and made our way to the bonzery. On seeing our trunks brought in and put down, the bonzes went out, looking anything but pleased. One of the youngest of them asked us in Chinese: ' Why do you come hither?' We answered: ' To stay here and learn the language.' Meanwhile our luggage continued to arrive, and the bonzes with the other authorities present held a conference. One of these priests of error, putting on a long black gown and assuming an air of gravity and severity, came and bade us pack up our trunks and begone. We gave an affirmative nod, but continued to receive and dispose of our luggage."

One of the officials told the foreigners that they must go to see the Regent. On reaching the latter's residence at the time appointed, they were told that the Regent was so vexed at their landing that he could not speak to them until two hours later. When they were finally admitted, a statement was read in which the Regent said that, since the people of Loochoo had a religion of their own, they did not need Christianity. If the Frenchmen were allowed to remain, other Europeans would come in such numbers as to cause great trouble to their country, which was so small, poor, and unproductive that it scarcely furnished sufficient food for its present inhabitants.

After the question had been discussed for a while, M. Girard said: " We are brought here by duty. The captain cannot take us on board again. You may be as severe as you please against us; but we cannot go away. You shall kill us rather."

The letter that we have been following says:

" At last the Regent, seeing our firmness and unshaken resolution, and fearing lest the French Admiral should refuse him his assistance against the pirates, permitted Messrs. Furet, Girard, and Mermet to occupy the bonzery on condition that in the course of two or three months they should be fetched away." *

When Admiral Laguerre heard of this arrangement, he sent orders to the commandants of the vessels under his

* " Annals Prop. Faith," 1855, English Ed., p. 322 sq.

charge that they should not go to Loochoo for the purpose of taking the missionaries away, but only to see that they were well treated.*

In May, however, M. Furet was taken on board a vessel of the French navy that was on its way to Nagasaki. Much to his disappointment, he was not allowed to proceed from that port to Hakodate, the commandant expressing his fear that the presence of a missionary on board would prove prejudicial to the interests of France. He was accordingly given passage to Hongkong, where he found M. Mounicou, another missionary assigned to Japan. Under the instruction of a Japanese from Nagasaki, they gave themselves earnestly to the study of the language. The next year both of them were permitted to go on a man-of-war to Hakodate, where they spent four days. They went on shore and took walks into the neighbouring villages, though they were always accompanied by policemen, who hindered their attempts to converse with the people.

In October, 1856, Messrs. Furet and Mounicou went to Loochoo. They found that their associates there had profited but little by the concessions that had been gained for them by the French naval officers. They had, indeed, succeeded in obtaining a house in the middle of the city; but it was soon found that, although guards were not posted on the premises, they were placed on the road that led thither so as to turn back intending visitors. M. Mermet wrote: "It is like living in a desert. This was formerly one of the busiest streets; now it is overgrown with grass and thorns. The houses that once faced ours have turned their backs upon us and have their entrance on the other side. The people are forbidden, under severe penalties, to come near us." Those appointed to teach them the language did their best to mislead and discourage them. Workmen and servants could be engaged only through the officials. Domestic servants were changed every month, and were ordered to talk about nothing that was not immediately connected with their work. Notwithstanding these pre-

* Bouix, "Martyrs du Japon," p. 241.

cautions, one of the servants, a young man twenty-two years of age, listened with interest to what the missionaries said about Christianity and was baptised by them. Soon after this he disappeared and the missionaries believed that he had been put to death.

With various changes in its personnel, the mission in Loochoo was continued until 1862. At times there were individuals for whose conversion hopes were entertained; but with the exception of the young man already mentioned, none went so far as to receive baptism.

M. Mermet's health was so impaired by his devotion to study that it was found advisable for him to remove, in 1857, to Hongkong. The next year he accompanied Baron Gros, who negotiated a treaty between France and Japan. This, which was similar in its provisions to the American treaty that had just been negotiated by Hon. Townsend Harris, permitted French citizens to reside in certain ports.

Unknown to the missionaries, descendants of the ancient Christians of Japan were being subjected to a new persecution the same year that this treaty was arranged. Eighty persons living near Nagasaki were suddenly arrested, and though the majority were at once set free, thirty of them were put in prison. There they endured tortures and privations under which ten of them died, while the health of others who were released in a year or two was so shattered that most of them did not long survive.*

M. Girard, who had been made the Superior of the Mission, was eager to improve the advantages to be gained through the new treaty. His letters to the Directors of the Seminary in Paris were filled with pleas for men and means. He urged that four missionaries be sent at once so that the ports, as soon as opened, should be provided with priests who could administer the sacraments to the European residents, and also seek out the Japanese Christians who, there was reason to believe, were to be found in different parts of Japan.

M. Girard himself arrived in Yedo, September 6, 1859.

* "La Relig. de Jésus Res.," vol. i., p. 547.

A few days later, at the formal ratification of the French treaty, he was present in ecclesiastical dress and was officially recognised as a priest temporarily serving as interpreter for the Consul-General of France. Apparently the fact of his being an ecclesiastic did not excite any prejudice, and the Government graciously furnished three persons to instruct him in the language. A few months later, he commenced to teach French to a number of young officials. Some of their superiors were always present during the lessons, probably to prevent too intimate relations with the pupils and the introduction of dangerous subjects.

In November, 1859, M. Mermet reached Hakodate. His experiences in Loochoo and the knowledge that he had already gained of the Japanese language enabled him to confer directly with the Japanese officials and to set aside the many obstacles that they at first put in his way. The vigour with which he began his labours is shown by a letter that he wrote only eight days after his arrival. In it he said:

"I wish I could tell you of being already settled in my house, which is to cost a hundred dollars; but that cannot be for another week. Every day the house is getting into shape. I spur on the workmen, and cheer them with *sake* at an expense of four hundred cash a week. I am very busy. I am giving lessons in English and French; I help the Consul; I go about among the ships; I measure rafters and beams; I plan out work that Mrs. Hodgson [wife of the English Consul] is doing for the adornment of my chapel, which will be very handsome, thanks to the cheapness of silks and embroideries. . . . I have had an audience with three Japanese princes. I have seen and conquered. A fine piece of land has been granted to me temporarily, that is, so long as I remain in Hakodate. This has made all the consuls jealous, since none of them had been able to procure it for even a term of six months."

A month later he had commenced the erection of a chapel. He appeared to have won the good will of all classes of people. He wrote:

"I have visited the principal officers of the city and have been visited by them. On showing them my modest chapel, I said that I had built it for them and for all the Japanese. . . . They have given me all necessary aid for the pursuit of my studies. Everybody knows me and salutes me with respect. All the Japanese strive to find some excuse for coming to see me. There are some sick people for whom I am caring, and they do not know how to express sufficiently their gratitude. My little chapel is frequented by Russians as well as by some American and English Catholics. Foreign residents, seeing that I am on such good terms with the authorities, come to visit me. I have opened a school for teaching French."

In March of the next year he wrote:

"Everybody comes to talk with me, even the bonzes, who in the bottom of their hearts hate me and who every week preach against me sermons whose invariable conclusion is: 'May the holy Amida drive out the erroneous doctrine of the Frenchman.' This, however, does not prevent them from coming to taste my wine nor from sending me presents of little cakes."

With all his interruptions, M. Mermet found time for study. He prepared an English-French-Japanese dictionary, and also a phrase-book. Obtaining from the Governor permission to visit a village of Ainu, he made a collection of the words of their language.*

M. Mounicou removed in 1861 from Loochoo to Yokohama and was entrusted with the work of superintending the construction of a church on land that had already been procured by M. Girard. This building was consecrated January 12, 1862. Though the church was nominally for the use of Europeans, it was hoped that ere long it would be frequented by the people of the country. As soon as it was thrown open to visitors, large numbers of Japanese came to see it. M. Girard wrote February 25:

"During a month our chapel has been visited every day by crowds of Japanese of every class and every rank; men, women, and children, old people, officers, bonzes. There have been a thousand on one day. We joyfully yielded to the pressing solicitations of their praiseworthy and pious curiosity; we explained the meaning of the religious pictures which adorned it, making

* M. Mermet withdrew from Japan in 1863, giving as a reason that family matters required his presence in France. He afterwards came again to Japan in the employ of the French Legation, but rendered no further service to the Mission.

use of them as an introduction to the more complete instruction of these people in our holy law; when suddenly there was communicated to us sorrowful news which threw us into consternation. Thirty-three of our listeners were seized coming out from our bounds, chained, and thrown into prison. On the morrow, nevertheless, the visitors continued numerous; the same anxiety was manifested to question, the same respect and docility to hear us. Was what we heard false? Unfortunately, our new hearers soon learned by their own experience that the arrests were too true. Twenty-two of them met the same fate as the former. Immediately the panic spreads in all directions. The news of the persecution is confirmed, and the strangers in the land are everywhere agitated. Our church is deserted." *

When the French Consul-General conferred with the Governor of Yokohama, the latter said that the Japanese subjects who had been arrested could not escape the penalty for violating the laws of their country. Finally, however, the prisoners were released after the missionaries had given a promise that they would not preach to Japanese until the French and Japanese governments had come to an understanding upon the matter. "We could not preach sooner," wrote M. Girard, "and we hope to secure freedom for the prisoners and to remove the odium with which their punishment has loaded us."

The Governor of Yokohama also tried to induce the Consul-General to order that the three Chinese ideographs signifying "Church of the Lord of Heaven" be erased from the front of the building. "Of what advantage," asked he, "is it to write the name of the edifice in Chinese characters which Europeans cannot read? I see in them only a means for tempting the Japanese, and you know very well what are our ideas on this point." The French representative did nothing to comply with this request.

Soon after the consecration of the church, M. Girard left the care of the mission to M. Mounicou during his own temporary absence in China and Europe. He took with him a young Japanese who, on Good Friday, 1863, received at Rome the three sacraments of baptism, confirmation, and the eucharist.

* "Annals Prop. Faith," 1863, English Ed., p. 259.

Though the number of missionaries in the open ports was increased in 1863 by the transfer of those formerly stationed in Loochoo, there was little to be done besides caring for the foreign residents, studying the language, teaching classes in French, and waiting for more favourable conditions. In Nagasaki, a church was commenced that was to be dedicated to the Twenty-six Martyrs who, in 1597, had suffered on a hill near the city. Already at Rome, June 6, 1862, Pius IX., in the presence of two hundred and fifty cardinals, patriarchs, archbishops, and bishops, summoned from all parts of the earth, had solemnly proclaimed the canonisation of these martyrs. To devout Romanists, the events occurring soon after at Nagasaki " seemed like a visible answer to the honours thus so splendidly rendered to these heroes of the Faith."

The construction of the church went on but slowly, and as it neared completion in December, 1864, the builder invented more difficulties than ever. He even threatened to suspend work altogether. Just at this time the Governor asked M. Petitjean, one of the missionaries, who after two years in Loochoo had come in 1862 to Nagasaki, if he would not become the teacher of French in a school that was about to be opened. " I should be glad," said the missionary, " to do what is desired; but until I am free from the cares connected with the construction of my building, it will be impossible to assent."

" When," asked the officers, " do you wish that your temple should be finished?"

" By the first of January."

The next morning three times the usual number of carpenters appeared. Work went on by night and day, so that the church was completed at the close of the year. " The gilded crosses on its three towers glowed in plain sight of all Nagasaki opposite the Sacred Hill [where the martyrdoms are supposed to have occurred]. Young and old, men and women, soldiers and citizens, came to visit what they called the French Church. The boys drew pictures of it with charcoal on the pavements of the public road. The old men repeated to each other stories about ancient Christians and their churches."

The dedication of the church took place February 19, 1865. The European vessels in the harbour were dressed out with flags. The French Consul and the commandant of a French naval vessel came with a guard of honour. The commandants of Russian, English, and Dutch vessels, each accompanied by a dozen Catholic marines, were present. A Russian naval band assisted in the musical part of the service. At noon, salutes were fired by all the men-of-war. To the great disappointment of the missionaries, the people of Nagasaki, usually so curious to see anything out of the usual course of things, appeared indifferent to all this ceremony. Shortly before this, their visits to the church had almost ceased. Evidently the authorities had warned them to keep away.

As we have seen, the missionaries from the first had hoped to find descendants of the early Christians still retaining a knowledge of the faith of their ancestors. Their enquiries, however, brought no intelligence that seemed trustworthy. To M. Petitjean was given the great joy of learning that their hopes had not been without foundation. The story is best told in his own words:—

"On March 17, 1865, about half past twelve, some fifteen persons were standing at the church door. Urged no doubt by my guardian angel, I went up and opened the door. I had scarce time to say a *Pater* when three women between fifty and sixty years of age knelt down beside me and said in a low voice, placing their hands upon their hearts:

"'The hearts of all of us here do not differ from yours.'

"'Indeed!' I exclaimed, 'Whence do you come?'

"They named the village, adding: 'All there have the same hearts as we.'

"Blessed be Thou, O my God, for all the happiness which filled my soul! What a compensation for five years of barren ministry! Scarcely had our dear Japanese opened their hearts to us than they displayed an amount of trustfulness which contrasts strangely with the behaviour of their pagan brethren. I was obliged to answer all their questions and to talk to them of *O Deusu Sama, O Yasu Sama,* and *Santa Maria Sama,* by which names they designated God, Jesus Christ, and the Blessed Virgin. The view of the statue of the Madonna and Child recalled Christmas to them, which they said they had celebrated in the eleventh

month. They asked me if we were not in the seventeenth day of
the Time of Sadness (Lent); nor was Saint Joseph unknown to
them; they call him O *Yasu Sama no Yofu*, 'the adoptive father
of our Lord.' In the midst of this volley of questions, footsteps
were heard. Immediately all dispersed; but as soon as the new-
comers were recognised, all returned laughing at their fright.
" 'They are people of our village,' they said, ' They have the
same hearts as we have.'
" However, we had to separate for fear of awakening the suspicions of the officials, whose visit I feared."

What follows is a condensation of M. Petitjean's account, omitting some minor details.*

" Saturday, March 18. From ten o'clock in the morning until
night there has been a constant stream of visitors. The Japanese
officers, not knowing what to make of this extraordinary concourse, redouble their vigilance, and there does not pass a quarter
of an hour without some of them coming into the church.
Warned by what happened in Yokohama, M. Laucaigne and I
hold ourselves somewhat aloof. About noon, however, I cannot
resist the entreaties of a man about seventy-six years old and two
women of nearly the same age who ask permission to adore the
crucifix. The good old man repeated some prayers in Latin,—
Te Sancte and others that I was not able to catch perfectly. The
entrance of officers interrupted us.
" Sunday, March 19. A crowd like that of yesterday. Some of
the Japanese remained in the church even during the mass.
Among them I recognised some of our Christians. To four or
five who came to adore the crucifix I was able to teach the sign
of the cross. They appeared, indeed, never to have made it as
we ordinarily do. ' We make it thus,' one of them told me as
with his right thumb he signed his forehead and breast.† Then he
told me: ' In the village of Urakami not all are like us. There
are some spies who watch us; and among those whose hearts are
one with ours, there are some who have received but little instruction.'
" Monday, March 20. The number of visitors increases. The
officers station themselves so as to guard the approaches of the
church. In order to protect the interests of these dear souls, who
would be compromised by a slight indiscretion on our part, we
abstain as much as possible from appearing in the church. When
able to slip in a word, we say to them: ' Return home. The officers are watching you. Come again later and not so many at
a time.'

* Fuller accounts of these and subsequent events may be found
in " La Religion de Jésus Ressuscitée au Japon."
† This is said to have been the method used by the Spanish and
Portuguese.

" Tuesday, March 21. Christians and pagans come in a crowd and mingle together. We recognise the former by their lifting their hands to their breasts when their eyes meet ours. We speak to many of them, telling them not to come again for fifteen days so as not to give alarm to the Government and thus expose themselves to danger.

" Wednesday, March 22. Our Christians have doubtless transmitted our advice to others. They come in smaller numbers. The officers have disappeared or else have laid aside their swords. We are able to speak to some persons and have made an appointment to meet three men to-morrow upon a mountain near the city. We hope to find out about many matters. First, have our people at Urakami always had baptism? If not, we will teach them the formula and get them to administer the rite to infants in danger of death. In the second place, have they preserved the essential mysteries of the Christian faith? In any case, it will be useful to recall these to their minds. Finally, we will learn how they recite their prayers, and teach them where they are ignorant.

" Thursday, March 23. We have returned from our appointment. Only one of the men was on hand, but what he told us is of the highest importance. In spite of persecutions, Urakami has never been without Christians. Baptism has always been administered. Paul, the man who gave us this comforting information, was not able to repeat the words used in the sacrament, for these are known to only a small number of persons. He told us: 'When a child is born, we call the person in the vicinity who knows how to administer baptism. He pours water on the head of the child while making the sign of the cross, gives it a name, and repeats some prayers that we do not know.' He added a number of points that confirm us in the belief that they observe the sabbath and feast days. They are now keeping Lent. Finally, in their prayers they frequently invoke God, the Holy Virgin, their guardian angels, and their patron saints. It was arranged that next Thursday we shall meet the baptiser of Urakami in a house that Europeans frequently visit and whose master is a Christian. It is a small house in the country where visitors go to admire the flowers and dwarf trees. We were there last year without suspecting that we were with a Christian family."

Various causes led to delay in meeting the baptiser. In the first place, the gardener, who had been imprisoned a few years before on suspicion of being a Christian, was afraid that he might again draw attention to himself. He therefore asked that the interview might be held elsewhere. On going to a mountain that was next appointed as the place of meeting, it was found to be occupied with parties of picnickers. Soon after this the baptiser came to the church, where he met M.

Laucaigne and made another appointment. The following condensation of M. Petitjean's narrative tells of how this was kept:

"Domingo, the baptiser, was surrounded by three or four relatives and friends. He told us that he had greatly longed for this day, for he knew we were their priests. Only the fear of compromising our holy cause had kept him from coming often to the church. But to the important point—the formula employed by him in baptism. Here it is: '*Kono hito wo paotizo in nomne Patero, Hilio, et S'ra Spiritou Sancto, Iamoun.*' The word *ego* is lacking, but in Japanese the pronoun is often understood. The *te* is replaced by *kono hito* meaning *this child, this person*. Before and after the formula are prayers to our Lord and to St. John the Baptist. Is this formula valid? Until a contrary decision has been made, we shall regard it so. At least, we shall keep ourselves from allowing the lightest doubt of it to arise in their minds. To make it agree with ours I have told Domingo that the words he employs are the same with a slight difference of pronunciation which the Japanese vocal organs have gradually introduced. He has promised that henceforth he will employ the formula which I have given him in writing and he has repeated over to me. Domingo assures us that he is the only survivor of the last baptisers of the valley. In case of death or disability he will be succeeded by his son, a young man of twenty-five.

"Domingo has given us much precious information concerning the Christian community of which he is the head. Every day there is family worship. On one week the father of the family repeats the prayer aloud; on the following week, the mother; and then the children do it in turn. When any person is at the point of death, his friends gather about him to pray. For eight days after his death, supplications are made to St. Peter to open the gates of paradise for the departed one, who after that is not forgotten in the daily prayers. Domingo recited to us in Japanese the *Salve Regina* and many other prayers. He has put into our hands a unique book of Christian doctrine that he possesses. It has for its title: 'The Commencement of Heaven and Earth' (*Tenchi no Hajimari no Koto*). It begins thus: 'The Lord of Heaven, Deus, to whom our adoration is due, is the Ruler of heaven and earth, the Father of men and of all created things.' It was written from memory in 1822 or 1823. We find in it accounts of the Creation, the Fall, the promise of the Messiah, etc. We have found in it some errors, but they are of little importance."

The missionaries soon learned of Christian communities in other places. A young man who came to Nagasaki from the Goto Islands followed a crowd of sightseers to the church. Great was his surprise on see-

ing the cross and other Christian symbols. Finding an
opportunity to speak to the missionaries, he told them
that in the island where he lived were a thousand Christians. Only a few days later they were told of fifteen
hundred more living among the mountains twenty-five
or thirty miles distant. By the eighteenth of June they
knew of twenty Christian communities, and were in direct relations with seven baptisers. In boats and on
foot companies of believers came to see the church and
to ask for crucifixes or medals. Their leaders often
spent the night in the house of the missionaries.

The organisation of the communities was nearly the
same in all the villages. There were usually two leaders.
When possible, the first of these was a man who knew
how to read and write. He presided at the prayers on
Sunday and came to the beds of the dying. The second
was the baptiser. He always had a pupil in training
to be his successor. The baptiser did not hold office
for longer than ten years; and the pupil, as a rule,
studied the formula and assisted in administering the
rite for at least five years before succeeding to the office. Sometimes the offices of baptiser and prayer-leader
were held by the same person. The Christians had some
books and religious emblems that had been handed down
from generation to generation. One treatise on " Contrition " had been composed in 1603.

Traces were still to be seen of the distinctions that
existed in the work formerly done by the different religious orders. One community often looked upon another as not belonging to the same religion. They used
the names Kirishitan sect, Bateren sect,* and Dogio
sect according as the original teachers had been Franciscans, Jesuits, or Dominicans. Saints honoured in one
village might be unknown in another, and there were
differences in the days observed for fasting.

Among the prayer-leaders that visited the church was
a fisherman named Michael, who came from an island
near Nagasaki. At the end of the interview, the mis-

---

* The name " bateren," as applied by Japanese to Roman Catholic priests, is a corruption of the Portuguese word *padre*.

sionaries gave him a discipline with which to scourge himself when imploring pardon for his sins. His zeal in its use soon led to his being known by the name "Michael of the Discipline." He offered to put his boat at the disposal of the missionaries and take them to his own or other islands for secret interviews with the Christians. In September, M. Petitjean thought that he might venture to accept this invitation. His account of the trip, with some abbreviation, is as follows:—

"At evening Michael came to the house at the appointed hour to conduct me, disguised as a Japanese, to his boat, which was waiting for us near the station of the harbour police. The night was so dark that I did not need the disguise. Wearing my cassock, I went to the shore with my guide. We set out at eight o'clock in the evening and by half past eleven had reached our destination. On arriving at the hut which was to be my hiding-place, I found there more than thirty persons. It was a meeting of the leading men of the place, who for a long time had been urging me to visit them. The remainder of the night and all of the next day were spent in religious conversation. People were constantly coming and going. The village numbers at least three hundred houses, in each of which live six or seven people. There is not one of them who has not been baptised. The general spirit of this Christian community is excellent. It is surprising to find among them so much knowledge of our Faith. The doctrines of the Holy Trinity, of the Fall, of the Incarnation, and of the Redemption, seem to be as familiar to them as to most of our French Catholics. They know and keep the Commandments. They lead a life of penitence and perform frequent acts of contrition, especially at the hour of death. There are no books in their village; yet most of the inhabitants know by heart the Lord's Prayer, the Angelic Salutation, the Apostles' Creed, the *Confiteor*, the *Salve Regina*, and the Act of Contrition. Many of them repeat the treatise on Contrition of which I have before spoken. In the house whose hospitality I received they showed me with much reverence an image representing the Fifteen Mysteries of the Rosary, and below it were represented St. Francis of Assisi, St. Anthony of Padua, and a third saint whose name I could not tell. I have learned from the leaders of the community that in their village and a number of others the ceremony of trampling on the cross had not been practised from time immemorial. This exemption was due to the feudal lords, who were willing to show their independence of the Court at Yedo. The same persons tell me that at the time when the ceremony was in vogue the Christian officers used frequently to substitute images of Shaka for those of Jesus Christ and the Holy Virgin."

As the officials in Nagasaki sent warnings to the people that they ought not to visit the foreign church, it was arranged that the prayer-leaders and baptisers should come to the residence of the missionaries once a month, by night, in order to receive instruction, which afterwards they should convey to the other believers. These visitors were required to give a password when they came to the garden-gate. The servants employed by the missionaries then admitted them to their own apartments as though they were personal friends, and then saw that all the gates were securely fastened so that there might be no danger of interruption.

In the last months of 1865, notwithstanding the commands given by the officials, many deputations of Christians came to the church, among them being several from the Goto Islands. M. Girard in sending to Paris for more missionaries said that in the communities known to be in the southwest of Japan the Christians were estimated at fifty thousand. M. Petitjean at about the same time put the number of those in and around Nagasaki at twenty thousand; but in 1868, he informed the United States Minister that, so nearly as could be estimated, the number in the whole empire was about twenty thousand. In 1892, the Vicar Apostolic of Southern Japan said that, in all, fifty thousand descendants of the ancient Christians were discovered, though only about one-half of them re-entered the church, the remainder—" the rich," as he put it,—refusing to do so.

As the missionaries became better acquainted with the conditions of the different communities, they were much perplexed over the difficult problems awaiting solution. The Roman Catholic Church places so much stress upon baptism that there was much anxiety concerning the validity of the rite as it had been administered. The formulas used by different baptisers were found to be more or less corrupted.* In some cases the

* Some examples of these corruptions are seen in the following forms.

" Iogo te baotiz'no mono i nomoune Paiter, iets Hirii, iets Seu Santi. Amen."

" Iego te paoteren'zo in nomidz Patiris, Hirii, iets S'birito Santi. Amen."

water had been applied without pronouncing the words: in others, the formula had been pronounced upon the water, which was then sent by a messenger, who sometimes poured it on the head of the child and sometimes made him drink it.

Difficult, too, were the questions connected with marriage; for the Christians, deprived of their teachers, had fallen into the ways of the people about them. It was estimated that one-fourth of the families were in an irregular condition, because of divorces; while the unwillingness to contract marriages with unbelievers had increased the number of those within the prohibited degrees of relationship.

It was thought that no time ought to be lost before beginning to prepare men to be teachers of these companies of Christians. The missionaries fitted up in their own house a room that they named "The Hall of the Immaculate Conception." This was used as the abode, or rather hiding-place, of boys and young men, who received instruction in Christian doctrine, and to some extent, in Latin. It also served as a retreat for visitors who needed to spend more than a single evening at the Mission.

Messrs. Petitjean and Laucaigne felt the necessity of having a catechism to be used by the leaders of the Christian communities. They thought it best to keep the terms that were already current among the Christians. Meanwhile, Messrs. Girard and Mounicou in Yokohama, were preparing a catechism in which these terms—half Portuguese, half Latin—were replaced by those used in China. The difference of opinion over this matter caused some friction. The Yokohama catechism was the first to be completed, but when copies of it were sent to M. Petitjean, he would not distribute them. M. Libois in China, made this difficulty an argument for urging the officers of the Seminary in Paris to try and obtain the making of speedy arrange-

"Ego te baterinzo in nomine Pater, et Hirio, et Spirito Santo. Amen."
"Iogo te baotizo mono ni nomine Pater, et Hirio, et Spirito nome eo Santi. Iesamen."

ments for the governing of the Mission. It was partly in consequence of this that, in 1866, M. Petitjean was appointed Vicar Apostolic of Japan.

On the feast of the Twenty-six Martyrs in February, 1866, the sacrament of the Eucharist was for the first time administered to the Japanese. The service was held in the secret Hall of the Immaculate Conception where, on the previous night, " conditional baptism " had been administered to the intending communicants, in order to set aside any question about the validity of that which had been received before. These communicants were three young men who desired to devote their lives to the service of their Church. The missionaries would gladly have sent them for study to the seminary in China; but at that time it was difficult for a Japanese to leave his country. In the vicinity of Nagasaki there was a strict registration of all the inhabitants, with a yearly inspection by the police to see that none were absent without due authorisation.

Other first communions soon followed. A regular organisation of the catechumens was made so that they should come for instruction at appointed times and in companies of not more than twelve or fifteen at once. Those that were taught became teachers in their turn, as they returned to the villages and communicated to others what they had been told. Especially in Urakami there was great zeal to receive instruction. It was soon said that every one there, from the children six years of age to the old men and women, knew the prayers and more or less of the catechism. Tomokichi, who was now the baptiser, had so many asking for instruction that he felt obliged to limit the numbers, and so he refused to teach the girls. Thereupon, several of them, aged fifteen to eighteen, came as a deputation to remonstrate.

" Have you received religious instruction in order to teach everybody except us? Do you not wish that our souls should be saved? If we die, what will become of us? "

As Tomokichi remained inflexible, they became more importunate and said:

"Wretch that you are, do you wish then to keep everything for yourself? Do you despise us because we are women? Have we not as much need as others for salvation? We have fully decided that we will remain unmarried in order that we may give ourselves, body and soul, to God."

They withdrew in tears, many of them resolving that they would learn to read in order that they might make use of the catechism. Copies of this, made in the Hall of the Immaculate Conception, were in circulation among the Christians. When the missionaries learned what had occurred, they advised Tomokichi to teach the girls, provided they came accompanied by some of the mothers and at a time when young men were not present. Afterwards he might choose one or two widows for special instruction, who should serve as catechists for the women.

The Christians manifested great solicitude for the souls of their ancestors. To one who came, asking if it would not be possible to obtain paradise for those that had died before hearing the Gospel, M. Petitjean said: "But your progenitors for several generations have been Christians." "Yes, for seven generations; but before that all were pagans." The missionary told him that he should confine his prayers to those of his relatives who, according to Roman Catholic theology, might be in purgatory.

In 1866, M. Furet came to Nagasaki, and the Mission was increased by four new missionaries. M. Petitjean was absent through part of the year, having gone to Hongkong for episcopal ordination. On his return he spent a few days in Tokyo, where he told M. Roches, the French Minister, of his fears that the believers might be persecuted, and received the assurance: "I give my word that in case your Christians are disturbed, they may count upon the French Minister."

M. Furet considered that M. Petitjean was altogether too timid in trying to prevent the Christians from flocking to the church in such numbers as would arouse the opposition of the Government; but it was not long before events showed the need for caution. In November the head officer of Urakami assembled the chiefs of the villages, together with some of the principal Christians, and addressed them as follows:

"I supposed that after the misfortunes coming upon you ten years ago you had ceased to be Christians. On the contrary, I know that you often go to the European priests. I know that for a year you have been going to them for instruction, that your children are employed as their servants, and that you have carried many plants to ornament the grounds about the church. I wished to warn you earlier, but was prevented by illness. Believe me, you are doing wrong. Cease from such acts if you do not wish to be severely punished. I say this to you, who are the principal men of our village, so that you may prevail on your people not to provoke the Governor's anger by continuing to frequent the church."

All listened in silence to this exhortation and departed without making any reply. The visits by day to the church became infrequent; but every night many men came to the residence of the missionaries to receive instruction and prepare for the communion.

In January, 1867, M. Laucaigne began to make visits to the Urakami valley, remaining several days at a time in the retreats that the people prepared for him in the different hamlets. He himself has given to us some details of the methods that he used:—

"When nearly every one had gone to bed and there were but few people in the streets, I would lay aside the cassock that I usually wore and put on a Japanese dress that our Christians had made for me, a wig that was a gift from one of them, and some straw sandals, which, if it were muddy, served for but a single trip. The girdle about the waist and a kerchief around the head completed my costume. In this disguise I went among the Christians accompanied by two young men who carried a lantern and what I needed for saying mass. When I reached the Christian quarters, I was sure of meeting a company of the faithful who came out in front of their houses or walked along the fields on the edge of the road that they knew I would take. As soon as I came near them, they would kneel and make the sign of the cross; it was their way of saluting and of asking the blessing of their spiritual father. The Christians prepared for my reception little hiding-places in the most retired parts of their houses. Sometimes the little altar before which I was to say mass would be set up in a barn that on the outside had all the appearance of a shepherd's hut. It was always in the middle of the night that I said mass; all was over by dawn. Those 'that had been in attendance returned at once to their homes; there remained with me only so many persons as I could hear confess during the day. It goes without saying that I took good care not to go out by day lest I should be recognised by the heathen. It was only by night that I went to visit the sick or changed my residence. I remained but little more than a week consecutively in one place. Those were the happiest moments of my life."

M. Cousin, a new missionary who had arrived the previous year, spent eleven days in the Goto Islands, where he administered baptisms and communions. By the first of March those in the islands and in Urakami who had been admitted to the Eucharist numbered about four hundred.

Many among the Christians showed much zeal in carrying to others the instruction that they had received. Michael of the Discipline used to set out in his boat every day, as though to engage in fishing, but in reality to visit the Christians. Though not possessed of much education, he had so thoroughly learned the catechism and some of the prayers that he could teach them to others. After a while he began hunting up believers in more distant places, as in Hirado, where there were said to be about a thousand Christian families.

As believers in remote communities learned of the presence of missionaries in Nagasaki, many of them came for instruction. Since the Hall of the Immaculate Conception could give shelter to only about twenty persons each night, others had to await their turn. The Urakami people, although most of them were poor, gladly offered hospitality to their fellow-believers. One of the leading Christians sometimes had more than twenty of these visitors lodging with him. Another was zealous in hunting up any Christian travellers who were ill. Often he would carry such on his shoulders to his house, which was thus transformed into a hospital. If any of these persons seemed in danger of death, M. Laucaigne was summoned to their side.

XI

PERSECUTION

1867-1873

IT had been the custom of the Christians to avoid trouble by joining with others in making contributions to the temples, and by allowing deceased friends to be buried with Buddhist rites. Those in Urakami now resolved that, whatever might be the consequences, they would make no more gifts to temples. In April, 1867, the relatives of a Christian who had died asked the missionaries what they ought to do about the funeral. The latter said that the Church, as the enemy of all superstition, disapproved of heathen ceremonies, and they advised that, without having recourse to the Buddhists, they give notice of the death to the officers of the village. Instead of following this advice, the relatives, as had been done in some other cases, buried the body without saying anything to either officers or priests. These last brought the matter to the attention of the Mayor, who summoned the brother of the deceased person, reproved him for what he had done, and threatened to make him exhume the body in order to have it properly buried by the bonzes. The Christians made no reply, and the menace was not carried into effect. A few days later another death occurred. In this case notice was sent to the Mayor, who gave an order for burial by a Buddhist priest. The relatives declared that they would not accept the priest's services, and the Christians of the different villages sent deputies to the Mayor saying that, while they were loyal subjects of the Government, they wished to have no dealings with the bonzes. A few days later, the son and another relative of the deceased person were summoned

to appear before a magistrate in Nagasaki. By advice of
their Mayor they asked the deputies of the villages to
go with them. At two o'clock on the morning of the
appointed day, they sought strength through the sacrament of the Eucharist, and afterwards went to the magistrate. He said to the son:

" You have buried your mother without notifying the
Mayor or the priest."

" I informed the Mayor but not the priest."

" Why did you not call the latter? You know the law."

From this point Dominic Zenemon, one of the deputies, took the place of the son in replying to the
magistrate. In response to the last question he said:

" We do not like the bonzes, and our aversion to them
we have received from our ancestors."

" Why do you dislike the bonzes? "

" We do not believe what they teach."

" Henceforth, you must conform to the customs of
the country and call them."

" We are citizens of this country and are disposed to
obey you in all respects. Our religion declares this to
be our duty. We cannot, however, call the bonzes, for
that would be contrary to our religion. You can command us in whatever relates to the body; but not in
what concerns the *anima*."

" What do you mean by that word *anima?* "

" The *anima* is the soul. It is that part of ourselves
that does not die, that is capable of doing good or evil,
and that, after life in this world is over, will receive
reward or punishment."

" What is this religion of yours? "

" It is that which we received from our ancestors.
It gives peace to our hearts in this life, and assures us
of perfect blessedness in the life to come."

As the magistrate made further inquiries concerning
their belief, Dominic said:

" Being but a poor farmer, I know only the most essential parts of the doctrine; but if you will go to the
French priests, they will tell you all about our religion."

The Governor also met the deputies, and after asking
a few questions dismissed them. The next day he sent

them his decision that they ought to call the bonzes to conduct funerals. The Mayor advised them to present a petition asking to be freed from the necessity of doing what was opposed to their beliefs. Of eight hundred families living in the Urakami Valley, seven hundred were included in the list of those asking this exemption. Four days later, there was another death, and to the surprise of the people the Governor then gave his authorisation for funerals to be held without recourse to the Buddhists. The police officers simply took note of the failure to have the customary rites performed, and said that the course to be pursued would be decided later. In other respects the Christians for a while enjoyed greater freedom. They went openly to the church in Nagasaki, and made no attempt to conceal the chapels in Urakami. The change in the attitude of the officials was probably owing to the unwillingness of the Shogun to have anything done that would offend the French Minister, whose support he hoped to gain against those who were trying to overthrow his power. The Minister himself, when visiting Nagasaki in May, had met the Christians who were concealed in the house of the missionaries, and had promised to use his influence in their behalf. He also took part in the service of dedicating an image of the Virgin Mary that was set up before the church. In the evening the front of the church was illuminated, and the Vice-Governor, in company with the French Consul, came before the image and presented his congratulations to Mgr. Petitjean.

This apparently favourable condition of affairs was but the calm preceding the outbreak of a storm. About three o'clock on the morning of July 15, M. Laucaigne, who was spending a few days in Urakami, was suddenly awakened by the master of the house where he was stopping, who called to him:

"They are coming to arrest us. Quick! We must flee."

M. Laucaigne hastily dressed and barely escaped from one side of the garden as armed men entered at the other. The rain was falling in torrents as he made his way to the cabin of a poor old woman who lived on the edge of a forest. He had been there but a few moments when the approach of a band of officers made it necessary to flee. Hastening through the forest he came to a deep and thickly wooded valley where he remained several hours. When all seemed quiet he returned to the cabin. Another alarm drove him back to the forest, where he spent the night and then made his way to Nagasaki.

The police had been conducted to the village by a traitor, a young man who a few months before had made his first communion, and who on account of some family quarrel had put himself at the service of the Mayor, that officer being no longer inclined to favour the Christians. The chapel that had been M. Laucaigne's retreat was pillaged and all of his effects that he had left behind were taken. Several of the villages in the valley were visited and a number of the people arrested. The prisoners were at first taken before the Mayor. A crowd of their friends followed them. It is said that the Mayor tried to stir up the people to resist the officers and even to use weapons, his object being to have them raise such a revolt as would in the eyes of foreigners be a sufficient reason for punishment. Some of the Christians were so indignant at the cruel way in which the prisoners were treated that they did come to blows with the officers, but there was no such general disturbance as the Mayor desired.

Sixty-four of the arrested persons, some of them being women, were taken to Nagasaki. Crowds watched them as they passed through the streets. The European residents were greatly stirred by the sight. The consuls of different countries uttered their protests. In an interview with the Governors, the French Consul said:

" It is not in the name of the treaties that I come before you; it is as a friend and in the name of humanity whose laws you violate. Europe will condemn your act. In her esteem you will descend to the rank of barbarous peoples, and your relations with her will suffer. It may even be that the foreign ministers residing in Yedo will oblige you to retrace your steps, a humiliation that can be avoided if you now of your own accord release the prisoners."

A few days after the arrest, General Van Valkenburgh, the American Minister, came to Nagasaki. In a report to his government, he wrote:

"I at once asked an audience with the two Governors of Nagasaki, and on the twenty-ninth of July they visited me pursuant to my request. I expressed to them my regret at the occurrence and endeavoured to induce them to release the poor prisoners. They declined, having arrested them as criminals under the laws of Japan upon complaint and proof, unless by direction from the Government. They assured me, however, that they had not been tortured, and promised that the wants of those confined, as well as their families, should be provided for, and that no future arrests should be made until directions were received from the Goroju (Shogun's Council)."

The missionaries were much disappointed by the attitude of the French Minister. In a letter written August 8, to Mgr. Petitjean, he said that he had hastened to confer with the Shogun's Council, and had been impressed with the sentiments of moderation and tolerance expressed by its members. He was told that orders would soon be sent to Nagasaki for setting the prisoners at liberty. Meanwhile he reminded the missionaries that the present moment, when the enemies of the Shogun were watching every opportunity to weaken his authority, was not a favourable time for seeking a definite settlement of the religious question, on which the Japanese felt so deeply. He added that he did not doubt the missionaries would use their influence with the Christians to induce them to observe certain external formalities that did not touch their religious beliefs.

Evidently the "external formalities" of which the minister wrote were those connected with funerals, and the missionaries were unwilling to withdraw from their decision that the Christians ought to have nothing to do with the Buddhist priests. Two more deaths had occurred, and those responsible for the funerals had been taken into custody. To the protest of the American Minister that this was a violation of the promise made to him that there should be no more arrests until orders came from Yedo, the reply was given that the persons in question had not been put in prison, but were simply held for examination.

Persecution now commenced in the villages of Omura, some twenty miles from Nagasaki. In connection with a registration of the inhabitants, they were ordered to seal with their own blood, a statement that they were not Christians, and also to drink water over which the Buddhist priests had pronounced certain formulas. In one village forty men who refused to obey were thrown into prison, the women and children being left at liberty. In another village, the Christians at first sealed the document; but when they realised its meaning, they declared that they had been deceived and that they wished to be known as Christians. Thereupon, seven of the men were taken into custody. When the believers in Urakami learned what had happened, some of their number went to these villages in order to guard the houses and otherwise help the women and children, who, however, were soon after imprisoned as their husbands and fathers had been. The whole number of arrests at this time in Omura was about one hundred and ten.

A few days later an attempt was made to procure a general apostasy in Urakami. The Christians of the different villages were told to send delegates to receive an official communication. They accordingly chose persons for this purpose; but the Mayor, who feared that those selected might be too immovable, replaced them by others. On the appointed day the Governor of Nagasaki met these people. He urged them to take such action as would secure the release of their friends and put an end to the trouble. The first two delegates to whom he appealed were frightened into promising to do what was required. The next seven would not yield. Disconcerted by their firmness, the Governor told them to put their statements into writing so as to send them to him in a few days. He then said it was necessary for him to return to Nagasaki where the prisoners were being examined. His place was now taken by a subordinate, before whom came the delegates that had been originally chosen by the villagers. They bore a petition that they asked him to present to the Governor. After he had examined it, the officer said:

" This of itself is sufficient to ruin you, for in it you

have used the word 'Christian,' a name which the Government does not permit."

Throughout the interview the officials themselves had always taken care not to use that word, but had replaced it by such terms as "the French religion," "the foreign religion," "the religion of the Lord of Heaven," etc.

On the same day in Nagasaki, five of the Christians were led in chains across the city from the prison to the place where they were to be examined. They were taken one at a time before the Governor, who among other questions, asked them how they had been instructed, who were their leaders, who among them had taken the first steps in getting the missionaries to visit their villages, and whether they were able to perform miracles.

These examinations were continued from day to day. On September 8, when twenty-two of the prisoners were brought before the officers, all but one of them apostatised. At their head was the chief of one of the villages, a man enfeebled by ill health, who was as yet only a catechumen. The apostates did not receive their liberty, though they were exempted from the severe treatment to which the others were now subjected. The latter were crowded into a little room and had their food reduced to a very small allowance.

At this time, for reasons not connected with the Christians, the Governors of Nagasaki were replaced by an envoy of the Shogun. In an interview with the French Consul the new official denied that the prisoners had been ill-treated. He said that he would release them if they would renounce their faith. Henceforth, too, the missionaries must cease to visit them. When the Consul asked why the prisoners had not already been set free in accordance with the promise made to the French Minister, he was told that the Shogun had never ratified the action of the Council in this matter.

One concession was granted a little later. Whereas, forty-seven persons had been confined in a room twelve feet long and six feet wide, the number was now reduced to thirty-three.*

* U. S. Dipl. Correspondence, 1867, p. 72.

On September 16, twenty-eight of the Christians in Urakami were called to the house of the Mayor, that they might be questioned separately by the Buddhist priests.

"Why," was the question put to one of them, "do you follow the religion of the foreign priests? Cannot you save your soul well enough through Buddhism, which likewise teaches about heaven and hell? We also adore one supreme being—Amida. It is only because you are not acquainted with our teaching that you reject it."

"No," was the reply, "it is because we are Christians and wish nothing to do with Amida."

"But what you believe is really the same as what we hold to be true. Tell me what your belief is."

The Christian repeated the Apostles' Creed, strongly emphasising the article, "I believe in the life everlasting."

"That is a very beautiful doctrine. You can follow it without calling yourselves Christians and thus doing what is forbidden by the laws of the land. Do not the commands of the Lord of Heaven require obedience to parents? Why then do you disobey the rulers, who are the fathers and mothers of the people?"

"We are quite willing to obey the rulers, but not to accept the doctrine of Amida," persisted the Christian.

Soon after this Mgr. Petitjean received from M. Roches, the French Minister, a note that contained the following passage:

"You will to-day receive an official letter, an authentic copy of which I have transmitted to the Japanese Government. It is only in consequence of receiving this document that it has consented to set the prisoners at liberty without demanding from them any act that could be regarded as an abjuration. I ought to add that it was not without great difficulty that I secured this solution of the problem. The daimyos, who, we have been told, are little favourable to the spread of Christianity, and who are perfectly well informed concerning all that has occurred at Nagasaki, have all sent protests to the Shogun against the present state of affairs. They expressed the opinion that the Shogun's Government had given tacit assent to their views, and they added that they were determined to resort to the most energetic methods for causing the fundamental laws of Japan to be respected. They declared that they had given stringent orders for the beheading of any European priest or Japanese Christian that might dare to enter their territories. These letters of the daimyos are by no means a pretext invented by the Japanese Government to cover the present necessity; I have read them and have been able to verify for myself their authority."

The official letter to which the personal note refers was likewise addressed to Mgr. Petitjean. It informed him that the Japanese Government had consented to pardon the persons arrested at Nagasaki who had violated the laws of the country by professing an unauthorised religion. " I ought to add," continued the Minister, " that, if the Shogun forgives the past, he understands that in the future the Japanese will observe the laws of the Empire. I therefore hope that as regards your Catholic Mission you will avoid every act that has for its purpose the encouragement of Japanese subjects who profess the Christian religion in continuing their resistance to the authorities under whom the laws of Japan place them."

The Minister also wrote to the French Consul in Nagasaki:

" After I have obtained the unconditional release of all the Japanese who have been imprisoned on the charge of having violated the laws of the country by professing the Christian religion, you will warn the Bishop in my name that he must henceforth avoid everything that can encourage Japanese subjects to break or defy the laws of the land. Hereafter no priest of the Catholic Mission should go to Urakami or elsewhere for the purpose of religious propagandism. In the great state of excitement that now prevails in the south of Japan, the presence of a Catholic missionary in the midst of the native population would be the cause of incalculable evils. A sound policy and the true interests of our religion admonish us to do all we can to avoid such a result. You will therefore aid, so far as you can, the carrying out what is written in this letter and the spirit of my instructions."

It is not strange that Mgr. Petitjean felt called upon to write to the Minister reminding him that he had been kept informed of what was happening, and that during his visit to Nagasaki, in June, when his attention had been called to the question of the funerals, he had tried to re-assure the missionaries by speaking of the liberal ideas of the Shogun, while at the same time he had promised the Christians that he would use his influence in favour of religious toleration. The letter closed with the state-ment that it would be impossible to follow the recom-mendations made by the Minister.

The prisoners were brought, October 5, before the Governor, who informed them that they could be set at liberty only on condition of their signing a document which admitted that they had been following a religion not sanctioned by the Government. Some of them con-sented, and after three days ten of the leaders of the Christians, who had been subjected to torture, yielded, and said to their companions:

"We have submitted; and if we, who are men, have done so, what can you women and children do? It is impossible for you to hold out. It is better to surrender at once rather than to suffer torture uselessly."

This advice was so far followed that the paper was signed by all of the prisoners with the exception of Dominic Zenemon, who still stood firm. Twice was he tortured; but each time he came forth victorious from the test. No less than seven times was he brought be-fore the Governor or his delegates.

"How have you been instructed?" he was asked.

"At first I went like the others to visit the church. There, I saw the priest praying and I asked him to teach me his doctrine."

"Were you not aware that the laws of Japan forbid its people to follow the religion of foreigners?"

"I did know it; but I thought the Emperor ought to permit us to follow this religion, for its doctrines are good, and it teaches nothing but what is right. Urakami has become much better since it has learned the Christian doctrines. Its people do not quarrel, nor drink; they busy themselves with taking care of the sick or with labour in the fields, which are more productive than ever before. It is asserted that Christians practice sorcery and perform miracles. This is a mistake. Sorcery is the work of devils; and if we could work miracles, we should have come out of the prison in spite of you."

"This religion may be good; but by following it you have broken the law and so done wrong."

"No, I have not done wrong; for God, who teaches men this religion, is my first Father and my first Mother. As for the law, if I have violated it, let the offence be washed out by my blood. I give up my body to satisfy the law; but I wish to save my soul."

Notwithstanding his steadfastness, Dominic was soon set at liberty. On his return to Urakami his house was crowded with those that came to hear from his own lips the story of the trials through which he had passed. Those who had not been so brave were ashamed of their weakness. Already, on the day of their deliverance from prison, thirty-eight persons had gone to the Governor's house, saying: "Our apostasy was only in words and not from the heart. We were overcome by fear of torture. To atone for our crime we are ready to go back to our chains, to suffer, and to die." A few days later, ten others wished to follow their example; but the official of their district refused to bring them before the Governor.

Officers had been sent to destroy all the chapels in the valley, and they compelled the Christians to assist in the work. Fifty policemen were stationed in the villages to watch over those who had withdrawn their acknowledgement of wrong-doing. At first these persons were not allowed to have any communication with others. While they were at home, guards stood before their doors; and when they went to work in the fields, they were followed by officers. Little by little this surveillance was relaxed, and in December the guards were withdrawn. A few days before this was done, the Governor himself came to the houses of those that had retracted, expressed his pity for what they had suffered, and in a paternal way advised them to be more careful in the future. He feigned ignorance of their protestations that they had never wished to renounce Christianity, and said that he was so satisfied with their submission to the Government that he could now take away the guards as being no longer needed. A patrol was kept in the village, however; daily visits being made to the houses of the persons who had retracted. The object of this seemed to be to prevent them from having any communication with the missionaries; yet hardly a night passed when some of them did not find means of going to the residence in Nagasaki, where they expressed great remorse for the weakness they had shown, and sought pardon for their sin.

Death could not be shut out from the valley; and those that were responsible for the burial of their friends without Buddhist rites were summoned before the officials, only to be dismissed with a reprimand or with the statement that their cases would be considered later.

The prisoners in Omura suffered much from insufficient food and, as winter came on, from insufficient clothing. Four adults and several children died.

There was persecution in other communities. Some of the Christians apostatised, while others tried to conceal their faith. Even Michael of the Discipline advised the Christians to assume the outward appearance of heathenism. When the missionaries learned of this, they were able to get him to come and see them, and as a result of the interview he put away certain Buddhist emblems that he had thought it right to use in order to avoid persecution. At Shittsu a number of Christians were beaten because they refused to attend Buddhist services. Afterwards ninety persons from this place and seventeen from Kurosaki, were sent to the coal mines at Takashima as convicts, sentenced to hard labour.

Though the Christians in the Goto Islands were not molested at this time, they were apprehensive that their turn would come. Six of their number, therefore, set out in a small boat to see if they could not find some uninhabited island that would serve as a retreat for the

Christians when persecution should arise. For several months nothing was heard from them. Driven about by the winds and disappointed by finding people living in all places at which they touched, they finally came to a small island belonging to Satsuma. Its inhabitants regarded them as shipwrecked sailors, confiscated their boat, and sent them to Nagasaki, whence they returned to their home, convinced that no island suited to their purpose could be found.

In October, 1867, Mgr. Petitjean went to France and Rome in order to plead the cause of his Mission. His attempts to induce Napoleon III. to make a benevolent intervention in favour of the persecuted Christians were of no avail, the Emperor saying that nothing could be done except in concert with the other Powers.

It was in the absence of the Vicar Apostolic, who did not return until June, 1868, that the Shogunate was overthrown and the old edicts against Christianity re-affirmed by the new Government. Even before this last action was announced, there were signs of the storm that was soon to break in its fury. March 16, twenty-two Christians of Urakami, eleven of whom had been among those arrested the previous year, were ordered to appear before the new Governor. One of them was Dominic Zenemon, who became their spokesman. About three hundred of their friends followed them to the open courtyard in front of the Governor's residence. While waiting for the door to be opened, they knelt upon the coarse pebbles that took the place of a pavement, and with rosaries in their hands, spent the time in prayer.

The officer that conducted the examination began by asking:

" Is it true that you adore Jesus and follow the religion of the French? "

His pronunciation of the word " Jesus " being different from that used by the Christians, Dominic was not quite sure of its meaning and so said:

" We follow the true Christianity."

"·Christianity [Roman Catholicism] is the religion of the French. If it were good, the other nations of Europe would accept it. Instead of doing so, they mock at it. Therefore, it is evil and you ought to give it up."

"We cannot do so. It is necessary to be a Christian in order to secure the salvation of the soul in another life."

"Do you believe that a naked man, a criminal fastened to a cross, can protect you? Ten years ago some of your people were put in prison and many of them have since died. Do you believe that any calamity has come to the officers that ordered their punishment?"

"God does not always punish men in this life. He waits."

Dominic was going on to explain some of the Christian doctrines when he was ordered to be silent:

"Who are you that you dare to talk in this way before your superiors? You must give up this religion or else resign yourself to death. Choose."

"I cannot give up being a Christian."

"Are you all of the same mind?"

"Yes, yes," cried the Christians, as they made low bows.

The question was put to them three times with short intervals for reflection; but they continued to give the same reply. The officer then said:

"You have come here with closed ears, fully determined not to listen. What would happen in your families if the women and children refused to obey the head of the house? Everything would go wrong, and it would be necessary to chastise them. In Japan there is only one Head of the Empire, and all ought to obey him."

"We are loyal to him. If we are only permitted to be Christians, the Government would have no more faithful servants than we are."

"You disobey the laws by following a foreign religion. Do you not see that you will be put to death and that your families will suffer for your offence? Withdraw from here. Consult with your friends, your wives, and your children. Perhaps they will be wiser than you are. Away with you!"

April 29, one hundred and eighty heads of Christian families in Urakami were called before the Governor.

As before, Dominic was the chief speaker. After all had declared that they could not give up Christianity, they were told:

"Instead of trusting your rulers, who are the father and mother of the people, you allow yourselves to be deceived by the French priests. They seek only the conquest of the land. That is the reason why your religion has for so long a time been prohibited, as it will continue to be, whatever changes there may be in the government. You are traitors, since you do not adore Ama-terasu, who came from heaven to create Japan and who perpetuates herself in the person of the Mikado, her direct descendant, and in the officials, who are his representatives. What have the French and other priests done that you should ally yourselves with them? What complaint have you to make against the Son of Heaven and his officials, that you will not submit to them?"

"If we are disobedient," said Dominic, "let us be put to death. It is what we desire."

Once more the Christians were dismissed that they might reflect on what had been said. There were many rumours about what would be done to them. It was said that twenty were at once to be put to death, while the others would be tortured. The day and the hour on which the execution was to take place were said to have been fixed, and people from the neighbouring country began to flock into Nagasaki in hopes to see the spectacle. The foreign consuls in a letter that they addressed to the Governor General of Kyushu, said that they had no desire to interfere with the rights of the Government, but since there were persistent rumours that a general persecution of the Christians had been planned, they desired to make an earnest remonstrance against what would certainly injure Japan's reputation with Western nations.

On May 14 the Supreme Council of the Emperor sent the following circular to the provincial governors:

"Among the inhabitants of the village of Urakami near Nagasaki there have always been some persons who have not ceased to follow the Christian religion; but in recent years their number has grown from day to day until the whole village, consisting of about three thousand inhabitants, practise that religion. The tribunal at Nagasaki is greatly troubled over this matter. It has vainly tried by all sorts of expostulations to bring these people to repentance. At the beginning of the new system of government we cannot, without exposing the country to most serious perils, permit this to continue. Measures of repression must be taken at once. The leaders must be called together and an attempt be made to detach them from their belief by kind exhortations. If they yield, they must be made to destroy their books and religious images and then to take a vow before the national gods. In case they do not heed the exhortations, nothing remains but to adopt strong measures. The leaders must be arrested and beheaded, their heads being exposed as a warning. Others must be transported to distant provinces where they shall be employed in various kinds of labour. In this way it will doubtless be possible to root out the beliefs that they cherish. Those that in time show signs of repentance shall be allowed to return to their villages. While the gravity of the crime may render these methods necessary, they are nevertheless extreme measures. Hence, before putting them into execution, each daimyo is requested to state without reserve his opinion upon the subject."

Okuma Shigenobu (afterwards Count Okuma, the well-known statesman) had been one of the officials in Nagasaki at the time when Christians were first arrested under the new Government. A few days later he was appointed an Assistant Councillor of State and called to Kyoto. Immediately after his arrival, the Supreme Council held a meeting to consider what action should be taken in connection with protests made by the foreign representatives against the treatment of the Christians. As no others had any definite plan to propose, they finally agreed with Okuma's contention that yielding to the demands of the foreigners would be such a lowering of national dignity that a refusal ought to be given, even though it should lead to war. Accordingly at a conference held at Osaka with the foreign ministers he was the chief speaker. His own account of the meeting will show the view taken by the Japanese and some of the difficulties with which the Government had to contend:

"I said: 'I am one of those who arrested and examined Christians in Nagasaki. . . . We cannot grant your request for releasing the prisoners and withdrawing the prohibitions against Christianity. Foreign countries are not justified in interfering when we punish our people according to our laws. Hence we do not think it necessary to discuss the matter with you.'"

"Sir Harry Parkes, the English Minister, was very angry. He shook his fist and struck the table as he said: 'This is insolence; this is going too far. Religion and truth are universal. Men are free to follow this religion or acknowledge that truth as they deem right. Among civilised nations, there is none that does not permit liberty of belief. To have laws punishing people who have done nothing wrong, to erect barriers for shutting out the truth, is a shame for even a barbarous country. You do not realise what you are doing. You are rejecting the friendship of other lands. You ought to consider the condition of Japan and think of its future.'

"I answered: 'You cannot hope to move us by such simple arguments as these. I know a little about religion and religious history. Christianity, indeed, contains some truth; but it must not be forgotten that its history is filled with evil. A historian has said that the history of Europe is the history of strife; and a religious writer says that the history of Europe is the history of Christianity. If these authors are correct, the history of Christianity is a history of strife. Christ has not given peace to the earth but a sword. After the birth of Christ came the age of the popes. What was it that gave rise to great tumults and continually plunged the people of Europe into deep misery? From ancient times the rulers of different countries have often done cruel deeds; but what is it that has gone beyond kings in cruelty? How about the dungeons and the torments for punishing those who, as you say, simply held opinions differing from those of others? Of late, this evil has somewhat decreased in the West. This is because men's minds are expanding and they are not controlled by religion alone. In our country, conditions at present are different. From the first, Shinto has controlled men's minds. Buddhism also has had great power for over a thousand years. We are not lacking a religion. If at this time we should remove the edicts against Christianity and at the same time release its followers who have been arrested, Shintoists and Buddhists would rise up in anger and there would be a great disturbance. Of all disputes, none are more violent than those connected with religion. They suck out the blood, crunch the bones, and are never satiated. We cannot tell what sort of strife would arise in our land. Our statesmen must carefully consider this. In what happened at Nagasaki our Government did not make the first move. The people of different places came with their complaints and urged us to take action against the Christians. We were forced by reasons connected with the internal affairs of the country to take action and strictly suppress Christianity. We thank you for your benevolent thoughts; but the facts being as stated, what else can we do?'

"Parkes became more angry and said: 'You are cowardly. If you wish to accomplish anything you must expect some loss. If you hesitate because of unwillingness to face difficulties, you can never attain success. Is not this an era of re-organisation? Why not destroy evil customs and come out into a broader world than you have yet known? Christianity is now accepted by all civilised countries. Though some evils may have appeared in its history, its fruits are seen in the civilisation of this nineteenth century. Its excellence and truth are evident. Nothing is worse than to regard as an enemy what the whole world knows to be good; nothing is so foolish as to reject the truth. You ought to open your eyes. It is truly said that Oriental officials are so in the habit of looking only at what is directly before them that they never turn their gaze upwards. If you repeal the edicts and pardon the prisoners, you will find that your fears were needless. If you do not take this action, I am sure that Japan is doomed.'

"I answered with a laugh: 'The day that we blindly follow the commands of foreigners will surely be the time of our nation's destruction. We are better acquainted than you with the state of affairs in our country. You think that what you desire can easily be done; but it is not so. Religious views that are the product of past centuries cannot be overcome in a single day. We cannot endure to add another to the many things that are disturbing our country. In making purchases, one should not pay more than a reasonable price. We do not like to pay too high a price, as we should by purchasing Christianity at the cost of many human lives.'" *

June 7, the very day that Mgr. Petitjean reached Japan on his return from Europe, another circular from the Supreme Council ordered the deportation of the Chris-

---

* "Sekijitsu no Monogatari" ("Talks about Former Days"), pp. 273-389. The *Fukuin Shimpo* of December 11, 1902, published an interview with Count Okuma in which he said that at the conference in Osaka the zeal natural to youth was increased by the fact that he had made up his mind at that time to construct a new religion that should combine the best elements of Buddhism, Confucianism, and Christianity, and he felt that the spread of Christianity would interfere with this plan. He added that the French Minister became angry and said that he should ask his Government to send men-of-war to protect the Christians. To this Okuma rejoined: "Your threat shows how good reason we have to fear Christianity; for as soon as trouble arises, there is instantly talk about gunboats."

tians. It was accompanied by a list that specified how four thousand and ten of them were to be distributed among thirty-four daimiates. It was directed that "these persons shall be rigidly excluded from social intercourse until it shall have been proved that their hearts are purified. They shall be employed as labourers on ground requiring improvement, such as mines, collieries, etc. They shall live in forests." The daimyos should take care "to induce them to renounce their evil way, and if there be any who refuse to repent, severe punishment must be inflicted." * Capital punishment was probably intended by this last clause.

The Governor-General of Kyushu now sent a tardy reply to the letter of the consuls in which he said: "We respect the humane feelings which dictated this letter, and we pity these perverse-minded Japanese subjects of the lower class who, in the face of an old established Japanese law, have committed the crime of apostatising to a strange religion. The practice of this is strictly prohibited, and we shall have no alternative but to punish them according to Japanese law if our repeated remonstrances do not cause them immediately to repent and retract their errors."

Kido, who had been one of the leaders in restoring power to the Emperor, was sent to Nagasaki to enquire concerning the Christians and to arrange for carrying the proclamation into effect. In an interview with the English Consul he said that so much animosity existed between the Christians and other Japanese of the lower classes that civil strife was feared by the Government, whose object was not so much to oppose Christianity as to preserve order. It did not wish to resort to extreme measures; but if the means now being taken did not produce the desired result, it would be necessary to punish the Christians severely. He believed that the missionaries still kept up secret communication with their followers in Urakami. A missionary seemed to him to be a man sent to Japan that he might teach the Japanese to break the laws of the land.†

* U. S. Dip. Cor., 1868, Part I., p. 771.
† Adams, "Hist. of Japan," vol. ii., p. 145. One charge made

The deportation of the Christians soon began. The first company, consisting of one hundred and twenty persons, was summoned July 20. Their friends, who followed them to the gates of the Governor's residence, were driven away with blows. The prisoners were taken on board a Japanese steamer, and at one time it was commonly believed that they had been taken to sea and drowned. It was afterwards learned that they had been divided among three provinces. Sixteen of them had been sentenced to death, but were reprieved in consequence of representations made by the foreign ministers.* It was partly perhaps because of these protests and partly because the Government's attention was occupied in repressing its opponents in the northeast that there was a lull in the persecution.

On the evening of the day after the first deportation, M. Cousin embarked on a steamer that was starting for Shanghai. The anchor had been weighed, the customhouse officers had departed, and the steamer was moving slowly as though picking its way with difficulty among the other vessels in the harbour, when the captain's boat, which had been sent to shore, came quickly alongside, bringing with it ten lads, the seminarists from the Hall of the Immaculate Conception. They were taken on board and the steamer hastened on its way. M. Cousin took his pupils to the college at Penang. Four of the boys died there, while three others were unable to keep on with their studies. The remaining three afterwards returned to Japan, where in 1882 they were ordained as priests.

The Christians in Urakami now openly practised their religion, for they knew that it could not be concealed. There was not a day when some persons belonging to the families of those that had been exiled did not go to the church in Nagasaki. M. Laucaigne, disguised as a Japa-

---

against the Christians by their opponents was that they held meetings at night in which gross licentiousness prevailed. Apparently the American Minister was inclined to think there was some ground for the accusation, though he gave no reason for such an opinion. U. S. Dip. Cor., 1868, Part II., p. 765.

* U. S. Dip. Cor., 1868, Part II., p. 796.

nese, often went by night into the valley in order to administer the sacraments to the dying.

Several Buddhist sects requested that the Christians be put in their chárge so that attempts might be made for their conversion; but Buddhism itself was not in favour with those now in power, and the petition was rejected.*

November 12, in Hisakashima, a small island belonging to the Goto group, twenty-two heads of families were arrested and taken to the chief town of the islands. Immediately afterwards, with the exception of six young men who escaped, the whole remaining population, men, women, and children, one hundred and eighty-one persons in all, were shut up in the house belonging to one of them, this improvised prison being so crowded that there were seventeen persons to a single mat.† The food given them was insufficient. One child and one old person soon died. There were arrests in other places. In January, 1869, a letter of instruction from the Supreme Council warned the Daimyo in Goto that in taking action against the Christians care should be exercised that nothing concerning it should become known outside.

At about this time a registration was made of all those families in Urakami from which no members had been deported. This proceeding led to fear that more arrests would soon be made. The number of the prisoners at Omura had been greatly lessened by death, there being in January, 1869, only seventy-eight survivors of the one hundred and twenty-three that had been incarcerated less than a year and a half before.

The persecutions at the Goto Islands became known to the foreign ministers, so that they sent a new protest to the Imperial Government. After a while the reply came that an officer sent to make an investigation had reported that there had been no persecution. Thereupon the ministers presented a detailed statement prepared by Mgr. Petitjean, which gave particulars concerning four hun-

---

* "Shin Nihon-shi," vol. ii., p. 255.
† This is the statement in "La Relig. de Jésus Res.," vol. ii., p. 129; but, as Japanese mats measure six feet by three, it seems almost incrédible.

dred persons who had been arrested. Many of them had been tortured, while two men, three women, and twelve children had died under the treatment received. The particulars concerning the death of the men was given as follows:

" 1. Paul Sakeichi, aged 79 years, arrested the 12th November, was beaten with an iron rod and thrown in prison, where he died toward the middle of December, of hunger, cold, and the blows he had received.

" 2. Francis Rikiso, aged 55, son of the above Sakeichi, arrested the same day as his father, was, after being beaten almost to death, submitted to the torture named *sangtshino seine*,* during which he fainted. On recovering consciousness, he was, on the following day, tortured again; the executioners beat him with iron bars, putting live coals into his mouth. Again it was thought he was dead. Thrown into a prison where he had scarcely room to rest his bruised body, he was soon nothing but one living sore, and died after three months of agony, on the 17th February, 1869. His body was left unburied for four days and nights in the midst of the prisoners." †

In the year 1869 arrests occurred from time to time. The protests of the ministers appeared to have little effect except that in the Goto Islands the number of those kept in confinement was reduced in June to twenty-seven, all of whom were heads of families. These were told that ere long they would be put to death unless they gave up their religion. The others were kept under surveillance, and those that were able to do so were made to work in the fields. Mr. De Long, the United States Minister, received from the officials of the Foreign Department the following communication:—

" In reply to the letter received in the fifth month of last year, we now beg to inform your excellency that we duly inquired into the alleged ill-treatment of Christians from the officers in charge of the Goto Islands; and as their statement did not appear to us sufficiently explicit, we directed some officers from Nagasaki to

* More properly, *sangi no seme*, or the punishment by three pieces of wood. The prisoner was made to kneel on two pyramids of wood and to sit back on his heels. His thighs were loaded with heavy stones. The third piece of wood was a long pole placed between the calves and the lower part of the thighs. Two attendants seated on the ends of the pole used it as a sort of seesaw.

† U. S. For. Relations, 1870, p. 453.

visit those islands and investigate the matter on the spot. Altogether there were more than one thousand persons on those islands who professed Christanity. Out of those, three hundred and thirty-five were reconverted to their own country's religion after having been gradually advised and disciplined. Five hundred and ninety-three were kept in prison, where they continued to receive advice, and one hundred and forty of these persons escaped from their prison.

"It having been reported that some of those had formed a conspiracy to rise against authority, they were caught and tried, and those who did not confess were coerced in the usual way in order to extort confession from them; but they have not been struck with iron rods, nor has fire been put into their mouths, as mentioned in your letter. Moreover, the prison, so-called, was simply a dwelling-house arranged in such a way that the persons kept in it could not go out during the night. During the daytime they were permitted to work on their farms. Of this large number, some have died from natural causes, but not from any cruel treatment administered. Those persons received a much gentler treatment than is usually accorded to criminals under the laws; and since special laws were issued during the last sixth month relative to Christianity, ill treatment of native Christians has been forbidden, and we believe therefore that the cruelties reported to have been practised are simply the result of rumours without foundation. . . ."*

January 7 another communication from the same officials said that it had been decided to transport all the Christians remaining in Urakami; "our reasons being that if those Christians remain undisturbed, from the unfriendly feelings of which they are the objects, difficulties will inevitably arise between them and their neighbours, and in this manner it will become troublesome to govern those country people. In conclusion, we beg to state that, all rumours that may be circulated notwithstanding, those people will not be subject to any severe labour." †

Early in January, 1870, all the Christians of Urakami, about three thousand in number, were embarked on two steamers. The men were first sent on board and were followed by the women and children. Those of the women who had been admitted to the sacraments wore upon their heads the white cloths that had been given to them as veils at the time of their baptism. Many were

* U. S. For. Relations, 1870, p. 455.
†Ib., p. 456.

seen to make the sign of the cross as they got into the boats that bore them to the steamers.

The foreigners in Nagasaki were moved with pity and indignation. Nothing was effected by a protest of the consuls; while Sir Harry Parkes, the English Minister, who arrived in Nagasaki while the Christians were being collected, asked in vain that the proceedings be delayed for fifteen days in order that he might have time to communicate with the Central Government. On his return to Tokyo, he joined with the representatives of the other treaty powers in asking for a conference with the highest officers of the state. The request was granted, and the meeting was held January 19. It was attended by Sir Harry Parkes, and Messrs. Outrey, De Long, and Von Brandt, the representatives respectively of Great Britain, France, the United States and Holland. Among the Japanese were Prince Sanjo, the Prime Minister; Sawa and Terashima, Ministers of Foreign Affairs; and eight members of the Imperial Council. Some extracts from the report of the proceedings will show the position assumed by each party in the controversy:

Sanjo. "Since last year the Government has had a full opportunity of discovering and understanding the character of the Japanese people who profess Christianity, and it has learned that they have become troublesome, and if allowed to proceed unchecked will subvert all governmental authority, interfere with trade, and seriously affect the relations of the Government with foreign nations. This Government does not move these people on account of their religious professions, but on account of their having been for a long time ungovernable and insubordinate, and on this account the Government has determined to change their residence. The Government heretofore removed some of them and has treated them with kindness, and those now being removed are being treated in the same manner, and consequently we do not think that we have destroyed or violated the promises made by this Government last year to the foreign representatives. This Government, in allotting to these people new residences, has not been persecuting them. . . ."

Parkes. ". . . My own judgment of this, and I am sure it will be of my Government, is that this was a most cruel proceeding, the only reason assigned being that these people professed the Christian religion, and that is the religion of my countrymen. Such an act when known in England will produce a bad effect and be looked upon as a most unfriendly act. . . .

If a few of these people commit wrongs, punish them; but to visit this punishment on families and on thousands is contrary to our view of right. . . ."

Outrey. "In my opinion there is a misunderstanding about a word. You said you would act ' mildly' towards native Christians. I suppose the greatest punishment you consider you could inflict is death, and I suppose what you mean by ' mild treatment' is that you will not *kill*. This is not our understanding of ' mild treatment.' In our country it is regarded that a man taken from his family and banished is most cruelly treated. . . . "

Iwakura. "There is a misunderstanding. We consider that we have acted mildly and as we promised. These persons recently deported have had their families sent with them, and this cannot be called severe punishment. They have lands assigned them and an opportunity given them to make a living as they had before. Heretofore the punishment for this offence was crucifixion. This we had moderated at the request of the foreign representatives, but you know that in Japan, where all the people believe in one religion, a sudden change or the sudden introduction of a new religion would produce great and constant political disturbances. Our object now is to converse on this subject. If in the future we understand and believe it to be necessary we will still execute this order. If it was only for those people at Urakami believing in Christianity, this Government would never have thought of moving them. Whether it is on account of their religious belief or because bad persons seek refuge there, we do not know; but trouble ensues and the only way we know of correcting it is dividing them up and sending them away. This is done solely on account of their acts of insubordination."

Outrey. "This is not in accordance with the letter you wrote us. I will ask what are those things in which they are disobedient? Is it because they profess Christianity or not?"

Sawa. "I was myself for a long time Governor of Nagasaki, and I know all about these people. What I now say is that it is not owing to the influence of missionaries that criminals from neighbouring daimyos' clans take refuge in these Christian villages and are there received; they then profess Christianity, are baptised, etc., and when the Government officers seek to apprehend them, collisions ensue between these Christians and the forces sent to apprehend them, while, in fact, these men are robbers."

Outrey. "I wonder that you have the power to punish a whole village and not a few persons in it. There is contradiction here."

Sawa. "I did not mean to say that we could not arrest them, but that the whole people of the village would resist our officers, pretending that the man was being arrested on account of his religious faith when really it was for some crime he had committed."

Terashima. "The villagers among themselves are extremely

hostile toward those in the same village not of the same religious faith; that is, among our people it is quite usual for one to help another in necessity by making little loans of salt or provisions. When asked such favours, these Christians would not grant them unless the others would profess Christianity; and many have thus been starved or driven into professing Christianity. Their conduct has been constantly overbearing. They have not come to open hostilities, but they have pursued a system of vexation and intimidation so oppressive that it has led many to leave. . . ."

*   *   *   *   *   *   *

Sawa. "The upshot of this matter is that we do not move these people on account of their profession of the Christian faith, but on account of their actions, and this Government would have pursued the same course with any other people; and unless we do this we do not know how we will govern them."

Outrey. "How many people?"

Sawa. "About five thousand."

Outrey. "How many Christians?"

Sawa. "About three thousand."

Outrey. "Three thousand are troubling two thousand, and you remove the three thousand?"

Sawa. "Yes."

Outrey. "I thought there were four thousand, according to this decree."

Sawa. "This included native Christians in neighbouring villages."

De Long. "Has the decree of deportation which was published last year been repealed or amended?"

Sawa. "It was left in abeyance for awhile on account of our internal troubles. It has not been repealed or amended."

Terashima. "We were prevented from carrying it out also on account of the expenses we should have had to incur, these Christians not being treated as criminals, but they were provided with houses and lands, besides their number being very large. We have hoped the respite given them would induce them to amend their ways. In this we were mistaken."

De Long. "Then the decree now being enforced is the original decree?"

Sawa. "Yes, but in a milder form; and we shall explain the difference to you."

Terashima. "Formerly only the men were to be deported; now they are not separated from their families, and they will even be furnished lands and houses."

*   *   *   *   *   *   *

Iwakura. "If this Government has prohibited the Christian religion in Japan, it is not because it is opposed to it, but because we foresee great troubles to ensue from it, as, for instance, if one man in a hundred becomes converted to that faith it would lead to a splitting up and dividing of the people.

Formerly the laws against this were very strict; now they are three or four degrees milder than formerly but we cannot allow it to be professed generally."

Von Brandt. "We do not ask you to allow the free exercise of it, but we do ask that men who do profess it shall not be punished for professing it; in this there is a great distinction. I ask no change of laws, but simply to allow those who do profess Christianity to remain without being tortured for their faith."

Iwakura. "You must consider the motives of our Government, as, for instance, the native Christians formerly sent from this village to Choshu are all to be returned now as they have recanted their professing of Christianity."

Outrey. "This is a contradiction. This proves that it was because they professed Christianity that they were punished, as now that they have recanted, their punishment ceases. If all would now publicly recant their professions of Christianity, would they all be allowed to remain?"

Iwakura. "Yes; if they follow the religion of their Emperor and obey the authority of the Government, no reason for their punishment exists."

    *   *   *   *   *   *   *

Terashima. "If I said that this was being done on account of the religion of these men, it was true in only one sense; but the main reason is that in consequence of their professing the Christian religion, they despise their own. According to the Shinto religion, the Mikado is the direct descendant of the gods. Thus he rules by divine right on account of his divine origin. Christianity teaches our people to despise and disbelieve this feature of our faith, and thus it brings this sacred thing into contempt. As, for instance, these Christians, instead of going to the Shinto temple in Urakami sacred to the Mikado and worshipping, they refuse to do it and thus treat the Mikado contemptuously and lead others to show disrespect to him."

Outrey. "How comes it, if this is the reason of your opposition to Christianity, that you do not punish the Buddhists? The Mikado is the chief of the Shinto faith, and he cannot be the chief of more than one religion."

Terashima. "The Buddhists show their respect to the Shinto faith by agreeing to this principle."

Outrey. "Yes; but they have their own temples and priests. Do they compel them to go to the Shinto temples and pay their respect?"

Iwakura. "In Japan, whether Buddhists or not, they have respect for and adore Tensho Daijin, the ancestor of the Mikado, as such, but Christians do not. They insult and ridicule her, and of course thereby insult and ridicule the Mikado."

Von Brandt. "How do they insult her?"

Terashima. "In Urakami, at this temple of Tensho Daijin, they have a peculiar gate sacred to the Mikado's ancestor. These Christians never will go through this gate, but go around it, and thus show all the people how they despise the goddess, and teach others to despise her also. Then, in all Shinto houses the people have idols, family gods, and also sacred writings; they insult these idols and put the sacred writings in indecent and filthy places to show the people how they despise them. There is a place there called Shibakaru, with several little red gates, and inside these grass grows, which people gather, and they will throw this grass through these gates and go around after it rather than pass through it. This action itself may be small, but the feeling exhibited is great and shows disrespect to the Mikado and his ancestor. The systems of government here and in Europe, you must bear in mind, are different. There the people have more or less to do with the government; here they have nothing to do with it; and to maintain this government it is absolutely necessary for us to compel all the people to believe in the divine origin of the Mikado, and respect and reverence him and his ancestors."

After consulting together the foreign representatives declared their belief that the people were being persecuted on account of their religion, and urged that such proceedings should be discontinued. The Japanese officials continued to insist that, as expressed by Iwakura, if Christianity were permitted, " the Government cannot be carried on, because the Government is based on the Shinto religion." They also complained as follows of the action of the missionaries:

Terashima. " In referring these religious questions to the treaties, it will be seen that the engagements are mutual; that foreigners in Japan can have their own places of worship and practise their own religion, and that neither foreigners nor Japanese shall disturb the other. This at least is the spirit of the treaty. Now, although we have given foreigners their own places of worship and have never interfered with them, we have found out that missionaries have established a place of worship at Urakami, not within the limits of the foreign settlement, where they go at night and preach their faith."

Outrey. " They must not have this; it is the first I have heard of it."

Terashima. " Although it is not, perhaps, according to the letter of the treaty that foreign places of worship should not be attended by Japanese, we consider that foreigners have no right to go outside of the settlement propagating their faith, as they are doing. It appears to this Government that these missionaries have also led these people so to act as to implicate them seriously. That they have promised them assistance if troubled by our Government is evidenced by the fact that when we attempt to control them they always rush to these priests and complain to them. That we ought sooner to have come forward with our complaints against these priests we admit, and we are very sorry that we have not done it; but thinking that the shortest way would be to deal with our own subjects, we have let the matter go on. Now we regret this; for if we had sooner complained, it would have resulted in only ten or a hundred persons being moved."

Outrey. "I regret that you have never informed us of this; but I wish to say that this persecution commenced four years ago, and this shows that the more they are persecuted, the more they increase. We know that at a place in the interior where there were no priests, you have had to persecute these people for Christianity; and this we know from your own official newspaper."

Terashima. "That is true; but there are Japanese who are preaching Christianity."

Outrey. "Do you not know that in the time of the Tycoon [Shogun] your Government suddenly heard of four or five thousand native Christians? Were they not Christians from their fathers? And does not this prove that the more you persecute, the more Christians there will be?"

Terashima. "It is possible that those were people who were Christians before this; if so, they kept it still. The Government was not going so far as to try and find out the sentiments of a man's heart and punish him for them; but these men are seditious, and we cannot tolerate them. We will not say the missionaries advise this; but the people do defy the Government. The officers from Nagasaki inform us that they have turned one of the ten temples into a place of worship, and there the people assemble and await the missionaries, who come in the night and perform religious worship."

Outrey. "Destroy the houses there and stop it if it is not within the treaty limits."

Terashima. "These missionaries employ two-sworded men, who are outcasts, as sub-instructors, who go about teaching and it is owing to these that Christianity is propagated inland. Now, the reason we move these people is to take them from under the influence of these missionaries. To say the truth, Urakami and other such villages have become the asylum of outcasts, and there they congregate and claim that they are under the protection of foreign powers. I know well these people have been led to believe so."

Outrey. "We certainly have never any of us or our consuls given them any such assurances, and we have never heard of this before. We trust you will reconsider your actions, because it will cause great feeling in Europe and America, and may lead to serious results. We ask postponement and due reflection."

Iwakura. "I can only repeat that we desire friendly relations, but we must be allowed to govern our own people. We thank you for your evidences of friendliness, and we will send orders to postpone further actions pending this conference, and on this

conference it will depend whether we go further or not. We have
spoken of the wrongs of the missionaries, which you ministers
cannot defend; and we hope it is in the power of you ministers
to control these missionaries."

Outrey. " We will do what we can do to make our people in all
cases do right."

De Long. "I state unhesitatingly that when any complaint is
made to me of a wrong done by any American citizen, I shall
always be as ready and willing to restrain or punish him as I
am prompt to demand redress for my countrymen from this
Government when I consider them aggrieved." *

Two days after this conference, the Ministers for Foreign Affairs sent to the foreign representatives the following report that had been made to them January 9,
1870, by the officials in Nagasaki:

" We beg to report that up to yesterday we continued sending
off the native Christians to various provinces as set forth in the
accompanying paper, taking good care, in conformity with the
instructions received, to treat them kindly and tendering them
advice. Heads of families were provided with money, and the
sick who applied for relief were sent into hospital. The old and
infirm were furnished with sedan chairs in places where the road
was rough, and sandals for travellers were given to all. Families
were not separated, in accordance with your instructions, but
some were sent to different places at their own request. We allowed them to take whatever they required of their own goods,
and such as were left behind were placed in strong warehouses
to await your further orders as to its disposal. As it was exceedingly cold and snow falling at the time, we furnished all with
sake to use on the road as and when they pleased. Strict orders
were given by us to those officers who accompanied them to provide whatever could contribute to their comfort. It was clearly
explained to them that all reasonable wants they may have shall
be duly supplied in the provinces whither they are sent, and they
all left cheerfully and in good spirits." †

As will be seen, the Japanese constantly asserted that
there was no cruelty, but in after years one of the officials
related the following incidents. It is not stated with
which of the successive banishments they were connected:

* U. S. For. Relations, 1870, pp. 462-468. I have made a few
verbal changes, correcting misprints and removing a few infeli-
cities occasioned doubtless by haste in preparing the report.
† *Ib.,* p. 472.

" Men and women were bound and passed from hand to hand across the gang-plank of the boat which waited to carry them, handled and counted and shipped like bales of merchandise. One woman, thrown amiss, fell into the water, and her hand waved farewell in the sign of the cross as she sank never to rise again. The other concerned a woman too, a mother with her infant at her breast. The officials determined to force her to recant, and failed. At last they took her infant, placed it just beyond her reach, and there let it wail its hungry cry two days and nights, with promises all the time of full forgiveness to the mother and the restitution of her babe, if only she would recant. Recant she would not, and at last her tormenters gave in, their cruel ingenuity exhausted." *

January 28 the Ministers of Foreign Affairs presented the following memorandum, which may be taken as the official statement of the Japanese side of the controversy:

" They [the Japanese ministers] understand that the foreign ministers are dissatisfied with the measures taken by the Japanese Government relative to the native Christians.

" Appreciating friendly intercourse and the respect of the treaty powers for Japan, they have deemed it their duty to explain their motives for these measures; that the inhabitants of the village of Urakami are wrong in worshipping a foreign religion is not the question, but as co-religionists they formed a party and thwarted the authorities. The Government would not treat these people severely simply because of their worship. The Government never inquire what religious opinions people inwardly profess and as long as they infringe no laws or offer no resistance, though there may be many who profess foreign religions, they will not be interfered with. And hence, since the conclusion of treaties with foreign countries, has the Government abolished the law of *fumi-e* [trampling on Christian emblems] which was established for the purpose of inspecting people's hearts.

" The Government have engaged in their schools to teach languages, etc., those who come here as missionaries and have permitted any one to translate and sell publicly all sorts of books, even such as relate to religions. This proves that the Government intends to change the law respecting religion; but when the people commit wrongs and misdemeanours, infringe the laws of the country, or resist the power of the Government on the plea of being Christians, or when they are told by missionaries that they will not be punished, as foreigners will protect them, then the Government must step in, as such things cannot be permitted. Advice must then be given to such people and they must be brought back to submission to the laws of their country.

* Quoted by Dr. G. W. Knox in New York *Independent,* June 21, 1894.

" The Government carries out the treaty in allowing foreigners to worship their own religions and build churches in Japan; but they are dissatisfied with foreign priests who induce the people to worship with them. They use soft speech and science, or give money to those who worship their religion, telling them that foreigners will aid them, and the people consequently become so outrageous as to insult the authorities, and this must be remedied. On investigation, it has invariably been found that these so-called native Christians are only so in name; their acts, however, are such as would undoubtedly be punished in all other countries. They conceal among themselves all sorts of criminals whom the Government wants to have arrested; they always disputed with others and caused disturbances; insulted our ancient religion, destroyed images of the gods, and defile the gods from whom his Majesty the Mikado is descended. If these people were left alone they would cause great trouble, the Government might be weakened, and the country endangered. It would have been quite proper to punish these people severely; but, as it was promised in January, 1869, by Higashi Kuse to the foreign ministers that they would hereafter be treated leniently, the Government had no other means in dealing with this matter than to remove these people to other places and thus cut off their communication with priests, whose desire of converting them may not be bad, but unfortunately the Japanese misapprehended the matter and insulted the authorities. The Government removed them in the manner as promised to the foreign ministers. No severe treatment was inflicted, but all necessary aid was rendered. This the Government is prepared to prove.

* * * * * * *

" The Japanese Government will not be obliged to resort to such measures as the unpleasant one referred to, if foreign missionaries would exclusively apply themselves to the teaching of their own people according to the treaty, instead of acting improperly as hitherto. Then the Japanese Government may not be obliged to cut off the communication of those of their people who seek information on religious subjects with the missionaries, and may further have no objection to send back to their village those who have been moved out of it.

" The Japanese Government are desirous that their people be instructed in arts and sciences, in which your country is superior, instead of being instructed in religion, and they are, above all, desirous that the existing friendship between our countries may increase more and more." *

A week later the foreign representatives presented the following memorandum:

" The Japanese Government having declared that the action of some foreign missionaries in preaching outside of the limits of the

* U. S. For. Relations, 1870, p. 473.

foreign settlement has caused serious disturbances, and is one of the reasons for which the Government thinks the removal of the native Christians from the neighbourhood of Nagasaki is a political necessity, the foreign representatives do not hesitate to declare that they, on their part, will do everything in their power to restrain the foreign missionaries from such acts, and will punish them therefor if such acts be persisted in; provided, that the native Christians who have already been deported from Urakami are all brought back." *

As might be supposed, the missionaries were far from pleased at the attitude taken in this last memorandum. Moreover, they put little faith in the promise that the exiles would be returned to their homes. M. Laucaigne decided to leave Japan for the present. He took with him thirteen of the young seminarists whom he had been instructing in the Hall of the Immaculate Conception, and went with them to Canton to continue their education.

It was at first difficult to find out anything about the condition of the exiled Christians. It was learned after the cessation of the persecution that their treatment varied greatly in the different provinces. The Buddhist and Shinto priests were charged with the duty of trying to bring about apostasy, and when their discourses failed to produce the desired effect, recourse was often had to torture. The worst treatment was suffered by those sent to Iwami and Nagato. Among those in the former of these provinces was Dominic Zenemon, who, it will be remembered, had been the spokesman of the Christians when they were called before the officials in Nagasaki. He was in the first company of exiles. With twenty-seven others he was enclosed in a small room connected with a Buddhist temple in the town of Tsuwano. Though the weather was bitterly cold, they were allowed no fire. The food served them was very insufficient. There was so much curiosity among the people of the town to see the prisoners that the officials decided to examine them in public. Four or five hundred people were present. The officer said to Dominic:

" Who is it that you worship? "

" We Christians worship the One who created Heaven and earth and all mankind. It is because He is the Lord

*U. S. For. Relations, 1870, p. 474.

of all that we worship Him. You, too, are under obligation to do so, since He created you also."

"No, no!" said the officers with a laugh, "we do not worship Him."

"It is true that you do not, for you do not know Him; but it is none the less true that you ought to do so."

"We follow the religion of our own country; but you, although a Japanese, follow the religion of foreigners. You are disobedient to the Emperor."

"It is not of much importance whether a person belongs to one country or another. He who made other lands made Japan also. Hence Japanese, like other men, ought to worship Him. The deities that are worshipped in Japan have created nothing, and, therefore, have no claim on our worship. You speak of the Emperor. We surely have no desire to oppose him; but the God who created the world created him also. The Emperor and his ministers, like all other men, ought to obey God. Moreover, we Christians pray for the Emperor's prosperity. Our religion commands us to do this."

"Nevertheless, if you do not renounce this religion, you will be put to death. On the other hand, if you are docile, you will be sent to your homes."

"Do with us whatever you will; we cannot renounce our religion."

This was the first of many occasions on which the Christians were summoned before their judges. On one occasion, when they had been urged in vain to give up their religion, the principal officer threatened to throw them all into a pond of ice-cold water that was near by.

"Do as you please," said the Christians, "we cannot give up our faith."

"Well then, go back to your prison. To-day only Zenemon shall be punished."

Thereupon Dominic, who was in a weak state of health, was led to the pond, while the people crowded around to see the sport.

"Take off your clothes and jump into the water," commanded the officer.

"No. If you wish, you may strip off my clothes, but I will not do it."

"What? You will not obey? Do you forget that it is in the Emperor's name that I command you?"

"I am not obliged to obey you in this thing, and I will not."

All the officers joined in ordering him to take off his clothes. He refused to do so, but made no resistance when one of the servants began to strip him. Exposed to the cold winter air, he stood in silence. To all the commands to jump into the water he simply said:

"I am in your power. Do to me whatsoever you will."

Some one finally pushed him into the water, which, as he recovered his footing, was waist-deep. Though his whole body shook violently from the chill, he joined his hands in prayer and remained silent. The officers commanded him to kneel. This time he obeyed; keeping his clasped hands above the water. Soon, however, the cold so weakened him that his hands fell of their own weight. His tormentors dashed water over his head, and it was only when his strength was nearly exhausted that he was taken back to the prison, where the officers showed a little mercy by allowing a fire to be made of straw, before which he lay as his companions chafed his limbs and covered him with their own garments. Afterwards other prisoners were thrown into the pond.

When the second company of exiles reached Tsuwano, they also were severely treated. Even the women were sometimes deprived of clothing and exposed for two or three days to the winter air, no food being allowed them during that time. By these and other means a few were led to apostatise. As it was thought that Dominic had much to do with encouraging the others to be steadfast, he and two of his companions were shut up in a dark room swarming with vermin, and were not allowed to leave it at any time. The two who were with him died ere long and were replaced by others. Their food was gradually diminished. They commenced to dig a tunnel, hoping to get out where they could find some nourishment. This was discovered by the guard, who with a spade struck Dominic over the head and shoulders, wounding him so severely that his two companions had much trouble in staunching the flow of blood. Some of those who by apostasy had gained a considerable degree of liberty learned of this and found means for sending medicine and food to Dominic.

It is not necessary to continue the narration of the sufferings of the prisoners in this and other provinces. The Central Government constantly asserted that the exiles were being treated with kindness; but when rumours came that those in Kaga were subjected to much cruelty, the British Acting Consul at Niigata was sent to investigate their condition. He found this much different from what was alleged by the officials. Husbands had been separated from wives, and children from their parents; no land had been allotted to the exiles; in many instances their food was insufficient, being increased only on condition of apostasy. At one place iron rings attached to the floor were fastened round the necks of men and women who would not give up their faith.*

Mgr. Petitjean, who had been in attendance at the Vatican Council, returned to Japan in December, 1870. He at once authorised the missionaries to renew their nocturnal visits to Christians living near Nagasaki, but enjoined them to use the greatest prudence. He decided to take up his own residence in Yokohama. On his way thither he visited Kobe and Osaka. M. Cousin in the latter city was having frequent visits from the exiles. In some sections of the country they enjoyed a considerable degree of liberty, being able to be away from their guardians for several days at a time. One came from a place so distant that it took him five days to reach Osaka, while two others were eight days on the road. Afterwards people came even from the province of Kaga. The intelligence that M. Cousin was thus enabled to obtain showed that most but not all of the Christians were standing firm. He was able to send out catechists whose chief duty was to strengthen those that were in danger of apostasy. The persons in Kaga who had yielded began to show signs of repentance. They would come together in the evening to receive instruction from the catechists, and they asked to have their children baptised.

* Adams, " Hist. of Japan," vol. ii., p. 215.

Though the officials must have known of what was being done, they did not interfere.

In Nagasaki a time of calm had succeeded the storm. Though most of the Christians of the immediate neighbourhood had been torn from their homes, many remained in the Goto Islands and other places. Young men, nominally employed as servants of the missionaries, were instructed by them and then sent out as catechists. Every evening people came to the residence, so that in the first eight months of 1871, five hundred and fifty persons confessed and received the communion. The missionaries went to the bedsides of the sick when these were near enough to be visited in a single night. Mme. Salmon, the mother of one of the missionaries, took a large house near the church in order that she might provide a lodging place for the female catechists and for women that otherwise would not have been able to receive the sacraments.

In December, 1871, there was a renewal of the persecution. Sixty-five persons living in the vicinity of Nagasaki were sent into exile. Again the representatives of foreign powers uttered their protests; this time with more effect than before, for further arrests that had been ordered were not carried out, and six weeks later the sixty-five exiles, with the exception of one who had died, were returned to their homes. One reason for this act of clemency is to be found in the desire of the Government to obtain a revision of the treaties. In furtherance of this object, an embassy started for the West at just about the time the last arrests were made, and those who protested against the violation of the promise that no more Christians should be deported were also able to show that intelligence of what had been done would make the Western nations very unwilling to make such concessions as were desired by Japan.

In March the Supreme Council issued to the local governments a notification concerning the persons who had been deported in 1869. This ordered: " If there are any of them who have manifested repentance, they shall be set free. According to their desires, they shall be registered among the inhabitants of your province or sent back to their former homes." A subsequent circular said: "Among the repenting Christians set free in accordance with the notification of March 9, 1872, are some who wish to be restored to their families, from which they find themselves separated. The prefects shall confer together in order to facilitate the re-union of households. If, notwithstanding such efforts, the location of members of the family cannot be discovered, the head of the family shall be sent to the place from which he was deported, and the local authorities of that place shall aid him to collect his household once more." *

It will be seen that this last circular contains a disproof of the Government's former assertions that families had not been separated. Foreign officials were told that these orders were intended to include all of the exiles, and that the apparent restriction to apostates was to avoid offending public opinion, which was still strongly opposed to granting any concessions to Christians. Nevertheless, up to July, only five hundred persons had been sent back to Urakami, and all of them had bought their release by apostasy. "It was announced in Kaga," wrote M. Cousin in October, "that those who wished to return to Nagasaki had only to ask permission; but the essential condition was that they should sign with their own blood a promise never to profess Christianity. Only ten had the weakness to apostatise, and these were sent back at once. Nothing was said to the others. A general prison is being prepared, which they can leave only in the daytime and by permission of the chief of the guards." In some other places those that stood firm were treated more severely than before. Their liberty was so restricted that the clandestine visits to the missionaries in Osaka became infrequent.

At this time, however, the missionaries had very much to encourage them. There had been several conversions at Hakodate, Yokohama, Osaka, and Kobe. The work about Nagasaki had been more completely organised. The following statistics were given for that region:

* "La Rel. de Jésus Res.," vol. ii., p. 226.

Children of Christians baptised in 1871-72.... 650 to 700
Adult baptisms in 1871 350
Adult baptisms in 1872 1220
Confessions in 1871 1170
Confessions in 1872 1920
Communions in 1871 1050
Communions in 1872 1569
Confirmations in 1871-72 429
Extreme unction in 1871-72 71

The number of persons receiving extreme unction was
lessened by the difficulty the missionaries found in reaching those at the point of death.   Persons dangerously ill
were often brought from distant places to Nagasaki, in
order that they might receive the ministrations of the
priests.   There were eighty-five catechists, men and
women, more than half of whom had received careful
instruction for four or five months; the men being sheltered at the residence of the missionaries, and the women
in the house of Mme. Salmon.   Twenty children, abandoned by their parents, had been placed in Christian
families.   In June, 1872, five nuns connected with the
Society of the Holy Infancy had come to begin the work
of gathering children into an orphanage.

Rumours of a change in the policy of the Government
increased.   By the end of 1872, the exiles were receiving more lenient treatment, and there were many indications that brighter days were at hand.

" EDICTS AGAINST CHRISTIANS REMOVED.
PRISONERS FREED.   INFORM ROME, PROPA-
GATION OF FAITH, HOLY INFANCY.   NEED IM-
MEDIATELY FIFTEEN MISSIONARIES."

Such was the message written in March, 1873, by Mgr.
Petitjean and sent to Hongkong for transmission by
telegraph to the Missionary Society in Paris.   Orders
had at last been sent for the return of all the exiles, and
ere long, companies of them began to arrive in Nagasaki.
What joy for them to come back to their beloved valley,
which some of them had not seen for more than three

years, and others for five years! What joy in the re-
union of families that had been long separated! What
tales they had to tell of their experiences during the
days since they had parted! Yet all the feelings were
not of joy. Many faces were missing. The statistics
are deficient; but according to a table made out by the
missionaries, those that had been deported from Urakami
numbered 3,404. There had been 660 deaths and 176
births in the time of exile, and the number of those
returning in 1873 numbered 1,981. Apparently this last
number does not include the 500 apostates of the previous
year.

Those that returned were in great poverty. Many at
the time of their departure had sold their lands at any
price they could get, and they were now forced to cul-
tivate less fertile ground on the sides of the mountains.
The Government constructed barracks for those that
had no other shelter. The Christians of other places
came to the help of their brethren, and as the first
harvest was bountiful, the severest stress was soon
relieved.

The Christians that had been sent into exile had not
suffered in vain. Not only had they been one of the
means for bringing about religious freedom, but they
had also impressed some people who saw them with
profound respect for their faith. Hon. Ebara Soroku,
a prominent Methodist and a leading member of Par-
liament, says that some of the exiles were placed under
his care by a provincial governor, who afterwards became, like himself, a Christian and a member of the
National House of Representatives. Various efforts, he
says, were made to lead the exiles to apostatise. They
were first brought into the presence of the officers, who
attempted in vain to overawe them. When this method
failed, young Christians were exposed to temptations
that it was thought would surely lead them to such
immorality as would bring disgrace upon their religion
and loosen its hold upon them. Another fiendish plan
was, after much thought, devised by the Governor. He
caused a mother to be shut up with her infant and deprived of food. The mother, growing weaker and

weaker, could no longer nurse the child. It cried from morning until night; but when food was offered to the mother on condition that she would renounce her faith, she replied: " I prefer to die and to kneel at the feet of my Lord." The Governor was so much moved by her steadfastness that he finally relented and ordered food to be given to the woman. Mr. Ebara says that the conduct of the exiles under suffering had great influence in leading him and others to become Christians in later years.*

Hon. Kataoka Kenkichi, who was several times Speaker of the House of Representatives, says that in his city of Kochi about sixty of the Christians, before being sent back to their homes, were taken to a Buddhist temple in order that the priests might make one more effort to persuade them to renounce their faith. Their steadfastness so surprised the priests that it is said some of them decided to become Christians. Mr. Kataoka adds: " To the exiles I attribute my first leanings towards Christianity and my subsequent Christian belief." †

It will be seen that at the end of the period of persecution, the Roman Catholic missionaries had several thousand adherents. They counted the Christians directly connected with them as fifteen thousand, while they knew that there were many thousands more who considered that they held the faith of the ancient Christians, but who had not yet entered, as many of them afterwards did, into formal relations with the missionaries. In comparing the results of what has been accomplished by the Roman Catholic, the Greek, and the Protestant churches, the great number of adherents that the first had from the beginning must be remembered. On the other hand, however, it cannot be forgotten that its missionaries have laboured under the great disadvantage of being the successors of those who were believed to have brought great evils upon the country two hundred and fifty years before. Though the common

---

* Quoted from *Koe* in *Japan Weekly Mail*, December 22, 1900.
† *Fukuin Shimpo*, quoted by Ritter, " Hist. Prot. Mis.," p. 230.

people were slow to learn of any distinctions, educated persons were aware that there was a great difference between Roman Catholicism and Protestantism. Many who were bitterly prejudiced against the former were not unwilling to examine the teaching of the latter.

XII

DEVELOPMENT OF THE CHURCH

1873-1900

THE telegram in which Mgr. Petitjean informed his society of the release of the Roman Catholic exiles called for the sending out of fifteen new missionaries. Evidently the officials of the society felt as he did, that the needs of Japan were very pressing. The thousands of believers now in connection with the missionaries ought to be instructed, other descendants of the ancient believers were to be gathered in, it was necessary to plan for the training of native workers, and there was reason to hope that the changes now going on in Japan would open the way for winning many new converts. By September, eleven of the fifteen missionaries that had been asked for were on the field. M. Laucaigne was raised to the episcopate and made an auxiliary of Mgr. Petitjean. A seminary for the training of evangelists was opened in Nagasaki. One was already in operation at Yokohama. In the latter city twenty young men received instruction in lithography, so that they might multiply copies of the catechism and other books.

At the close of 1873, there were connected with the Mission two bishops, twenty-nine missionaries, six sisters, two hundred and twenty-seven catechists, and two hundred and fifty baptisers. There were three churches and twenty-seven oratories, two seminaries with seventy pupils, six boys' schools with two hundred pupils, one girls' school with fifteen pupils, and two orphanages with thirty-six inmates. The baptisms that year of "heathen adults" numbered one hundred and twenty; of "converted schismatics," five; of children of Christians, two thousand and seven; and of children of heathen, one hundred and ninety-seven.

The year 1874 brought severe trials to the Christians of Kyushu. An epidemic of dysentery in Urakami and other places caused the death of about one hundred of their number. The missionaries gave medical aid, while catechists and others nursed the sick. While the epidemic was still raging, a severe typhoon accompanied by heavy rains caused much damage. The barracks put up by the Government for the returned exiles yielded to the fury of the storm, which also blew down a large part of the houses in Urakami and some other villages. The fishermen in one place lost all but one of their boats. The rice-fields, which had given promise of abundant crops, were devastated. The price of food at once rose rapidly, and the condition of the Christians was so pitiable that an appeal to European charity was made by Mgr. Petitjean.

Another trial to the Mission was the burning in December of the residence of the missionaries in Yokohama. Religious utensils, books, and printing presses, were lost in the conflagration.

One consolation in the midst of these trials was that some of those descendants of the ancient Christians who had formerly held aloof from the missionaries now showed an inclination to enter into relations with them. Some of these " separated ones " (*les séparés*), as they were called, had known so many cases of betrayal by pretended brethren that they were very suspicious, fearing that, if they did not keep their faith a complete secret, they might be arrested and put to death. Even their children were left without instruction until they had arrived at the age of discretion, so as to avoid any danger that might come from their not keeping silence. After these persons were convinced that the missionaries were indeed the spiritual successors of those who had taught their ancestors, they held aloof because of hesitancy about associating with other Christians. Some even united with unbelievers in inimical acts towards those whom they ought to have regarded as their brethren. Yet some of them, when at the point of death, sought the services of the priests. The kindness shown to them by other believers at the time of the epidemic did more than almost anything else to lead many of them to give up their policy of separation.

Not only in the open ports, but also in the interior, there was an increasing number of conversions. In August, 1875, one of the missionaries baptised in the village of Matsunaga (Suruga) thirty persons who had received instruction from a catechist. Soon after this, the number of worshippers at the annual festival of a Shinto shrine in the neighbouring city of Numazu was much smaller than usual, whereupon those that mourned over the diminution of revenue decided that the advent of Christianity must be held accountable. They accordingly induced the officials to call together the heads of families to read to them the following document:

"Every one knows that Japan is the Land of the Gods, and that the one hundred and eighty-two Emperors, commencing with Jimmu Tenno, have for 2,535 years ruled the country. Certain foreign religions that came from India and China have already spread through the land and have lessened the respect paid to the gods. In our days the religion of Jesus also, although its followers are still few, is striving to possess the land. From a patriotic point of view this is greatly to be regretted, since it is not right that a person by allying himself with a foreign faith should become unmindful of the claims of his own country. Therefore we have this morning assembled the inhabitants of Numazu in order that we may administer to them a solemn oath, which shall be confirmed by the ceremony of offering a cup of *sake* at the shrine. By this oath they shall make a promise that neither they nor their descendants will ever accept the Christian religion. If any one violates the promise, may the gods crush him under the weight of their curses."

The people, with the exception of one man, signified their willingness to take the oath. This one declared that, since he was a Christian, he could not do it. That evening he was called before the officers, who told him that he must write a statement declaring that he was a Christian. When he had done this, they asked him what were the chief teachings of his religion, whereupon he produced a catechism, from which he read the Ten Commandments and other important sections.

When the Christians of Matsunaga heard what had

happened, they informed the missionaries, who at once
sent two catechists, one of whom was well known in that
region, as his father was the chief officer of Matsunaga.
The catechists went to see the officials who had been
responsible for forcing the oath upon the people, and
got from them an acknowledgment that they had not
received from their superiors any authorisation for such
an act. Having also procured a copy of the document
to which the names had been signed, the catechists next
went to the Governor of the prefecture and gained his
assurance that he was not responsible for what his
subordinates had done. Returning to Numazu, they
advertised that for a week they would hold preaching
services in the house of the man that had refused to
take the oath. Though the people at first were timid,
the house was afterwards crowded with persons wishing
to listen.

In other places there were similar attempts to get the
people to sign promises that they would not accept the
foreign religion. In one village, when a Christian refused to obey the summons to attend the assembly
where the document was to be presented, half of the
other villagers followed his example. The Buddhist
priests in Numazu were now aroused to action. They
did their best to decry Christianity, urging the people
not to have even business relations with its followers.

"Paganism is not the only enemy of Catholicism,"
wrote one of the missionaries about 1874, as he commenced to describe the missionary efforts of the
Protestants and of the Russo-Greek Church. He considered that the work of the latter was inspired by the
political ambitions of Russia, and said:

"The popes exert all their efforts to gain adherents to schism
and thus to Russian ideas. . . . For three years the Russian
schism has established its centre of action at Tokyo, from which it
extends its influence to the most distant provinces. The pope,
with a zeal worthy of a better cause, has educated many catechists
whom he sends into the interior, where he supports them at great
expense."

In 1876, Mgr. Osouf wrote that the Russian schism
was losing ground, while Protestantism was "increasing

and was paralysing the efforts of our missionaries by means of the publications that it lavishly scatters, and of the schools that it multiplies."

To meet what it regarded as dangerous heresies, the Mission published several books in opposition to the Protestants and Russians. Indeed, its literary efforts at this time were largely expended upon works of this kind. The most elaborate book was one in four volumes, " Seikyo Bumpa Ron " (" A Discussion of the Divisions of Western Religion "). This, which was written as though by a Japanese, described the founding of the Christian Church, the way in which the Greek and Protestant divisions arose, and the evil nature of these great heresies. The spirit in which the book was written may be judged by the opening sentences of Vol. III., which treats of Protestantism:

" Having already in the Second Volume investigated the origin of the Russo-Greek Sect and shown its falsehood, evil, sin, and error, it is necessary in this Third Volume to speak of the myriad sects of Protestantism so as to show their falseness, stupidity, error, sin, and atrocious evil. Protestantism had its origin in such great sins as uncleanness, licentiousness, robbery, and tyranny. If I describe it, Japanese will look on it as so shameful and un- clean that they will not wish to listen to its teachings or give their assent to it."

In speaking of the evils of schism, the writer says, that in America there are more than three thousand sects. Of Luther he writes: " From the creation of the world, never has such another wicked person been seen." Henry VIII., however, is described as being a close second, and Cobbett's " History of the Reforma- tion " is utilised as a valuable witness for showing how even Protestant writers acknowledge the evils that ac- companied and followed England's separation from Rome. The Greek Church does not fare much better than Protestantism in this exceedingly bitter polemic. Though the book may have furnished weapons for the opponents of all forms of Christianity, it may be doubted whether it helped the cause of those who issued it.

In 1876, the Propaganda decided that Japan should be divided into two vicariates; that of the south being committed to Mgr. Petitjean, who now removed to Osaka; and that of the north to Mgr. Osouf, who now made his residence in Tokyo.

At first but few converts were gained in Osaka. After having his hopes in many persons disappointed, M. Cousin in 1877 baptised seventeen adults; in 1878, twenty-one; and in 1879, forty. Hoping that descendants of the ancient Christians might be discovered in that part of the country as they had been in Nagasaki, he took care to follow up every promising clue. Information was received of several villages where it had been the custom for the officials to attend every burial in order to thrust a stake into the grave so as to prevent the resurrection of the dead person. It was thought that the apprehension implied by this act might be due to some misinterpretation of the Christian doctrine, and catechists were sent to explore the region. They found there a woman that knew the *Ave Maria*. She said that the officers still kept up the practice of driving stakes into the graves. When her husband returned from the fields, he declared that all the people of the village had once believed in Christianity; but he professed to have forgotten all that he ever knew about it. A few days after this, one of the missionaries went to see if he could find any believers; but the chief of the village, after learning of the visit of the catechists, had so threatened the people that only two families could be found whose members were willing to acknowledge that they were Christians.

In March, 1879, there were church buildings " worthy of the name " in the six cities of Tokyo, Osaka, Yokohama, Nagasaki, Kobe, and Hakodate. There were also fifty-five chapels and oratories. The Christians connected with the Mission numbered 20,146.

In 1880, Mgr. Petitjean removed to Nagasaki, he having become convinced that it was still the most important centre for the work of his vicariate. In the city itself some conversions had occurred, so that the number of Christians was about two hundred and fifty. A judge, who had taken part in the persecutions, expressed, shortly before his death, a desire to receive instruction, and he was finally baptised. The patience and resignation that he showed during his last days were so marked as to astonish the physician, who asked him how he was able to endure his sufferings without complaint, and to face death so courageously. "You would not be able to understand the reason, were I to tell you," was the reply; "let it suffice for me to say that I count myself happy in being permitted to suffer and then to depart from this life." In the Urakami Valley the Roman Catholic population was then reckoned as 3,370. Although one hundred families once included among the "separates" had returned to the pale of the Church, two hundred other families still held aloof. To a considerable extent the village had recovered its former prosperity. Strengthened by the persecutions through which they had passed, the Christians were fervent and zealous in good works. A missionary wrote of the valley as being one of the most Christian places in the world. There were chapels, schools, orphanages, a hospital, and a community of women who, while supporting themselves by tilling the ground or other occupations, also cared for the sick and orphans, taught the catechism to the children of the valley, and held themselves ready to do any work of charity to which they might be called. A large building, which had formerly been the residence of the officers charged with enforcing the laws against Christianity, where the ceremony of trampling on the cross had formerly been performed, and where ten years before the Christians had been convoked to hear the decree for their banishment, was purchased, and on July 7, 1880, the Feast of the Japanese Martyrs was celebrated by beginning the work of transforming this building into a church. Dominic, the old hero, who had stood so firm throughout the persecutions, obtained from the Governor of Nagasaki permission to erect a large stone cross on the summit of one of the hills that overlooks the valley.

At Nagasaki, on the last day of the year 1882, three young men, who the previous year had been made deacons, were ordained as priests. They had been in that company of boys that M. Cousin had taken to Penang

in 1868. One of them was a son of Dominic. It is the
belief of the Roman Catholic missionaries that, as a rule,
it is unwise to induct to the priesthood those who have
been converted from heathenism or even their children,
since they yet bear in their blood, as it were, such corruption as makes it doubtful whether they will not
bring dishonour to the sacred office. The candidates for
the priesthood should have behind them at least two or
three generations of Christian ancestors. The discovery
of the descendants of the ancient Christians has made
it easier to follow this policy in Japan.

In Hirado and its neighbourhood were five or six
thousand Christians under the care of the missionaries.
They had constructed several chapels, and in 1883 they
built a large church in the centre of the city. When they
petitioned the local authorities to support them in their
refusal to make contributions for Buddhist temples and
festivals, not only was their request granted, but the
Buddhists were ordered to restore property that they had
taken from the Christians ten years before.

A letter written in 1883, by M. Fraineau gives such
a vivid picture of some features of missionary life that
the following abridgement of it will not be out of place :—

"I started, May 30, for Ichimanda, which is about twenty
leagues south of Oita. In that village there were a few catechumens. A peasant who possessed the best house in the place had
consented to take out an inn-keeper's license so that I might lodge
there. He was led to do this by no desire for religious instruction, for which he has always shown the most complete indifference, but by the love of the twelve *sous* that I promised to pay
him daily for food and lodging.

"I installed myself in his house, with fleas, mosquitoes, and
lice for my companions; for never have I seen a richer collection
of these pests. It is the season when work in the fields is at its
height, the farmers being busy harvesting wheat and preparing
the fields to be planted with rice. The people that now serve as
our landlords are labourers. In the morning, after absorbing a
kettleful of a kind of vermicelli boiled with cabbage-leaves and
wild greens, the whole household, including the cows and the
horse, set out for the field without paying any attention to my
catechist and me. I ought to say in excuse for my hosts that the
person who came to Oita to consult about my entertainment arrived on a fastday and so reported that I ate only one meal in
the daytime. Thus, unknown to us, the fast had become a *sine*

qua non. Behold then the catechist and me condemned to an enforced Lent three weeks long. I at one time thought of installing
myself in the kitchen and leaving the people of the house free
to reap their wheat and plant their rice in peace; but in the midst
of heathen I could not indulge myself in such liberty. Dignity is
more precious than life, and here it would be better for a person
to perish with hunger than to lose prestige by condescending to
occupations not appropriate to his sex and condition. Moreover, let us be patient; we shall be obliged to wait only until
about two o'clock in the afternoon. It is at that time every day
that the woman of the house, who has neither clock nor sun-
dial, leaves her work and comes to see if we are still alive. In
accordance with the rules of Japanese etiquette she always begins
by bowing her head three times to the mat, asking us at the same
time if we are in good health. She then makes many excuses,
though without any real contrition, for having kept us waiting so
long, and says that we shall be served with food immediately, this
meaning about an hour later, since it is now that she lights the
fire and begins to heat water for cooking the rice.

"In the evening it is about half past ten before we get anything more to eat. Here, as in a regiment of cavalry, the animals take precedence of the men. Before our needs are supplied,
it is necessary that food should be prepared for the cows and the
horse, to say nothing of the five goats that have been left from
morning to night without food and are now stunning us with the
noise they make in one corner of the house. However, a person
that has had dinner at two o'clock can wait until half past ten
for his supper. These two grand meals whose preparation has
given our hosts so much trouble consist invariably of a dish of
rice and some boiled bamboo-roots that have no other seasoning
than an ancient flavour of salt fish with which the wooden cover
of the family kettle seems to be saturated as the result of years
and perhaps ages of use. Apart from such trifling defects, this
is a very palatable dish. By adding vinegar and wearing green
spectacles a person might make himself think he was eating
asparagus.

"Let us come to more serious matters. The bonzes follow
me everywhere, and I at least have the consolation of being able
to say that, if they make me trouble, I also on my side give them
abundant anxiety and annoyance. It is certain that at night they
do not lie down in so tranquil a state of mind as I do. Yet it is
not my laurels that keep them from sleeping; for thus far, in
appearance at least, my labours have not been crowned with very
great success.

"I had hardly set foot in the village of Ichimanda at ten
o'clock of a dark night and in a pouring rain, before the temple
more than a league distant that cares for this section of the
country learned of my arrival and prepared a pastoral letter to
warn its people of the danger that menaced them. At daybreak
the next morning this letter was carried from house to house,

read to the members of each family, and re-enforced by the comments of its bearer. This letter was the fifth or sixth edition of what the bonzes had already said or written elsewhere. Not only was it a tissue of calumnies, but it also contained menacing prophecies and invoked the anger of Japan's guardian deities upon all that dared to come near me. It said I was the cause of the rain whose constant fall for fifteen days had made the grain rot; the cause of the thunder which, as it appears, is more frequent than usual, while lightning has set fire to a farmhouse more than two leagues from the place where I am stopping; the cause of the floods that after the heavy rains inundated the fields to the destruction of the crops; etc., etc. These calamities are but the preludes of yet greater ones; for since my arrival flocks of crows frequently pass over the village by night with mournful croaks, and this is regarded by the heathen as a very evil omen.

" To the written lies are added such as the bonzes did not dare to put on paper, probably because they would appear too absurd; but these are propagated by word of mouth and are readily accepted by the credulous peasants. Here are some samples. Leaves of trees are changed in my hands to bank-notes that afterwards resume their original form, so that a merchant who at the day's close shuts up in his safe the money received from me is likely at some future time to find in its place only a handful of oak-leaves. Hence it is always with fear and but poorly concealed hesitancy that people receive paper money from me, and I have to take special care that the notes are not of too high denominations. One day the people of a wayside inn where my catechist and I had eaten rice preferred to make us a present of it rather than give us change for a one _yen_ bill. It is said that my glance will cause all sorts of evil to people that happen to meet me on the road when I am in ill humour; their bodies are likely some day to crumble into dust as suddenly as though they had been struck by lightning. By my mere wish I can poison the water in the wells, and I can confound my enemies while they are at a long distance from me.

" In the midst of these ill-disposed and hostile people I have found some friendly persons. There are some souls here that the good God seems to have chosen, and it was for their sakes that I came. Their instruction had been begun by Peter, a poor labourer who was baptised in March. On his return home he tried to teach others and succeeded in leading some families of the neighbourhood until there were more than a dozen applications for baptism. To them I was not a mysterious being, half man and half demon; I was not even a stranger; but I was the Lord's messenger, whose coming they awaited with impatience and who was able to induct their souls into a new life. I was also received as a priest that had come among his children. It was a great joy for me to see the ardour with which, notwithstanding the labours of the day in what was a busy season of the year, the poor people came every evening to hear an explanation of the truths of our holy religion. The catechetical instruction began immediately after our supper, that is to say, according to the custom of our hostelry, between half past ten and eleven o'clock in the evening, and it always ended after midnight by all reciting the evening prayer, which, as you see, ought to be the morning prayer. I need not tell you of the annoyances and troubles to which my new catechumens were subjected. Knowing already that the disciple is not above his Lord, they were resigned to all. There was only one thing that they could not bring themselves to accept. They did not wish that any one should insult them by calling them Christians. The doctrine of the Lord Jesus Christ appeared to them too good and its morality too pure for them to be able, notwithstanding what the bonzes said, to confuse it with the tissue of crimes and magic of which the reports had come down to them from ancient times; and they persuaded themselves that the 'Religion of the Lord of Heaven' was certainly not the same as that preached by Saint Francis Xavier to their ancestors. With all their favourable disposition and their ardour to receive instruction, they would have been ready to give up everything the day they should learn positively that they were on the point of joining the sect of ancient Christians, so much does that name, sullied by the calumnies of the bonzes, arouse hatred and repugnance in the popular mind. In the beginning I had respect for their weakness and took the greatest care to avoid what would enlighten them too quickly. They needed to be prepared for the reception of that unwelcome truth.

"Finally the time came when I could no longer leave them in ignorance. It was a very solemn moment when on a beautiful sabbath evening, in commencing a catechetical exercise on the First Commandment, I told them that the religion they were about to embrace by receiving baptism was the very one that had been reviled for three hundred years, and that the God whom they ought to worship was even the same Jesus Christ who had been so despised in their country. This declaration came to them like a clap of thunder. The questions and cheerful remarks that had made our lessons so pleasant came to an end; all the heads sank in consternation to the mats; and the deep sighs that escaped from the breasts of these poor men attested the terrible struggle going on in their hearts. I was the only one to speak and often my voice betrayed even to myself how great was my emotion. It might be that this evening would see the end of all the hopes I had been cherishing. At the close of the meeting, when I asked them whether they were willing to give way before the calumnies of the bonzes or whether they would not have the courage to make a momentary sacrifice of their reputation for the sake of God who had so loved them and had died for them, all replied with a magnificent profession of faith :—

"'Not only of our reputation, but also of our property and of our lives. If we must be called Christians, we will use that name ourselves; and far from being ashamed, we will glory in it.'

" The news of this caused a great commotion in the village. The annoyances took a new turn and became a real persecution. The village mayor and the physician, the two great men of the village, were induced by the bonzes to put themselves at the head of the movement against the Christians. Especially did the mayor, aided by a subordinate, display an ardour worthy of a better cause. When he learned that our catechumens, instead of yielding, had thrown away their idols and were preparing for baptism, his anger could no longer be kept within bounds. Unmindful of the fact that he was acting not only against human rights but also against the laws of his country, which placed him in office to serve as a peacemaker rather than as a judge, he called all the heads of families to his office and opened a court as a Roman governor in the time of Nero or Diocletian might have done. He ordered our people to apostatise under penalty, in case of refusal, of having all their goods at once confiscated and given into the hands of their creditors, and of having all the village cease from having friendly relations with them. They would be forbidden to draw water from the village well, to cut wood on the mountains, to hold communications with other people, etc., etc. The mayor thought that in view of such threats the catechumens would hasten to submit. None of them, not even of the women, appeared alarmed or affected by his words, and all openly declared that, although they had not yet received baptism, they were already Christians at heart, so that, even though their heads were to be cut off, no one could make them give up their faith.

" Our catechumens held meetings by themselves—holy assemblies in which they exhorted one another to preserve carefully in their hearts the gift of faith which God had bestowed upon them and which the devil was trying to take away. Let me cite especially the noteworthy meeting where the patriarchs of the band addressed the little company to the following effect:—

" ' Since our relatives and friends reject us, let us form a new family. Persecuted as we are for the same cause, let us unite our efforts so as to sustain each other. Let us have only one heart and one soul. Let us strengthen our courage by a mutual agreement, and though men may try to force us to deny Jesus Christ, let us here take an oath that we will remain faithful and be ready for any sacrifice rather than abandon Him.'

" Ere the meeting adjourned the form of the oath was settled upon, and the paper on which it was written was passed around the assembly. The men affixed their seals, while each woman pricked the point of a finger with a needle and so signed with her own blood."

Soon after this M. Fraineau returned to Oita. The last of July the catechist brought intelligence of the progress of events in Ichimanda. The threats made against the Christians had to some extent been put into execution.

One man had been deprived of all his property, and it had been divided among the people of the village. Probably he had been in debt to the community. After having been driven from his house, this man was cared for by his fellow-believers. Two families, whose members were preparing for baptism, had been frightened by a visitor from Nagasaki, who said it was well known in that city that when any Christian was sick the priest knelt at his side and either sucked out his blood or drove a nail into his head. After this, whenever the catechist visited these families, the women and children kept out of sight, while the men made it evident that his presence was unwelcome.

During M. Fraineau's sojourn in the village the man in whose house he lodged had overheard much of the instruction that was given to the catechumens, and had himself shown some interest in Christianity. After the departure of the missionary he had ventured to take down his idols. Two nights later his horse suddenly died. Regarding this as a punishment for his rash deed, he had called a bonze to appease the anger of the deities, whose images he now restored to their former place.

The Christian charity of the believers had been shown by their treatment of a leper who had come to their village. The daughter of a *samurai,* she had become the wife of an Osaka merchant. Soon after the death of her husband, she found that she was a victim of the terrible disease of leprosy. Her brother shut her up in a sort of cage in order to keep her from the rest of the family, and she saw no one except the servant that brought food to her. After two years of this seclusion, she broke out from her cage with the intention of drowning herself. It was January. On reaching the river's bank, she could not get up courage to jump into the cold water. She therefore decided to make a pilgrimage to noted Buddhist temples in order to pray that she might be healed. As she was begging her way, she came to Ichimanda, where the Christians were so moved by pity, that one of them took her into his house while others saw that she was always supplied with food.

The two missionaries that had taken the most prominent part in the events connected with the discovery of the Christians in Nagasaki were taken at about the same time from the scene of their earthly labours. Mgr. Petitjean had for some time been aware that he had not long to live. It was his hope that before passing from earth he might be able to establish a station of his mission in the Loochoo Islands, where he had begun his labours for the Japanese. He had gone to Kagoshima with the intention of taking passage for those islands, but became so ill that he was taken back to Nagasaki, where he died October 7, 1884. Three months later, January 10, 1885, Mgr. Laucaigne, who had shared with him the hopes, the disappointments, the joys, and the perplexities of the early days of the Mission, also passed away.

M. Cousin was then made Vicar Apostolic for Southern Japan. M. Osouf, who was appointed to the like office in Northern Japan, was raising funds in America at the time these deaths occurred. He was at once summoned to Rome. Leo XIII. had just addressed a letter to the Emperor of China, and he now put a similar one for the Emperor of Japan in the care of Mgr. Osouf. The new Vicar Apostolic arrived in Yokohama in August, 1885, and through the French Minister made arrangements for being presented to the Emperor, by whom he was graciously received as the bearer of the Pope's letter.

About 1886, there was begun a charitable work that soon attracted the notice and admiration of European residents in Japan. A woman suffering from leprosy, and for that reason abandoned by her husband, had found shelter beneath a miserable roof that was built over the wheel of a rice-mill. Her bed was a coarse straw matting spread over the boards that formed the cover of the sluiceway. Her food consisted of a cup of rice bestowed daily by her relatives, who otherwise did hardly anything for her relief. The disease made rapid progress and she was soon totally blind. It is not strange that the temptation to take her own life often presented itself to her mind. In some way, however, she gained a knowledge of Christianity and desired to receive baptism. M. Testevuide, who was asked to administer the rite, says:

" While I was seeking upon her brow, disfigured as it was with leprosy, some place to apply the water, the woman wept; but it was now with a joy that brightened up her face, notwithstanding the sores with which it was entirely covered."

He could not bear to leave her in such a place. Her brother, who was displeased that a foreign priest had come to see her, showed no disposition to help in bettering her condition. M. Testevuide wished to get her into a hospital; but at that time there was in all Japan no place where such a patient would be received. His interest in this woman led him to reflect on the sad lot of thousands of Japanese who were suffering from the same disease. The desire grew strong in his heart to do something for the relief of these unfortunate persons. In a letter telling the bishop of his wish to devote his life to such work he said:

" I am not ignorant of the dangers to which I shall expose myself. Some day, perhaps, I shall see myself shut off from your society and that of my brethren. If God in His just and merciful designs should permit me to be infected with the evil that I desire to heal in others, I will remind myself of the promise of our Lord Jesus Christ not to leave without reward a cup of water given in His name, and I will present myself at His tribunal with a greater degree of confidence. I will ask of you as a last favour only this, that you will permit me to live and die among my poor lepers."

Some friends gave him a small sum of money with which he hired a house in the neighbourhood of Gotemba, a town at the base of Mount Fuji. Though the house was far removed from other habitations, the people did not like the idea of having a leper hospital so near them, and they tried to get the owner to refuse to rent the house. M. Testevuide insisted for a time that the bargain already made should be kept; but finally, in order to avoid trouble, he sent away the few lepers he had gathered and set himself to collect money for the erection of a building of his own. The foreign communities in the open ports, always quick to respond to charitable appeals, soon furnished him with funds that enabled him to purchase a tract of about six acres, on which he erected a small hospital. There he lived in close intimacy with the lepers, alleviating their sufferings, cheering their hearts by his kind words, and giving them religious instruction. The best known methods of medical treatment were used. In some cases the external signs of the disease so far disappeared that the patients could go back to live once more with their friends. As M. Testevuide did not believe that complete cure could be effected, he always told such persons to come again for treatment the moment that there was a reappearance of trouble. Such patients as were able to do so, worked in the garden, which was thus made to furnish much of the food needed by the community. Japanese Christians were found who gladly gave themselves to the work of nursing the sufferers. Mention is made of one man that shut himself up for life among the lepers, making only the one condition that food should be provided for his own family. Such kindness as was shown by M. Testevuide and his associates could not fail to touch the hearts of its recipients and make them willing to listen to the Gospel that had inspired such love and self-sacrifice. Though M. Testevuide did not become infected with the dread disease, his years of labour for the lepers were but few. He died in 1891, but the work begun by him has been continued with similar devotion by others.

An extract from the *Japan Weekly Mail* of November 26, 1887, gives a bird's-eye view of the educational work of the Roman Catholic Mission at that time:

" The missionaries . . . are exclusively French. It is a large and powerful mission, numbering nearly sixty fathers and over forty Sisters of Charity. Most of the staff is attached to the seminaries and convents in the capital and the outports. The rest are scattered over the country. The two parent seminaries of the Mission, which were established simultaneously at Nagasaki and Tokyo, date from the year 1872, and the Yokohama Convent School was founded in the same year. Tsukiji Convent School followed in 1874, Osaka and Kobe Convent Schools in 1877, and

Nagasaki Convent School in 1880. There are also convent schools in Hakodate and Niigata, besides stations at Sendai, Morioka, Okayama, Kyoto, Hiroshima, and Kochi. . . . The educational work of the Mission in its higher branches is devoted almost exclusively to the training of youths for the priesthood and does not suffer itself to be diverted into secular channels. Instruction is ever restricted to a subordinate place as the hand-maid of religion. Even where a technical education is given, as at Osaka, the lads are trained to be carpenters and smiths for the service of the Church. In the convents it is somewhat different; since many girls attend these establishments merely to receive a foreign education. Great attention is paid by the sisters to sewing, crocheting, and all kinds of fancy work. Many of the pupils are enabled to pay something for their board by the sale of their handiwork; a contribution which is welcome, seeing that almost everything has to be supplied gratis to the pupils. In Protestant mission schools it is a question under debate whether pupils shall be admitted before the age of nine or ten; in these Catholic homes there are babes two months old. The orphans whom the sisters adopt are mostly placed with Christian women outside the convent who receive a small fee for their services. Some of the most difficult or delicate cases are attended to within the convent walls. The care and attention which the good sisters bestow on these wretched waifs, the diseased and unsightly off-spring of poverty and sin, is beyond all praise. The Mission has no less than nine orphanages with nearly a thousand inmates."

An interesting event in 1888 was the discovery of descendants of Ishikawa Kizaemon, one of the Twenty-six Martyrs of 1597. There were now two branches of the family; one living in Okayama and the other in a neighbouring village. The tiles on the roofs of Japanese houses are often decorated with some emblem, and in the house occupied by the Okayama branch of the family the decoration included a cross. Though the present members of the family had apparently lost all knowledge of Christian doctrines, some of them were soon afterward baptised.

In 1879, the Propaganda had established several districts between which the vicariates of China and adjacent countries had been distributed. For the promotion of unity in ecclesiastical matters it had been ordered that each district should hold synods at regular intervals. Since the conditions in Japan and Korea did not justify their inclusion in this arrangement, it was not until 1884, that these countries were set off as together forming one district. In March, 1890, the first synod was held in Nagasaki. The time was so chosen that the twenty-fifth anniversary of the discovery of the Urakami Christians occurred while the synod was in session. To increase the importance of the occasion, the Pope accorded a plenary indulgence to all Christians who should at that time make a pilgrimage to the Church of the Twenty-six Martyrs in Nagasaki, and he accorded to the bishops the power to bestow the papal benediction upon the people. The first solemn session of the synod was held on Sunday, March 2. On that day also, the pilgrimages were inaugurated by twenty-five hundred Christians from Urakami. Early in the morning six hundred of them had received the communion in their own valley and then, forming a procession, they had marched over the same road that had been trodden by many of them twenty years previously, as they went into exile. The women, as before, wore the white head-dresses received at the time of their baptism; but now, if tears were in the eyes of any, it was as a sign of joyful thankfulness, and not of grief. With banners and songs the pilgrims made their way through the streets of Nagasaki and up the flight of steps that led to the church.

Certain days had been appointed for the coming of Christians from other communities. As the ancient Jews made their way to Jerusalem at the time of the Passover, so the Japanese believers came from different parts of Kyushu. Some journeyed by land, bands of happy pilgrims rejoicing in the religious liberty that had been assured to them a year before, by the National Constitution. Dwellers on the islands came by boats, on which they lived during their stay in Nagasaki. At early dawn and in the evening, their prayers and songs could be heard floating over the placid waters of the bay. On the day assigned to a company for its visit to the church, its members gathered upon the shore and awaited the summons for climbing the hill. When the bell sounded, the missionaries in charge of the section of the country from which the pilgrims came would put themselves at the head of the procession as it made its way to the church.   Often the number of those who came was too great to allow all of them to enter the building at one time.   It was estimated that in all, some ten or twelve thousand Christians took part in these pilgrimages.

The great day of the feast was March 17, the anniversary of the discovery of the Christians.   Throughout the commemorative service that was observed, two women remained kneeling before the tomb of Mgr. Petitjean.   Twenty-five years before, this mother and daughter, the latter then but a little girl, had been in the company of visitors who had said to him whose body was now lying within that tomb: " We have the same heart as you."

In 1888, a third vicariate—that of Central Japan—had been created, and this was followed in 1891, by a fourth, comprising Yezo and the Kurile Islands, that was named the Vicariate of Hakodate.   Almost immediately after this, the Pope established an episcopal hierarchy in Japan.   The vicariates were replaced by three bishoprics and one archbishopric.   In carrying out this arrangement, Mgr. Osouf became the Archbishop of Tokyo; Mgr. Cousin, the Bishop of Nagasaki; Mgr. Midon, the Bishop of Osaka; and Mgr. Berlioz, the Bishop of Hakodate.

At this time the prospects of rapid growth seemed bright.   In Oshima there were thousands * asking for instruction preparatory to baptism, and in a short time the rite was administered to about fifteen hundred of them.   From 1880 to 1890, the " Catholic population " had grown from 23,909 to 42,378.   Included in this increase were many people that had formerly been reckoned among the " Separates," and this source of enlargement was from the necessity of the case becoming of less importance, so that the growth of the next five years to 50,302 was very encouraging.   The effects of the reaction that retarded the advance of Protestant Christianity were not felt so quickly by Roman Catholi-

* " Milliers d'ames." " La Relig. de Jésus Ressus.," vol. ii., p. 540.

cism. They appeared later in the slower growth of the next two five-year periods, the population in 1900 being 54,602, and that of 1905 being 59,437.

The following account, abridged from that given in 1895, by M. Marnas,* will serve to show some of the methods by which the work was carried on:

"In each diocese there are useful auxiliaries to second the efforts of the bishops and missionaries, who without them would be unable to perform the many duties of their apostolate. Some are Japanese. These are priests, catechists, and school-teachers. In the south, eight native communities of nuns devote themselves to the religious instruction of children and to charitable efforts of the most varied forms. Other nuns have come from Europe. The Marianites, a congregation of men, including both priests and lay brothers, devoted solely to education, have established a college. The Dames of Saint-Maur, the Nuns of the Holy Child Jesus of Chauffailles, and the Sisters of Saint Paul of Chartres have seminaries and schools for girls, direct the orphanages of the Holy Infancy, and give themselves to labours among poor, sick, and needy persons of all kinds.

"History will not be able to bring against modern missionaries in Japan the reproach urged by Rohrbacher against those of former times that they did not pay sufficient attention to raising up a native clergy. This work, which holds the first place in the solicitude of the bishops, is in excellent condition. Up to the present time twenty-three priests have been ordained. Three of these have died: one of them by disease after a service of four and a half years, and the other two by being drowned at sea in a typhoon.

"Whoever has seen the first native priests of Japan engaged in their labours can bear of them the general witness that they are as well instructed, as pious, and as devoted to God's service as could reasonably be expected. Since 1890, as a result of an understanding between the bishops, a single seminary—that in Nagasaki—receives from all four dioceses those who by previous examinations have been judged fit persons for ecclesiastical studies.

"The studies are exacting. The pupils show much interest in them. They apply themselves closely to their work and are successful. In the lower classes they study Latin, the Japanese language, and the Chinese ideographs. In the following grades, history, geography, literature, the sciences and philosophy are added. Finally they come to the study of dogmatic theology, moral theology, and the Holy Scriptures. The entire course requires over fifteen years. In rare cases, candidates for holy orders are admitted before reaching the age of thirty. They are tested before being made sub-deacons. The rules require that they shall leave the seminary for one year and be sent into the

* "La Relig. de Jésus Ressus.," vol. ii., 554 sq.

country districts as catechists under the direction of missionaries. If any then feel appalled at thought of the irrevocable vows that every priest must make before ascending to the altar, they have the option of remaining in an inferior position. Those that persist in their desire for ordination are tested at the seminary for one more year before being allowed to take the decisive step.

"These young men are attractive in appearance. They are simple-hearted, refined, good-natured, and animated. They show the same zeal in their sports as in their studies. They have clear brows and frank faces. At the altar they are reverent and grave. They carry out the ceremonies with great perfection and chant the liturgy in a very appropriate manner. For the most part they are sons of confessors of the faith. At the time of the last persecution many of them shared the prisons of their parents, and in childhood had the honour of suffering for Jesus Christ. The children of heathen are fewest in number and belong to dioceses that have not the advantage of possessing descendants of the ancient Christians.

"The catechists, a class of helpers whose preparation is easier and quicker, have not for that reason failed to render most important service. Not only did they at first give effectual aid in the restoration of the ancient Christian communities, but they have been and still are indispensable agents for the conversion of the heathen. It is doubtless true that the work of the catechist cannot supply the place of that done by the missionary; but it supplements the latter and serves to extend its influence. It can readily be seen that a Japanese layman, who is ordinarily a married man not distinguished from others by his dress or behaviour, can mingle much more easily with his fellow-countrymen, talk with them on matters of common interest, and gradually lead them to a religion of which he himself is already a convert. A foreign priest, especially at first, is the object of a certain amount of suspicion. Heathen have no idea of the spiritual motive that has brought him to them, and they often think that he has been led by some secret and selfish purpose.

"In Japan two methods are employed for the training of catechists. The first is that of having them study for a while in special schools. The other is to choose from the most talented and earnest members of a Christian community one or more men who are willing to serve in the desired capacity, and the missionary himself instructs these persons, furnishes them with books, replies to their own doubts or to those proposed to them by others, has them preach in public when he is present, and otherwise directs their education. While in the case of a native priest, who to a sufficiently thorough knowledge of the sacred sciences must add the practice of lofty and stern virtues, there must be a special call well tested by means of long studies and training, a catechist, since he is not constrained to celibacy or to a particular form of life, can be prepared for effective service in a few months, especially if he has had some previous education.

" One very remarkable thing in Japan is the taste that the people have developed for public speaking Perhaps there is no country in the world where there is more of this and where the people listen so well without signs of weariness.* The Japanese are naturally eloquent and it is not rare to find, even among men of meagre education, a real talent for extemporaneous speech. Whoever has anything to say can always find an attentive audience. All that it is necessary to do is to hang out through the day before the gate a paper lantern on which is written in Chinese ideographs a notice of the lecture; and at evening the speaker, whether he be a politician, a preacher, or a simple story-teller, finds seated on the mats before him an audience made up of people of all ages and classes, who smoke their tiny pipes and sip tea while they willingly listen until late at night to whatever may be said.

" The catechist's mission does not end here. He remembers the Chinese proverb: ' A chance word often accomplishes more than a well-prepared discourse.' All the time not given to study is devoted to interviews with the heathen and especially with the catechumens. He teaches them the holy doctrine; he prepares them for baptism; he shows an interest in children, invalids, and poor people; he takes part in the joys and sorrows of the family whose confidant and friend he becomes; and it often happens that it is by his deeds rather than by his words that he gains for God the souls of his brethren. The work of the catechist therefore completes that of the missionary. He prepares the way for the latter by winning for him the minds and hearts of men. Without him the evangelisation of the people, if not impossible, would at least be very difficult. In the midst of the Christian communities the catechist fills a different place but one no less useful. In the absence of the priests it is he that gathers the Christians for the recital of prayers, that exhorts them to remain faithful, that instructs the children, and prepares them for the reception of the sacraments.

* This interest in public speaking of which M. Marnas writes is a matter of recent growth, and to a considerable extent it is due to Christian influence. In former times there was, of course, no public discussion of political questions, and Buddhist priests did but little preaching. Among Japan's noted men it would be hard to select any who were famous as orators. As soon as the public proclamation of Christian doctrine became possible, Protestant missionaries and afterwards the native evangelists began to preach. Those of the Roman Catholic and Greek Orthodox churches did the same somewhat later to a less degree. The Buddhist priests found that in order to retain a hold upon their followers it was necessary to do more than formerly for their instruction. The advocates of popular rights soon saw the advantage of public discussion as a means for arousing the people, and so political lectures became common.

"Women can serve as catechists for persons of their own sex. While keeping within their sphere, they often prove no less successful than the men. The communities of nuns in the Nagasaki diocese are veritable nurseries of female catechists. At the direction of the bishops these workers often go to the most distant places; for in Japan women are not shut up as they are in China, and they are often better able than men to exert a helpful influence upon families.

"Important as is the part taken by catechists, they do not suffice for fully attaining the end sought by the Catholic apostolate. Schools are also needed. These are necessary for Christian children, whose faith and morals must be safeguarded. They are necessary for the heathen themselves, since the schools often furnish the only means for reaching these persons. The Japanese Government has established educational institutions of all grades. Before the movement that makes Japan to-day enthusiastic in educational matters had become so marked, the Catholic missionaries, when as yet they had no Christians, gathered many heathen pupils or accepted positions as teachers in the government schools. The institutions founded by them did not survive the persecution of 1870-73. After that outbreak few efforts were made in the same direction. Although the zeal of the missionaries was chiefly directed to the care of the Christian communities and the evangelisation of the heathen, they opened primary schools wherever their resources made this possible. These primary schools have continued to increase in number until the present day. The teachers are Japanese chosen and supported by the Mission. The pupils pursue the same studies as those of the government schools, with the single addition that the catechism is taught outside of the regular class-hours. Heathen children are usually admitted to these schools in the same way as Christian children, and it often comes to pass that they and their parents ask to become Catholics.

"In order to reach the upper classes of society the bishops appealed to the Marianites to establish colleges in the principal cities. The first members of this order, who arrived at Tokyo in 1887 under the direction of the Abbé Heinrich, were favourably recommended to the Japanese authorities by the French Minister. When permission had been obtained for opening a school in the capital, they rented a building and commenced their first term with sixty pupils. These belonged to the best families in Tokyo and Yokohama, Protestant as well as Catholic. Among them were some Japanese. In 1895 the pupils numbered one hundred and sixty, divided about equally between Japanese, Europeans, and Eurasians. In 1891 the Marianites established a second institution in Nagasaki with the intention of having it serve for a novitiate as well as for a school.

"Long before the Marianites arrived in Japan, the Dames of Saint-Maur, the Nuns of the Holy Child Jesus, and the Sisters of Saint Paul had been called for the purpose of opening girls' schools. There are in Japan no communities of nuns that do not have schools. Besides the orphanages under their care, where Christian education is given to about fifteen hundred children, they have established several schools for daughters of well-to-do families. It is remarkable that after a little while most of those who come as heathen ask of their own accord to be Christians.

" Some missionaries have engaged in literary labours. They have published in Japanese fifty books that treat for the most part of religious matters. Since 1880 they have conducted under various names a review which discusses important theological, philosophical, historical, and scientific questions, besides giving the religious news of Japan and the Catholic world. There is also a weekly journal.*

" If words are powerful, works are much more so. When an epidemic breaks out, when the cholera rages as it did in 1886 and 1890, missionaries, nuns, and Christian believers are to be seen carrying help to the sick in the unostentatious manner of persons that are performing the most elementary duties. In 1890 MM. Brotelande, Vigroux, and Lecomte saw their devoted labours in the hospitals of the capital rewarded by the baptism of five hundred cholera patients. In Tokyo the older orphan girls under the care of the Dames of Saint-Maur aroused the admiration of the physicians and hospital officers, who gave to these improvised nurses the recompense usually bestowed on attendants of the first class; but what was more pleasing to these orphans was the number of baptisms that they were able to administer. In 1891 and 1892, when influenza prevailed, a single Christian obtained the baptism of four hundred adults. It is not only under unusual circumstances and at the time of great epidemics that Catholic charity is manifested. Among the nuns are some that care for the sick, either visiting them in their homes or bringing them to the convent. They have pharmacies and dispensaries where every year they give remedies and help to thousands of people and where they obtain many conversions or prepare the way for them. Others have small hospitals where they receive sick people who have no other refuge and who for the most part find there the benefit of a Christian death. But the most extensive work conducted by the three sisterhoods is that done in the orphanages. Thanks to the Society of the Holy Infancy, they are bringing up in ten institutions about fifteen hundred orphan girls who find all the care that could have been given by their own parents, the affection that such parents often refuse, and beyond all this the inexpressible advantage of a Christian training and education. The nuns teach these children such industries as will give them a means of support in future days. Nea·ly all these young girls are Christians when they

* Among the books issued at about this time was a translation of the New Testament made from the Vulgate. The translator was a Protestant Japanese.

leave the orphanages. The greatest obstacle to their continuance in the faith is the difficulty of finding suitable husbands; the number of Christian young men being much less that that of Christian young women. Most of them are compelled to marry heathen, and this gives rise to many inconveniences.

"There are also orphanages for boys. Every diocese has its own, but the number of inmates is much less than that in institutions for girls. One reason, and perhaps the principal one, is that in Japanese families boys are always preferred to girls. Hitherto the young men going out from the orphanages have shown little inclination to marry the orphan girls.*

"Infirm and friendless old people cannot fail to have a claim on Catholic charity. At Nagoya, M. Tulpin has brought together on land belonging to the Mission about forty old persons whom he lodges, either in families or singly, in detached buildings, thus leaving them at liberty and under the pleasant illusion of dwelling in their own homes. Finally, there is the work for lepers inaugurated by M. Testevuide, and since his death in 1891 continued by M. Vigroux."

At about the time described by M. Marnas, the Roman Catholic missionaries were feeling, with others, the results of the reaction against Western ideas. M. Bulet wrote: "The characteristic note of the period we are passing through is, if I am not mistaken, a real religious indifference, which is more difficult to overcome than the ancient hostility, which made martyrs." Archbishop Osouf reported: "Nearly all the missionaries complain of a want in their Christians, the absence of zeal to propagate their religion around them." One missionary wrote of a place where about thirty catechumens had

---

* Father Steichen, writing in 1904, says that the Catholic Church then had 21 orphanages, where 1,378 girls and 182 boys were sheltered at an annual expense of 100,000 *yen*. He questions whether the results correspond to the expenditure. "It may be asked," he says, "whether it is really practical to confer baptism on these waifs. Some persevere, but the great number when once put back into the pagan environment forget little by little that they are Christians. In general the Japanese have not much will power, but in the environments from which come the children of our orphanages it is even impossible to give it to them. . . . This essentially Christian work is the despair of the missionaries. On the one hand they would not abandon these poor unfortunates to their sad fate and on the other hand they ask themselves whether with the same resources they might not undertake some less ungrateful work."—"The Christian Movement in Japan," II., p. 195.

" fallen away during the year, under the influence of political excitement and the revulsion of feeling against foreigners;" while another said: " This year has been the most painful of my life. To judge by the number of baptisms I have to report, one might doubt of the zeal of my five catechists. Nothing could be more unjust. . . . St. Paul (2 Tim. iv.) has well described the state of my district: ' There shall be a time when they will not endure sound doctrine, but will turn away their hearing from the truth and will be turned unto fables.' " *

* Casartelli, " The Catholic Church in Japan," pp. 37-38.

XIII

THE MISSIONS IN THE TWENTIETH CENTURY

1901-1909

HOWEVER it may be to those more directly concerned with the progress of the Roman Catholic Church in Japan, its later history presents, to one outside of its communion, but few striking events. Such a person can not be greatly interested in the coming and going of individual missionaries, or even in the appointment of new bishops to take the place of those who have passed away. Year by year, whether those in attendance be many or few, the Church's services of worship are conducted in the same way; it carries on its educational and charitable institutions with some increase in their number, yet with little change in their methods; and it adds slowly though steadily to the number of its adherents; but, except that its edifices are often prominent features in the appearance of the cities where they are located, the missions are carried on in ways that but slightly attract the attention of the outside world. There have been, however, some events connected with the development of the Roman Catholic Church in the twentieth century that demand a place in this history.

The interests of the Church in Japan, as has been seen, were for a long time entrusted to the Société des Missions-Étrangères of Paris, and thus, nearly all of the missionaries were French. After the Spanish-American war many of the Dominicans removed from the Philippine Islands, and in 1904, the Propaganda having caused the Island of Shikoku, which then had three hundred Roman Catholic Christians and four chapels, to be given into the care of their order, six of these Spanish friars went to this field. A company of Franciscans have settled in Sapporo, where considerable of their time is given to the teaching of English, German, and French, probably with the hope suggested in a report of the Société des Missions-Étrangères, which says: "If the teaching of languages has as a result a students' hostel and later a real college, it may be believed that the *élite* of the next generation will be led to our holy religion."

The desire of the Jesuits to re-enter Japan has at length been granted, and in 1908, members of that Society went thither, entrusted with the task of founding an educational institution of high grade. Thus three of the orders that long ago laboured in Japan have returned to the scenes of their former triumphs and sufferings.

A company of Trappists that had come to Japan in 1896 and established a monastery near Hakodate, began, about 1901, to attract considerable attention because of accounts that were published by journalists who had visited them and been impressed by their austere method of life. At first the community had experienced great difficulties from the severity of the northern winter, from sickness and even death, from the hostility of the people among whom they settled, from unfriendly articles in the newspapers, from the interference of officials, from the destruction of one of their buildings in a typhoon, and from insufficient funds. They gradually disarmed prejudice, and by 1902, about fifty persons, children and adults, living in the neighbourhood, had been baptised by them. The products of the farm that they cultivated were of such excellent quality as to gain a ready sale, so that a report made in 1902 said that, if means for clearing more land could be found, the community might hope that after a while it could be supported by its own labour. The same report says:

"The principal object of our foundation was to introduce the religious life into Japan. In fact, we are the first and only religious order here. If it is true that it is as well worth while to make one native priest as to make a thousand Christians, how much more is this true of a religious destined for the priesthood? We have now eleven Japanese, of whom five are professed religious and six novices; three more will enter soon." *

* "Annals Prop. Faith," Amer. Ed., July-Aug., 1902.

Near the monastery is a company of nuns belonging to the allied order of Notre Dame des Anges.

In Kyushu many descendants of the ancient Christians still hold themselves aloof from the missionaries; the Report of the Société des Missions-Étrangères for 1903, says that they are more difficult to reach than the pagans, though most of the forty-four adults baptised at Urakami the previous year were from this class. The Report for 1906 says that in Ikutsukishima—the island formerly under the rule of " Prince Anthony "—there were still six thousand of these " séparés."

M. Ferrand has taken much interest in the establishment of hostels for students attending higher institutions of learning. This work he began in 1899, when a small building for the purpose was obtained in Tokyo. Soon afterward another was opened in Kanazawa (Kaga). In these hostels the students paid for their lodgings, but, in addition to being under helpful influences, they received from the missionaries gratuitous instruction in foreign languages. Obedience to rules, such as that forbidding the inmates to be absent at night, was required. The directors learned by enquiries at the different schools whether the students were regular in their attendance and whether their conduct was good. In 1906, M. Ferrand, in writing of what had been accomplished, said of the boarders in these hostels:

" Under a gentle, paternal surveillance, a rule easy to accept, they live in an atmosphere really Christian, where they receive instruction adapted to their needs from a religious, philosophical, historical, and scientific point of view. Little by little, thanks to the lectures they follow and to private conversations, the errors and prejudices imbibed at school are disappearing; ignorance and doubts are vanishing; the true religion and its ministers are better understood and appreciated. Many souls who have remained upright come nearer to us and make the decisive step for which they are prepared; the light shines for them and it is thus that more than a hundred students have been converted and baptised.

" We have also established a club of Catholic students to group together all those who are in Tokyo and through them attract the non-Catholic young men. This little society counts in all about eighty members; they meet once a month for conferences given by the missionaries and the older students. . . . For more than a year the members of the Catholic students' club have published a little monthly review of about seventy pages, called the *Shin Riso* (New Ideal), which treats from a Catholic point of view all serious questions which may interest the student." *

The Japanese are very fond of theatrical representations, and in some places the missionaries have taken advantage of this fact for reaching the people by means of what bear some resemblance to the mystery plays of the Middle Ages. At one of the first exhibitions of this kind the drama was founded on the history of the Twenty-six Japanese Martyrs. A report of it says:

" The actors performed their parts with faith and true piety. From the fifteen or sixteen pagans that the building could contain not a single unpleasant word was heard. On the contrary, the pagan women wept with emotion, while the men waxed indignant over the cruelty with which the executioners treated the martyrs. The effect that was produced has exceeded our hopes. Many pagans who for some years have been inclined towards Catholicism were converted." †

M. Angles, writing from Osaka, says that, as the exhibitions are conducted there, the actors are usually selected from the young men of the parish or from inmates of the orphan asylum. Among the most effective pieces are those founded on the story of Joseph and on that of the Twenty-six Martyrs. Large audiences listen with close attention, not only to the dramas, but also to the short addresses on religious themes that are introduced between the acts.

Many publications have been issued in recent years. M. Ligneul has been specially active in preparing a number of books on subjects more or less directly connected with religion. These have established for him a reputation as a scholar, and probably led to his being invited to give a series of lectures at Tokyo, before the Imperial Educational Society. He took for his subject " The Philosophy of Teaching," and the lectures were published by the society. Afterwards he delivered an-

---

* " Annals Prop. Faith," Supplement to Amer. Ed., December, 1906.
† " L'Evangile au Japon au XXᵉ Siècle," p. 160.

other course before the students of philosophy in the
Imperial University of Tokyo, upon " The Place of
Philosophy in Contemporary Society."

The war with Russia probably affected the Roman
Catholics less than it did the Protestants and Greeks,
though they shared the work done in behalf of the
soldiers and their families.   The Mission's request that
it be allowed to send one or more priests to care for the
spiritual interests of Catholic soldiers and to engage in
beneficent efforts for others, was not granted by the
Government.   Among the Russian prisoners brought to
Japan were many Polish Catholics, and the missionaries
gained permission to visit these.   The Bishop of Osaka,
when visiting one of the prisons, spoke to an audience
of twelve hundred men of different races.   At that time
he confirmed three hundred and fifty Poles.*

Of another place a missionary wrote :

" Our five hundred prisoners have all made their confessions
and been communicated. We say mass for them regularly every
Sunday and nearly every Thursday, so that they are really better
provided with services than they were in Russia. In the two
places where mass is said for them the prisoners have fitted up
proper chapels; the sergeants serve at the mass, and some of them
would take rank with the most experienced servers." †

Father Steichen thus describes how the interest taken
in the prisoners excited the suspicion and distrust of
ultra-patriotic Japanese :

" Some of our Christians abandoned their religion because the
missionary had gone to visit the Russian prisoners in order to
offer his services to some Polish Catholics among them. Another reason for this abandonment of their faith was that the
missionary had incurred the suspicion of being a Russian spy,
because he had gone to witness the departure of troops for the
front." ‡

In November, 1905, Archbishop O'Connell of Maine
(afterwards of Boston) went to Japan as a legate from

* " Annals Prop. Faith," Am. Ed., December, 1905.
† " Christian Movement," vol. iv., p. 210.
‡ *Ib.*, vol. iii., p. 182.

the Pope to return thanks for favours that had been shown to Roman Catholics in Japan, and for protection given at the time of the war to those in Manchuria. He was given an audience by the Emperor, and at a reception tendered to him in the Y. M. C. A. Hall of Tokyo, several Protestants were among the speakers.

Roman Catholicism has been, to a greater extent than Protestantism, subject to the charge that it tends to weaken the spirit of loyalty. This is partly because of the prejudice occasioned by the events of three centuries ago, because fewer of its followers have been among those taking a prominent part in national affairs, and because of what is thought to be its attitude in some European countries. One French missionary speaks of having the objection thus thrown at him:

" Catholicism is not a religion fitted to Japan, because a Catholic is deficient in patriotism."
" What proof have you of that?"
" What proof? Why is it that Clemenceau makes war on the French Church? Is it not because French Catholics are not patriots?"

Another effect of the troubles in France was that the contributions from that country to the work of missions were greatly diminished. Letters of the missionaries abound in regrets that lack of funds prevented their utilising the opportunities that were before them. They were inclined to contrast their condition in this respect with that of the Protestants, whom they supposed to be provided with immense sums. Little had been done to develop self-support in the Japanese churches. Father Steichen, writing in 1904 of the self-sacrificing spirit of the missionaries, said:

" Instead of requiring the faithful to come to their aid, whether for the maintenance of the churches or for other running expenses, as is done in all other parishes throughout the world, they deprived themselves of necessaries in order to defray the expenses themselves. So the 58,086 Catholics of Japan contribute hardly 2,000 *yen* for the maintenance of the Mission." *

The greatly increased cost of living in Japan combined with the lessening of the contributions from France

* " Christian Movement," vol. ii., p. 197.

to cripple the work. The Report of the Société des Missions-Étrangères for 1906, in speaking of the reduced number of seminarists studying at Nagasaki, said that the mission, alarmed at the financial outlook, did not dare to call to the service of the Church young men, to whom after ordination it would be unable " to furnish such sustenance as is required by the canons. The mission at Nagasaki has no resources of its own, and the best Christian communities will long be incapable of undertaking the support of the native clergy that is already in existence." M. Sauret wrote, in 1905, that the cost of living had so increased that most of the missionaries had dispensed with their catechists, and he went on to say:

" This means an absolute stand-still in our missionary labours, properly speaking, as it is impossible for us Europeans to do any direct work among the pagan element of the population. To reach it we need the catechist as an intermediary; the very fact that we are foreigners is an insuperable obstacle to our being admitted in a pagan family, much less gaining its confidence."

The same letter says:

" The diocese of Nagasaki is rather behind in regard to the evangelisation of the pagans; this is due to the fact that the old Christians of St. Francis Xavier, discovered by Bishop Petit-jean in 1865, are all in this part of the country. For many years the missionaries had all they could do to minister to those Christians, who numbered several thousands. Although they had kept the faith, they were very ignorant and had to be instructed and trained in the practices of religion. I was the first one to attack the pagans and not without some success. I formed a catechist to clear up the ground for me, and that man has brought to the faith a number of pagans."

After speaking of the need for a dispensary, the letter continues:

" But if we want a dispensary to do some good to the soul, we must also employ Catholic Japanese nurses. They are indispensable and would alone be able to make conversions. Sisters might have direction of the institution, but they could do no effective work for the evangelisation of the pagans. Their habit and their nationality would always stand in their way. The Japanese keep strangers at a distance. In their heart of hearts they despise them more or less, though exteriorly they preserve a respectful silence. There is no possible intimate association under such conditions and consequently the heart is not won over and it is difficult to effect a sincere conversion. In dispensaries and in hospitals a Japanese woman could do a great deal of good. A sick man or woman would speak to her with sincerity and would not hesitate to ask her about the character, life, and religion of the foreigners at the head of the dispensary. From admiration it will be easy for them to pass to imitation. The patients would not dare to ask similar questions of the Sisters; and, even if they did, they would not pay much heed to the answers; in their opinion all foreigners must have a motive of human interest for coming to Japan and it must be for their advantage to keep it concealed. With such a feeling of distrust, no mutual confidence can be established. After they are once converted, the men will speak frankly to me of their disposition before baptism. Nurses, therefore, will not only do good at the dispensaries, but they will dispose men to study the Christian doctrines by visiting them in their homes. . . . Moreover, if a child is dying in the neighbourhood, it can be baptised unknown to the parents. My woman catechist baptises a number of pagan children every year in this way. Every one knows that she is in my employ, and as I have the reputation of being a good medical doctor, the people imagine that, by being associated with me, she has learned to take care of the sick. She can present herself anywhere where there are sick children. As she has a weakness for finding fever and always discovers microbes in a dirty skin, she, of course, needs water to lower the temperature or bathe the parts affected by the microbes. Whilst the pagans admire so much scientific knowledge in a Japanese woman, she profits by the occasion to administer the Sacrament of Baptism, making use of the Latin formula. The unknown language sounds rather strange to pagan ears; they imagine her words to be some kind of incantation to add efficacy to the remedies." *

Imperial recognition of Christian philanthropy was shown, about this time, by the conferring of the Blue Ribbon on M. Bertrand and Sister Marie Colombe, for what they have done among lepers, and on M. Corre for his works of charity. This honour is bestowed on persons that have performed noteworthy deeds of public utility. On M. Vernier, who has been engaged in education, was conferred the decoration of the Order of the Sacred Treasure.

Perhaps the most successful enterprises under Roman Catholic auspices have been the schools of the Marianites. The first of these, as has already been

* "Annals Prop. Faith," Supplement to Am. Ed., June, 1905.

mentioned, was established at Tokyo in 1887. Up to 1906, Japanese and European boys were educated together; but, as it was found advisable to make a division, the latter, with most of the Eurasians, were then sent to a new school that was opened in Yokohama. The next year it had 130 pupils, representing sixteen or eighteen different nationalities. Statistics of the Tokyo school for 1907 show that it was attended by 685 Japanese, 17 Chinese and Koreans, and 8 Eurasians. The enumeration by religions shows " Catholics, 71; Catechumens, 29; Pagans, 610." That it was reaching the upper classes of society is shown by its having thirty pupils from families belonging to either the old or new nobility of Japan. There were twenty-eight sons of generals or admirals; while others were sons of ambassadors, ministers of state, consuls, judges, members of the Diet, etc. Two of the Marianites were professors in the Imperial University, one taught in the Nobles' School, and two in military schools. The order also had a school at Nagasaki with 388 pupils, another (begun in 1906) at Kumamoto, and a commercial school at Osaka with about 600 students. The account from which these figures are taken, says that an " Apostolic School " had just been opened at Urakami, and already had more than thirty pupils. " It will have for its end the recruiting of religious, whether priests or not, who will devote themselves to teaching. If some prove unfitted for religious lives, they will be employed as free teachers, and thus, while living in the world, will be able to render valuable service." *

One difficulty attending missionary work at this period was probably felt in a greater degree by the Roman Catholics than by the Protestants. It was that which came from the changes in population. The young people were moving from the country into the manufacturing and commercial centres. Coming into new and sometimes unfavourable surroundings they were tempted to conceal their religion or to grow weak in the

* " Annals de la Société des Missions-Étrangères," July-August, 1908.

faith. After the war with Russia, many Japanese re-moved to Korea and Manchuria, where the chances of their being in helpful religious surroundings were small. The Report of the Société des Missions-Étrangères for 1907, makes frequent mention of the weakening of small communities of Christians by such removals.

The Report of the same society for 1906, in explain-ing the reason for slow progress, mentions, besides other things to which reference has already been made, the fact that the Catholic doctrine rests upon the principle of authority, and says: " This principle our Japanese would perhaps admit if the seat of that authority were Japan; but their national pride opposes itself to permit-ting that a foreigner should, apart from the Emperor, have control over them."

What has been accomplished in the half century since Japan has been re-opened to the missionaries of the Roman Catholic Church, so far as this can be told by figures, is shown by the following statistics for 1908, taken from the Annual Report of the Société des Mis-sions-Étrangères (Paris, 1909):

DIOCESE	Tokyo	Nagasaki	Osaka	Hakodate	TOTAL
Catholic population	9,625	44,931	3,711	4,427	62,694
Churches and chapels........	36	122	27	32	217
Bishops	1	1	1	1	4
Missionaries	32	36	26	25	119
Native priests	3	26	3	1	33
Catechists	21	335	39	21	416
Seminaries	1	1	—	1	3
Seminarists	2	16	—	2	20
Communities of men........	2	2	1	3	8
Religieux	34	18	6	35	93
Communities of women	5	17	5	3	30
Religieuses	87	221	23	58	389
Conversion of heretics	5	—	4	1	10
Baptisms of pagans *	705	522	243	342	1,812
Baptisms of pagan children in articulo mortis	300	767	511	267	1,845
Baptisms of children of Chris-tians	195	1,657	97	65	2,014

* Of the " Baptisms of pagans " those in articulo mortis were at Tokyo, 521; Nagasaki, 175; Osaka, 67; Hakodate, 145; Total, 908.

DIOCESE	Tokyo	Nagasaki	Osaka	Hakodate	TOTAL
Schools	12	8	5	8	33
Pupils	1,989	1,186	1,694	1,033	5,902
Crèches and orphanages	3	8	5	3	19
Inmates	432	188	174	133	927
Industrial schools	7	6	7	—	20
Children in same	111	105	258	—	474
Pharmacies and dispensaries.	3	7	—	4	14
Hospitals and leper asylums..	1	2	—	—	3

The Official Catholic Directory (United States) for 1908, gives the following additional statistics of the previous year for the work of the Dominicans in the Prefecture Apostolic of Shikoku:

Prefect Apostolic	1
Missionaries	6
Catechists	3
Churches or chapels	5
Baptisms of adults	29
Baptisms of children of Christian parents	4
Baptisms of children of pagans, *in articulo mortis*...........	32
Catholic population	300

PART II

THE GREEK ORTHODOX MISSION

XIV

THE BEGINNING OF THE MISSION

1861-1872

JAPAN'S nearest neighbour is Russia. For a long time subjects of each nation had settlements in Saghalien, and the resulting disputes over territorial rights continued until 1875, when Japan waived its claims to that island, and at the same time received the islands of the Kurile group that had hitherto belonged to Russia. The Kuriles had been visited in the eighteenth century by Russian priests, and not long ago there were still living on one of the islands about a dozen families of Christian Ainu, the descendants of those that had been taught by these missionaries. It is said that some of the priests penetrated into Yezo.*

There was a professorship of the Japanese language in a school that was established by Catherine II. in Irkutsk. It was filled by Japanese who had been shipwrecked on the coast of Siberia. When Klaproth was sent in 1805, as interpreter of an attempted embassy to China, he remained for a while in Irkutsk, where, among other things, he studied Japanese at this school. The occupant of the professorial chair at that time had become a member of the Greek Church.

In 1854, the Chaplain of the Russian ship *Diana,* then anchored at Shimoda, was one day walking on the shore, when a Japanese, whose attention had been attracted by the cross on the priest's breast, asked to be taken on board the ship, and there, when secure from the observation of any of his countrymen, he drew from beneath

* "La Rel. de Jésus Res.," vol. i., p. 193; "Nihon Seikyo Dendoshi," vol. ii., p. 2. From the second of these books has been drawn most of the material for this chapter.

his robe a cross, repeated the names of Jesus and Mary, and said that he was a descendant of Roman Catholic Christians. He was taken to Siberia, where he probably joined the Russian Church.*

M. Mermet, the French missionary who visited Hakodate in 1861, was vexed at the growing influence of the Russians. In one of his letters he wrote that their houses and shops were springing up on all sides, as though by magic, that Russian men-of-war were numerous in the harbour, and that " an army of popes," having large sums of money at their command, was spreading over the country. These popes, he said, were very zealous and by their benefactions were purchasing the good will of the people.† The Frenchman's zeal for his own church and his desire to arouse the emulation of his supporters must have led him to an exaggerated view of the activity of the Russians. It may be doubted whether his army of popes equalled in number that of the band that set upon the doughty Falstaff; certainly, there seems little reason to believe that, with a single exception, any Russian priests connected with the navy or the consular service were deeply imbued with a missionary spirit.

A Russian consulate had been established at Hakodate in 1859. The priest that served as Consular Chaplain had been there less than a year when poor health compelled him to withdraw. The Holy Synod, when called upon to appoint his successor, asked the authorities in the St. Petersburg Ecclesiastical Academy to find a suitable person. The one chosen was Ivan Kasatkin, a young man twenty-four years old, of deep faith and fervent piety, who had been earnestly praying that God would show him the work he ought to undertake. Before this, he had become deeply interested in Japan through reading Golownin's account of his captivity in that land. Moreover, he longed to preach the Gospel to those that had not yet heard it. Hence, the position of Consular Chaplain at Hakodate was attractive, as it

---

* *The Mission Field*, October, 1860
† " La Relig. de Jésus Res.," vol. 1., p. 389.

might possibly open the way for him to carry out his desires.

He was soon ordained to the priesthood, taking at that time the name of Nicolai, by which he has since become so well known. In July, 1860, he left St. Petersburg, and with only two days' delay at his home, pushed on through Russia and Siberia until, at the end of September, he reached the town of Nicolaievsk at the mouth of the Amur River. Since it was too late to get a boat to Japan, he remained in that place through the winter. His missionary zeal was strengthened by intercourse with Bishop Innocent, who was seeking to convert the tribes of eastern Siberia.

When spring came, Père * Nicolai proceeded on his journey and reached Hakodate in June, 1861. His duties in connection with the consulate were so light that he had abundant time for studying the Japanese language. Among the teachers that he employed was Joseph Neesima, who, after being with him about a month, told him of his purpose to leave Japan, and asked his assistance in carrying it out. Père Nicolai warned him of the danger and offered to teach him English; but on returning from a summer vacation, the Chaplain found that the young man, in whose care he had left the house, was no longer to be found in Hakodate.

Another person who was engaged as a teacher failed to appear at the appointed time, and when Père Nicolai sent to enquire the reason he said: " Please excuse me; for if I go to your house, I shall be killed." Père Nicolai afterwards thought that some young men who were studying Russian had frightened away the teacher, so that more time might be devoted to them.

A *samurai* by the name of Sawabe, who was a native of Tosa in the island of Shikoku, had come to Hakodate and there married the daughter of a Shinto priest. After the death of his father-in-law, he succeeded to the care

---

* It may seem somewhat inconsistent to use this word in connection with a Russian when it has not been used of the French priests; but, until raised to the bishopric, he was so universally known as Père Nicolai that no other designation has so familiar a sound to old residents of Japan.

of the shrine. He did not take much pleasure in the duties of the priesthood and, like so many others of the military class, his thoughts were much occupied with the political questions of the time. Hakodate had become a rendezvous of the *ronin*—military men who had detached themselves from the service of their feudal lords, and who were restlessly agitating various plans for advancing what they considered the interests of their country. Many of them had adopted the watchword "*Hono joi*" ("Honour the Emperor; drive out the foreigners"). They were waiting some favourable opportunity for action. Sawabe was on intimate terms with many of these men.

The Russian Consul wished his son to take lessons in fencing, and Mr. Sawabe, who had formerly been a teacher of that art, was employed for an instructor. In his visits to the consulate he often saw Père Nicolai, whom he regarded with special dislike as being not only a foreigner, but also a priest of the European religion. For a long time he refused to have any conversation with the Chaplain, though he took every opportunity to show his aversion by scowling upon him. Believing that the danger of intercourse with foreign lands came largely from their religion, he, as an ardent patriot, desired to do what he could towards warding off the threatened evil. He decided to have a discussion with Père Nicolai and to slay him if it proved impossible to defeat him by argument. Wearing the two swords belonging to the military class, he one day broke abruptly into the Chaplain's room, calling out in an angry voice:

"Is it because you wish to get possession of our country that you have brought hither your corrupt doctrines?"

"Are you acquainted with the doctrines that I teach?" quietly asked Père Nicolai.

"I at least know that they are evil."

"How can you be sure of that? Before making such an assertion, ought you not to examine my religion to see whether or not it is so hateful as you suppose?"

"Well, then, tell me about it and I will listen."

Père Nicolai therefore began to speak about the Creator of the universe. Gradually Mr. Sawabe became so interested that anger gave way to respectful attention. After a time he began to jot down notes of the principal points. At the close of the conversation he asked that he might come again for further instruction. This was the beginning of earnest study that finally led Mr. Sawabe to the conviction that Christianity is true. He did not conceal from his old friends the change that had come in his views. They were amazed that one who had been prominent in advocating the expulsion of foreigners had become a believer in their religion. Some of them thought he had become insane.

Among the friends to whom Sawabe told his new faith was a physician named Sakai, an upright man who had the reputation of standing firmly by whatever he believed to be true. He brought forward many objections against Christianity, some of them being such as Mr. Sawabe was unable to refute. He was therefore in the habit of repeating them to Père Nicolai, who supplied him with answers to carry back to his friend. Finally Dr. Sakai became sufficiently interested to go himself to the Chaplain for instruction. A third inquirer was a man named Urano.

There were rumours that a new official that had been sent to Hakodate was about to enforce the old laws and punish as rebels those persons that had anything to do with Christianity. This frightened some of those who had hitherto been ready to listen to what Mr. Sawabe told them. Some went so far as to cut off all social relations with him and Dr. Sakai. They would probably have been ready to give information against their former friends. Mr. Sawabe had most reason, however, to fear his mother-in-law. She was bitterly opposed to Christianity, and would not have hesitated to betray him to officials searching out followers of that religion.

Sawabe, Sakai, and Urano, following the advice of friends, decided to seek safety by flight to some place where they were not known. They earnestly desired to receive baptism before leaving Hakodate. On an April night in 1868 they slunk through the streets to the house occupied by Père Nicolai, where all the preparations had been made for the ceremony. A young Russian, who was accustomed to act as reader in the consular chapel, was stationed on the stairway to guard against intrusion, while within a dimly lighted room the rite was administered. Following the custom of the Greek Church, the three men received Christian names, and were henceforth to be known as Paul Sawabe, John Sakai, and Jacob Urano.

At the close of the ceremony, Père Nicolai bade farewell to these men, the first fruits of his missionary labours. It was doubtful whether he would ever look upon their faces again. They as yet knew but little of Christian truth. They greatly needed the instruction that it would be impossible for him to give. He was indeed sending them forth as sheep—nay, as new-born lambs—into the midst of wolves.

The three men went out into the darkness and made their way to the house of a friend by whose aid passage had been secured on a junk that was about to sail. Joined by Dr. Sakai's wife and daughter and by Mr. Sawabe's serving-man, they were soon on board; but the wind and waves were so high that the captain did not dare to set sail. For a whole day they remained in the harbour, apprehensive lest their absence would cause a search to be made for them. The next day they started. Hardly had they cleared the harbour when the violence of the sea made it impossible to proceed. The ship put back to port. Dr. Sakai with his wife and daughter went to the house of a friend who had helped them to escape, and there lay concealed in the attic. The others found refuge elsewhere. On the fourth day they again set forth and after three days at sea reached a port in the northern part of Hondo.

As it was thought safer to divide into two bands, Dr. Sakai with his family at once set out toward his native town in the province of Rikuzen. Mr. Sawabe's servant, who was an intemperate man, gave so much trouble that it was found necessary to discharge him. Mr. Sawabe decided that Yedo would be the safest refuge for himself; and as Mr. Urano's home was in Rikuzen, the two travelled thus far in company and then separated.

At this time the country was in a troubled state, the
northern daimyos, who sided with the Shogun, being in
arms against the Imperial forces that had been sent to
compel their submission. The Tosa clan, to which it
will be remembered that Mr. Sawabe belonged, had
taken a leading part in the overthrowal of the Shogunate.
It is not strange that, being betrayed by his dialect, he
was soon arrested on suspicion of being a spy. Fortu-
nately he was able to obtain release by presenting satisfactory proof that he had come from Hakodate. Soon
afterwards he reached the home of Dr. Sakai, who gladly
welcomed his friend and fellow-believer. The house,
however, was small and not well fitted for concealing a
stranger, whose presence was likely to give rise to unpleasant enquiries; therefore, Mr. Sawabe was sent to
Mrs. Sakai's parents in a neighbouring village. They at
first received him kindly; but when it became known that
he and Dr. Sakai were Christians, the family feared
that they would be punished for giving shelter to a follower of the proscribed religion. The relatives had
several consultations over the matter, and though they did
not openly refuse to keep Mr. Sawabe, there were various
indications that he was no longer a welcome guest.
Among other gentle hints, they frequently discharged
muskets before the house, saying that they were trying
to frighten away evil spirits. Mr. Sawabe, being well
aware of what they had in mind, was unwilling to cause
them annoyance, and soon decided that it would be better
for him to move on towards Yedo.

He had not gone far when he was again arrested as a
spy. The officers that examined him differed among
themselves as to whether his story about coming from
Hakodate ought to be believed. They finally decided
that in any case the best plan would be to send him to
the city from which he professed to come. He was
therefore sent under escort to the northern boundary of
the province and there left to pursue his own way. As
all places seemed dangerous and the direct road to Yedo
was not open to him, he decided that he might as well
obey orders by returning to Hakodate. Before landing
there he heard that such a strict search was being made

for all persons that had any connection with Christianity that it would be perilous to go to his own house, and difficult to find a safe retreat anywhere in the city. He sent some one to call his wife, and then with her and his child went to the house of her uncle, a petty official living in a village not far away. The fact that this official was giving shelter to the refugees probably became known to his superiors, for he was soon summoned to the office, where his attention was called to the regulation by which any person who concealed a Christian became liable to severe punishment. He did not like to send away his relatives, but Mrs. Sawabe happened to learn what had happened and told her husband, whose unwillingness to have others suffer on his account made him decide to return to Hakodate. There he called on Père Nicolai who, in surprise at seeing him, asked why he was so rash as to venture into the very jaws of the tiger that was waiting to destroy him.

"There is no place," said Mr. Sawabe, "where I am safe. After seeking various refuges, I have been forced to return to Hakodate. Here everybody knows me and it will be useless to hide. I shall simply go on my way to meet whatever may be God's will."

At this time the remnants of the Shogun's army were gathering at Hakodate, where it was said they planned to make the last stand. The city was in confusion and the excitement over military and political matters prevented the paying any attention to the enforcement of the laws against Christianity. Mr. Sawabe was therefore left undisturbed.

Père Nicolai saw reasons for believing that the time was near at hand when it would be possible to engage in active evangelistic efforts. He was teaching Russian to some of the officials, and when he occasionally referred to Christianity, he saw no indication that they wished to evade the subject. Conversations that he held with *samurai* coming from different parts of Japan showed that a great revolution was taking place in the thoughts of the people. The movement in favour of adopting Western civilisation had begun and some people were saying that there must be a new religion, since Buddhism was losing its influence and the attempt to revive Shinto was not arousing much enthusiasm. It would be impossible for a consular chaplain, working as an individual and having no resources beyond his own salary, to utilise properly the great opportunity that was close at hand. He therefore sent to Russia asking for a furlough, during which he could appeal to the Holy Synod and to his friends for help. Having thought much about the way in which missionary work ought to be conducted, he had already prepared a set of rules for a society of evangelists that he hoped sometime to organise. These rules are interesting as showing his early recognition of the importance of making converts work for the salvation of others, and also because the plan here marked out is in the main the same that was afterwards used with good results.

RULES

" The evangelists shall be organised as a deliberative body.

" These evangelists shall teach Christian truth to other people while still continuing to study it for themselves.

" There shall be two kinds of meetings. In the first, the evangelists, together with others who know the essential doctrines but desire further study, shall meet to read and explain the New Testament. Such meetings shall be held twice a week, the evangelists taking turns in conducting them. None of the number should fail to attend; if any person is unavoidably prevented from coming, he ought before the next meeting to learn from some one else what was said. The second meeting is for the benefit of those—whether men, women, or children—who are commencing to study Christian doctrines. The evangelists shall explain to them the Creed, the Lord's Prayer, and the Ten Commandments. This meeting shall be held twice a week. The evangelists shall divide the people into classes for instruction. If for any reason a person is not present at a meeting, the evangelist shall ask some one of the absentee's family to inform him of what was said or shall go himself to the person's house for that purpose.

" In neither kind of meeting shall there be discussion until after the explanation is finished, although the meaning may be asked of anything that has not been understood.

" Besides conducting the two kinds of meetings already mentioned, the evangelists shall go about the city every day trying to win new enquirers. If among those interested are persons unable to attend the meetings, the evangelists shall go to their houses in order to explain the Creed, the Lord's Prayer, and the Ten Commandments. This is to be regarded as of prime importance and should be done even if, for lack of time, the evangelist is obliged to omit the meeting for reading the New Testament.

" When persons have thoroughly learned the Creed, the Lord's Prayer, and the Ten Commandments, and are established in the faith, they shall be presented to the priest for baptism.

" Whenever any point of doctrine is not understood, it shall be brought to the priest for explanation, and, if it is a matter of importance, the explanation shall be written down in a notebook.

" On Sundays the Association of Evangelists shall meet at the house of the priest to report what has been done during the previous week, as well as to consult together and decide on what shall be done in the week to come.   These decisions shall be recorded by the evangelists in their notebooks.

" A record shall be kept of baptisms, births, marriages, and deaths.

" A book for recording receipts and expenditures shall be prepared and put in the care of a person to be chosen by the Association.

" The money first collected shall be used for the propagation of Christianity.

" When sufficient money has been gathered, a young man shall be taught the Russian language and sent to a theological school in Russia.   On the completion of his education, he shall return to Japan and there establish a school for teaching Christian doctrine and the sciences.   He shall also translate religious books. Another young man shall be sent to a medical school in Russia and on completing his studies shall return to found a hospital and a medical school.

" When the number of baptised believers reaches five hundred, one of the evangelists shall be chosen for sending to Russia that he may be ordained to the priesthood.   Afterwards, one person shall be ordained for every additional five hundred converts. When there are five thousand believers, a request shall be made for the appointment of a bishop.

" The evangelists who go to teach Christianity in the different provinces shall strictly observe the above rules."

While Père Nicolai was awaiting the reply to his request for a furlough, Mr. Sawabe brought him two men whom he was trying to interest in Christianity.   One of them was Mr. Kannari, who afterwards became a prominent evangelist.   The second, named Arai, though only a youth, had the reputation of being a talented scholar. Both were deeply impressed by what they heard, and until Père Nicolai's departure for Russia they frequently came for further instruction.

These new enquirers were taking an active part in the

political movements of the time. With others of the Sendai clan, to which they belonged, they favoured an attempt that was being made to rally the adherents of the Shogun and establish a republic in Yezo. Seeing that their numbers were insufficient for the impending conflict with the Imperial forces, they returned in April, 1869, to their province in the hope of getting others to join them. They found Sendai occupied by the Imperial troops and such a sharp watch being kept that they were obliged to remain in concealment. In conversation with those whom they met clandestinely they repeated what they had learned about Christianity.

As education had been highly valued by the Sendai clan, it possessed many men of superior ability. They were now, however, regarded as rebels. A few of the more prominent were put to death and the others had no opportunity of using their talents in the direct service of their country. Many of them became farmers or else went into retirement while they watched the course of events and hoped for better times. It was among such men that Mr. Arai found persons ready to hear about a religion whose nature they did not clearly understand but which seemed to offer a ray of hope for their own future and for that of their country, which they considered to be in a deplorable condition. The speedy defeat of the rebels in Yezo overthrew the plans of those opposed to the new order of things. Might not the Christian religion be used as a means for averting some of the evils that threatened the land?

In January, 1870, Mr. Arai went again to Hakodate. Père Nicolai was in Russia ; but Mr. Sawabe heard with joy that the *samurai* of Sendai were ready to listen to Christianity. It seemed to him that by their help a movement could be commenced for the spiritual and political renovation of Japan. He therefore had Mr. Arai write a letter in which these men were urged to come to Hakodate for the study of Christianity. The reasons presented were chiefly political ; the argument used being that the new religion would be the best instrument for uniting the hearts of men who, discontented with the present trend of national affairs, were working for the good of their country. With Mr. Sawabe himself at this time, patriotic motives were probably more powerful than those that were directly religious.

Several of Mr. Arai's friends decided to heed the call. Some of them thought that a movement could be inaugurated that would restore the clan to its former position of influence, others agreed with Mr. Sawabe's view that a new religion would provide a bond of national unity, and some had the idea that by association with the foreign priest in Hakodate a way might open for their going to Europe. The writer of the Japanese history of the Mission compares these men to those who at first followed Christ because they thought He would free Judea from the Roman yoke, but who afterwards learned to know His real mission and became the pillars of the early Church.

Those who decided to go to Hakodate sold their goods, bade farewell to their friends, and set out in two or three small companies. They had somewhat misunderstood Mr. Arai's letter. It had not, as they supposed, urged them to come at once. When the first party, consisting of three men, reached their destination, they learned to their surprise that Père Nicolai, who was to be their teacher, was not in Japan. On going to Mr. Sawabe's house, they found that he was temporarily absent, and, moreover, that, instead of being, as they had supposed, a wealthy man able to become their patron, he had hard work to provide for his own support. Mrs. Sawabe sent a messenger to call Mr. Arai, who was surprised to learn that his friends had come so promptly. Until late at night he talked with them about what should be done, and answered their questions concerning Christianity; for during his own stay in Hakodate he had gained from Mr. Sawabe considerably more knowledge than he had possessed when talking with the same men a few months before. He also had a small manual of doctrine which he read and explained. The next day this instruction was continued. The new-comers soon saw that Christianity was much different from what they had supposed, and some of the doctrines they found difficult to understand. There was some talk among them about the advisability of returning to Sendai; but they thought they would be ridiculed by their friends if they returned so soon, and so they decided to remain long enough to give Christianity a thorough examination.

The Japanese historian remarks that if these men had found Mr. Sawabe in flourishing circumstances and had immediately met Père Nicolai, it is probable that they would have been unable to see anything save in the light of the motives that had brought them to Hakodate, and thus their selfish purposes would have been so strengthened as to blind their eyes to the truth. Disappointed as they were, they were now willing to listen humbly to what was taught them by Mr. Arai and by Mr. Sawabe, who soon returned home. Ere long they became deeply interested in their study of Christianity. Before this, Mr. Sawabe and Dr. Sakai had come into possession of a Chinese translation of the New Testament. This they had divided into two parts, each taking one. The men from Sendai spent much time in making copies of the half that Mr. Sawabe possessed.

Meanwhile four others were journeying towards Hakodate. On their way they passed through the village where one of their friends named Kageta was in hiding. Being one of the prominent *samurai* of the clan, he was in special danger of being punished as a rebel. On going to the house where he was supposed to be, they were told that he was not there. They had not proceeded far on their way when a messenger came running after them to say that Mr. Kageta was really in the house and desired to see them. They turned back and after some persuasion induced him to go with them to Hakodate.

These new additions to the company were heartily welcomed by Mr. Sawabe. His house had been burned a short time before, so that he was living in a shed on the grounds connected with the shrine where he had once served as a priest. Though everything was in a confused state, there was considerable room in the building, and he gladly gave shelter to all of the men from Sendai except two who found lodging elsewhere.

Mr. Sawabe is described as having been at this time a rough, fierce-looking man, who from his outward appearance might have been taken for one of the blood-thirsty swashbucklers whose riotous conduct gave so much annoyance in the troublous times of revolution. He looked like a man who in argument would never rest until he had completely silenced his opponent. His heart, however, had already been so softened by Christianity that his words and acts were gentle. He was particularly careful not to do anything that could offend these new friends. As they were well-educated men, they asked many questions that he found it difficult to answer. Hitherto he had despised learning, considering it a sign of effeminacy to spend much time over books. Now he mourned over the difficulty he had in understanding the meaning of his Chinese Testament. He saw that he needed to study if he did not wish to be put to shame, and he recognised that his lack of literary culture would greatly limit his usefulness. Hence he set himself to studying the Chinese classics, and also borrowed books on various subjects in order that by their perusal he might remedy some of his defects.

Of all the men from Sendai, Mr. Kageta was the least ready to give assent to the new teaching. While the others busied themselves in copying the Bible, he said that he would not take the trouble to do so until he had found out whether its doctrines were true or false. When some of his companions who thought they were making great progress attempted to argue with him, he would meet them with a few simple, but keen questions that sufficed to show them how little they really understood the subjects under discussion.

It would be instructive if we had a record of what was said in this interesting class whose very teachers had so slight knowledge of the doctrines they taught, doctrines so different from anything these men had before believed. One day, for instance, a discussion arose over Christ's words, "Love your enemies." Did this mean that revenge should not be visited upon the enemies of one's feudal lord? Some one asserted that it could mean nothing less. Then there was great excitement. These men had from childhood been taught the Confucian precept, "Live not under the same sky with the murderer

of thy lord or father." They said that they could not accept the new teaching which was so contrary to the
fundamental principles of loyalty and filial duty. It
would be a shame even to sit in the same room with a
person that could approve such a doctrine. When one
of their number, who had at first kept silent, ventured to
say that this new idea ought not to be set aside so lightly
without due consideration, the others glared at him as
though he too were one with whom they ought not to live
under the same sky.

Mr. Ono, the man who had thus spoken, had from the
beginning been very susceptible to Christian ideas. Even
with such imperfect teaching, he had become convinced
that the fundamental doctrines of Christianity were true,
and he had become desirous of teaching them to others.
He had been very earnest in trying to convince Mr.
Kageta, who came to Hakodate later than he, of the existence of God. To the latter this teaching seemed at
first the height of folly, and he could not understand how
an educated person like Mr. Ono could hold such silly
views.

After a time the funds of these men ran low. Messrs.
Ono and Arai therefore returned to Sendai, hoping to get
some help for the support of the company and also to
interest others in the new thoughts they had received.*

The others also began to talk about the necessity of
returning. Mr. Sawabe was anxious to detain them
until Père Nicolai should reach Japan. In providing for
their support he went so far as to sell his sword, a great
sacrifice for a *samurai* to make. At last he proposed, for
he was still imbued with the old ideas of his people, to
sell his wife in order to gain funds for the same purpose.
The others would not consent to this, and all but two of
them went back to their homes. They were so far convinced of the truth of what they had heard that they began to teach it to their relatives and other friends. As a
pardon was extended about this time to the hitherto
proscribed members of the clan, Mr. Kageta was at

* Mr. Arai soon went to America in the suite of Mori Arinori,
the Japanese Minister. While there, he joined a Methodist
church.

liberty to go wherever he pleased. He had become an earnest believer, and he now openly collected people together that he might read and explain to them the manual of Christian doctrine.

The two men that remained in Hakodate were still troubled for means of living. They opened small shops and succeeded fairly well in business; much better than Mr. Sawabe, who commenced to brew and sell rice-beer, but whose manners were not such as to attract custom.

When Père Nicolai arrived in Russia, the Holy Synod was considering the establishment of a bishopric in Pekin, and the Metropolitan asked him to be its head. He replied that he had no desire to be a bishop, and that he was too much interested in Japan to leave it for another country. The Holy Synod now approved of his plans and many persons promised financial support. The largest single subscription was ten thousand rubles brought to him by a merchant of Moscow who, when asked his name, refused to give it and said, " God knows." Père Nicolai was raised to the rank of Archimandrite. It was at first hoped that four priests might be sent to reside in Yedo, Hakodate, Nagasaki, and some other city to be chosen later. One priest did indeed accompany Père Nicolai on his return; but he fell ill on the journey and was obliged to go back to Russia only two months after reaching Japan.

Père Nicolai reached Hakodate in February, 1871. He soon sent a letter to Sendai in which those who had become interested in Christianity were invited to come to him for further instruction. He also asked that they bring with them some scholar well versed in Chinese, who could help him in the translation of books. The recipients of the letter, who had been eagerly waiting to hear of his return, at once prepared to follow his words. They found a Confucian scholar to accompany them and soon all were on their way to Hakodate. On their arrival they were lodged in a building connected with the consulate and were formed into a sort of school. The Archimandrite not only instructed them in Christian doctrines, but also taught the Russian language to those desiring it. At the same time he worked upon an adaptation of the Chinese New Testament to the needs of the Japanese. The school was soon increased by the coming of more persons from Sendai, and by the reception of others in Hakodate who wished to study Russian.

While Père Nicolai had been absent Dr. Sakai had come again to Hakodate, where he soon gained an extensive medical practice. Although the company of enquirers in Mr. Sawabe's house received help from members of the Sendai clan who had no interest in Christianity, Dr. Sakai seemed indifferent to their needs. Mr. Sawabe and the others were indignant at what they considered his stinginess. Some of the younger men went so far as to force their way into his house and show by their rough behaviour how much they disapproved of his conduct. Whatever may have been the reason for his indifference, he afterwards showed that he was not miserly, for soon after the coming of the Archimandrite, Dr. Sakai brought to him a large package of silver coins, saying he had been saving this money in order that it might be used in the service of the Church. Père Nicolai, while commending the zeal thus displayed, told him that perhaps the money would have been more acceptable to the Lord if it had been used for helping the brethren in their time of need.

At about this time Dr. Sakai and another man disappeared. For several days no trace of them could be found by their anxious friends. At last they came to Père Nicolai, pale and emaciated, as though they had passed through a severe illness. They said that, being possessed by the desire to become preachers of the Gospel, they had hidden themselves in an attic where they had spent the time in fasting and prayer, beseeching God to accept them for His service. The Archimandrite was pleased with their earnestness, though he told them that any person desiring to practise religious austerities ought first to seek the advice of a priest so as to do all in accordance with ecclesiastical rules.

Soon after Père Nicolai's arrival, but before the Sendai students reached Hakodate, Mr. Sawabe left that city for a short visit to Tosa, his native province. While on the journey he tried to learn what he could concerning the trend of public thought, and he was convinced that conditions were becoming favourable for an active propagation of Christianity. This made him enthusiastic in urging the immediate and vigorous prosecution of the work. On coming back to Hakodate, he was displeased to find that most of the men from Sendai were learning the Russian language instead of giving their whole time to the study of religious truth. " Is this the time," he remonstrated, " to be learning a foreign tongue? You should be preparing to go out as evangelists at the earliest possible moment." In this view he was seconded by Mr. Kageta, who had not entered the classes in Russian.

Mr. Sawabe urged Père Nicolai to remove to Tokyo, saying that Hakodate was too far removed from the center of influence and activity to be a favourable place for inaugurating any movement that was to affect the whole nation. Père Nicolai agreed with this opinion, though he felt it necessary to remain a few months longer where he was. He had an abundance of work. Besides the students who lived at the consulate, he had several other pupils in the Russian language. The superintendence of the work of the translator took much time. With the aid of the students he used a lithographic press for printing copies of the Lord's Prayer and of doctrinal manuals. He prepared a Russo-Japanese dictionary, which his pupils copied by hand. The dictionary continued to be reproduced in this way until 1881, when it gave way to one published by the Educational Department.

Near the close of 1871 several of the men from Sendai were baptised. Soon after this Père Nicolai asked one of them, John Ono, if he would be willing to return to his native province as an evangelist. Mr. Ono replied that the proposition accorded with his earnest desires. Being further asked whom he would like for associates, he chose Peter Sasakawa and Jacob Takaya. The Archimandrite therefore began to give the three young men special instruction in Christian doctrine and evangelistic methods. In November they set forth on their mission.

No definite arrangement was made for their support. They had no desire to receive financial assistance from others, but expected on reaching Sendai to provide their own sustenance.

Soon after this, Mr. Sawabe was sent to Tokyo to make arrangements for the removal of Père Nicolai to that city. On his arrival he found lodgings near Nihonbashi, the very centre of the metropolis, and set himself to studying the state of affairs. There were all sorts of rumours concerning the attitude the Government was about to assume towards Christianity. Some said that the old edicts were soon to be removed. Already two scholars of growing influence, Nakamura Masanao and Fukuzawa Yukichi, had expressed sentiments in favour of religious liberty, and others were approving their views. Mr. Sawabe met some high officials of his acquaintance who expressed their willingness to have Christianity taught. He believed that, whatever the real sentiment of the Government might be, the favourable time for evangelistic efforts had come and that, since American and French missionaries were already in Yokohama and Tokyo, the Greek Church ought at the earliest possible moment to enter a field that to the enthusiastic pioneer seemed full of promise. He was living at this time with some friends belonging to his own clan, who invited him to join them in a business enterprise that they were sure would make them rich. He refused, saying, " Money-making is all very well in its way; but I have some business of far greater importance. I have consecrated myself to God for the work of preaching the Gospel." In December, when Mr. Ono came on private business to Tokyo, Mr. Sawabe thought that his friend was the one best fitted to prepare the way for Père Nicolai, and he therefore insisted on an exchange of places by which he himself was transferred to Sendai.

On the coming of Père Anatolius, another Russian priest, to Hakodate, Père Nicolai gave the work there into his care, and in January, 1872, set out for Tokyo. When he arrived in Yokohama he sent a messenger to call Mr. Ono, who reached him the next day. After consultation about various matters, Père Nicolai said:

"I shall go to-morrow to Tokyo, so you must return at once." Mr. Ono reached Tokyo in the middle of the night and the next morning waited upon Soejima, the Minister for Foreign Affairs, whom he told of Père Nicolai's intention to reside in the city.

In Tokyo Père Nicolai at first went to a hotel that had been opened on the Foreign Concession. As this was too expensive, he accepted the use of a room that an American offered to let him have until he should be able to find a house. He soon obtained a Japanese building that was only about twelve feet square. Thither, on Mr. Ono's invitation, came four or five persons to hear what the foreigner might have to tell them. An appointment was made for a second meeting, but on the day it was to have been held, one of the great conflagrations for which Tokyo is noted swept over that section of the city. With the exception of a few things that were thrown into the well, and two books, nothing was saved from the building. Père Nicolai now found temporary shelter with a South American until he could rent another house.

News from Sendai caused much anxiety. The three evangelists that had been sent to that city went about among relatives and friends, telling of their new faith and inviting those that wished further information to come to Mr. Ono's house. This continued to be used as the chief preaching-place even after the owner went to Tokyo. Meetings were often held also in the houses of enquirers, whose numbers rapidly increased. Soon there were each day more than a hundred hearers—men, women, and children—some of them coming from neighbouring villages.

Reports of what was going on spread through the city. It was commonly believed that the evangelists practised magic. In February one of the hearers, who was well acquainted with the prefectural officers, heard reports that the latter were beginning to think they ought to prohibit the teaching of Christianity and were preparing to make arrests. To his suggestion that the meetings be temporarily discontinued, Mr. Takaya replied:

"From the first we were well aware that the officials

might interfere with our work.   If at the st rumour of trouble we cease proclaiming the Gospel, ν en will the time ever come for making God's mercy known?   It is not our business to consider whether the officials will make arrests.   So long as we are left free, we shall continue our work."

On the evening of February 13, while Mr. Sawabe was preaching at the house of an enquirer, he was interrupted by a messenger who had come to tell him that several policemen were prowling about Mr. Ono's house and that one of them, disguised as a merchant, had gone to enquire for Mr. Sawabe.   The evangelist went on with his meeting, and at its close returned to Mr. Ono's house.   Soon three policemen entered, and after binding him took him to the prefectural office.   About forty policemen had been lying in wait about the house.   They probably feared that the Christians would resist them, and perhaps remembrance of stories told about the arrests of Christians two hundred and fifty years before made them fear that magic would be used for effecting an escape.   As a further precaution, they had barricaded the streets by placing ladders across them.   After Mr. Sawabe was taken away, they entered the house, took possession of the books, and trampled on the icons.

At the prefectural office Mr. Sawabe was asked why he was breaking the laws by teaching an evil doctrine. In reply, he tried to tell them about Christianity; but the officers cut him short, saying that he should not be so insolent as to dispute with his superiors.   They took away the religious emblem hanging from his neck and committed him to jail.

Peter Sasakawa, on hearing of this arrest, said to the Christians: "When Mr. Sawabe came to Sendai, I reported him to the officials as being my guest; hence, it is a very irregular method of procedure for the police to seize him without giving me any notification.   I must go to the office and make enquiries about the matter. As I cannot hope to escape arrest, it will be better for me to give myself up at once."

He did as he had said, and was put in jail.   Jacob Takaya had set out to Tokyo on the day of Mr. Sawabe's arrest; but being overtaken by a messenger who told him what had happened, he returned to Sendai, spent the night in Mr. Ono's house, and the next morning was taken by the police, who were surprised that he should come back to face the danger that he knew to be threatening him.

The three evangelists were not allowed to see each other. Mr. Takaya was put in a room with several common criminals. It contained a Buddhist image, and the rules of the prison required that all should repeat prayers before it every evening; but the keepers excused him from doing this, and even allowed him to repeat aloud his Christian prayers.

Several persons who had attended the meetings were put into prison, while others were summoned to the office for examination. Their names were learned from a list in Mr. Sawabe's notebook. One hundred and fifty persons were put under the surveillance of relatives, who were made responsible for their conduct. Among those interrogated were several children, who astonished the examiners by asserting their willingness to suffer punishment for the sake of Christ.

The prison was conducted after the old methods, the supply of food being insufficient, except as it was supplemented by gifts from friends. The believers rallied to the help of their brethren. The chapel in Mr. Ono's house was appointed as the place whither contributions of food should be brought. One of the Christians had a friend among the police, who let him know beforehand, when any of the company were to be apprehended. These persons would then come to the chapel so that all the arrests might be made there. The police showed considerable clemency, and in order not to cause inconvenience to those who might be busy in collecting supplies for the prisoners, would postpone their arrest until a later day.

Intelligence of these events soon reached Père Nicolai, who was greatly troubled at thought of the danger to which the Christians were exposed. He would say to Mr. Ono:

" If we cannot devise some way of saving them, they

will certainly be subjected to the severest punishment. You must save them.   If you do not, it will be the same as though you killed them."

Mr. Ono could not bear to think of his brethren as groaning in captivity, while he remained at liberty.   He said that he ought to go and share their imprisonment, or even their death, if it should come to that.   Père Nicolai frowned upon such an idea, and told him that he ought to remain in Tokyo, devising some plan for the rescue of his brethren.   Mr. Ono had an interview with the Minister for Foreign Affairs, and through the agency of friends got Mr. Fukuzawa Yukichi to plead with the high officials against a persecution that would bring disgrace upon the nation.   Some *samurai* from Sendai, who were in Tokyo, consulted with Dr. Verbeck, then an adviser to the Council of State, who appealed to Mr. Okuma and others connected with the Government.

When the prefectural officials presented a report of their action, the matter could not longer be disregarded by the Central Government, and though there were differences of opinion among those in authority, orders were sent to Sendai for the release of the prisoners. They were brought before the local officers that they might receive their sentence as follows:

"Although you are blameworthy for having studied the foreign religion, you are mercifully pardoned because you have repented of your fault.   Take heed that you do not offend again."

On hearing this, the Christians protested that they had repented of nothing, and therefore could not assent to this statement; but the officials would not listen, and ordered them to leave the place.   Those that had been under surveillance were also called to the office and told that they were pardoned, but that they must henceforth be more careful to obey the laws.

It was a happy day for the released prisoners and their friends when they met in the chapel to return thanks for their deliverance.   The persecution had its natural effect in dividing the chaff from the wheat. Some of the former attendants at the meetings had denied having any interest in Christianity; others had fled from home. The real enquirers had been bold, and considered it an honour to suffer persecution. The number of hearers was for a time diminished; but those that remained were more earnest than ever. After a while, there were additions to their ranks. In 1873, there were in Sendai twenty Christian families, besides about a hundred others in which were one or more believers. In all, there were about two hundred persons who had accepted Christianity, though few of them were baptised until 1875, when Mr. Sawabe, having been ordained as a priest, administered the rite to one hundred and twenty-nine persons.

As has been already mentioned, Père Anatolius was left in charge at Hakodate. It was his purpose to make the school in the consulate a place for the training of evangelists. Calling together the Christians, he asked them to select persons who should at once enter upon the work of spreading the Gospel. The choice fell upon Matthew Kageta, John Sakai, and Paul Tsuda. Houses were at once obtained in different parts of the city for the use of classes that met to study Christianity. The number of attendants increased so rapidly that other Christians were called to help the three evangelists.

In March, 1872, the Easter services in the consular chapel were attended by about thirty believers, besides a number of other persons. The reports that these gave of the services aroused general curiosity. As the bell of the chapel rang for the meetings that were held each day of that week, crowds collected about the door. The students acted as ushers to lead the people into the chapel. Since there was room for only about a hundred persons at a time, the people were admitted in companies, a short explanation of Christian doctrine being given to each band ere it gave place to the next. Throughout the city men and women were talking about Christianity; some saying that it seemed to be a good religion, while others denounced it as immoral or dealing in magic.

Yezo, unlike the more populous parts of Japan, had not been given a prefectural government. Its affairs were administered by a Colonisation Commission, and the officials were imbued with the old-fashioned ideas. In issuing orders for the registration of the people, they required that the names of men, women, and children should be reported to the Shinto shrines. Each person would then receive an amulet that he was to preserve with care, and that was to be returned to the shrine at his death. When the officials heard that Christianity was being openly taught, they decided that it must be immediately suppressed. Dr. Sakai was arrested and asked why he had become a follower of the evil religion. When he tried to explain the teachings of Christianity, his examiner refused to listen and sent him to prison.

Three days later, Messrs. Tsuda and Kageta were ordered to appear at the office. After some delay, they were brought into the room where criminals were examined. On every side were displayed instruments of torture, whose very sight was thought sufficient to make persons tremble. With several police to guard them, the prisoners were placed before a platform on which were seated the examining official and his clerk. After the names and ages of the evangelists had been recorded, they were asked:

" On what business did you come to this city? "

" I came," answered Mr. Tsuda, " for the purpose of studying the Russian language."

" Under that name you are also studying Christianity. Why are you doing so? "

" In these days, when Japan is having dealings with other nations, I am likely to be asked by foreigners why their religion has been prohibited. It seemed to me that inability to give a reason would bring disgrace upon me and upon my country. Hence, I thought it necessary to examine their doctrines. In doing so, I soon found out that there was nothing to justify opposition. The religion at which this prohibition was aimed must have been something other than that of Jesus, whose excellent teaching has brought the countries of Europe and America to their present state of civilisation. Convinced of its truth, I was led to study it more thoroughly."

"This religion of Jesus, as you call it, is just the same as Christianity, and is not Christianity strictly forbidden by the edicts that are posted throughout the land?"

"I, of course, know what is written in those edicts. Moreover, I have from childhood been acquainted with Shintoism and Confucianism, as also with Buddhism, which has been the religion of my family. Since, however, it was in the religion of Jesus that I first found the way of salvation and righteousness, I have desired to learn all that I could about it."

"Since you are a student, there may be some reason for making an investigation of Christianity; but why have you been teaching it to others?"

"Jesus said that we should bestow on others the same blessings that we desire for ourselves. Hence, it is my wish to teach this religion, not merely in Hakodate, but in all parts of Japan."

"The people of Hakodate are unintelligent. Hitherto they have been satisfied with Buddhism. To teach them something new, even though it may be good in itself, will only confuse them."

Mr. Tsuda seemed vexed at these words and said: "Intelligence and lack of intelligence depend largely on the degree of instruction that a person receives. Hence, I am specially desirous to teach those that are ignorant."

The officer, who seemed to be seeking some ground for pronouncing a sentence of condemnation, again asserted: "The religion of Jesus is certainly the same as that which has long been prohibited."

"Is it prohibited because it is evil, or because it is good?" asked Mr. Tsuda, thinking that if the answer was that it was evil, he would ask to be shown what points in it were evil; while if acknowledgement were made that its doctrines were good, he would ask why then it was to be suppressed.

The officer, however, waived the question, and simply said: "Law is law, and you as a law-breaker should tremble at thought of your wrong-doing."

"I am not conscious," said Mr. Tsuda, "of being a law-breaker, for I have done nothing but study a good religion."

After some further questioning, the two evangelists were sent to the military prison to await trial. They were closely guarded to see that they did not make use of magic arts to effect an escape. They relieved the dulness of their imprisonment by prayers, hymns, and conversation. Finally they gained permission to receive some books from their friends. When arrested, Mr. Tsuda had hidden a portion of the Scriptures in his bosom, but had not dared to read it until now, when he slipped it among the volumes received from outside. After a while the guard happened to notice it, and all the books were taken away.

As Dr. Sakai was not a *samurai,* he was put in the criminal prison, where, with fifteen other persons, he occupied a room fifteen feet long and nine wide. He made for himself a rosary by stringing pellets of boiled rice on a thread drawn from his clothes, while a chopstick furnished the wood for a cross.

The arrests of the evangelists caused so much alarm that the people no longer flocked to the chapel. Even the street merchants, who had formerly furnished supplies for the school, did not dare to enter the premises. When believers appeared on the street they were avoided by their acquaintances. One young man was expelled from a government school, and some other students were not allowed to live in the dormitories.

The Colonisation Commission tried in vain to make the evangelists recant, and then, not knowing what to do with them, sent a report to the Department of Justice with a request for instructions. The report arrived at about the time the case of the Sendai Christians was decided, and orders were sent for the release of the evangelists. They were set free on May 1, after an imprisonment of about two months. At the same time the officials of the Colonisation Commission sent word to the prefectures to which these men belonged, asking that they be summoned to return to their homes.

An official messenger soon came from Sendai for Messrs. Kageta and Tsuda; but, knowing that they had committed no crime, he consented to postpone their return, he himself waiting for them until the last part of

August. He then accompanied them to the prefectural office in Sendai, whence they were sent to their own villages after being told that, as their trouble had come from their connection with Christianity, they must be careful to avoid further offence in that respect. They paid so little heed to this warning that they were soon actively engaged in propagating their faith.

Dr. Sakai's home was north of Sendai, in what was then the Tome Prefecture. There was still more delay in his return, but he finally reached his native town, where he was put under the care of a relative, who had strict orders that Dr. Sakai was not to go elsewhere without permission, and was not to teach Christianity. In spite of these directions, he tried to tell his friends about his new belief; but they feared to have anything to do with a religion that had brought him into so much trouble. He therefore turned his attention to neighbouring villages. In one of these he was encouraged by the conversion of a young man named Semba, who soon afterwards visited Tokyo, where he received baptism.

In 1872, Père Nicolai procured, in the name of the Russian Legation, the lease of a piece of ground on Surugadai, a hill situated in a central and populous part of Tokyo. The location seemed a favourable one for his school, and also for the church that he had faith to believe would be erected before many years. The buildings already there were low and dingy; but the funds at his disposal were insufficient to provide anything better. He took one of them for his own residence, and in the others soon gathered a number of students. Most of them came for secular instruction. Père Nicolai taught them Russian by day, and in the evening he explained Christian doctrines to those that were willing to listen. A number of the pupils soon asked for baptism, and it was administered September 24, 1872, to ten persons. As the attitude of the Government towards Christianity was still doubtful, it was deemed advisable to use the greatest secrecy. A few days later, Père Nicolai, who had become well acquainted with one of the Buddhist priests in the Shiba Temples, was calling upon him, when the priest passed over a piece of paper saying: " See what I have here." Père Nicolai, little suspecting what it was, unrolled the paper and saw to his amazement that it contained a plan of the room where the baptismal service had been held. The places where he and each of the neophytes had stood were designated, as well as the position of the utensils used in connection with the ceremony. He was greatly disturbed at this, apprehending that some evil was about to fall on the young men, whose secret profession of Christianity had evidently been discovered. The priest, with a smile, told him not to be alarmed. A report of the matter, he said, had reached the Government, and on account of the connection of the temple with national affairs, a copy of the plan had been given to him, but there was no intention of making any trouble over what had been done.

It was afterwards found out that the sketch had been drawn by a friend of one of the persons baptised. He was a spy who, having in some way learned of what was to be done, gained permission to be present.

This occurrence, which at first caused anxiety, became a source of assurance, for the inaction of the Government seemed to show that it was not inclined to prevent its subjects from embracing Christianity. In December, ten more persons were baptised.

Père Nicolai's name was becoming well known among all classes of people, and various stories concerning him were in circulation. Some said that he belonged to the Imperial Family of Russia; many considered him a spy; and others believed that he had been sent to win men's hearts in order to facilitate the military conquest of Japan. Knowing that some of the officials suspected him of political designs, he sent to the Foreign Department a memorial, in which he denied that the doctrines of Christianity tended to shake the loyalty or patriotism of those that accepted them. The suspicion of the Government was not easily allayed. It had several spies enter the school to see whether anything taught there was likely to be a source of danger. One of these men became a Christian, and prepared a petition in favour of the public recognition of Christianity. Contrary to the advice of Mr. Ono, he tried to have this presented to the Emperor; but probably it did not get far beyond the first official into whose hands it came.*

* In 1877 a student in the Theological School confessed to Père Nicolai that he had been sent by the police as a spy. He also became a believer.

XV

THE EXPANSION OF THE CHURCH

1873-1882

JOHN SAKAI had not been very long in his native province before he obtained permission to make a visit to Tokyo. Instead of returning home from that city, he went in May, 1873, to Hakodate. Though he sent word to the officials of the Colonisation Commission that he intended to reside there, he received nothing from them to show that they objected to this or were taking any notice of his presence. He was soon engaged as busily as ever in evangelistic work. At the beginning of the next year, however, the officials of his own prefecture sent a messenger to escort him back. He was brought to the prefectural office and asked why he had gone to Hakodate. To this he replied that, as his wife and child were living in that city, he had found it necessary to go there in order to provide for their support. He was then accused of using the name Sakai illegally. The name was, indeed, that of his ancestors; but his father had "married into another house" and so taken his wife's name. After his son's birth, the father had left his adopted house. The boy, after remaining for some years with the mother, had gone to the father, and on the latter's death succeeded to his practice as a physician, at the same time assuming the name of Sakai. As there was some irregularity in this procedure, the officials took advantage of the opportunity it gave for bringing a charge against him. That this was used only as a pretext, was shown by the fact that the one who conducted the examination offered to release him on condition that he would renounce Christianity; but since he refused to do this, he was sent to prison for a month.

Soon after the expiration of this sentence, Dr. Sakai was again summoned to the office and asked:

"Why is it that since being let out of prison you have broken your promise not to preach Christianity?"

"I never made such a promise," was the reply; "nevertheless, since my release, I have not attempted to do missionary work. When I go about my duties as a physician, people ask me questions concerning my religious views, and I must make some reply. I could not refuse to answer if they asked about Buddhism or Shintoism; still less, when their enquiries are about Christianity. If you forbid this, I am willing, for my disobedience, to suffer whatever you may inflict upon my body, but my spirit will not yield to such commands."

At a later examination he was asked: "Why not give up Christianity until the Government approves of it? Ought you not to do what it commands?"

"Not if it commands what is wrong. If it ordered me to steal, I should not obey."

He was condemned to eighty days' incarceration. At that time it was customary to let out the labour of prisoners. Dr. Sakai was employed in the garden of a man who often came out to converse with him while he was at work. Religious subjects were introduced, and the man became so much interested that he continued to hire Dr. Sakai from day to day, often inviting him into the house, where they could converse more at ease. The officials said in one of their reports that it was useless to imprison such a person as Dr. Sakai, for while at work he was preaching to his employer, and after the day's labour was over he taught his doctrines to the other prisoners. Among the latter he gained considerable influence. They thought him a strange person, but could not fail to honour his upright character. When disputes arose among them, he was chosen to act as their judge. To keep him in prison was nearly equivalent to placing a Christian chaplain there.

While Dr. Sakai was in Hakodate, Mr. Semba, the young man whom he had led to Christianity at the time of his first recall to Tome, was teaching his new faith to the people about him. The Buddhist and Shinto priests soon accused him of sacrilegious acts, and had him sentenced to prison for three months. He also was earnest in teaching his fellow-prisoners. One of them became a believer, and promised that as soon as released, he would go to Tokyo for baptism. This person, however, was soon sentenced to death for his crimes. He was much distressed at the thought of not receiving the rite that would admit him into the Church. Therefore, on the morning that the man was to be led out for execution, Mr. Semba took some water from a teakettle and baptised him. Then, kneading some boiled rice into dough, he strengthened it with threads drawn from his clothes, so as to mold it into the form of a cross, which the criminal wore about his neck as he went to meet death.

Preaching places were gradually opened in different parts of Tokyo, and these were manned by those who were receiving instruction from Père Nicolai. Some of these also made visits to Nagoya, Kyoto, Osaka, and other places. They reported that everywhere abundant openings for the Gospel were found.

With the increasing number of evangelists, a difference arose in the views of those in Tokyo and those in Sendai, concerning the policy that should govern missionary operations. Père Nicolai, therefore, called all of them together for a council that met in May, 1874. Several days were spent in consulting about the interests of the work, and in drawing up a new set of rules. According to these regulations, there were to be two classes of workers; viz., evangelists and assistant evangelists. The duties and salaries of these persons were prescribed. Changes in the location of evangelists were to be decided by the Tokyo Church as the metropolitan. While making the proclamation of the Gospel their chief work, the evangelists might employ their spare time in any occupation for which they were fitted, and thus, by their industry, be an example to believers. They could admit persons to the number of catechumens. They ought to give lodging in their houses to persons from other places who came with a desire to learn about Christianity. If such a person were poor, he might be fed for three days at the expense of the general fund. If among the poor students should be found such as appeared proper persons to become evangelists, they might be supported for three months or more from the general fund; and after examination, the Tokyo Church should decide upon the time when they should come to it for further study. Those selected to become evangelists should be between seventeen and forty years of age, pious, intelligent, and without such hindrances on account of family affairs as would keep them from making missionary tours. Young men between twelve and seventeen years of age, of upright character and good mental ability, might be sent to school in Tokyo; those of them that intended to enter the service of the Church must have their parents' permission for spending seven years in study. Plans should be made for schools where children could receive both secular and religious teaching. For the instruction of women and girls there should be women evangelists and special schools. Evangelists should appoint in each church under their care two or three persons to serve as assistants; these should labour for the spread of the Gospel and the strengthening of the churches, besides caring for the families of the evangelists when the latter were absent on missionary tours. Though local churches should manage their own affairs without interference from others, the salaries of evangelists in some of the smaller places were to be sent through the superintendent of the district in which they belonged. At this meeting the fields of labour for over thirty evangelists were determined.

One of the rules that Père Nicolai had drawn up about 1869 for the Association of Evangelists that he hoped to form, was to the effect that when the number of baptised believers reached five hundred, one of the evangelists should be selected for ordination to the priesthood. The prosperity that had attended the work of the Mission had been such as to justify the carrying into effect what this rule prescribed, and the visit of a Russian bishop to Hakodate in 1875 was utilised for securing the ordination of Mr. Sawabe as a priest and of Dr. Sakai as a deacon. In 1878 five evangelists went to Vladivostock for ordination to the priesthood.

The most marked progress of the period under consideration was in the section of the country that has Sendai for its centre. The number of Christians in the city of Sendai and their influence were constantly increasing. In May, 1876, they took upon themselves the financial support of one of the evangelists. Some of the other evangelists in that place were unwilling either to be a burden to their brethren or to receive help from the Mission. They therefore decided to support themselves by labour or trade, giving only their spare time to teaching Christianity. Their withdrawal to this extent from evangelistic labours was regarded with so much concern by the Church that a meeting was held in which it was decided to ask them to devote themselves as before to the propagation of Christianity. Mr. Ono consented to become an evangelist again, though he continued to provide for his own support, as he was in possession of some property. The others refused to comply with the request, whereupon Père Nicolai sent them a letter in which he commended their desire not to be burdensome to the Church, but said that, while they needed little for their support, it took most of their time to gain that little, and it would be better for them to present this time to God by using it for the benefit of the Church. Some of them finally consented to follow his advice that they accept support from the general fund used for the work of the Mission. When Père Nicolai visited Sendai in 1877, a meeting of the Christians was held to consult with him concerning evangelistic efforts, one of the decisions being to divide the city into five parishes.

In 1877 Mr. Ono began to publish what is said to have been the first magazine in Northeastern Japan. The articles, which dealt with moral, literary, and educational, as well as strictly religious subjects, attracted considerable attention and did much to put new ideas into the minds of the educated classes. The evangelists also arranged a course of public lectures that were held twice a month.

Though the subjects were largely secular and some of the speakers were not Christians, the lectures of the evangelists often turned to Christian themes, while their efforts in seeking the enlightenment of the people helped to recommend their religion.

In 1874, when Dr. Sakai and Mr. Semba were under arrest in Tome, two merchants from Sanuma were in the former town on business. Hearing of what had happened, their curiosity was aroused to know the nature of the religion that brought upon its followers the opposition of the officials. In an interview that they managed to obtain with Dr. Sakai they were much impressed by what he told them. After his release he visited them in Sanuma, which was only seven miles from Tome. Fearing that they would bring trouble upon themselves, the merchants were at first very careful not to let others know that they were studying Christianity; but, after they became believers, they no longer wished to keep it to themselves, and so they commenced telling others of their new faith. The town was visited by different evangelists, one of whom took up his abode there. From the first the work progressed so rapidly that in 1875 fifty-three persons were baptised; in 1876, one hundred; in 1877, ninety-three. In 1876 considerable opposition was aroused against Christianity because one of the believers, with the idea of showing the folly of idol worship, dragged an image from a shrine that stood on his land, chopped it to pieces, and then destroyed the shrine. He and eleven others that had taken some part in the matter were brought before the courts and fined. In 1879 a church building was completed at a cost of some three thousand *yen*. Rev. Paul Sawabe then urged upon the believers the desirability of having the building provided with the various utensils used in the ceremonies of the Greek Church, whereupon the women brought their hair-ornaments, some of which had considerable value, as contributions towards the cost of what was needed.

Besides Sanuma, several other towns in the vicinity of Sendai were visited by evangelists, so that there were few places of any importance that did not have believers in Christianity. In some places church buildings were erected and schools established. In several towns the Christians raised funds that were invested so that the interest might be used for the support of the church or else added to the original fund until a sufficient amount should have been gained for a church edifice or some other object. In some cases land was purchased and cultivated by the Christians. At one time the fund at Sanuma amounted to several thousand *yen*.

In 1879 Père Anatolius, having been appointed Chaplain to the Russian Legation, removed from Hakodate to Tokyo. After this, other Russian priests went to Hakodate, but none of them stayed for any great length of time, and ere long the care of the Church in that city and the work of carrying Christianity to other parts of Yezo were committed to Japanese priests and evangelists. It is one of the noteworthy features of the Holy Orthodox Church in Japan that it has depended so little upon the personal labours of foreigners. Much of the time Père Nicolai was the only one in the country, and at no other time has he had more than five or six European assistants.

As with the Protestants and Roman Catholics, the members of this Church early began to show that they had learned from the second of Christ's great commandments the duty of charity. About 1873 the Christian women of Hakodate formed a society whose purpose was in part to help the poor. Their zeal stirred up that of the men. Among the gifts of that year was a sum of money sent for the relief of those who were suffering from a famine in Russia. In Sendai and other places there were societies that lent money, sometimes with and sometimes without interest, to members of the churches. Some of the funds were given outright to those that would be unable to repay. In 1875, when the overflowing of a river caused great distress among the poor in Sanuma, the Christians of that place took measures for their relief. Rice was purchased, and at night members of the Church, covering their faces so as not to be recognised, carried this to about a hundred poor families and gave it over without letting it be known whence it came.

Trouble frequently arose in connection with the burial of the dead. In January, 1875, the father of a young girl that had died in Hakodate gave the usual notice to the officials and told the Buddhist priests of his intention to have a Christian burial. He was soon summoned to the office and told that only Buddhist or Shinto rites could be allowed. To this he replied:

" My daughter was a Christian and so am I. To have a heathen ceremony would be to disobey the commands of the true God, and so I cannot permit such to be performed."

" But Christian rites are contrary to law."

" I must obey God. If by so doing I offend against the laws of the land, I must submit to the punishment that awaits me."

Some of the friends advised that the burial should be in a cemetery that had been set apart for the use of foreigners, over which the priests had no control; but the father said that this was something to which a Japanese ought not to consent, and rather than do it, he would suffer the penalty that might be incurred by violating the law. Finally the burial took place in a piece of ground that Père Anatolius succeeded in renting for a cemetery, and though the father was afterwards summoned before the officials, no punishment was inflicted upon him.

About the same time a similar case occurred in Sendai, where the person responsible for the burial was sentenced to thirty days' imprisonment. The relatives sent in a petition that led to an amelioration of the punishment, so that the man was not taken to prison but confined in his own house. In another place a man was sentenced to prison for forty days; but in view of the fact that he had followed the dying wish of his relatives, he was released on the payment of three *yen*.

The following statistics dated July, 1883, show the remarkable progress made in the period we have been considering:

Priests (3 foreign, 11 native) 14
Foreign teachers 2
Unordained evangelists 106
Believers * 8,863
Baptised during last year 1,391
Scholars 395
Organised churches 148
Church edifices 110
Preaching places 281

	Yen
Fixed contributions	148.69
School contributions	98.12
Church contributions	4,373.39

* It should be remembered that baptised children are included under this designation.

XVI

RECENT HISTORY OF THE MISSION

1883-1909

MATERIALS for writing the later history of the Greek Church in Japan are not such as can be utilised to any great extent in the present work. The news columns of the periodicals that it publishes will be of great value to its own historian, but the facts recorded need to be collated by some one so intimately acquainted with the inner working of the Church that he can select those that have proved to be of the most importance. It is to be hoped that the excellent history (in Japanese) whose earlier volumes have helped in the preparation of former chapters will ere long be brought down to a later date.

In a general way it may be said that, while the Orthodox Church continued to grow in numbers and strength, its rapid progress was checked a little earlier than was the case with Protestantism. Bishop Nicolai continued to be a marvel of executive ability and personal influence; the evangelists were active and earnest; in many places they gathered companies of believers; and yet, with the exception of northeastern Hondo, the degree of success attained was not such as attracted much notice from people at large. Persons that became interested in Christianity were inclined to examine it in its Protestant forms. The relations of the Orthodox Church to the Russian Government doubtless had much to do with this. Suspicion of Russia's movements and of what it might be planning to do in Korea made the former country and everything connected with it unpopular with the young men of Japan. This feeling was greatly increased at the close of the Chino-Japanese War (1895) when Russia took the lead in preventing Japan from retaining any territory on the Asiatic continent and soon after took for its own use the Laiotung Peninsula, which had been Japan's most important conquest in the war. The following statement prepared in 1903, by one of Bishop Nicolai's assistants, shows what response was made to the objection that came from the prejudice felt against Russia:

" From the present political situation of Japan and Russia, since the Japanese Orthodox Church is aided by the Russian Missionary Society, some are led to believe that the Church is necessarily Russianised and given to Russian forms. This is indeed a misapprehension. Such misconceptions have occurred in every age and we rather pity those who thus misunderstand us. It will be evident to one who has observed both the Russian Orthodox Church and the Japanese Orthodox Church, that the Japanese Church is not Russianised at all, even though it be aided by Russia. Bishop Nicolai, who is the apostle to Japan, did not introduce customs which were exclusively Russian at all. He only handed down the doctrines and customs of the Eastern Church of the Holy Catholic Apostles. In 1893 Archbishop Deonishi of Zante, an island off the west coast of Greece, visited our Japanese Orthodox Church. The Archbishop is a Greek and belongs to the Greek Church. However, he came to the Cathedral at Surugadai and worshipped with Japanese priests without changing his form of worship. He thus proved by his action that the Japanese Orthodox Church, which was established by the Russian Missionary Society, is just the same as those Orthodox Churches found in Greece and neighbouring countries. In the year 1895 Archbishop Gerashim of Jerusalem sent to our Japanese Orthodox Church a holy image that our reciprocal and harmonious relations might thereby be manifest. This shows plainly that the Orthodox Church established in Jerusalem is wholly like the Orthodox Churches found in all Eastern Europe."[*]

Besides the objection growing out of its relation to Russia, the Orthodox Church shared with others the popular dislike of Christianity. The following instances will show how this dislike manifested itself.

In 1894 an evangelist visited a village in the province of Ise where there were two converts. The villagers were soon aroused to active opposition, and drew up a covenant containing the following articles:

[*] " Christian Movement in Japan," II., p. 189.

"Christians shall be deprived of their former rights in the common forests."

"Christians shall not be admitted into our houses, nor will we enter theirs. If it is necessary to transact any business with them, we will stand outside of their houses while talking with them."

"We will prevent the Christians from working in the mountains. We will not turn aside for them when we meet them upon the street." *

In a village of Akita Prefecture under similar circumstances Buddhist priests from abroad were summoned to oppose the hated religion, and a document was drawn up pledging the villagers to break off all relations with Christians, not to allow them to hold any office, not to rent land to them, not to furnish lodging for the preachers, and to treat as Christians all persons that would not set their seal to this agreement. There was an attempt to break up the meetings, stones were thrown, and blows struck.†

In Shirakawa, Fukushima Prefecture, a town of ten thousand inhabitants, enmity was excited against the Christians because of their refusal to contribute towards the expenses of a religious festival. Some of their houses were injured by stones thrown against them. One believer and his wife were dragged out from their house and received several wounds. Three of the men that made the disturbance were arrested by the police, but were soon released.‡

In places where both Greek and Protestant evangelists were working, their relations, though not very close, were usually cordial except as sometimes feeling was aroused by the converts of one passing over to the other. In case the removal was from the Greek Church, the severe terms of the ban of excommunication prescribed by its ritual were not calculated to promote harmony.

In the city of Wakayama the workers of the Greek Orthodox, the Episcopalian, and the Presbyterian churches, thirteen in number, and including four foreign missionaries, had a society which met once a month.

* *Seikyo Shimpo,* May 15, 1894.
† *Ib.,* December 1, 1894.
‡ *Ib.,* October 1, 1898.

The church-members also had an alliance that provided for public lectures once a month. When attempts were made in 1898 to introduce into Wakayama Prefecture the system of licensed prostitution, from which it had hitherto been exempt, the Protestant churches proposed to the Greek and Roman Catholic that they should unite in opposing this effort. This was done; letters signed by representatives of each church were sent out, officials and legislators were interviewed, and a mass meeting was held in a theatre with addresses by the Protestant and Greek evangelists.*

When war broke out in 1904 between Japan and Russia, Bishop Nicolai was in a very trying position. Two Russian priests attached to the Russian legation, who had assisted him in his work, returned home. The Bishop, urged by the Russian Minister, to decide at once whether or not he would leave the country, called a council of the workers and leading Christians to ask their opinion about what he would better do. They were unanimous in adopting a resolution in which they said: " We earnestly hope, whatever may happen, that you will not return to your own country, but that for the sake of the Orthodox Church in Japan you will remain here." This decision having been reported to him, he addressed them the next day as follows:

" I did not make up my mind until yesterday whether I should remain in Japan or not in case of a Russo-Japanese war. If I returned to Russia, I should still have much business to attend to on behalf of our missions, but I have decided to remain in Japan. I am very glad to hear that your members unanimously decided that I should not return to Russia. I believe this is God's will. Especially I felt this to-day when I was praying during the service. My indecision up till yesterday belonged to my private convenience and not to the public. To say the truth, it is about twenty-three years since I left my native country, and a longing crept over me to return to my sweet home. But thinking the matter over more seriously, I realised that this was only my private inclination and that my public life belonged to Japan where our Church is yet in its infancy. Now I am thanking my God that your members have decided the question for me as you have. And again, I thank you for your kindness and that of your members in providing for my safety in case personal danger threat-

* *Seikyo Shimpo,* January 1 and June 15, 1899.

ened. You say that I need not enter a foreign legation, that you will protect me. But I think such a promise is not necessary. Our Russian Minister will provide for the protection of Russian subjects in Japan by either the French or German Ministers when he withdraws from Tokyo, and, moreover, the Japanese Government will protect such Russians who have no relations with the war. But it will be necessary to ask for the protection of the authorities for the safety of our Cathedral and all the buildings of the Church. These buildings are the property of the Japanese Orthodox Church, and in case they are violated (which I think will not be the case) your members would suffer a great loss.

"I hope there will be no change in our Church through the outbreak of war. Evangelists must propagate the Master's Gospel, students must attend the Mission School as usual, and I will devote myself to the translation of the Prayer-book with my assistant, Mr. Nakae. And if an Imperial Proclamation of war is issued, your members must pray for the triumph of Japan, and when the Japanese army has conquered the Russian forces you must offer to God a prayer of thankfulness. This is the obligation laid on the Orthodox Christian in his native country. Our Lord Jesus Christ teaches us patriotism and loyalty. Christ Himself shed tears for Jerusalem. That was because of His patriotism, and you must follow in your Master's steps.

"I prayed as usual to-day in the Cathedral, but henceforth I will not take part in the public prayers. This is not for the reason that it might be dangerous for me to appear in the Cathedral, but for the reason that until now I prayed for the victory and the peace of the Japanese Emperor, but now in case of war I can not pray as a Russian subject that our native country should be conquered by an enemy. I have, as you also have, an obligation to my country, therefore I am glad to see that you realise your obligation to your country. For myself, I will not for the time being serve in the public prayers of the Japanese Church." *

The decision of Bishop Nicolai was generally commended both by Japanese and by foreign residents. Doubtless it was also pleasing to the Government, since it gave an opportunity to show to the Western World its unwillingness to have the war regarded as in any sense a conflict with the Christian religion. Another address made by Bishop Nicolai about five months after the beginning of the war expressed his appreciation of the attitude of the Japanese Government, and spoke of the difficulties experienced by the Church. It will also serve to show us something of his own spirit. He said:

* *Japan Weekly Mail*, February 20, 1904.

"Dear brethren and co-workers. Our meeting is at an unfavourable time for the Church, but from our hearts we give thanks and praise God that through His mercy the Church remains in peace unmolested and that its members still maintain their good faith, each worker doing his duty faithfully. We also give thanks to the Japanese Government for its kind protection. From the beginning of this war, the Government declared that religion and politics or war should not be confounded, that no one should be hindered in religious rites or faith. As you know, this declaration has been kept. Only one or two suspicious persons have disturbed the peace of our Christians, and they have since been suppressed by the local governors. But the protection of the Government is only from the outside storm, and if in the inner life of the Church troubles should arise, the Government cannot protect us. A rotten boat is easily sunk by the waves; a worm-eaten tree falls easily by the wind. Toward our Church there is at present no heavy storm, but there are winds of hatred brewing by which we have so far been unmoved. No Christians have broken faith, no workers have left their posts of duty. As the blood flows through the whole body and gives life, we have evidence that just so the mercies of God are flowing through our Church body and that the Greek Church of Japan is not built upon the sand but is founded upon the Corner-stone for eternity. Brethren, observe this and know that God has accepted and blessed our little service, and rejoices that our labour is not in vain. Is this not a great comfort and consolation to us? Our Church is not only existing in the midst of this troublous time, but it is growing. Of course, the number of additions this year is less than last. The voice of the Gospel of Peace is drowned by the shouts of war. It is hard to reach the ear, but some few have heard and accepted, and these are precious fruit to the Kingdom of God." *

The members of the Orthodox Church did not fall behind others in patriotism. At the beginning of the war they organised a society to give aid to the families that were in distress because the chief wage-earners had been called to the army. Teachers and students in the theological schools collected money with which to print several thousand copies of " Japanese-Russian Military Conversations," and these they presented to the War Department.

When, as a result of Japanese victories, large numbers of prisoners were brought to Japan, a new and interesting work devolved upon this Church. By the permission of the War Department, priests with an understanding of

* " The Christian Movement," III., p. 178.

the Russian language were sent to all the towns where captives were detained, and temporary places of worship were set up within the camps. To many a homesick man it must have been a great comfort to listen to the familiar liturgy and to take part in the rites to which he had been accustomed from childhood. As the number of priests was insufficient for this new service, several persons were ordained sooner than they would otherwise have been. Much liberty was given to the Russian officers. Those that wished to do so could attend the ordinary churches, if such there were in the cities where they were held as prisoners. The following report gives a brief account of the work among the captives:

" Owing to the war, our evangelistic work among the Japanese people was hindered because of the especial work God had for us among the 73,000 Russian prisoners. Since our Church in Japan is small, we could not comfort the prisoners as we would have liked to do. Seventeen priests and six assistant priests who understood the Russian language devoted their full time to the work. Beside these, the older priests who could not speak the language had with them assistant priests as interpreters. These men conducted prayers and administered the sacrament in such a manner as to afford the prisoners all the religious comforts of their home land. The prisoners received the Japanese priests in all love and respect as if of their native blood, counting them all God's workers. As a proof of their deep appreciation of the work done among them, Bishop Nicolai has received many letters requesting him to extend to these Japanese workers most hearty thanks. Not only these letters have been received, but also presents of very valuable cloth. While the Japanese workers have given their time to comforting the prisoners, they have in return been greatly strengthened in faith by witnessing the devotion of these men even in hours of deep trial. The Russian men raised yen 11,700 for Bishop Nicolai's work. They built several chapels where they happened to be quartered, and paid all expenses in connection with the religious work among them. Bishop Nicolai gave to the prisoners 68,000 copies of the Gospels in the Russian language and several thousand copies of religious and literary books, also many prayer-books and silver-woven cloth. He also gave winter clothes to sick prisoners. All of these expenses were met by Christians from abroad." *

A society was also organised for helping the Japanese prisoners in Russia. Three thousand " comfort bags " were sent to these men.

* " The Christian Movement," IV., p. 208.

At a time when Protestant and Roman Catholic Christians were often suspected of being spies in the employ of the enemy, the members of a church closely related to Russia could not well escape being charged by the common people with disloyal acts. In some cases they were in danger of violence, and occasionally damage was done to church property. There was reason to fear that in Tokyo an attack might be made on the Cathedral, whose location on one of the most commanding sites in the city had long made it an object of popular dislike. The land on which it was built had originally been granted to the Russian Legation, in whose name it was still held, and some argued that it ought now be seized as the property of a hostile nation. The Japanese Government, however, took care to frown upon all such expressions of hatred. The Cathedral was carefully guarded by the police and, so far as known, no serious attempt to harm it was made by the populace.

During the time of withdrawal from the more active duties of his episcopate, Bishop Nicolai was largely occupied with literary labours. A report for 1904 says:

"In the publication department of the Church, we have nine men who are engaged solely in translation, and besides these there are three editors of magazines and church literature. The official organ of the Church is the *Seikyo Shimpo,* published fortnightly. The *Seikyo Yowa,* a monthly magazine, is devoted mostly to sermons and religious instructions for the edification of the Christians. The *Uranishiki* is a monthly periodical especially for women." *

This work was under the close supervision of Bishop Nicolai. Previously to this he had prepared a translation of the New Testament. The Orthodox Church had for a long time used the version made by the Protestants. Bishop Nicolai was not fully satisfied with this, partly because he thought it had been too much influenced by the English translation and partly because he considered its style as too near that of the colloquial language, and thus as lacking in the dignity that was desirable in such a book. His own translation made more use of Chinese terms and archaic forms.

* "The Christian Movement," III, p. 179.

In 1906 Bishop Nicolai was raised to the rank of Archbishop, and Père Andronik, who some years before had spent a short time in Japan as a member of the Mission, was made a bishop. The latter had hardly reached Japan the next spring when his health gave way and he was obliged to return ere he had fully entered upon the duties of his office. In 1908 another bishop was sent out to take his place.

After the war with Japan, the disturbed state of Russia, and the financial stringency existing there, led to a great falling off in the receipts of the Russian Missionary Society. This necessitated a reduction in the activities of the Japanese Church. At the Annual Convention held in July, 1907, it was decided to lessen expenses by diminishing the number of evangelists and students. This difficulty was bravely met by the Archbishop. A statement prepared under his direction says: " Faced as it is by the necessity of attaining self-support, the Japanese Church will rather look upon this necessity as a providence of the Most High, which is designed to be a strong stimulus to further progress."

Hitherto, this Church had made but little advance in the way of self-support; and it may be that, as has been the case with some others, the lessening of foreign aid will prove a blessing, and that what now seems a misfortune will hereafter be looked upon as one of the best things that could have happened to it at this stage of its development.

The statistics of this Church for 1907 include the following items :*

Missionary   1
Japanese ordained ministers   37
Japanese unordained ministers and helpers   129
Total membership 30,166
Adult and infant baptisms during year   838
Churches and preaching places   265
Church buildings   175

Estimated value of churches, land, and parsonages 83,236 *Yen*
Amount raised by Japanese churches last year...... 10,711 "

* " The Christian Movement in Japan," Sixth Annual Issue, Tokyo, 1908.

Amount expended by Mission in aid of churches or
evangelistic work, not including missionary salary and expenses .... 55,279 *Yen*

Boys' boarding school I
Students in same 44
Girls' boarding schools................................ 2
Students in same 99
Orphanage I
Inmates in same 54

INDEX